MAKING HISTORY

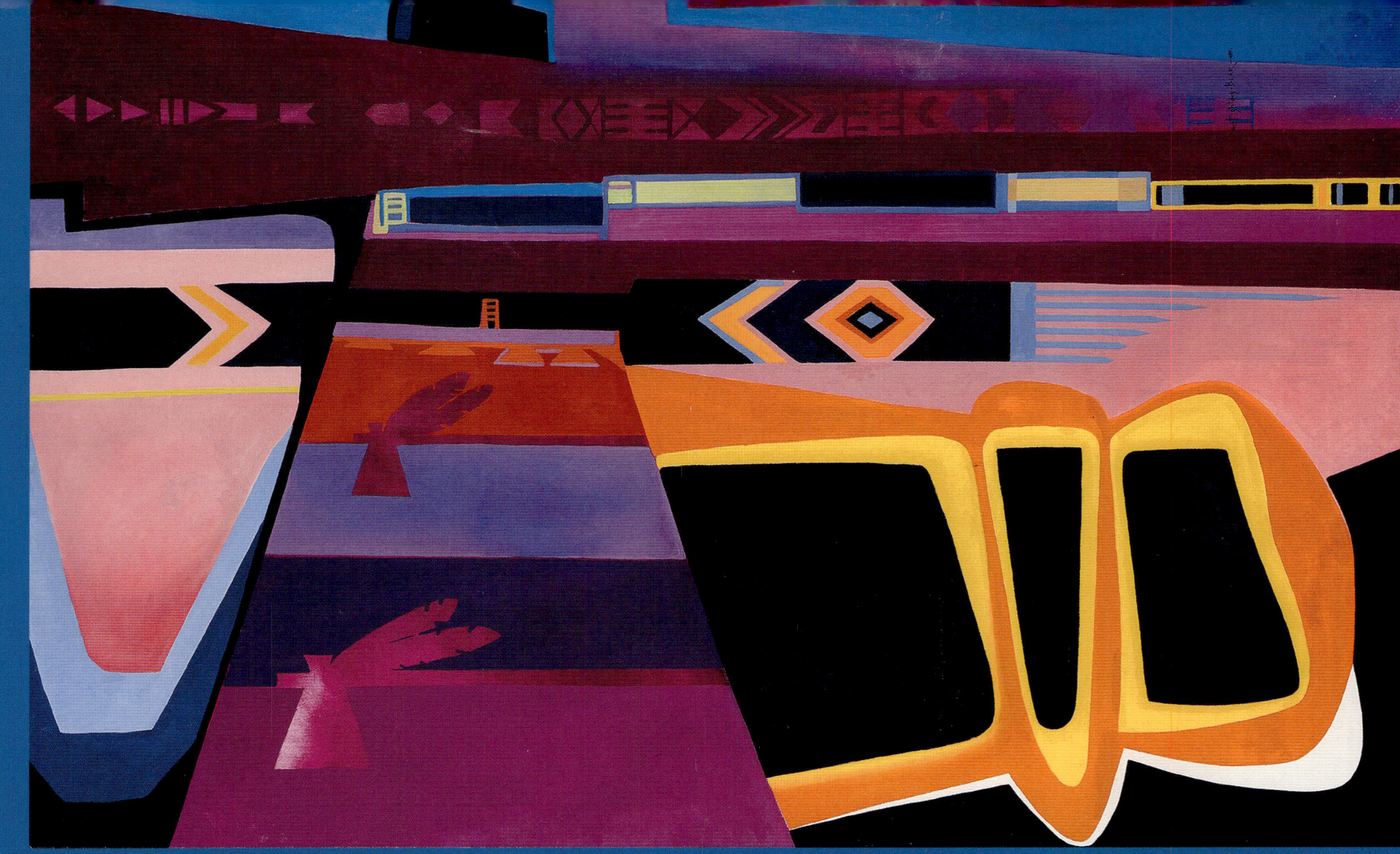

University of New Mexico Press / Albuquerque

MAKING HISTORY

IAIA Museum of Contemporary Native Arts

Institute of American Indian Arts

Edited by Nancy Marie Mithlo
Foreword by Robert Martin

Thank you to the Elizabeth Firestone Graham Foundation and the Institute of American Indian Arts for funding support.

Printed in the United States of America

Library of Congress Cataloging-in-Publication Data
NAMES Mithlo, Nancy Marie, editor.
TITLE Making history: IAIA Museum of Contemporary Native Arts: Institute of American Indian Arts / edited by Nancy Marie Mithlo; foreword by Robert Martin.
DESCRIPTION First edition. | Albuquerque: University of New Mexico Press, 2020. | Includes bibliographical references and index.
IDENTIFIERS LCCN 2020013742 (print) | LCCN 2020013743 (e-book) | ISBN 9780826362094 (paperback) | ISBN 9780826362100 (e-book)
SUBJECTS LCSH: Museum of Contemporary Native Arts. | Institute of American Indian Arts. | Indian art—Study and teaching—United States. | Art criticism—Study and teaching—United States.
CLASSIFICATION LCC N6538.A4 M35 2020 (print) | LCC N6538.A4 (e-book) | DDC 704.03/97—dc23
LC record available at https://lccn.loc.gov/2020013742
LC e-book record available at https://lccn.loc.gov/2020013743

COVER ILLUSTRATIONS *front* Bill Soza War Soldier (Cahuilla/White Mountain Apache), *Self-Portrait*, 1968, oil on canvas, 21 in. × 21 in., MoCNA Collection, MS-22 (Photo by Addison Doty). *spine* Janet Nipi Ikuutaq (Nunavut, Baker Lake), *Fighting over the Dead Seal*, Edition 10/14, 1997, woodcut on paper, 21 in. × 25.5 in., MoCNA Collection, CAN-27 (photo by Jason S. Ordaz). *back* Jeff Kahm (Plains Cree), *Converse*, 2012, acrylic on canvas, 90 in. × 90 in., MoCNA Collection, CAN-43 (photo by Addison Doty)

TITLE PAGE ILLUSTRATION: Raymond Winters (Hunkpapa Sioux), *Giant Symbols*, 1971, oil on canvas, 96 in. x 60 in., MoCNA Collection, S-124 (photo by Addison Doty).

DESIGNED BY Mindy Basinger Hill

COMPOSED IN 10.5 × 15 point Parkinson Electra Pro

DEDICATED TO CHARLES A. DAILEY (1935–2019)

FOR LIGHTING THE FIRE

CONTENTS

List of Illustrations / ix

Foreword / *Robert Martin* / xv

Introduction / American Indian Curatorial Practice: State of the Field / *Nancy Marie Mithlo* / 1

Introduction to the IAIA Museum of Contemporary Native Arts Collection and the IAIA Archives / *Tatiana Lomahaftewa-Singer and Ryan S. Flahive* / 5

Indian with a Watch / *Poem by Alex Jacobs* / 11

1 The Gaze in Indigenous Art: Depictions of the Body and Nudity / *Nancy Marie Mithlo* / 15

2 Mapping Indigenous Space and Place / *John Paul Rangel* / 45

3 Presentations & Representations: Images of Dances from the Southwest and West / *Suzanne Newman Fricke* / 75

4 Transforming Art History in the Classroom / *Lara M. Evans* / 95

5 "No Rules Make Art": The Work of C. Maxx Stevens / *Patsy Phillips* / 121

6 Historical Essays

About Professor Charles Dailey / *Jessie Ryker-Crawford and Stephen C. Fadden* / 141

Major Influences in the Development of Twentieth-Century Native American Art / *Charles A. Dailey* / 145

Cultural Self-Determination: A Conversation with David Warren / *Nancy Marie Mithlo and David Warren* / 155

Teaching from Three Knowledge Spaces: The Native Eyes Project / *David Wade Chambers* / 163

Illumination / *Poem by Elizabeth Woody* / 177

Contributors / 179

Index / 187

ILLUSTRATIONS

FIGURES

FIGURE 1 David Bradley, *Indian Affected by Anti-Indian Backlash*, 1978 / 6
FIGURE 2 America Meredith, *Bambi Makes Some Extra Bucks at The Studio*, 2002 / 6
FIGURE 3 Phyllis Fife, *Mist in the Morning*, 1965 / 6
FIGURE 4 Rick Bartow, *Inside Joke*, 1992 / 7
FIGURE 5 Heidi Brandow, *Object: Hand + Mechanism*, 2014 / 8
FIGURE 6 Alex Jacobs, *Santa Fe Dude #4*, 1999 / 12
FIGURE 7 Wesley Wolf, *Untitled*, 1973 / 17
FIGURE 8 Melvin Brown, *Mother and Child*, ca. 1982 / 20
FIGURE 9 Alex Jacobs, *Thursday Blues*, 1976 / 20
FIGURE 10 Yvonne Thomas, *Dawn's Glow (Northwest Woman II)*, 1984 / 21
FIGURE 11 Courtney Moyah, *Diplomacy*, ca. 1968–1969 / 22
FIGURE 12 Courtney Moyah, *Distortion*, ca. 1969 / 23
FIGURE 13 Courtney Moyah, *To Cry in the Dark*, 1969 / 24
FIGURE 14 Rick Bartow, *Cry I*, 1989 / 25
FIGURE 15 Rick Bartow, *The Change*, 1989 / 25
FIGURE 16 Clara LaRose Gaseoma, *Watcher*, 1985 / 26
FIGURE 17 Peggy Deam, *My Backyard Larry*, 1969 / 27
FIGURE 18 Bill Soza War Soldier, *Ghost Dance II*, 1969 / 29
FIGURE 19 Bill Soza War Soldier, *Self-Portrait*, 1968 / 31
FIGURE 20 Bill Soza War Soldier, *John Wesley Hardin, Killer of Men . . .*, ca. 1969 / 31
FIGURE 21 Allan Houser, *By the Water's Edge*, 1987 / 35
FIGURE 22 Allan Houser, *Dawn*, 1989 / 35
FIGURE 23 Shan Goshorn, *Vessel*, 2015 / 38
FIGURE 24 Shan Goshorn, *Feminine Sacred*, 2015 / 38
FIGURE 25 Keli Mashburn, *Water Study #1*, 2016 / 41

FIGURE 26 Marcella Ernest, *Nibiin Water Song* still, 2017 / 41
FIGURE 27 Jason Garcia, *Feast Day Selfie*, 2016 / 48
FIGURE 28 Mateo Romero, *Corn Dance Series*, 1991 / 51
FIGURE 29 Edgar Heap of Birds, *Telling Many Magpies, Telling Black Wolf, Telling Hachivi*, 1989 / 53
FIGURE 30 Jesus Barraza, *Indian Land*, 2004 / 55
FIGURE 31 Marie K. Watt, *When More Than Knees Have Been Wounded*, 1990 / 56
FIGURE 32 Anthony Gauthier, *Freedom*, 1976 / 59
FIGURE 33 Richard Ray Whitman, *Do Indian Artists Go to Santa Fe When They Die . . . ?*, 1989 / 60
FIGURE 34 Anita Fields (née Luttrell), *Untitled*, 1973 / 64
FIGURE 35 Norman Akers, *Sorting Out Blind Sensations*, 1998 / 66
FIGURE 36 Harry Fonseca, *Dance Land #2*, ca. 1980 / 76
FIGURE 37 *Christ, St. Vitalis, Bishop of Ravenna, and Archangels*, 547 / 78
FIGURE 38 Allan Houser, *Crown Dancer*, 1954 / 80
FIGURE 39 Allan Houser, *Fire Dancer*, 1990 / 83
FIGURE 40 Allan Houser, *Evolution*, 1993 / 83
FIGURE 41 Fritz Scholder, *Snake Dancer*, 1979 / 84
FIGURE 42 Melanie Yazzie, *Picture Tour Map of Arizona*, 1992 / 85
FIGURE 43 Mateo Romero, *Red Meridian*, 2012 / 87
FIGURE 44 Heidi BigKnife, *The Night after Columbus*, 1991 / 113
FIGURE 45 Geronima Cruz Montoya, *War Dance*, 1967 / 113
FIGURE 46 Melanie Yazzie, *Education*, 1992 / 114
FIGURE 47 David Neel, *Life on the 18th Hole*, 1990 / 114
FIGURE 48 Nani Chacon and Jaque Fragua, *Civil.War.*, 2014 / 114
FIGURE 49 Unknown Artist, *Untitled* (*The Boxer*), ca. 1962–1968 / 116
FIGURE 50 Lara Evans photographing *The Boxer*, 2014 / 116
FIGURE 51 Shawn Bluejacket, *Combattant de Liberté*, 2002 / 117
FIGURE 52 T. C. Cannon, *On Drinking Beer in Vietnam in 1967*, 1971 / 117
FIGURE 53 Dorothy Grandbois, *America on Alert*, 2003 / 117
FIGURE 54 Charlene Teters, *War Makers Back in Town*, 2003 / 118
FIGURE 55 Teresa Kaulaity Quintana, *Soldier Boy Ring*, 2013 / 118
FIGURE 56 Jean LaMarr, *Untitled* (Cover Girl Series), 1990 / 118
FIGURE 57 Jack Malotte, *Screaming Eagle Blues*, 1990 / 118
FIGURE 58 Hulleah Tsinhnahjinnie, *My Father was a World War II Warrior*, 1979 / 118
FIGURE 59 Floyd Solomon, *Deceptus Magnus-October 12, 1492*, 1990 / 119
FIGURE 60 Seth Picotte, *Economic Sovereignty*, 2016 / 119

FIGURE 61 Heidi BigKnife, *Medal of Dishonor*, 2003 / 119
FIGURE 62 Shan Goshorn, *Words Are Our Weapons*, 2015 / 119
FIGURE 63 Family portrait, late 1940s / 122
FIGURE 64 T. C. Cannon, *Instructor In Green*, ca. 1966 / 123
FIGURE 65 C. Maxx Stevens, *Aunt Nelly: My Story*, 1994 / 125
FIGURE 66 Children's Iron Lung / 126
FIGURE 67 C. Maxx Stevens, *Childhood*, 2004 / 127
FIGURE 68 C. Maxx Stevens, *House of Constant Rotation*, 2010 / 129
FIGURE 69 C. Maxx Stevens, *Last Supper*, 2011 / 132
FIGURE 70 C. Maxx Stevens, Detail from *Last Supper*, 2011 / 132
FIGURE 71 C. Maxx Stevens, *Wichita House*, 2019 / 134
FIGURE 72 IAIA portrait class, 1963 / 140
FIGURE 73 IAIA seniors, 1963 / 140
FIGURE 74 IAIA music students, ca. 1965 / 143
FIGURE 75 IAIA dormitory, ca. 1965 / 143
FIGURE 76 Students in the Commercial Arts class at IAIA / 143
FIGURE 77 IAIA student group, ca. 1965 / 144
FIGURE 78 IAIA faculty meeting, 1967 / 144
FIGURE 79 IAIA physical education class, ca. 1970 / 154
FIGURE 80 IAIA student group, 1972 / 154
FIGURE 81 IAIA Rodeo Club members Robin Fohrenkam, DeVere Manning, and Leo Martinez prepare to ride in the All Indian Rodeo, 1973 / 160
FIGURE 82 IAIA protest, 1973 / 160
FIGURE 83 IAIA students on the Santa Fe Indian School campus, ca. 1975 / 161
FIGURE 84 Group of students at Soleri Theater, 1978 / 162
FIGURE 85 Protest by IAIA students, 1981 / 162
FIGURE 86 Elizabeth Woody, *My Humanness Is an Embellished Tongue*, 1988 / 176

PLATES

Gallery 1 / FOLLOWS PAGE 10
PLATE 1 Jeff Kahm, *Converse*, 2012
PLATE 2 C. Maxx Stevens, *Memory Prom Dress*, 2005
PLATE 3 Dyani White Hawk, *Sioux Blue*, 2011
PLATE 4 Shawn Bluejacket, Combattant de Liberté, 2002
PLATE 5 Fritz Scholder, *The Offering*, ca. 1957–1958

PLATE 6 Sonya Kelliher-Combs, *Tangerine Walrus Family*, 2015
PLATE 7 Alex J. Peña, *Untitled Lines #19*, 2010
PLATE 8 Carly Feddersen, *Tooth and Twine Necklace*, 2016
PLATE 9 T. C. Cannon, *Tale of a Bigfoot Incident in American Vernacular*, 1966
PLATE 10 Raymond Winters, *Giant Symbols*, 1971
PLATE 11 Earl Eder, *Forms in Beadwork*, ca. 1963
PLATE 12 William Thoms, *Tamahnous Proto-Being*, 2016
PLATE 13 Tony Lee, *Wisdom*, 2008
PLATE 14 Anong Beam, *Revolution (The Evolver Series)*, 2002
PLATE 15 Anong Beam, *Simultaneous Advance (The Evolver Series)*, 2002
PLATE 16 Carl Beam, *Deontic Koan (The Whale of Our Being Series)*, 2002
PLATE 17 Carl Beam, *Chaos Theory (The Whale of Our Being Series)*, 2002
PLATE 18 Carl Beam, *Residential School (Nightmare Koan I)*, 2002
PLATE 19 Harry Fonseca, *Hopi Clowns*, n.d.
PLATE 20 Robert Gress, *Absaloka Parfleche Belt*, 1993
PLATE 21 Alfred Clah, *Untitled*, 1964
PLATE 22 Bobbie Kitsman-Jenike and Arone Raymond Meeks, *Across Time*, 1994

Gallery 2 / FOLLOWS PAGE 74
PLATE 23 John Hoover, *Hawk Woman*, 1970
PLATE 24 Carol Frazier Aikens, *Untitled*, 1963
PLATE 25 Helen Hardin, *Changing Woman*, 1980
PLATE 26 Robert Tsabetsaye, *Katchina No. 1*, ca. 1965
PLATE 27 Lawrence Lewis, *Self-Portrait*, n.d.
PLATE 28 Anita Fields (née Luttrell), *Gina Gray*, n.d.
PLATE 29 Ken Tohee, *Maiden Voyager*, 1999
PLATE 30 Marwin Begaye, *Kill the Indian Save the Man*, 1992
PLATE 31 Michael McCabe, *Big Guy*, 1983
PLATE 32 Brenda Holden, *Untitled*, 1969
PLATE 33 Tronto Malaya Akulukjuk, *Wanting Fish*, 1974
PLATE 34 Fritz Scholder, *One Navajo*, 1968
PLATE 35 Grey Cohoe, *Mesa Mirage from Tocito Rain*, 1983
PLATE 36 Laura Gilpin, *17 Navajos Gathered*, ca. 1968
PLATE 37 Laura Gilpin, *Making Frybread at Crownpoint School 1960*, 1960
PLATE 38 Kenojuak Ashevak, *My Mother, Myself*, 1995
PLATE 39 Otellie Loloma, *We Come as Clouds*, n.d.
PLATE 40 T. C. Cannon, *Self Portrait in the Studio* (1975), ca. 2005–2006

PLATE 41 Darren Vigil Gray, *Unrelenting-Number 1*, 1983
PLATE 42 Magdelene Ukpatiku, *Frightened Baby Becomes a Ptarmigan*, 1997
PLATE 43 Grey Cohoe, *Spirit Dance of the Moon and Sun*, 1967
PLATE 44 Bob Haozous, *Yellow Cat*, 1995
PLATE 45 Charlene Loneman, *Women in Mourning*, ca. 1966–1969

Gallery 3 / FOLLOWS PAGE 120
PLATE 46 Kirby Feathers, *Blue Feathers*, ca. 1966
PLATE 47 Ernest Cachini, *Untitled*, 1983
PLATE 48 Henry (Hank) Delano Gobin, *Red Print II*, 1965
PLATE 49 C. Maxx Stevens, *Dream Home*, 2016
PLATE 50 Reg Davidson, *Box Drum*, 1991
PLATE 51 Jean LaMarr, *Sometimes It Happens That Way*, 2004
PLATE 52 Evans Boone, *Untitled*, 1969
PLATE 53 Raymond Winters, *Somewhere in South Dakota*, 1968
PLATE 54 Roy Pablito, *Zuni Shalako Dancer and Mudhead*, 1965
PLATE 55 Norman Akers, *Warning Call*, 2002
PLATE 56 Margaret Wood, *Bag Series #3: Cree Tobacco Pouch*, 1993
PLATE 57 Margaret Wood, *Onyx Mosaic*, 1997
PLATE 58 Melanie Yazzie, *Little Dog*, 1998
PLATE 59 Larry Yazzie, *Ye'ii Impersonator*, 1984
PLATE 60 Nancy Sevoga, *Beginning of Winter*, 1997
PLATE 61 Linda Lomahaftewa, *Circle of Life*, 1990
PLATE 62 T. C. Cannon, *New Mexico Red*, ca. 1967
PLATE 63 Don Whitesinger, *Apache Crown Dancers*, 1983
PLATE 64 Harry Fonseca, *Deer Dancers*, ca. 1980
PLATE 65 Parker Boyiddle, *Birth (New Life)*, 1978
PLATE 66 Selina Farmer, *Butterflies in December*, 1998
PLATE 67 Maxine Gachupin, *Pueblo Dance*, ca. 1964–1968
PLATE 68 Marcus Amerman, *Fringed Cuffs*, 1980
PLATE 69 Fritz Scholder, *Artist at 40 as a Buffalo*, 1977
PLATE 70 Darren Vigil Gray, *Extra-Terrestrial Life Series*, 1987

Gallery 4 / FOLLOWS PAGE 178
PLATE 71 Frank Day, *Stalking Deer*, 1967
PLATE 72 Frances Makil, *Triangle Painting*, 1968
PLATE 73 Otellie Loloma, 1971
PLATE 74 IAIA student graduate Frances Makil, 1971

PLATE 75 Otellie Loloma, *Tall Man with Bird*, ca. 1960–1971
PLATE 76 Otellie Loloma, *Bird Woman*, 1962
PLATE 77 IAIA student on pottery wheel, 1963
PLATE 78 IAIA students in class with instructor Manuelita Lovato, ca. 1972
PLATE 79 Jacquie Stevens, Vase, 1985
PLATE 80 Laura Fragua Cota, *Womb Bowl*, 1999
PLATE 81 James McGrath and Manuelita Lovato hanging 1966 IAIA Faculty exhibit, 1966
PLATE 82 Manuelita Lovato, *Untitled*, ca. 1964
PLATE 83 Imogene Goodshot, 1973
PLATE 84 Imogene Goodshot, *Beaded Child Dress*, 1975
PLATE 85 IAIA graduation with Lloyd New, ca. 1975
PLATE 86 IAIA photography students screen printing, 1972
PLATE 87 Mike One Star, *Untitled* (bear paws on stripes), 1976
PLATE 88 Former students of IAIA return to join the instructional staff, 1977
PLATE 89 Linda Lomahaftewa, *Parrots Prayer Song*, 1989
PLATE 90 David Bradley, *A. I. M.*, 2002
PLATE 91 David Bradley, *The Married Woman*, 1980
PLATE 92 Tammy S. Rahr, *Endangered Species*, ca. 1993
PLATE 93 Dolores Guerrero-Cruz, *El Veso*, 1990
PLATE 94 R. C. Gorman, *Iris*, 1991
PLATE 95 Lucy Martin Lewis, *Beetle Design Bowl*, 1968
PLATE 96 Susan A. Point, *Black Bear Children*, 1992
PLATE 97 Linda Lou Metoxen, *Elk Spirit*, 1999
PLATE 98 Edward Wapp, *Make Me Dance Ivories*, 2003
PLATE 99 Janet Nipi Ikuutaq, *Fighting over the Dead Seal*, 1997
PLATE 100 Charlene Teters, *Oñate's Toaster*, 1999
PLATE 101 Roxanne Swentzell, *A Day at Cochiti Lake*, 2006
PLATE 102 IAIA students on stage at Soleri Theater, 1975

Osiyo! It is a privilege and honor to welcome you to this publication, *Making History*, a first-time collaboration between the Institute of American Indian Arts (IAIA) and the University of New Mexico Press. IAIA, established in 1962, is celebrating its fifty-eighth year as the birthplace of contemporary Native art. We continue to build on this legacy and illustrious history, which led to the emergence of a Native arts movement and a truly unique institution. It is at IAIA where Native students take pride in their heritage while their artistic creativity is nurtured and encouraged to flower. We are pleased to participate in the creation of this publication, a groundbreaking contribution to the field of contemporary Native art.

The United States Congress acknowledged our prominence when it chartered the IAIA in 1986 as the only federal college charged with responsibility for supporting and fostering scholarship and research in Native arts and cultures. In essence, Congress acknowledged that Native arts and cultures are this country's only Indigenous art and cultural forms, a contribution of tremendous importance to the richness of the United States.

IAIA offers certificates and associate's and bachelor's degrees in Studio Arts, Film, Creative Writing, Museum Studies, and Indigenous Liberal Studies. In 2013, we expanded our mission to include an MFA in Creative Writing, which has graduated ninety-five students since the program was launched. Moreover, IAIA is the only institution of higher education in New Mexico offering fine arts degrees accredited by both the Higher Learning Commission and the National Association of Schools of Art and Design.

IAIA's enrollment has grown to more than five hundred students, representing an average of one hundred Indigenous nations from the United States, Canada, and Mexico. With enrollments generally decreasing at colleges across the country, IAIA continues to be a very attractive choice for students interested in a world-class contemporary Native arts education. Our growth is due to a combination of factors, including expanded academic programming and new initiatives in recruitment and retention.

In addition to the MFA, a performing arts program that was eliminated in the 1990s due to severe budget reductions reemerged in 2014 as a minor. At the same time, IAIA launched a successful fundraising campaign to build a $9.5 million Performing Arts and Fitness Center, which opened in January 2018. This newest building on campus will enhance IAIA's ability to expand academic programs in both performing arts and in fitness, thus permitting the college to create the first bachelor's program in performing arts in the country offered exclusively from an Indigenous perspective.

A new IAIA student success initiative, the "15 to Finish Program," created financial incentives to encourage students to complete their degrees in a timely fashion—four years instead of five or more. Senior-year tuition and a book-fee waiver are awarded to students who maintain satisfactory progress over four years by completing fifteen credits per semester.

In establishing strategic partnerships with Walt Disney Imagineering, the Margaret A. Cargill Foundation, the Great Lakes Higher Education Corporation, the Stagecoach Foundation, the Santa Fe Institute, the University of New Mexico Press, and others, IAIA provides its students with expanded opportunities for scholarships, internships, artist-in-residence programs, and employment.

The aforementioned affords the context for IAIA's compelling mission to empower creativity and leadership in Native arts and cultures, and is manifested in more than four thousand alumni who have achieved success as prominent artists, writers, museum professionals, scholars, filmmakers, professors, attorneys, tribal leaders, and business entrepreneurs. Our distinguished alumni include Roxanne Swentzell, recipient of the 2016 Heard Museum Spirit Award; Dan Namingha, recipient of the 2016 Museum of Indian Arts and Cultures Living Treasure award; Jody Naranjo, recipient of a 2018 New Mexico Governor's Award for Excellence in the Arts; and Terese Mailhot, author of the *New York Times* bestselling memoir *Heart Berries*, just to name a few. We are proud to recognize also the first Native American United States Poet Laureate, Joy Harjo, as an IAIA alumna.

The writers of *Making History* have been educated by or have contributed to IAIA as educators, artists, and art professionals. Of special note is Nancy Marie Mithlo, PhD, a renowned professor and Native American art historian and scholar, who is both the editor of and a contributor to this book. This publication is the product of Dr. Mithlo's visionary leadership, energy, and passionate commitment to the field of contemporary Native art.

IAIA's Museum of Contemporary Native Arts, an integral component of our mission, has assumed a leading role in raising the profile of contemporary Native art in national and international venues and is the only museum in the world focusing exclusively on exhibiting, collecting, and interpreting the most progressive work of Native American artists. Its more than eight thousand contemporary Native artworks form the largest and most noteworthy collection of its kind in the world. This book is a resource that will showcase this amazing collection to a much broader audience.

Making History appropriately illuminates the vibrant spirt at the forefront of contemporary Native arts and offers invaluable insights from a Native perspective. As a result, it is an invaluable teaching tool for tribal audiences and an essential resource for all arts readers. I am confident that this book will enlighten and empower the creative spirit for generations to come.

Wado,

Robert Martin

DR. ROBERT MARTIN, CHEROKEE NATION
PRESIDENT, IAIA

MAKING HISTORY

Introduction

American Indian Curatorial Practice

STATE OF THE FIELD

NANCY MARIE MITHLO

The book you are reading is the result of eight years of planning, fundraising, group meetings, endless drafts, conference calls, and midnight worry. For myself, this effort is the culmination of thirty-five years of experience working with the Institute of American Indian Arts. From my student days in the mid-1980s to the present, the IAIA has continued to provide me with inspiration and drive in my role as an American Indian educator in the arts.

The group that generously agreed to participate in this project collectively wished to make an educational resource for learning about Native arts that did not alienate American Indian students. We wanted to provide educational materials in a form that reflected Indigenous knowledge systems—materials that are holistic, embracive, and free of jargon. Even small details such as the use of "we" or "us" were examined throughout to ensure that readers would be excited by the information provided and feel welcomed and spoken to, not about. The Indigenous Studies approach pursued does not follow strictly chronological or regional premises, but rather seeks out "defining moments of conflict" in the history of Native North American arts.[1]

It is important to note that this book is not a historiography of contemporary Native art that documents key performances, artists, collections, and pivotal events such as the establishment of Native arts organizations. While such documentation is surely needed, this specific project is not that encompassing, nor is it directed solely to internal scholarly debate concerning significance or value. *Making History* also does not address the systematic exclusion of Indigenous art paradigms and history in Western art discourse. Rather, our focus is on providing a scaffold of resources for emerging Native arts scholars, Native and non-Native readers, students, and academics who wish to understand the tenor and tone of what this field is about and how to approach teaching and learning about American Indian arts.

Making History specifically foregrounds the ideas and works that emerge from the IAIA experience in an effort to highlight the often-unknown histories of this central resource for Native arts production, teaching, and research. In planning the book, we referenced our desired approach to guiding readers as creating "embedded conversations." "Conversations" here connotes a dialectical give-and-take. Readers should imagine a guide walking a visitor through familiar territory, taking pains not to alienate or lose the guest while also pointing out amazing vistas.

The impetus for this volume grew out of the 2007 Ford Foundation "Advancing the Dialogue on Native Arts in Society" portfolio. Supported by Ford Foundation funding, I hosted the 2008 symposium *American Indian Curatorial Practice—State of the Field* at the University of Wisconsin–Madison, where I served as an assistant professor of art history. This gathering of twenty-four scholars and professionals identified the current challenges of American Indian arts scholarship and produced the online educational resource "Visiting: Conversations on Curatorial Practice and Native North American Art."[2]

The initiative's final joint report cited the need for an Indigenous *intellectual apparatus*: "a mechanism by which Indigenous artists and scholars can inform/transform the contemporary arts landscape and thereby the broader democratic project . . . The central aim would be to develop a common ground of understanding and intellectual framework through which to theorize Indigeneity and its relationship to other arts discourses and movements."[3] Our project has emphasized the "ground of understanding" implied in the portfolio's goals. Certainly, much work is left in establishing a relationship to "other arts discourses and movements."

This book follows four defining methodological principles that guided the initial UW–Madison symposium. I term this approach *American Indian Curatorial Practice*—research that is long-term, mutually meaningful, reciprocal, and includes mentorship. As one participant in the 2008 gathering noted, "Longevity and reproduction of knowledge is vital to growth, otherwise the cycle is constantly starting over. Textbooks are vital to the success and establishment of the field in academia."[4] Participants recognized the importance of a generational approach to developing and maintaining a politicized, intellectual, and community-engaged field of Indigenous arts practice. This approach is ideally suited for an educational environment, as it allows for sustained engagement with future practitioners.

On December 2, 2011, President Barack Obama announced the White House Initiative on American Indian and Alaska Native Education to ensure that the unique cultural, educational, and language needs of AI/AN students were met. Tribal Colleges and Universities were identified as critical partners in Executive Order 13592, "Improving American Indian and Alaska Native Educational Opportunities and Strengthening Tribal Colleges and

Universities." This order cites the development of educational resources as an urgent need: "Recent studies show that AI/AN students are dropping out of school at an alarming rate, that our Nation has made little or no progress in closing the achievement gap between AI/AN students and their non-AI/AN student counterparts, and that many Native languages are on the verge of extinction."[5] The White House initiative called for the development of a national network of individuals, organizations, and communities to share best practices in AI/AN education, including culturally sensitive curricula. This executive action inspired my development of *Making History* with the Institute of American Indian Arts. I am very grateful for the support of IAIA President Dr. Robert Martin, who approved my visiting researcher project proposal "American Indian Curatorial Practice—Establishing the Field" in 2012, and for the flexibility that the University of Wisconsin-Madison exercised in granting me leave status so that I could devote fuller research time to this vital project.

My experience working in "majority" colleges and universities over the past few decades has convinced me of the essential and timely need for a proactive intervention in the academy that provides a clear methodological and theoretical approach to integrating American Indian arts into existing curricula as well as providing resources for the establishment of quality interpretative materials in public educational settings, including the museum. My experience with editing *Manifestations: New Native Art Criticism* (Santa Fe: IAIA Museum of Contemporary Native Arts, 2011) and the 2012 "American Indian Curatorial Practice," a dedicated volume of the *Wíčazo Ša Review*, informed my strategy as senior editor of this textbook.[6]

Scholars have only recently pursued the articulation, codification, and legitimation of American Indian arts. Formal and descriptive considerations alone are no longer acceptable to the intellectual and legal mandates of the past three decades dealing with the contextual and political ramifications of American Indian arts production, circulation, and interpretation (including the Indian Arts and Crafts Act of 1990 and the same year's Native American Graves Protection and Repatriation Act). Resources and infrastructure such as reference collections, instructional image banks, graduate training programs, professional organizations, and textbooks are markedly missing from the study of contemporary American Indian arts. The publication of *Making History* is thus positioned within a transitional period that is establishing new pedagogies, practices, and interpretative frameworks.

While one book or project cannot redress the cumulative lack of resources available to teach American Indian art from an Indigenous perspective, this resource, generated by the IAIA, a national leader in producing, theorizing, and training the next generation of educators in American Indian arts, can serve as an example of best practices, new pedagogies, and fresh theoretical approaches to the rich creative life of Indigenous peoples.

NOTES

1. Over time, the individuals participating in or advising this project have included Patsy Phillips, Tatiana Lomahaftewa-Singer, Dyani Reynolds-White Hawk, America Meredith, Steve Wall, Lara Evans, heather ahtone, Suzanne Newman Fricke, and John Paul Rangel. I am extremely grateful to these scholars and other collaborators who have devoted their tremendous talents to see this project come to fruition. A special thanks to James Ayers, Katherine Harper, and Elise McHugh of the University of New Mexico Press, who have shepherded the project with grace, patience, and superb expertise. I am grateful also to editors Rose Marie Cutropia, Rupert Jenkins, and Sallie Wesaw Sloan, who provided diligent expertise in the final steps of manuscript submission. Thanks also to the University of California, Los Angeles, for assistance with the index.

2. This resource is available on my website: http://nancymariemithlo.com/American_Indian_Curatorial/index.html.

3. Elizabeth Theobald Richards, JoAnn K. Chase, and Sandy Grande, "The Ford Foundation's Indigenous Knowledge and Expressive Culture Portfolio Final Report: *Advancing the Dialogue on Native American Arts in Society* Initiative Convening, held at the Ford Foundation on April 29, 2008." Author's files.

4. American Indian Curatorial Practices Symposium, University of Wisconsin-Madison Department of Art History, Meeting Notes September 25–27, 2008, compiled by Nancy Marie Mithlo and Danielle M. Majors, November 15, 2008. Author's files.

5. https://obamawhitehouse.archives.gov/the-press-office/2011/12/02/executive-order-13592-improving-american-indian-and-alaska-native-educat.

6. Readers can purchase the *Manifestations* book I edited at https://iaia.edu/iaia-museum-of-contemporary-native-arts/vision-project/. For a review of my past scholarship on the IAIA, see my 2001 essay, "IAIA Rocks the Sixties: The Painting Revolution at the Institute of American Indian Arts." *Museum Anthropology* 24(2/3): 63–68.

Introduction to the IAIA Museum of Contemporary Native Arts Collection and the IAIA Archives

TATIANA LOMAHAFTEWA-SINGER
AND RYAN S. FLAHIVE

Within this textbook, imagined and designed to demystify the complex concepts and varied histories of contemporary Native American art, are works from a single museum collection housed in Santa Fe, New Mexico. The Institute of American Indian Arts (IAIA) and its associated IAIA Museum of Contemporary Native Arts (MoCNA) have collected contemporary Native art since 1962. This collection is perhaps the most important of its kind. Since its inception, the museum's holdings have challenged and redefined society's preconceived notions of Native art aesthetics.

The Institute's teaching philosophy emphasizes "cultural difference as the basis for creative expression," a concept developed by IAIA's first art director and philosophical leader, Lloyd Kiva New, and others. It stresses the development of the whole individual through academic training and the study of the world's arts and cultures.[1] This approach represented an about-face from the philosophies of previous American Indian boarding schools that were established in the late nineteenth to mid twentieth centuries.

While early boarding schools attempted to assimilate Native students into American society, IAIA promoted and encouraged a sense of pride in one's culture and declared that "difference is good."[2] IAIA students were encouraged to create works that reflected a contemporary, personal expression drawing inspiration from their own Native heritage, other world cultures, and American modern art movements such as abstraction. This new educational model represented an *intentional* departure from the dominant style of Indian art practice, particularly the flat "Studio Style" painting of the 1930s, developed at the Santa Fe Indian School under Dorothy Dunn.[3]

This aesthetic departure was explosive and immediately evident to the administration and faculty.[4] IAIA developed a collecting practice to capture this new form of Indian art that was intentionally *contemporary*. Known as the Honors Collection, this first collecting initiative from 1962–1972 documented the progression of student art work "as an active and dynamic group of paintings, graphics, textiles, sculpture and jewelry . . . to be used creatively for (a) artifactual record of student work while at IAIA (b) a unique and widely

FIGURE 1 David Bradley (Chippewa/Ojibway), *Indian Affected by Anti-Indian Backlash*, 1978, alabaster on wood base, 9.5 in. × 7.5 in., MoCNA Collection, CHP-77 (photo by John Joe).

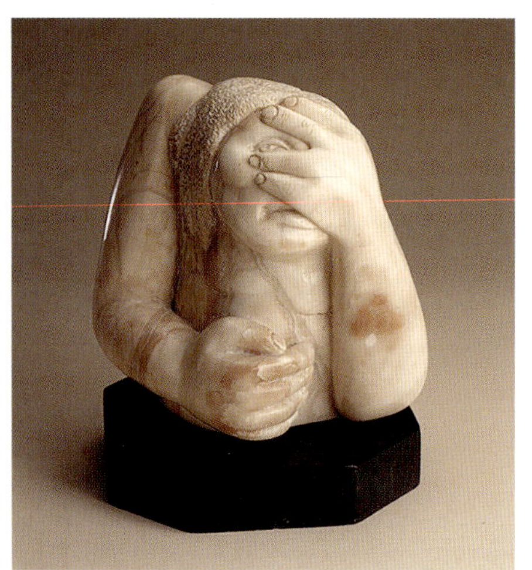

FIGURE 2 America Meredith (Swedish/Cherokee), *Bambi Makes Some Extra Bucks at The Studio*, 2002, acrylic on Masonite, 26.5 in. × 32.5 in., MoCNA Collection, CHE-111 (photo by John Joe).

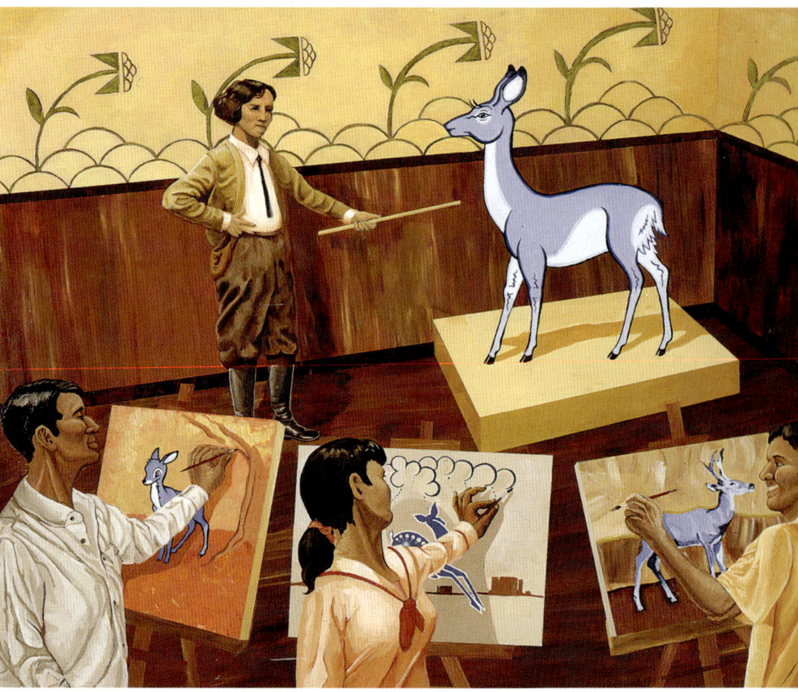

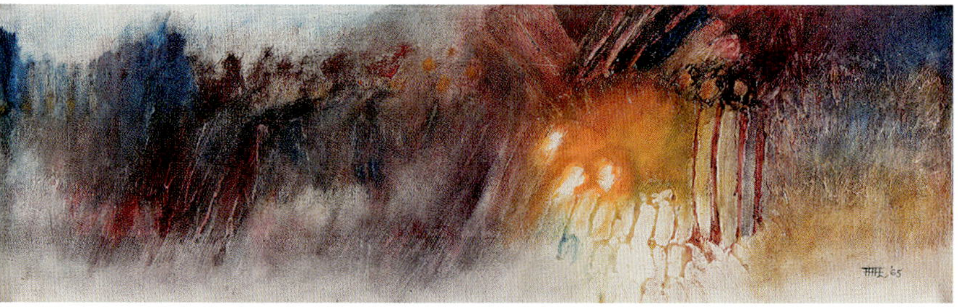

FIGURE 3 Phyllis Fife (Muskogee Creek), *Mist in the Morning*, 1965, oil on canvas, 10.25 in. × 28.25 in., MoCNA Collection, CK-7 (photo by Addison Doty).

diverse 'tool' to show, interpret and draw upon to reflect the wealth and vast resource of the young artists' social, cultural and historical backgrounds."[5] In addition to the Honors Collection, the school collected artwork by faculty and staff of the Institute that attested to the guidance and influence of this revolutionary program.

As IAIA moved into the twenty-first century, its program continued to rapidly develop. The high-school curriculum was dropped in 1979. Associate degrees were conferred as early as 1975. Baccalaureate accreditation was granted by the North Central Association of Colleges and Schools in 2001, and graduate degrees began in 2012. As the education program grew and changed, so did the museum collection. In the early 1970s, a large collection of IAIA graduate (alumni) work and ethnographic objects was transferred to the museum from the Bureau of Indian Affairs (BIA), which had obtained the pieces during the 1960s. This addition has provided researchers some insight into the impact of IAIA on its artists, particularly in terms of helping to direct artists toward contemporary and experimental forms. Today, the museum has expanded its focus and collects contemporary Native American art more extensively.

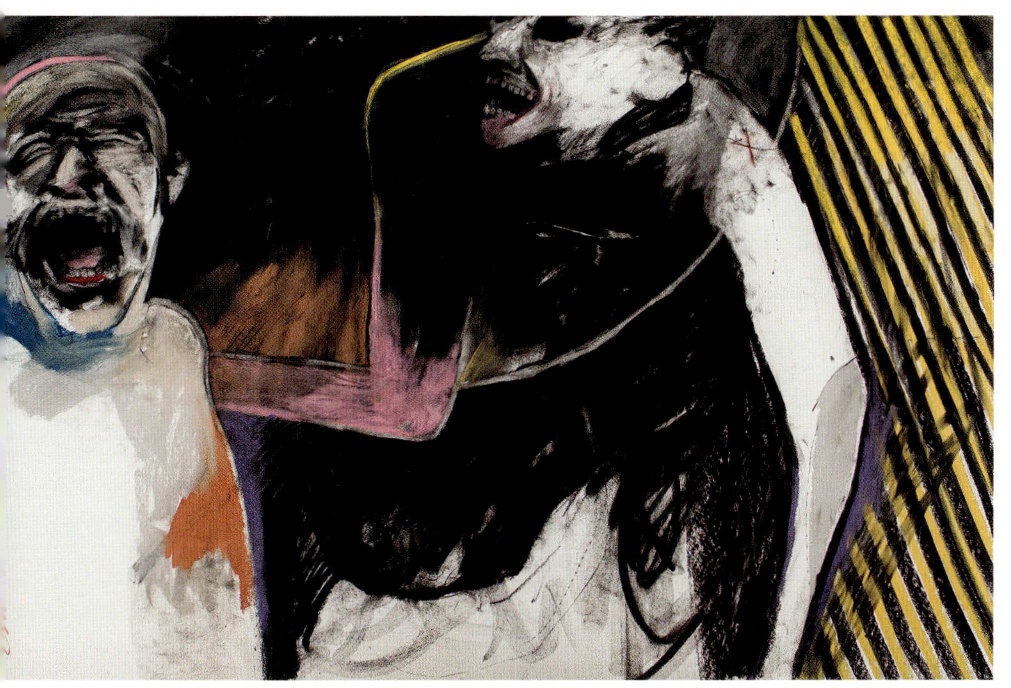

FIGURE 4 Rick Bartow (Yurok/Wiyot), *Inside Joke*, 1992, graphite, pastel on paper, 26 in. × 40 in., MoCNA Collection, CAL-20 (Photo by John Joe).

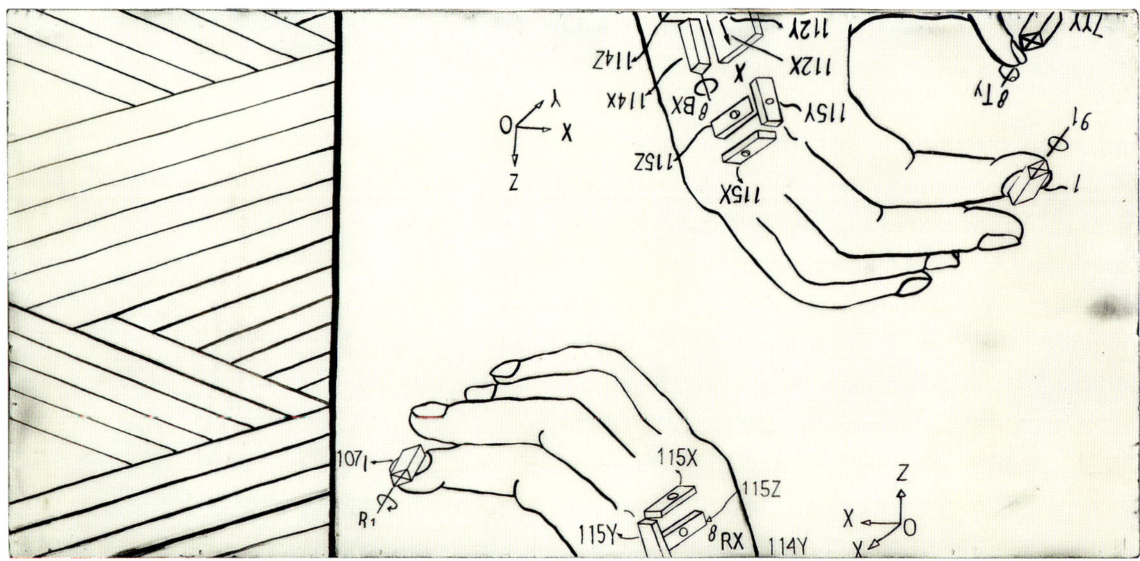

FIGURE 5 Heidi Brandow (Diné/Hawaiian), *Object: Hand + Mechanism*, 2014, encaustic on panel, 24 in. × 48 in., MoCNA Collection, N-1235 (photo by John Joe).

The work in the museum collection is evidence of the creative and open artistic climate that allowed Indian art to take on new directions and redefine itself with each generation. IAIA sparked elemental change in Native art aesthetics and still challenges students to experiment and explore their personal interactions with the modern world.

USING INDIGENOUS AESTHETICS

The following resources are exemplary of the diverse collections available for research that are housed in the Institute of American Indian Arts Archives on the campus of IAIA in Santa Fe, New Mexico. Many of these resources are also available online through the New Mexico Digital Archives: https://econtent.unm.edu/.

SELECT HOLDINGS OF THE IAIA ARCHIVES, SANTA FE, NEW MEXICO

Collections

MS03. James A. McGrath Papers.
MS15. Lloyd Henri New Papers.
MS23. Charles Dailey Papers.
MS27. Seymour Tubis Papers.
RG01. IAIA Records Compiled by Chuck Dailey. 1962–2007.
RG02. Printed IAIA and gallery ephemera.

Manuscripts

Boyce, George. "Criteria for Selection of Artwork for the Honors Collection." October 1963. RG01, 1963.

Cohen, Ernest, to Lloyd New. Correspondence regarding copyright of students' work in the Honors Collection. 15 May 1972. RG01, 1972.

Dailey, Charles. "The Institute of American Indian Arts Museum: 1962–1992." 1992. MS23, Charles Dailey Papers.

———. "Inventory of Art Collection: Institute of American Indian Arts." 6 August 1985. RG23, Charles Dailey Papers.

———. Memorandum to Lloyd New, "Honors Collection Policy." 1972. MS23, Charles Dailey Papers.

———. "The Quiet Renaissance" (draft). c. 1984. MS23, Charles Dailey Papers.

Institute of American Indian Arts. "An Evening with the Young Indian Painters from the Institute of American Indian Arts." 1966. MS03, James A. McGrath Papers.

———. "IAIA Basic Statement of Purpose." RG01, 1964, IAIA Records Compiled by Chuck Dailey.

———. "Institute of American Indian Arts Policy: Acquiring Art for the Permanent Collection." January, 1987. RG01, 1988.

———. "Permanent Institute Honors Collection Policy Statement." 1963. RG01, 1963.

Institute of American Indian Arts Museum. "Curatorial Assessment of the Collection." July 1990. Unprocessed Collection.

New, Lloyd H. "Cultural Difference as the Basis for Creative Expression." 1964. MS15, Lloyd H. New Papers.

———. "Report on a Proposed Philosophical Approach to the Art Education Program of the Institute of American Indian Arts, Bureau of Indian Affairs, Santa Fe, New Mexico." 5 Feb 1962. MS15, Lloyd H. New Papers.

New, Lloyd Kiva. "The Institute of American Indian Arts and Its Significance in the Development of Modern Indian Art." 1984. MS15, Lloyd H. New Papers.

Touchette, Charleen. "IAIA Rocks the '60s: The Painting Revolution at the Institute of American Indian Arts." 2001. RG02.

NOTES

1. Lloyd Henri New (1916–2002), known professionally as Lloyd Kiva New, was a groundbreaking Cherokee artist, fashion designer, and art educator. For more information, see Lloyd Kiva New, *The Sound of Drums: A Memoir of Lloyd Kiva New* (Santa Fe: Sunstone Press, 2016) and MS15, Lloyd Henri New Papers, IAIA Archives, Santa Fe, New Mexico.

2. The IAIA staff continue, "Differences are not just to be tolerated. Uniqueness which has merit deserves widespread support in time, energy, money, and courage." "IAIA Basic Statement of Purpose," 1964.

3. For more information on "The Studio" at the Santa Fe Indian School, see Dorothy Dunn Kramer, "Notes on the Paintings Done by the Studio," Museum of Indian Arts and Culture Archives, Dorothy Dunn Kramer Collection, Box 20; Bruce Bernstein and W. Jackson Rushing, *Modern by Tradition: American Indian Painting in the Studio Style* (Santa Fe: Museum of New Mexico Press, 1995); J. J. Brody, *Indian Painters & White Patrons* (Albuquerque: University of New Mexico Press, 1971); Michelle McGeough, *Through Their Eyes: Indian Painting in Santa Fe, 1918–1945* (Santa Fe: Wheelwright Museum of the American Indian, 2009).

4. From the start, IAIA staff and faculty curated exhibitions to showcase the progressive work being created by the students. For more information, see Joy L. Gritton, *The Institute of American Indian Arts: Modernism and U.S. Indian Policy* (Albuquerque: University of New Mexico Press, 2000); Institute of American Indian Arts, "An Evening with the Young Indian Painters," 1966; *The Institute of American Indian Arts Alumni Exhibition* (Fort Worth: Amon Carter Museum of Western Art, 1973).

5. For more information on the history of the art collection at IAIA, see Boyce, "Criteria for Selection of Artwork for the Honors Collection"; Dailey, "Inventory of Art Collection"; Institute of American Indian Arts, "Institute of American Indian Arts Policy"; and IAIA Museum, "Curatorial Assessment of the Collection."

GALLERY ONE

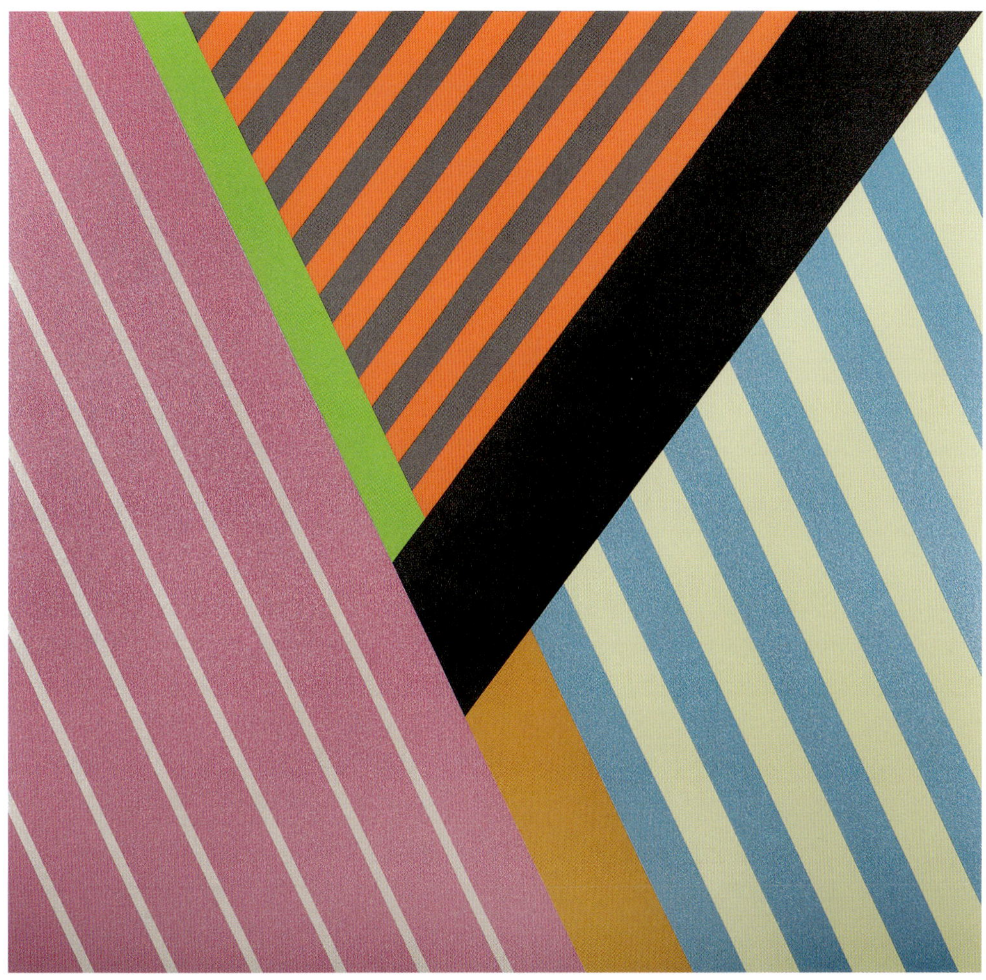

PLATE 1 Jeff Kahm (Plains Cree), *Converse*, 2012, acrylic on canvas, 90 in. × 90 in., MoCNA Collection, CAN-43 (photo by Addison Doty).

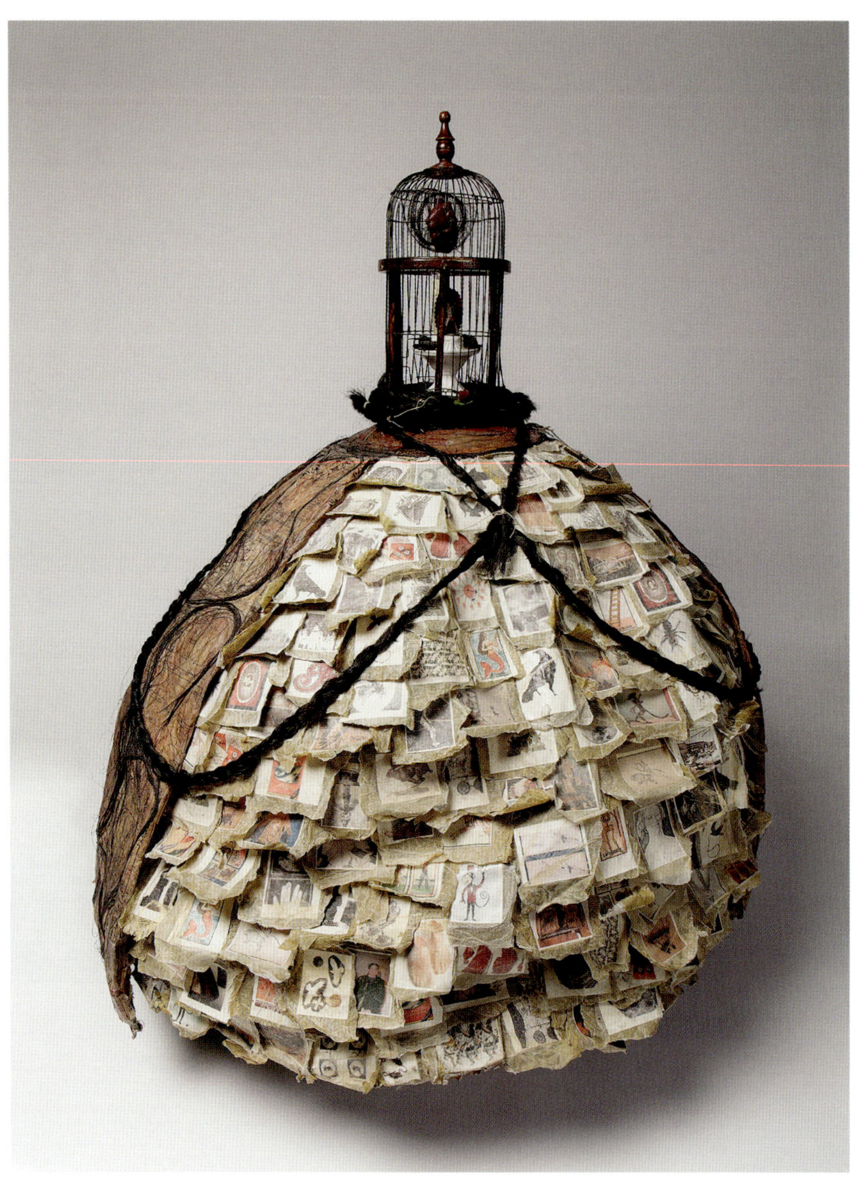

PLATE 2 C. Maxx Stevens (Seminole/Muscogee Nation of Oklahoma), *Memory Prom Dress*, 2005, mixed-media sculpture, 60 in. × 53 in., MoCNA Collection, 2012, SE-92 (photo by John Joe).

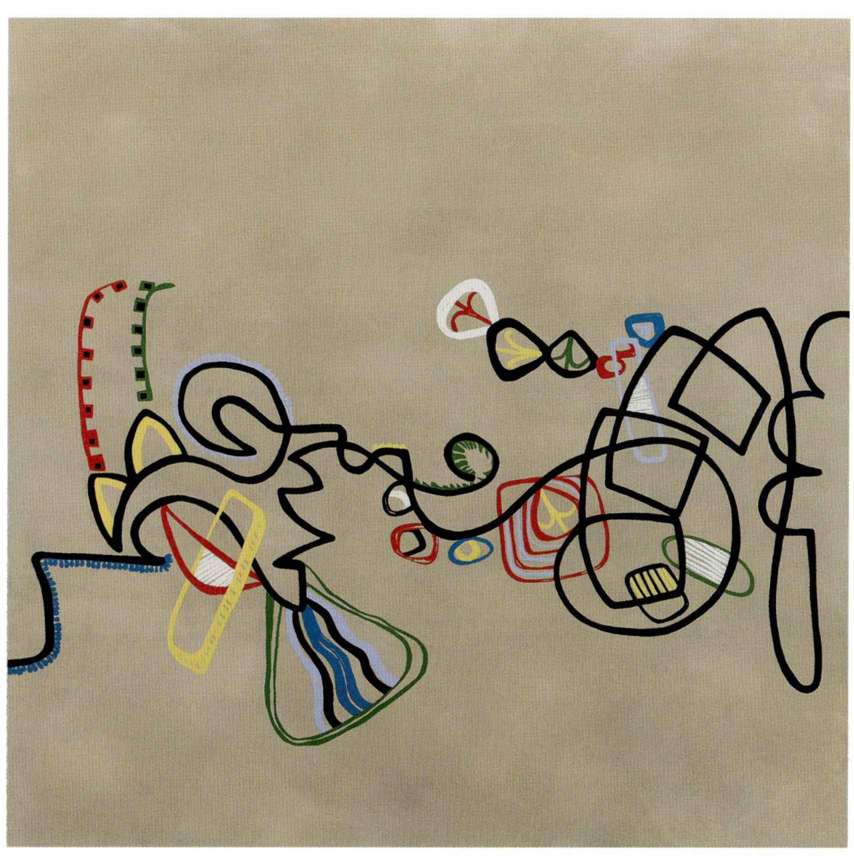

PLATE 3 Dyani White Hawk (Sicangu Lakota), *Sioux Blue*, 2011,
oil on canvas, 48 in. × 48 in., MoCNA Collection, S-320 (photo by Addison Doty).

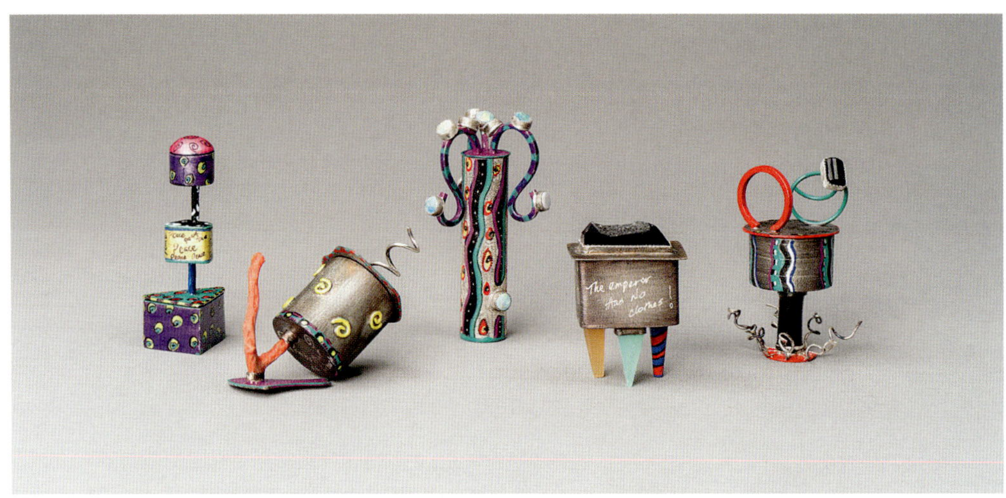

PLATE 4 Shawn Bluejacket (Shawnee), *Combattant de Liberté*, 2002, set of 5 containers, mixed media, silver, gem stones, acrylic paint, 4 in. × 3 in. × 9 in., MoCNA Collection, SH-3 (photo by Jason S. Ordaz).

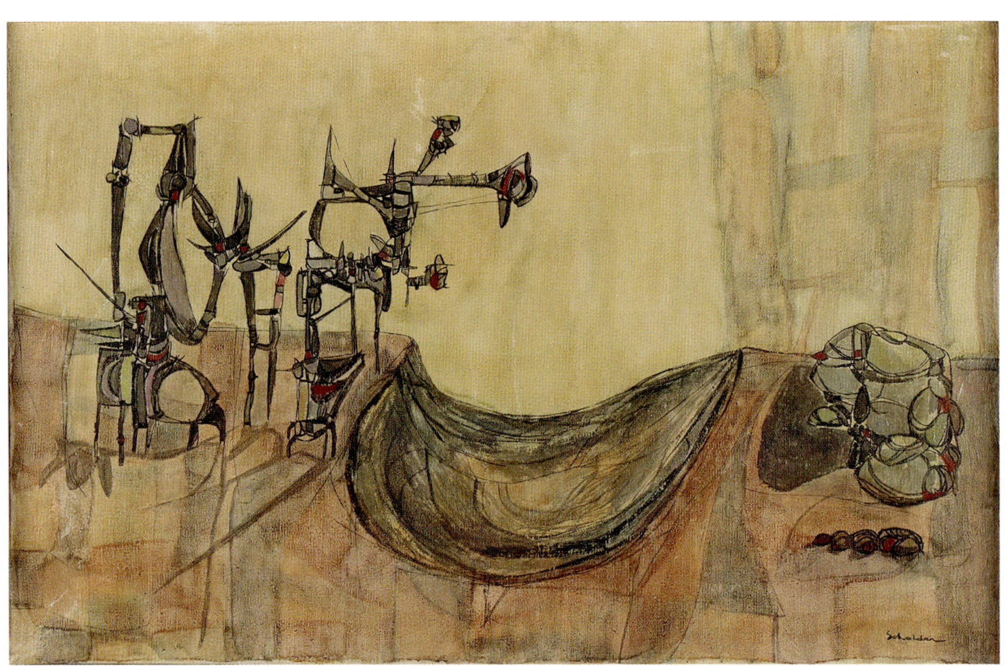

PLATE 5 Fritz Scholder (Luiseño), *The Offering*, ca. 1957–1960, oil and ink wash on canvas, 20 in. × 30 in., MoCNA Collection, MS-78 (photo by Addison Doty).

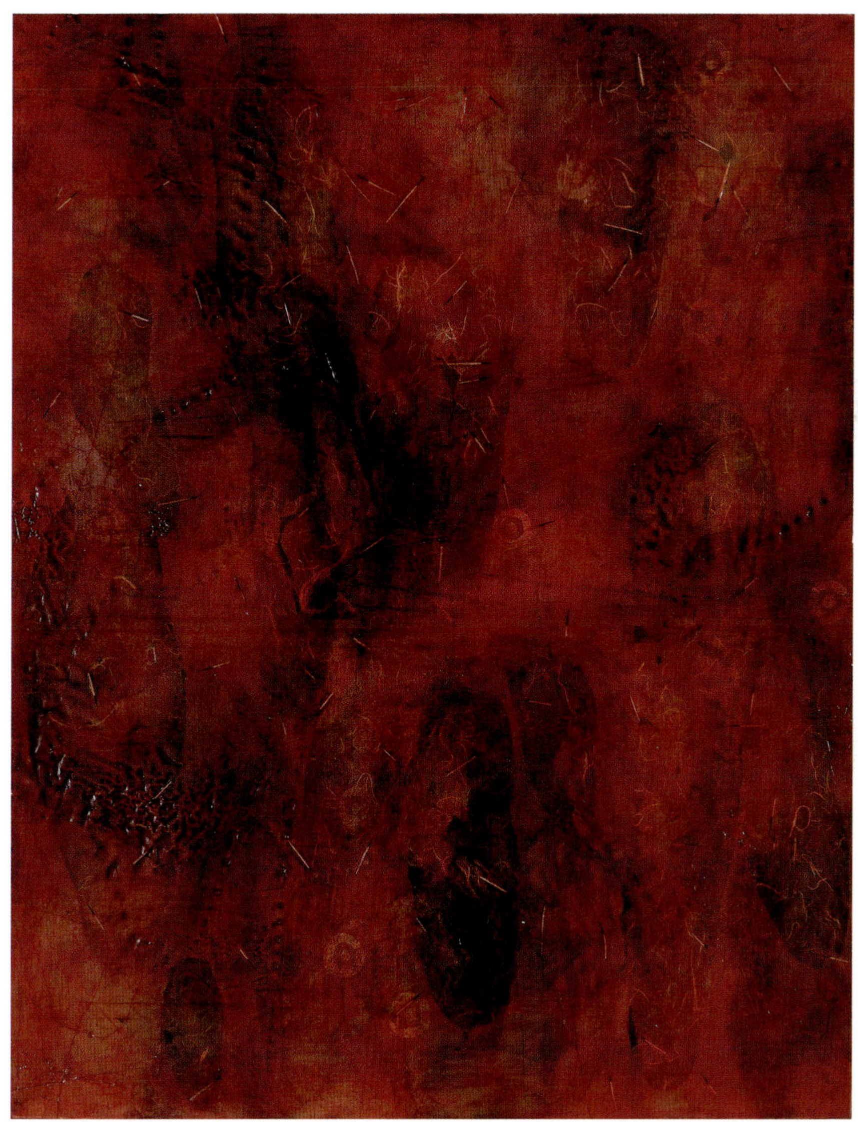

PLATE 6 Sonya Kelliher-Combs (Athabascan/Inupiaq), *Tangerine Walrus Family*, 2015, acrylic polymer, walrus stomach, paper, nylon thread, porcupine quill, 40 in. × 30 in., MoCNA Collection, AK-9 (photo by Addison Doty).

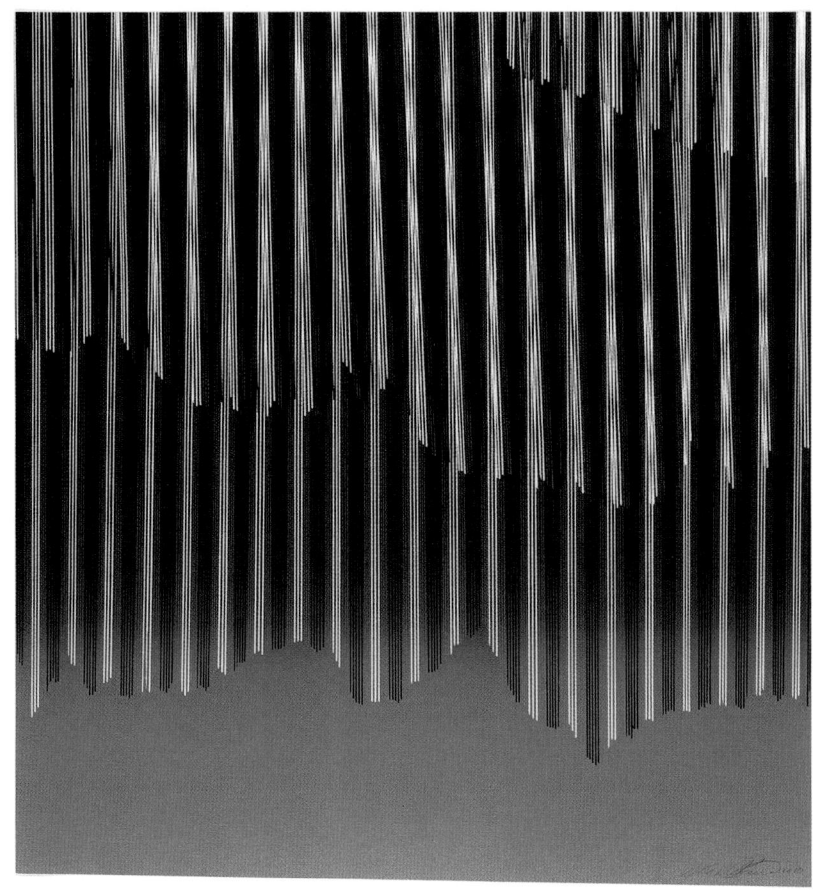

PLATE 7 Alex J. Peña (Comanche), *Untitled Lines #19*, 2010, monotype, graphite, enamel metallic ink on paper, 22.5 in. × 20.5 in., MoCNA Collection, CM-32 (photo by Jason S. Ordaz).

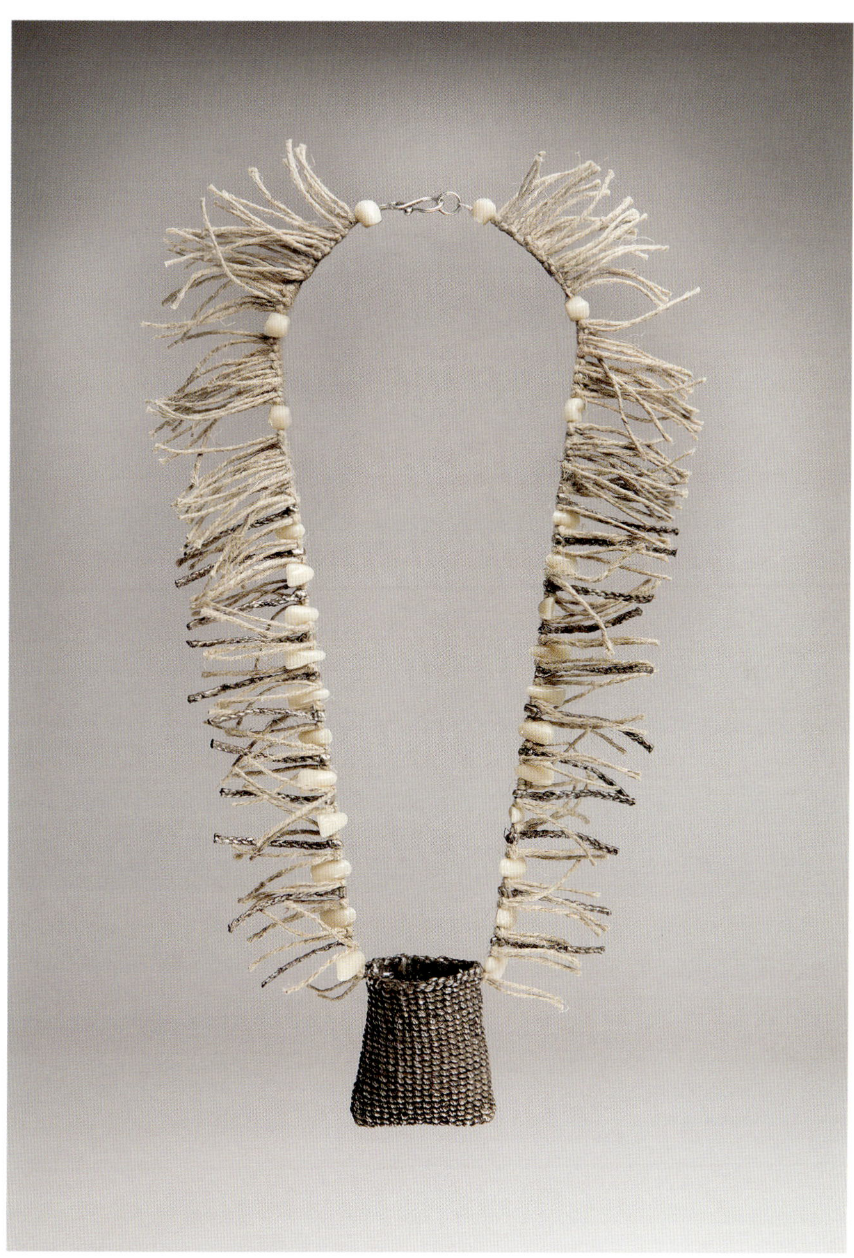

PLATE 8 Carly Feddersen (Colville), *Tooth and Twine Necklace*, 2016, prosthetic teeth, hemp on silver, 1 in. × 2 in. × 24 in., MoCNA Collection, CLV-55 (photo by Addison Doty).

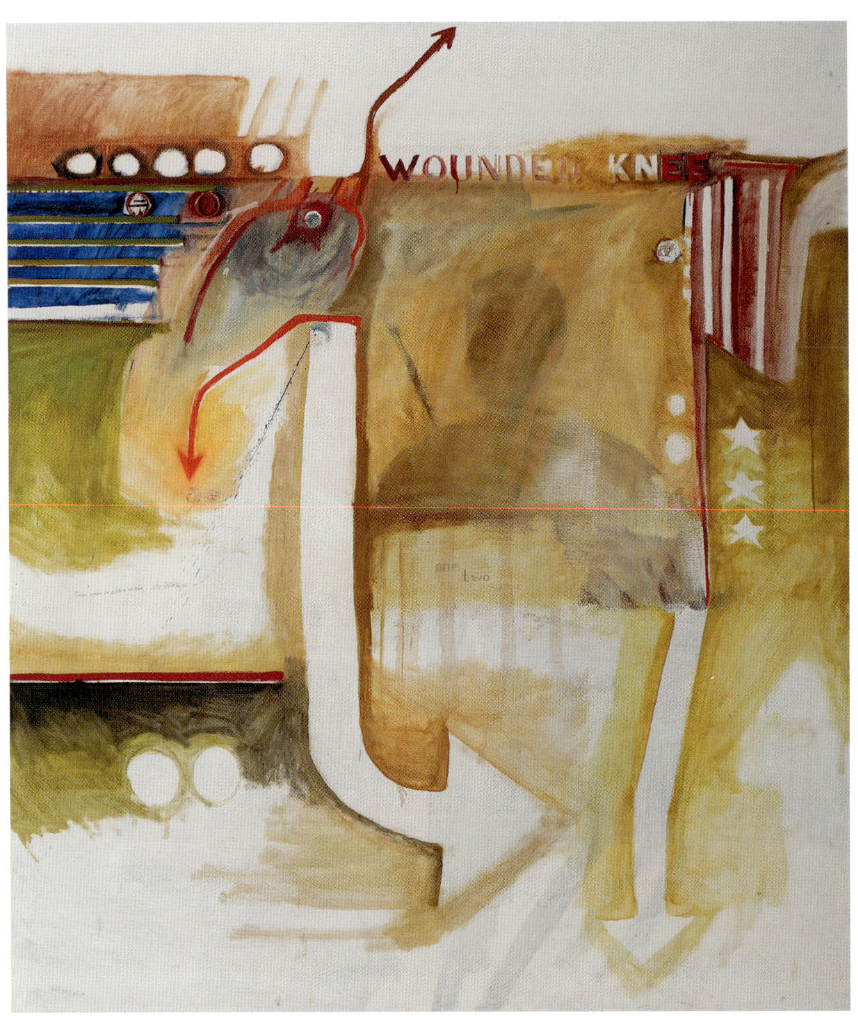

PLATE 9 T. C. Cannon (Caddo/Kiowa), *Tale of a Bigfoot Incident in American Vernacular*, 1966, oil on canvas, 72 in. × 59.5 in., MoCNA Collection, CD-7 (photo by Addison Doty).

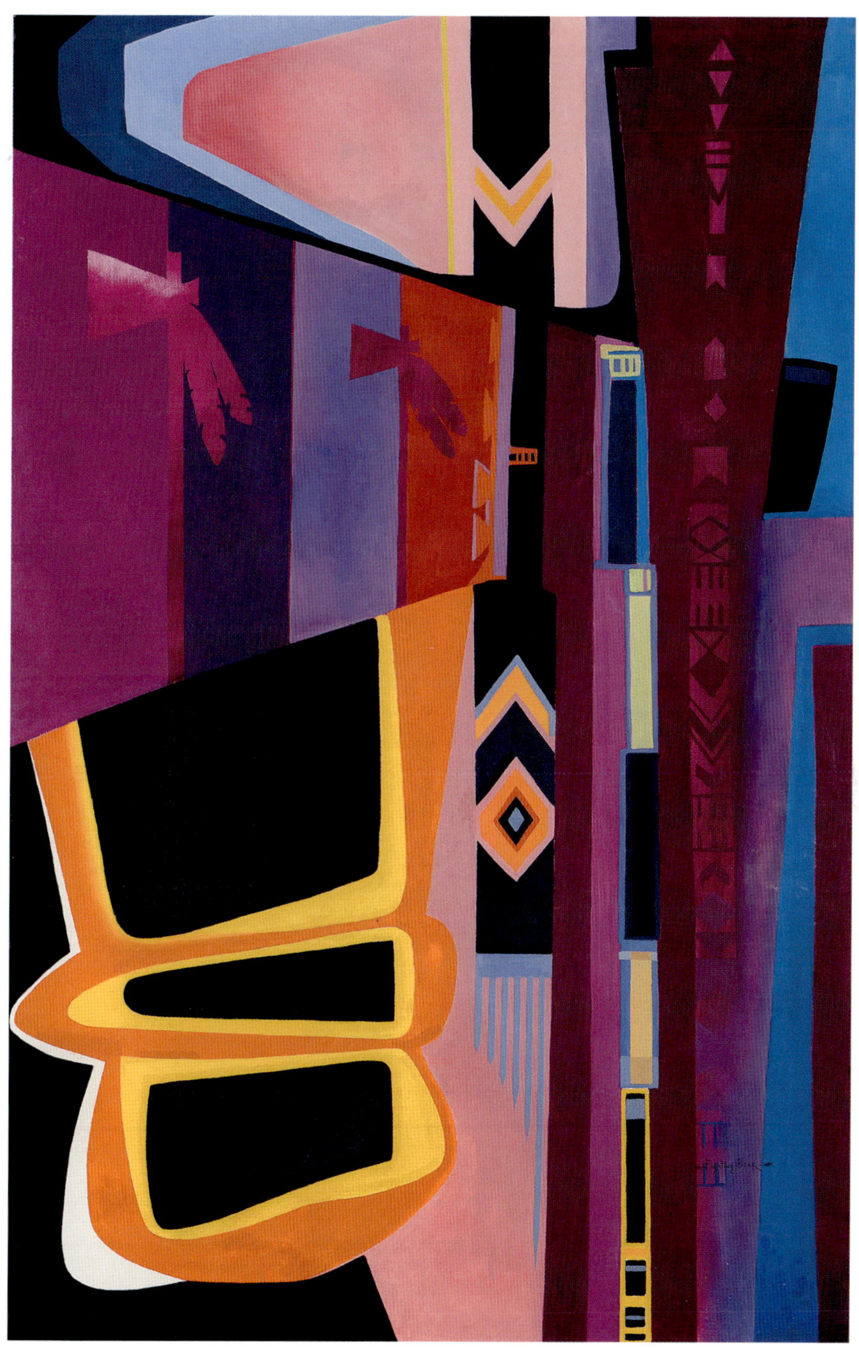

PLATE 10 Raymond Winters (Hunkpapa Sioux), *Giant Symbols*, 1971, oil on canvas, 96 in. × 60 in., MoCNA Collection, S-124 (photo by Addison Doty).

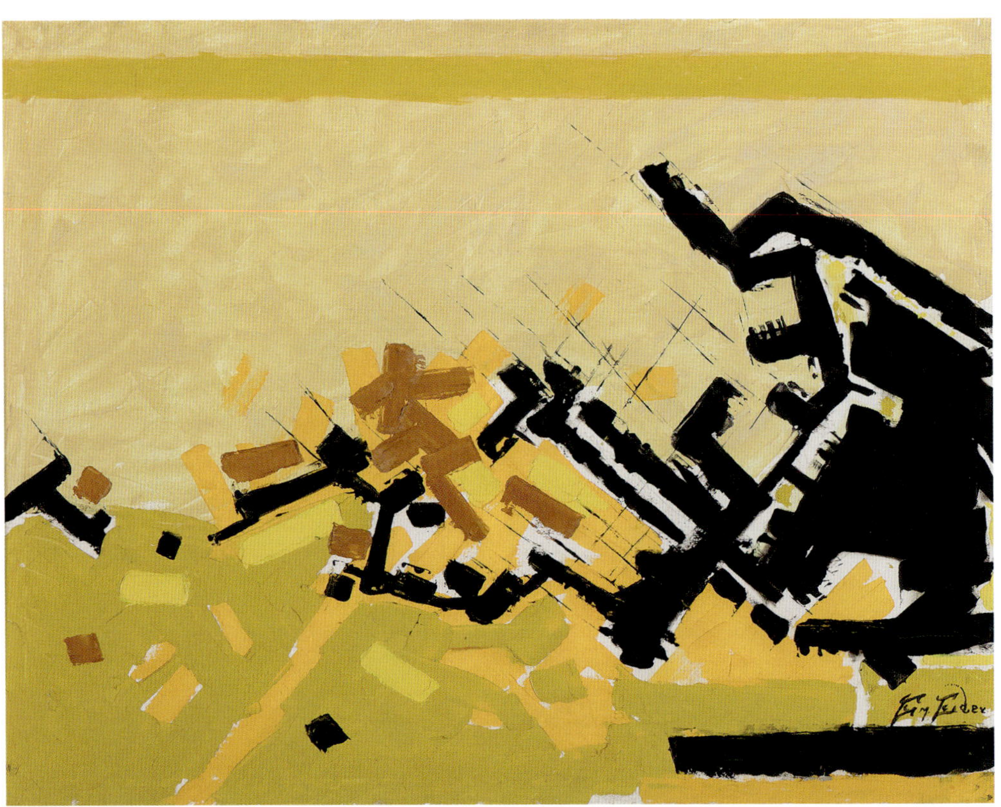

PLATE 11 Earl Eder (Yanktonai Sioux), *Forms in Beadwork*, ca. 1963, oil on canvas, 37.5 in. × 47 in., MoCNA Collection, S-60 (photo by Addison Doty).

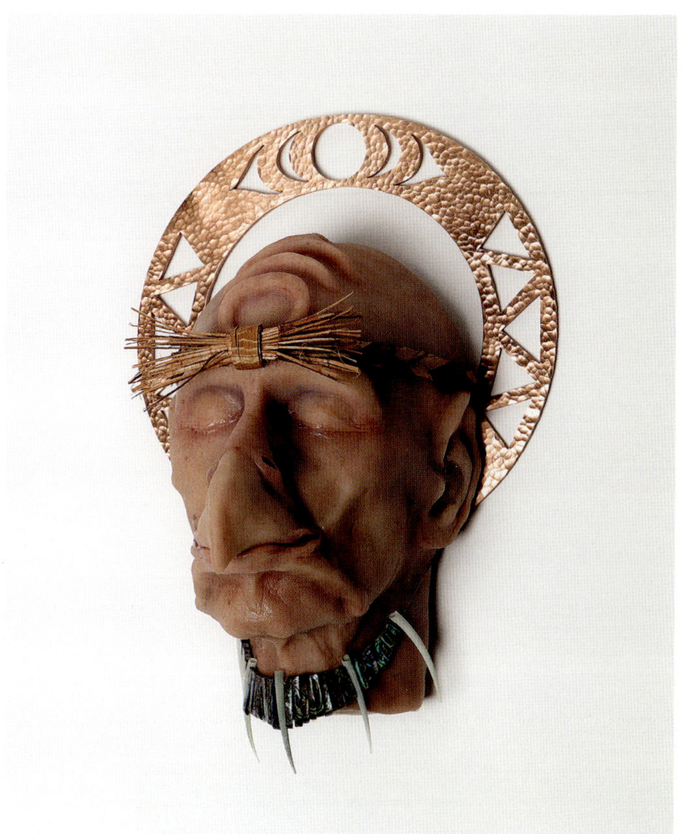

PLATE 12 William Thoms (Chehalis), *Tamahnous Proto-Being*, 2016, silicone, copper, urethane, cedar, abalone, sinew, 12 in. × 7 in. × 8 in., MoCNA Collection, NW-53 (photo by Addison Doty).

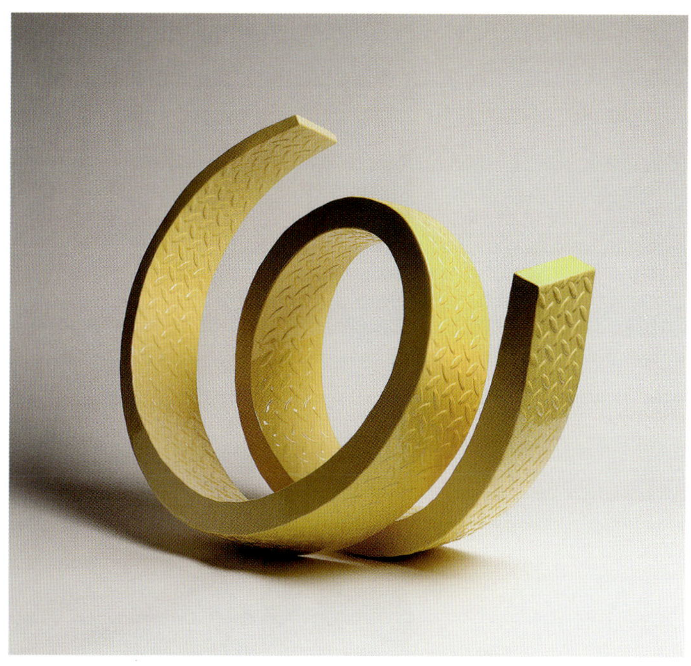

PLATE 13 Tony Lee (Navajo), *Wisdom*, 2008, powder-coated steel, 24.75 in. × 28.5 in. × 10.5 in., MoCNA Collection, N-1247 (photo by Addison Doty).

PLATE 14 Anong Beam (Ojibway), *Revolution (The Evolver Series)*, Part 1 of 5, 2002, mixed media on paper, 5.75 × 5.75 in., MoCNA Collection, OIJ-22 (photo by Jason S. Ordaz).

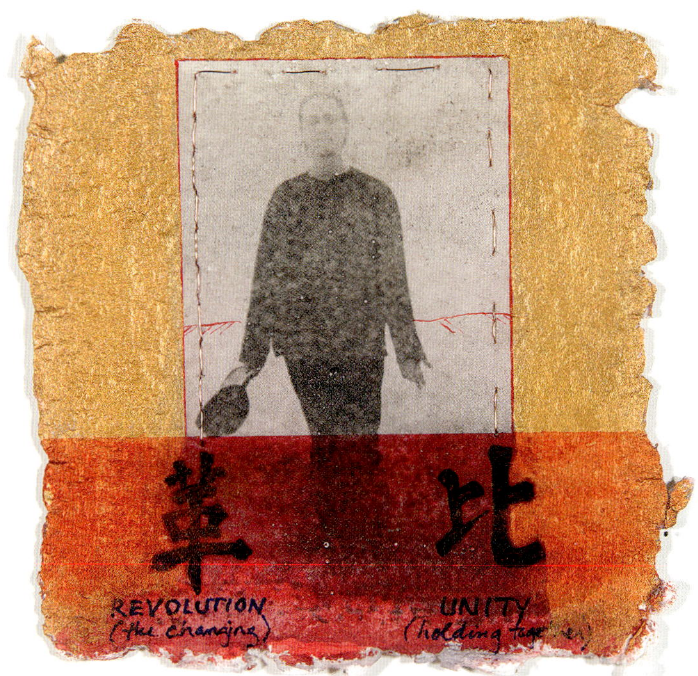

PLATE 15 Anong Beam (Ojibway), *Simultaneous Advance (The Evolver Series)*, Part 4 of 5, 2002, mixed media on paper, 9.75 in. × 7.5 in., MoCNA Collection, OIJ-25 (photo by Jason S. Ordaz).

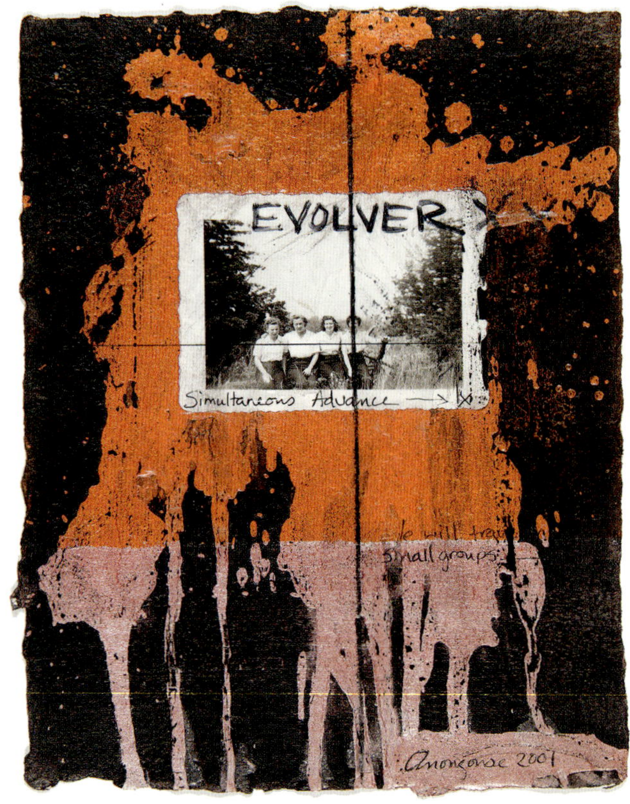

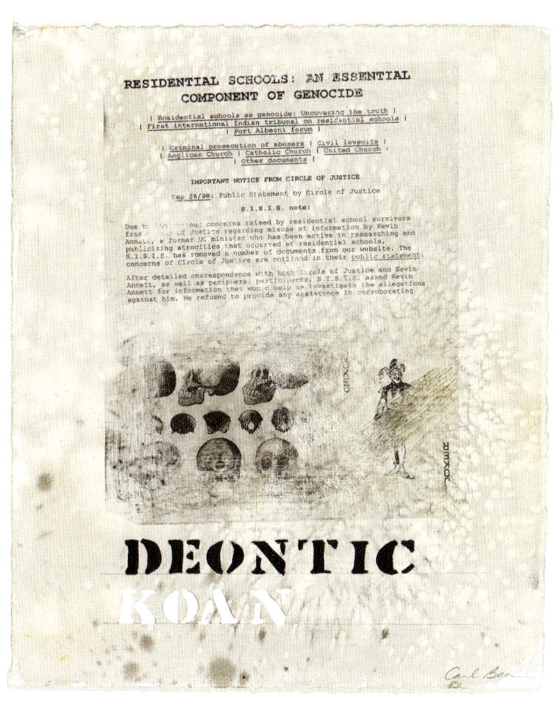

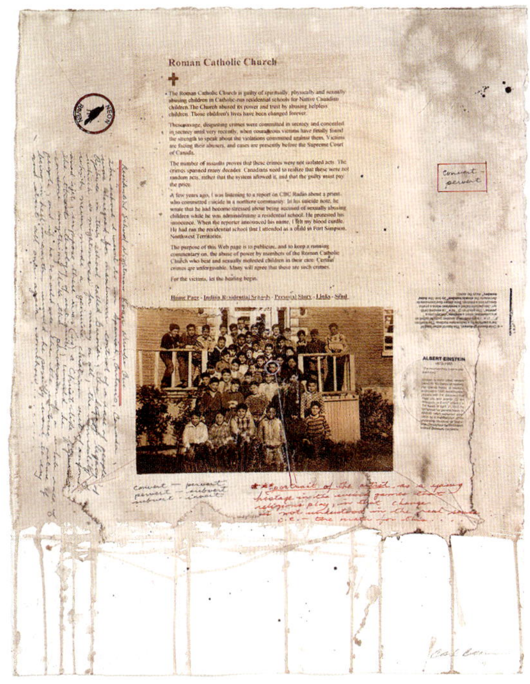

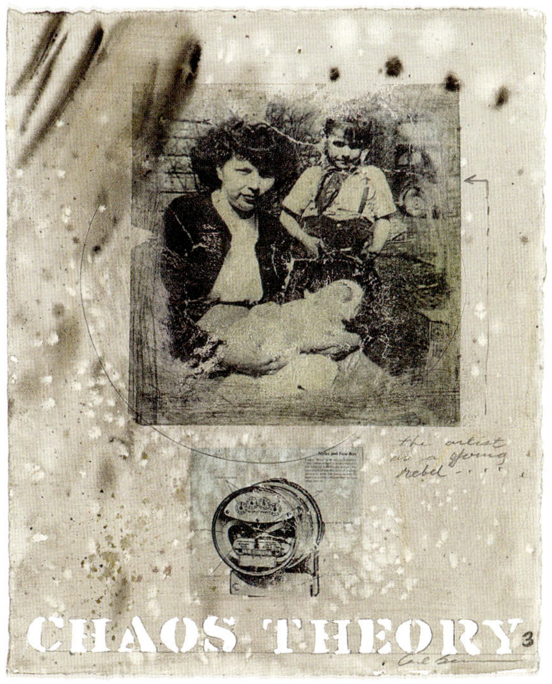

PLATE 16 *left top* Carl Beam (Ojibway), *Deontic Koan (The Whale of Our Being Series)*, Part 3 of 4, 2002, photo transfer, watercolor on arches paper, 15 in. × 11 in., MoCNA Collection, OIJ-29 (photo by Jason S. Ordaz).

PLATE 17 *left bottom* Carl Beam (Ojibway), *Chaos Theory (The Whale of Our Being Series)*, Part 2 of 4, 2002, photo transfer, watercolor on arches paper, 15 in. × 11 in., MoCNA Collection, OIJ-28 (photo by Jason S. Ordaz).

PLATE 18 *above* Carl Beam (Ojibway), *Residential School (Nightmare Koan I)*, 2002, photo transfer, watercolor on paper, 25 in. × 19 in., MoCNA Collection, OIJ-35 (photo by Jason S. Ordaz).

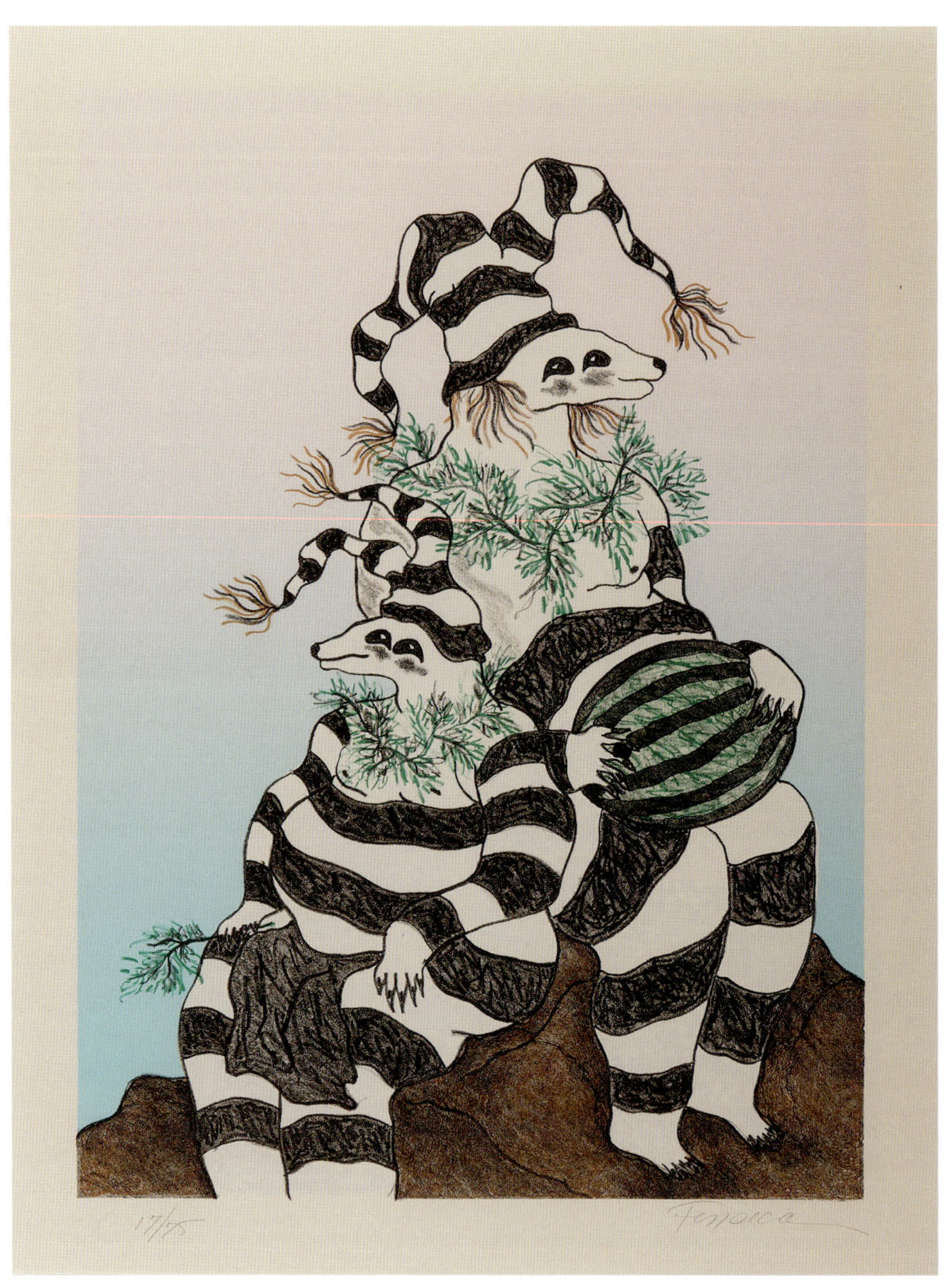

PLATE 19 Harry Fonseca (Nissan Maidu/Hawaiian/Portuguese), *Hopi Clowns*, n.d., lithograph on paper, 16 in. × 12 in., MoCNA Collection, MA-18 (photo by Addison Doty).

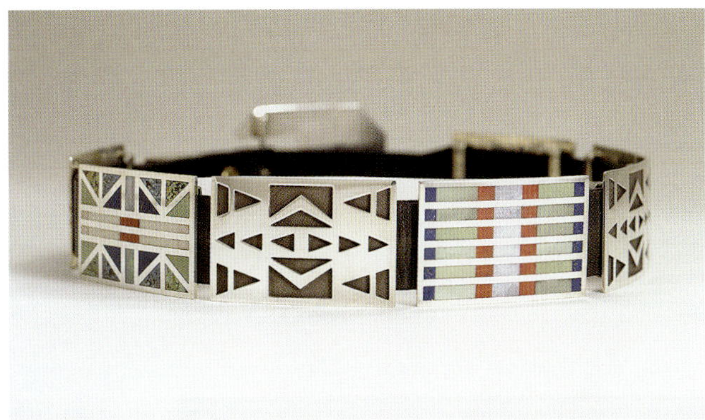

PLATE 20 Robert Gress (Crow), *Absaloka Parfleche Belt*, 1993, silver and gemstones on leather, 37 in. × 2.5 in. × 0.88 in., MoCNA Collection, CR-91 (photo by Walter BigBee).

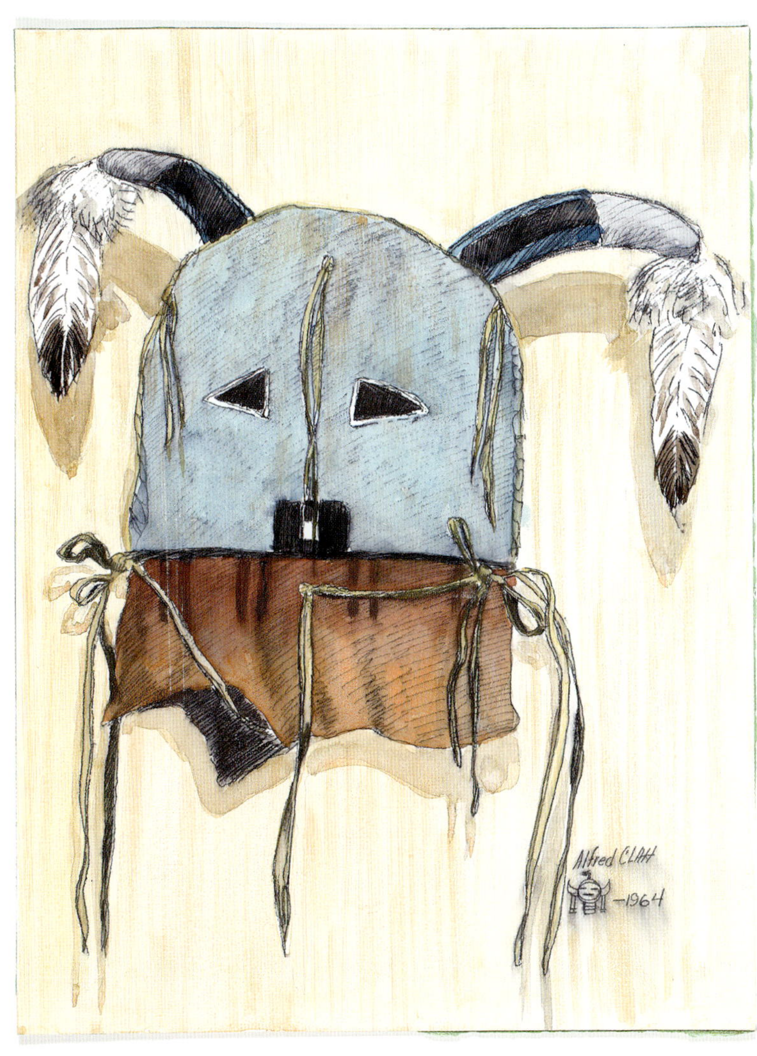

PLATE 21 Alfred Clah (Navajo), *Untitled*, 1964, watercolor on paper, 18 in. × 13.5 in., MoCNA Collection, N-1226 (photo by Jason S. Ordaz).

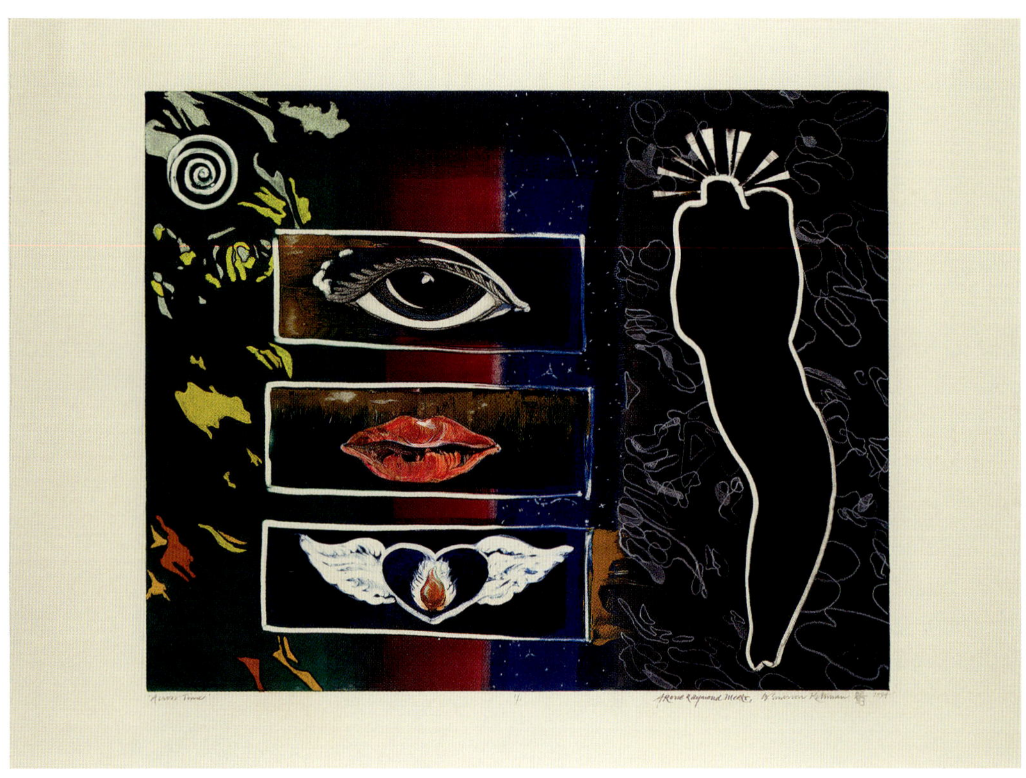

PLATE 22 Bobbie Kitsman-Jenike (Navajo) and Arone Raymond Meeks (Aboriginal), *Across Time*, 1994, monotype on paper, 22 in. × 29.75 in., MoCNA Collection, ABR-2 (photo by Jason S. Ordaz).

Indian with a Watch

POEM BY ALEX JACOBS

You could call me . . . haircut dude, he's so quiet, he never shuts up,
loner, lone wolf, ol weezer, ol war horse, he walks a lot, bus rider,
black bagger . . . or you could call me . . . Slammer Jammer, poem
slinger, gun for hire, poet mercenary, the godfather of Indian Soul,
the doctor of style, physician of funk, voice of authority,
tribal daddy, Mohawk terrorist, even the angry Indian comic . . .
but no they call me "The Indian With A Watch."

And it's not just Indians, but artists and poets too,
like they work with a watch on all day long but take it off when
they go out, like no one wants to be identified as "time manager,
time dispenser, time alluder," they all want to be timeless, like time
never affects them, like you never see a picture of an Indian with a
watch on in those "Time-Life Books," it's an unsolved mystery
anyone can be a part of, just by removing your watch . . .

It doesn't matter that this watch cost $3 and it has Batman on it and
it's one hour slow and seven minutes fast and I can't figure out
how to get it back on time. I only wear it to catch that elusive Santa
Fe Trails bus or count the minutes until my next dang bus is too
late or too early . . . so even if my watch works and I get to the bus
stop, I could still be late for court, late for work, late for a date, late
to wait for my connection, late for my deadline, too late for that
phone-call, too late to buy a 12 pack of Tecate on special, too late
to buy my canned tuna, ramen noodles and tortillas.
Just late again, like always, living this dang Indian Time.

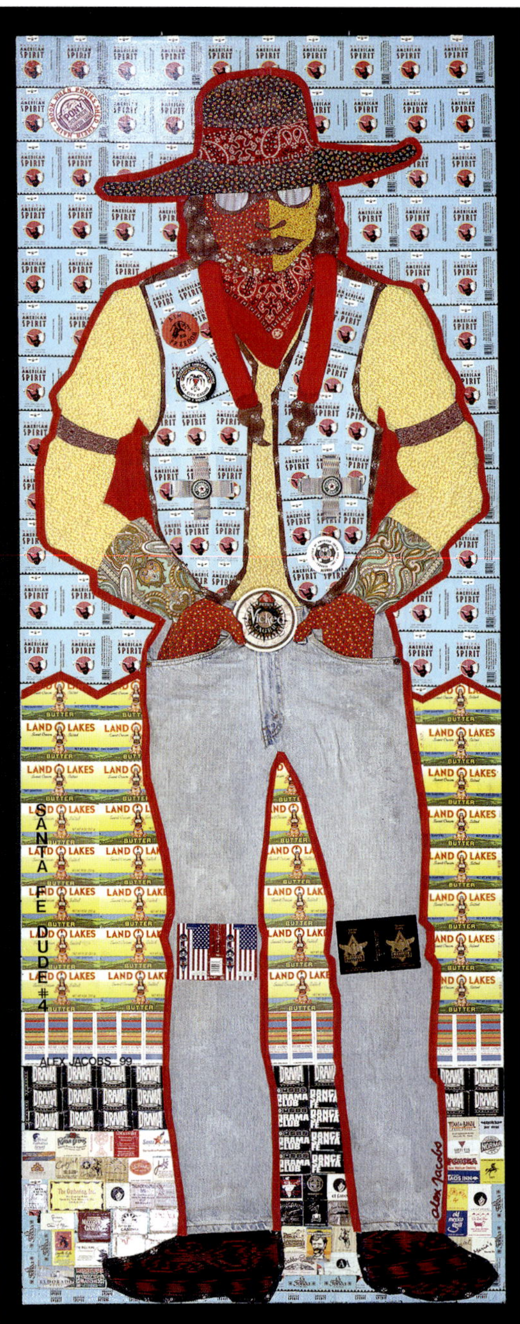

FIGURE 6 Alex Jacobs (Akwesasne Mohawk), *Santa Fe Dude #4*, 1999, mixed media on canvas, 78 in. × 29.5 in., MoCNA Collection, MH-26 (photo by Walter BigBee).

Hey, I could be the angry Indian, the shaman, the medicine man,
I could be the Indian on the nickel, tonto, chief, I could be so
sensitive that the trees reach down to touch me and animals lick
my sweet skin, birds sing their mating songs and the wind blows in
my hair so I get these tangles that always need untangling, baby . . .
I could be the Indian gone home to help his people
But I am currently in Santa Fe spending my casino millions!

So what if I'm the Indian with a watch
I'm clocking, man, I'm on the clock, I'm working, man,
I'm the man working for a living
Waiting for myself to make my own connection
Ain't nobody gonna come up and say:
"Oh wow man, sorry about the last 200 years, here's some free
shit, brah!"

You see, people see an Indian with a piece of art, they give him
money, they see an Indian with a six pack, they give him a hard
time, they see an Indian with a headband, they say: Right on Bro!
they see an Indian with a far off look in his eye, they give him a
donation, they see an Indian gal, well, they want a date, they see an
Indian with a briefcase, they want to give him a grant, maybe
but they see an Indian with a watch and everything is suddenly
equal, like they might even have an edge, an inside to start talking
all kinds of stuff, but hey, it's just a watch, got to get to my job, to
pay my court costs, to keep the judge happy, to keep the police
away from my door, and if I got a watch, I must got all kinds of
time to talk to you all . . .

Hey man, don't get me wrong, I'll talk history, philosophy,
sovereignty, gambling, symbolism, warriorism, shamanism,
I'll do the 'skin walk cause I can do the 'skin talk . . .

Man, I ain't no American Indian, cause that's what they call us in
the newspaper and media . . . and I ain't no Native American cause
that's what they call us all polite-like at the dinner table
("Uh, Mr. Native American could you please pass the peas.")
Man, I'm just a 'skin, a damn 'skin with a damn watch!
*(Und was soll es? Ich bin ein verdammter Indianer, mit ein
verdammten Uhr! Wieviel Uhr ist es?)*

What time is it?
It's just TIME, man, it's my time!
And I ain't waiting another 500 years, bro!
I choose my time!
And it's my time! Right Now!

Alex Jacobs

AUGUST 8, 1997
SANTA FE, NEW MEXICO

The Gaze in Indigenous Art

DEPICTIONS OF THE BODY AND NUDITY

NANCY MARIE MITHLO

In this chapter, I am interested in knowing how American Indian artists depict the human body, including nudes. I chose this topic because I found in my research that damaging images in popular culture had an impact on the self-esteem and life choices of Native peoples, especially women.[1] What, then, do Native artists choose to depict when making new representations from within Indigenous communities? I am also interested in knowing whether there is a relationship among the variables of the body, women, nudity, and the philosophical concepts of American Indian communities. In other words, do Indigenous artists have something unique to contribute to the dialogue of human nudity and images of the body in art? I have endeavored to use artworks from the historic archive of the Institute of American Indian Arts Museum of Contemporary Native Arts (MoCNA) in Santa Fe, New Mexico, a place that has been a part of my life for thirty years.[2]

METHODOLOGY

Seeing is not only seeing. Seeing is also thinking, processing, comprehending, and remembering. Often we think we recall something—a childhood memory, perhaps—but it is only a family photograph that holds the memory for us. Viewing something and thinking about how we view something are intimately linked.

"The gaze" is a bit more complex as a concept.[3] While this approach to understanding art encompasses the mind/memory part of seeing, it is additionally concerned with social aspects, such as who is seeing whom. In a heteronormative fashion, a male gaze on a female body is a particular dynamic, one often charged with notions of desire, control, or consumerism. Under regimes of power, the gaze of a police officer toward a person of color may connote suspicion, fear, or hate—or protection and concern. "The gaze" as a concept is also mutual. The person viewed gazes back, reinforcing or challenging the original intent. This, in turn, changes the social dynamic between the viewer and the viewed, altering it into something unknown and new.

Indigenous research prioritizes the "seen face."[4] I find this approach of speaking in person to be congruent with my training as a visual anthropologist. I prefer to talk to people, interact with them, and work with the same people for long periods of time. This is what I term American Indian Curatorial Practices—work that is long-term, mutually meaningful, and reciprocal, and that involves mentorship.[5] Working with collections and archives, researchers may or may not have access to living producers of the art or archival records they are studying. The Institute of American Indian Arts (IAIA) has an exceptional archive and the objects all have catalogue records, but these resources do not tell the whole story of a person's life, their intent, or their meaning in creating a work of art. The MoCNA collection at the IAIA consists largely of student works produced from the inception of the school in 1962 to the present. These students, especially in the early years of the school in the 1960s, were engaging in challenging issues and beginning to articulate just what Indigenous education in a government-sponsored boarding school could look like. In the pages that follow, I complement these early works with artistic endeavors through the past sixty years in an effort to create theory and meaning for what we have come to know as the contemporary Native arts movement.

Attending to the variables of the time the work was produced, the medium, the artistic intent (or what we may know of it), and the gender, age, or tribal affiliation of the artist while engaging equally in the content of the work is a sophisticated act of interpretation. As an educator, I suggest that students remain modest in their claims for what a particular artwork signifies. By "modest," I mean to encourage a spirit of inquiry that is open-ended and without any particular outcomes in mind. Interpreting art is a social act and, like viewing itself, is informed by the role of the viewer and his or her relationship to the maker and the subject matter.

PATTERNS OF SEEING

Let's start our discussion with an untitled painting by Wesley Wolf from 1973 (figure 7). When I first encountered this work, I was a bit shocked. I have in mind that elders, especially elder Native women, are conservative in the display of their bodies. Why would an IAIA student from the 1970s depict a nude elder with downcast eyes? Was this drawn from a photograph? If so, then why was a photograph made of a nude elder? What does the star shaped

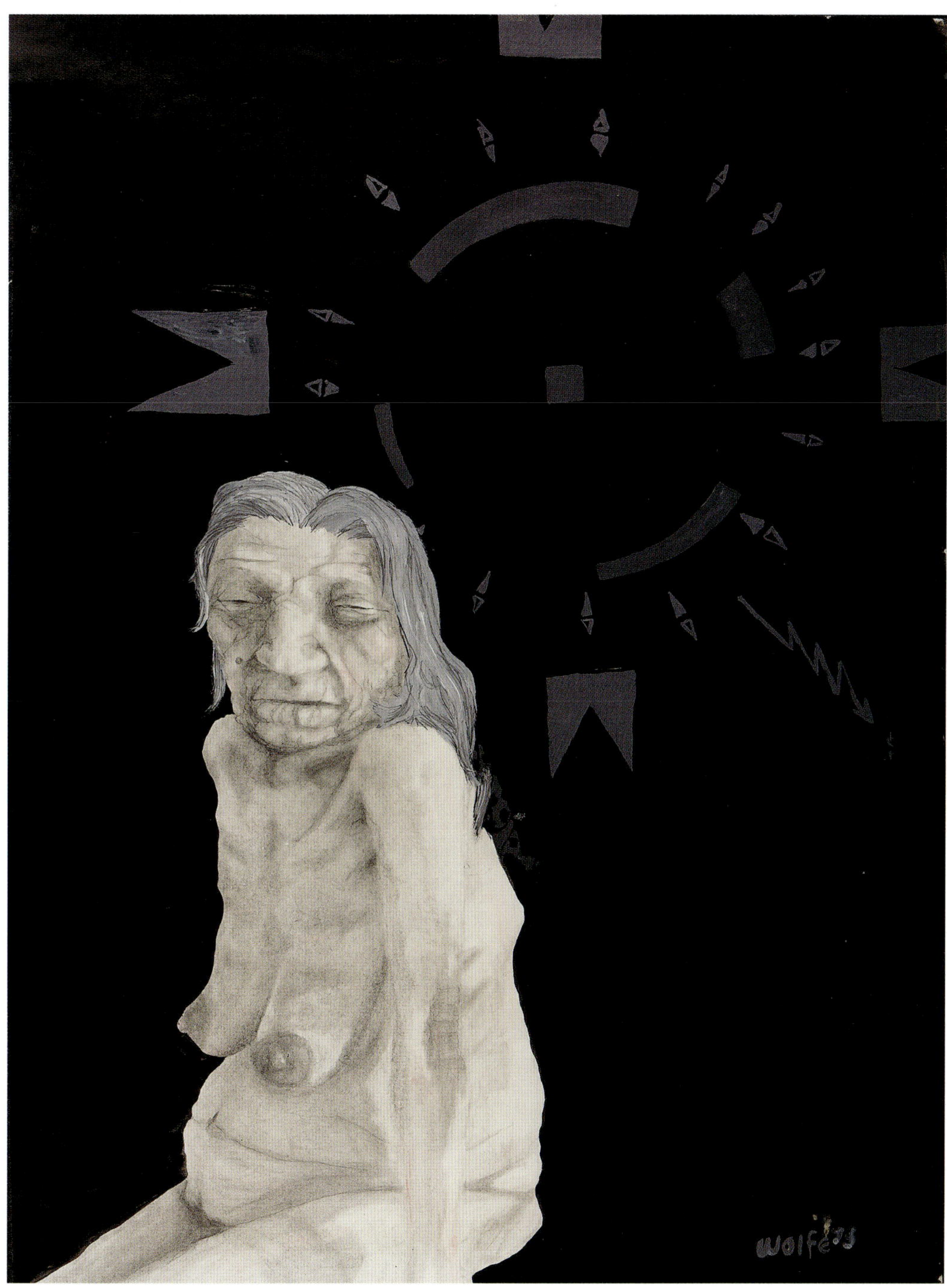

FIGURE 7 Wesley Wolf (Sioux), *Untitled*, 1973, acrylic and pencil on paper, 30 in. × 22 in., MoCNA Collection, S-154 (photo by Addison Doty).

design behind her signify? Without a full history, how am I to approach understanding this mixed-media work on canvas? What tools do I have at my disposal to interpret and appreciate the work?

Former IAIA Museum Director Richard Hill has stated, "Like many other indigenous cultures, Indians used the female form as a symbol of fertility, of an association with the female forces of the universe and as a part of the duality associated with that universe."[6] I like this interpretation; it gives me confidence to hear this in writing from one of the college's past leaders. As I say this, however, I realize that, had I been writing for a more mainstream academic audience, this perspective about women and fertility would be seen as essentialist and therefore bad writing or at least outdated. By "essentialism," I am referencing the idea that a person's race or ethnicity fully informs his or her perspective, experience, and life choices. While this kind of association can be used to harm, as in the example of someone associating a negative trait with one's identity (e.g., "Girls are bad at math"), there is also something real and truthful about making a generalization tying women and nature under an Indigenous knowledge system. I may disagree with what Hill has to say—and at times, as an intern working at the IAIA Museum under his leadership, I did!—but I consider him an elder and his concepts are useful in my work to understand the meaning of this particular canvas.

Hill states there is a duality to the universe and that women form a part of that duality. The artist Wesley Wolf's *Untitled* tells the viewer something about dualities in his choice of color: this is a black-and-white piece, not a colorful canvas. These qualities then—duality and the black-and-white palette—are in agreement, they are congruent. *Untitled* uses both figurative and abstract components, "figurative" meaning the use of a human body and "abstract" the geometric design in the upper part of the piece, almost in the position of a sun or moon above the woman's head. These dualities work to create interest and meaning.

But let us return to the nudity and the gender of the figure. We know this is an elderly woman by the exposed breasts and nipples that hang close to the figure's soft, rounded belly. Her bony shoulders are hunched up as if it were a struggle even to sit upright. Her hair is loose, and she averts her eyes downward from the mutual gaze of the viewer. In some ways, this gives her what some art critics may term agency—the ability to guide or be in control of the image-making. Averted eyes can also signal shame or modesty.

Human figures are complex to interpret and the artist leaves us much to ponder. Let's return to the Richard Hill statement above: "Indians used the female form as a symbol of fertility." As viewers, we can see that the figure depicted is beyond fertility: she is in a different life phase. Perhaps she has conceived and borne children, we do not know, but she is in her twilight years, on her way to her return to the earth. She even looks downward, as if signaling that she is ready to go back to the earth, as the sun design seems on its way upward, rising into the right-hand corner of the canvas. This sense of movement is accomplished both by the figure's being grounded to the lower left and slightly cut off and the design to the upper right, also slightly cut off. The viewer does not have the luxury of seeing either feature in full, but is rewarded with a sense of movement, of the earth rotating in time and space. There is a successful resolution to the piece as it floats between realism and abstraction, movement and tranquility, even acceptance.

But this reading of *Untitled* has not dealt fully with nudity. Could the canvas have succeeded as well if the figure were clothed? Hill asks this question in the same essay by directly confronting two systems of aesthetics, Native and European: "Have Indian artists, and therefore Indian communities, adopted a more European view of sexuality and nakedness in the arts?"[7] Let's consider two pieces, Melvin Brown's *Mother and Child* from 1982 and Alex Jacobs' *Thursday Blues* from 1976.

Mother and Child (figure 8) seems to address exactly opposite issues from *Untitled*. Here we have a fully fertile woman, in the life phase of mothering, demonstrated by her act of breast-feeding the young child. As in Wolf's work, her eyes are downcast and her hair is loose. Is she a victim to a male gaze or is she empowered? And what does the tribal designation of the artist as Navajo (Diné) signify? Are tribal specifics vital to reading this particular work?

The textiles depicted in *Mother and Child* are generic: this is a Pendleton trade blanket and an unspecified wrap around the child. There is modest jewelry—a string of beads on the mother's wrist. As an arts critic, I would not immediately prioritize the artist's tribal background as informing this piece. More important, I think, is the posing of the figure in a manner similar to Christian iconography, as in the Madonna cradling the Christ figure in the *Pietà*. Christian iconography would generally feature the Madonna as clothed, not naked. Like *Untitled*, the nudity of *Mother and Child* enables a more universal reading. Is this accessibility the desired outcome of both artists in using the nude? Or, as Hill inquires, is this a European view of sexuality?

Alex Jacobs's *Thursday Blues* (1976, figure 9) utilizes a vivid palette of greens, blues, and yellow to depict a female nude lounging with her face averted from the viewer. It is difficult to avoid a direct sensual reading of this piece—the woman's legs are open and her breasts jutted forward. Even her placement as

FIGURE 8 Melvin Brown (Navajo), *Mother and Child*, ca. 1982, oil on canvas, 30 in. diameter, MoCNA Collection, N-634 (photo by Addison Doty).

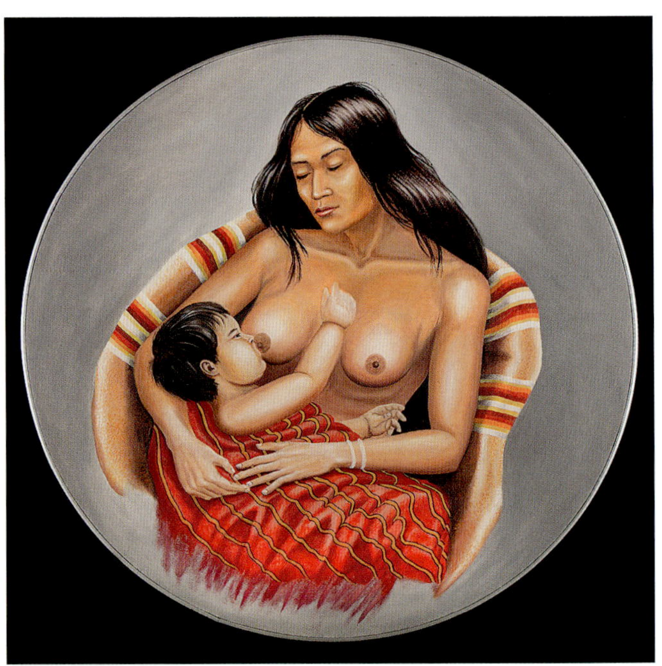

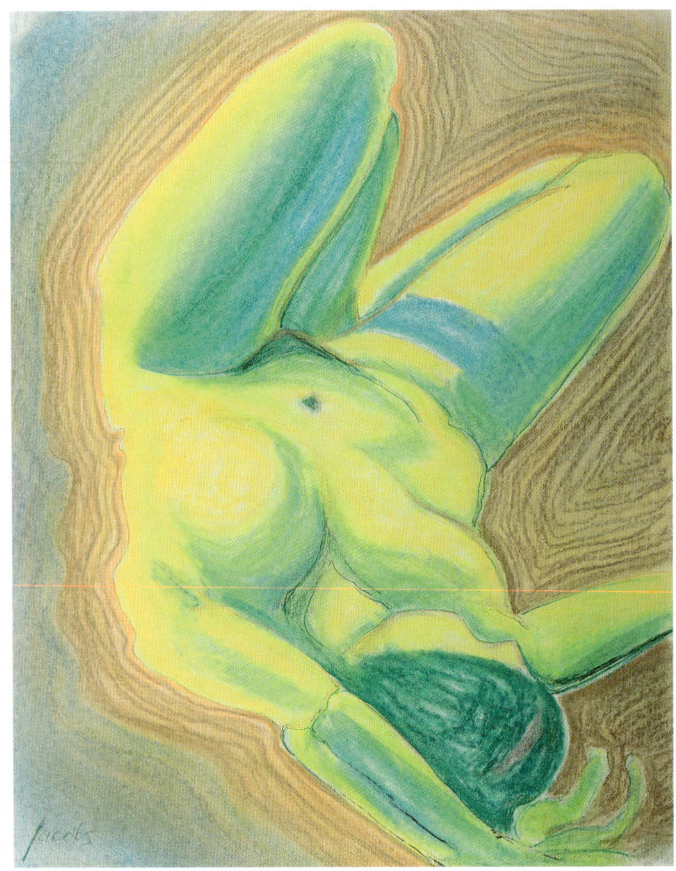

FIGURE 9 Alex Jacobs (Akwesasne Mohawk), *Thursday Blues*, 1976, pastel, ink on paper, 23.5 in. × 17.5 in., MoCNA Collection, MH-8 (photo by Addison Doty).

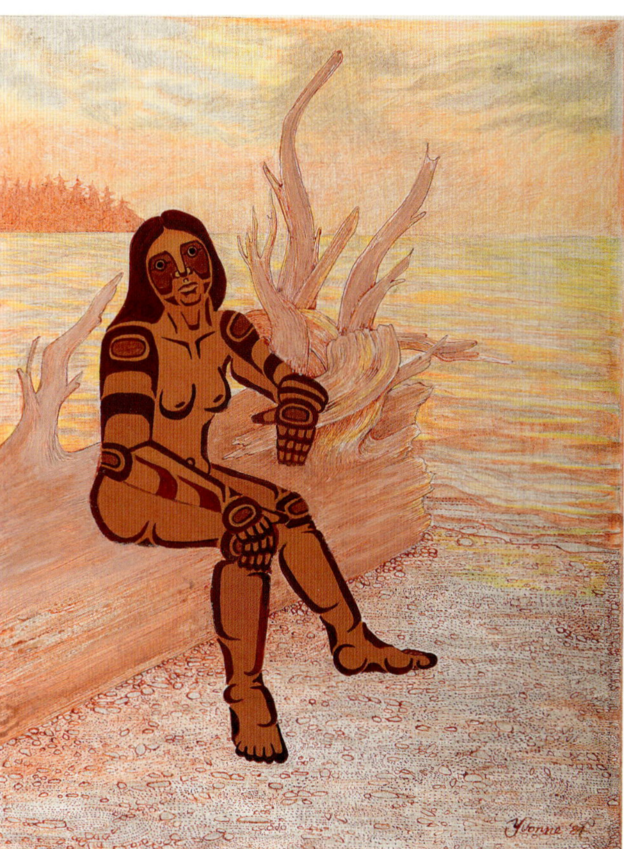

FIGURE 10 Yvonne Thomas (Lummi), *Dawn's Glow (Northwest Woman II)*, 1984, mixed media on paper, 16.5 in. × 20.5 in., MoCNA Collection, LU-10 (photo by Addison Doty).

upside-down, with her head at the bottom of the frame, suggests vulnerability and availability. The striking bold pastel colors and repeated lines emanating from the form convey a rawness and a vitality typically associated with the subjected female in a pornographic representational manner.

But this is not pornography. A situated reading, given the context of this collection as a component of an arts school, is that this piece was likely produced in a drawing class or influenced by a live-model drawing ethic. *Thursday Blues* can be interpreted in the frame of a classical nude study, a requirement of the Western fine arts canon. Jacobs' nude is not any studio sketch: it is a product of its generation, a result of the IAIA's first decades and before there was an established Native fine arts canon. A gifted and prolific writer and visual artist, Jacobs has channeled the vivid and energetic strokes and colors of this early canvas into the pulsating rhythms of the works he is best known for today.

Let us consider, then, another example, that of artist Yvonne Thomas (Lummi) and her 1984 mixed-media work *Dawn's Glow* (figure 10). This

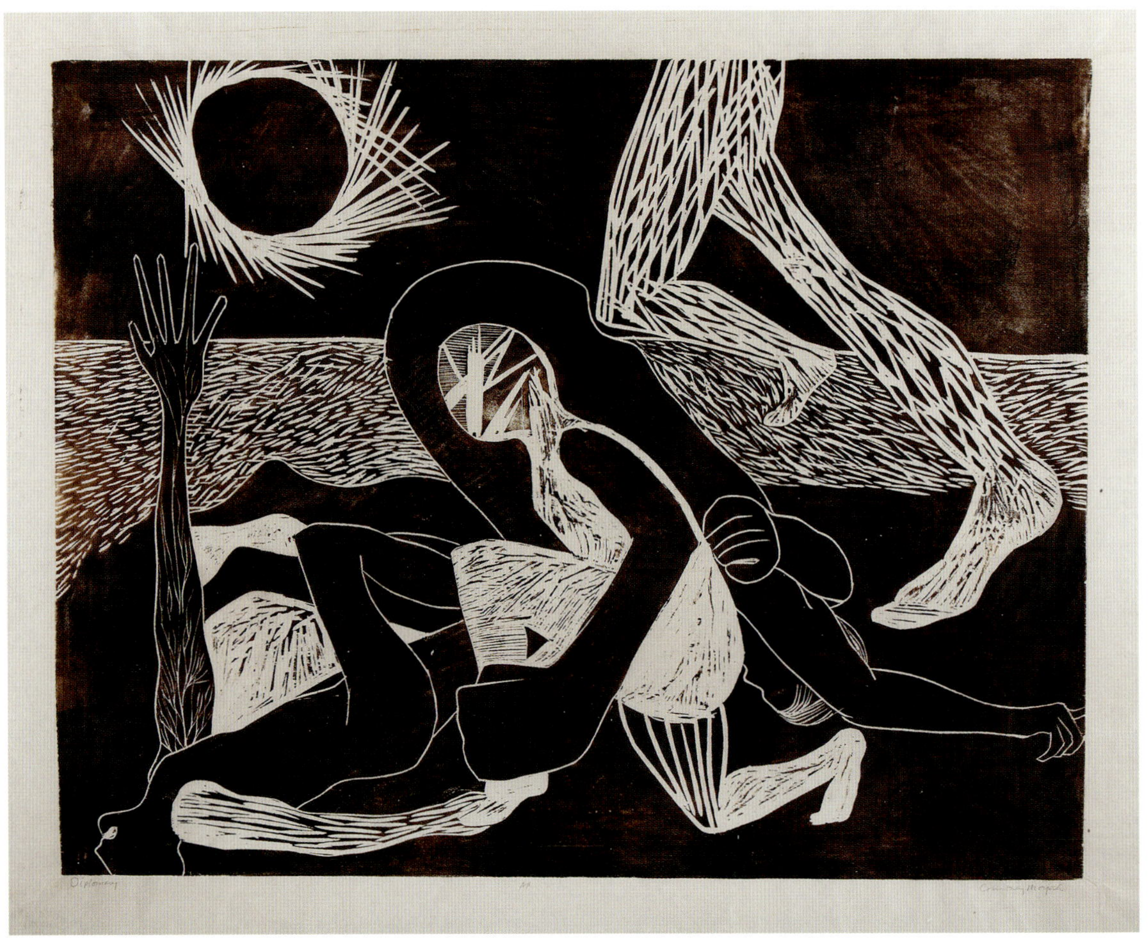

FIGURE 11 Courtney Moyah (White Mountain Apache/Akimel O'odham/Tohono O'odham), *Diplomacy*, ca. 1968–1969, linocut on paper, 34 in. × 28 in., MoCNA Collection, A-125 (photo by Addison Doty).

striking female is featured in full form, sitting confidently on driftwood by a body of water. She makes direct eye contact with the viewer as her arm rests assertively on a branch. The figure is nude, with breasts exposed, but is uniquely constructed in a method that combines Western figurative traditions and classic Northwest Coast line drawings. Crest figures are evident on her face as well as her upper and lower arms, but her hands, joints, and feet are rendered in a graphic style (not anatomically) mirroring three-dimensional carvings. The figure's genital area is modestly concealed by an arm resting on one knee. This remarkable nude figure is strikingly different from the three nudes discussed previously. Is this because the maker was a woman, is it due to a specific tribal reference, or is it the time period in which it was created? All of these variables are essential to investigating this work further. The use of regional motifs may suggest that the figure is a component of a storytelling tradition or an emergence story. Clearly, Thomas wishes for us as viewers to understand a specific place and humans' relationship to that place. This geometric figure is unlike a studio drawing or a universal portrait: it is a cultural interpretation that incorporates tribally specific designs with realism, with neither tradition taking precedence.

A series of works by Courtney Moya strike an altogether different chord. While the title and form of Thomas's *Dawn's Glow* are affirmative in tone due to figure, palette, and posing, Moya's depictions of grief and even terror are sobering reminders of violence against women and a lack of power and control.[8] These graphic works from the 1960s use ink and the medium of

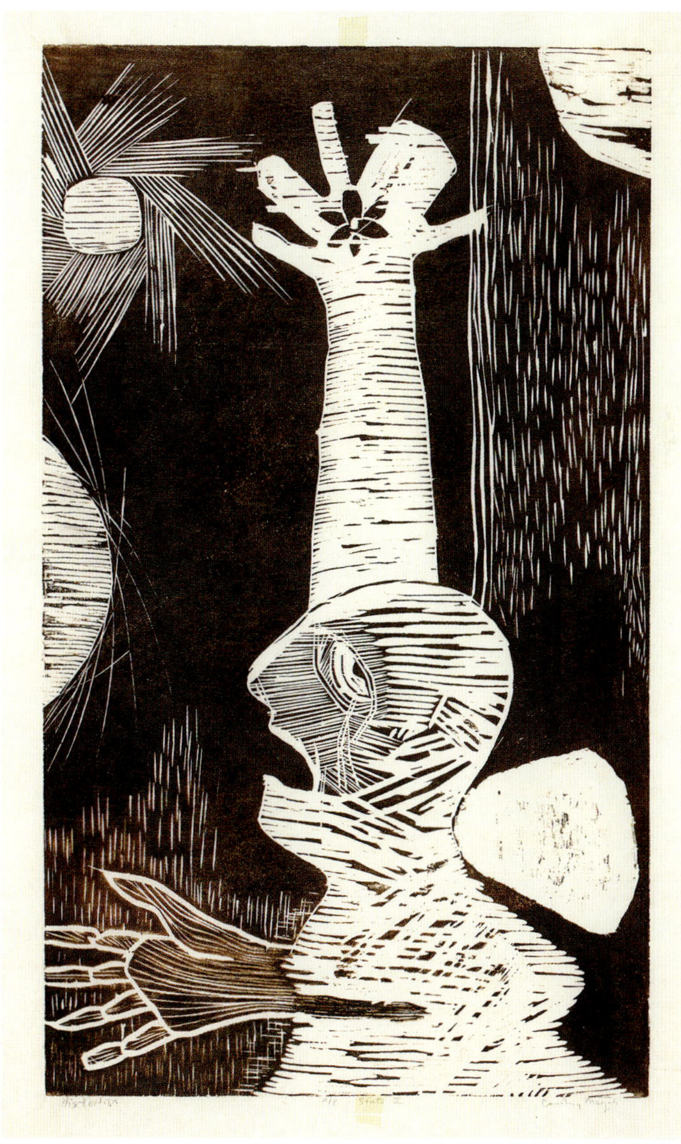

FIGURE 12 Courtney Moyah (White Mountain Apache/Akimel O'odham/Tohono O'odham), *Distortion*, Edition A/P, State II, ca. 1969, linocut on paper, 16.5 in. × 27.5 in., MoCNA Collection, A-75 (photo by Jason S. Ordaz).

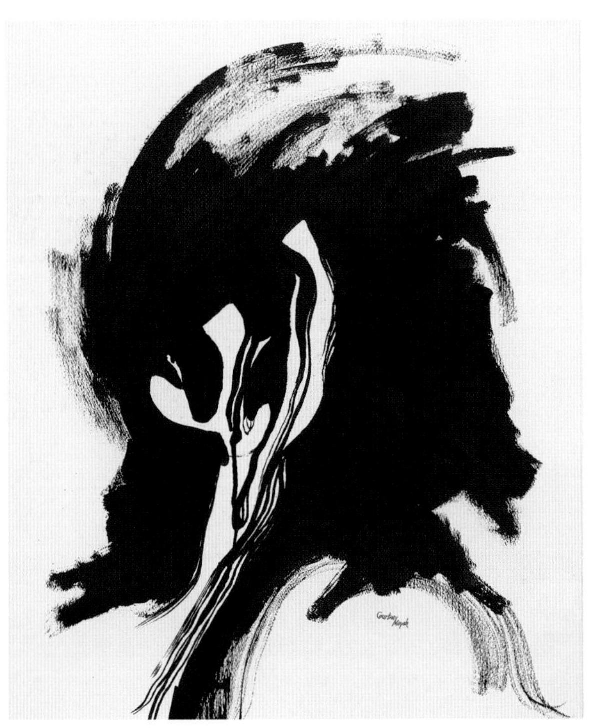

FIGURE 13 Courtney Moyah (White Mountain Apache/Akimel O'odham/Tohono O'odham), *To Cry in the Dark*, 1969, ink on watercolor paper, 26.25 in. × 22 in., MoCNA Collection, A-127 (photo by Jason S. Ordaz).

linocut press to convey stark scenes of conflict and sorrow in black and white. The complicated multifigured work *Diplomacy* (figure 11) features a prone body stretched horizontally, head lowered and open mouth grimacing in pain, while a threatening figure hovers above, a large clenched fist seemingly ready to strike. The victimized figure has one hand raised in a desperate cry for help, outstretched to a sun over the horizon line. Two other ambiguous figures are featured in fractured renderings: legs running toward the rising sun and an abstracted body faced downward that appears to envelop the aggressor. This narrative is accentuated by straight geometric lines emanating from the sun and throughout the bodies, making the figures' actions urgent and erratic.

This chaotic scene is accompanied by a similar linocut arranged vertically, presumably made at the same time, titled *Distortion* (figure 12). A lone figure also seems to beseech the sun, with a raised arm and open hands. A gaping mouth cries with eyes looking upward. This androgynous body offers one glimpse of hope in the form of a flower in the palm of the upraised hand. A vertical tree supports the figure, with geometric forms emanating from its core. While these works may have been executed in the context of a classroom, likely a printmaking course, their content can surely not be said to have been assigned. Moya's *Diplomacy* and *Distortion* are highly personal vignettes that cut to the core of trauma and suffering. Given the high rates of sexual violence against Native women,[9] a viewer might surmise that the title *Diplomacy* ironically references the historic use of rape during warfare. *Distortion* is more ambiguous. Is this a form of torture we are witnessing or a more metaphorical message?

Moya's pen-and-ink drawing *To Cry in the Dark* (figure 13), executed in the same time period, uses abstraction and the force of positive and negative space to vividly express human suffering. The bold ink lines surrounding the figure's face feel almost violently slashed across the paper, while rivers of tears and a downward-gaping mouth convey palatable grief. Are these artistic narratives biographical? Are they evidence? Are they healing? As viewers, we are unable to know exactly (and as a writer in this instance, I am solely refer-

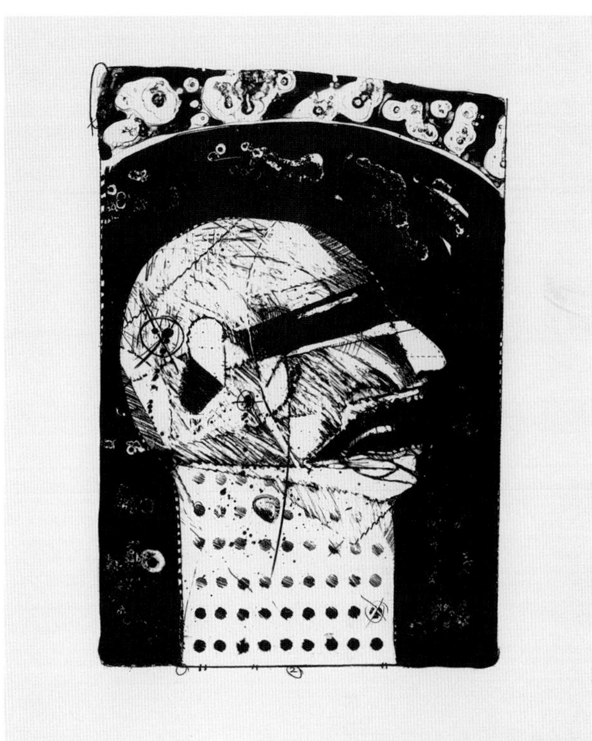

FIGURE 14
Rick Bartow (Yurok/Wiyot), *Cry I*, Edition 36/40, 1989, offset lithograph on paper, 30 in. × 22 in., MoCNA Collection, CAL-6 (photo by Jason S. Ordaz).

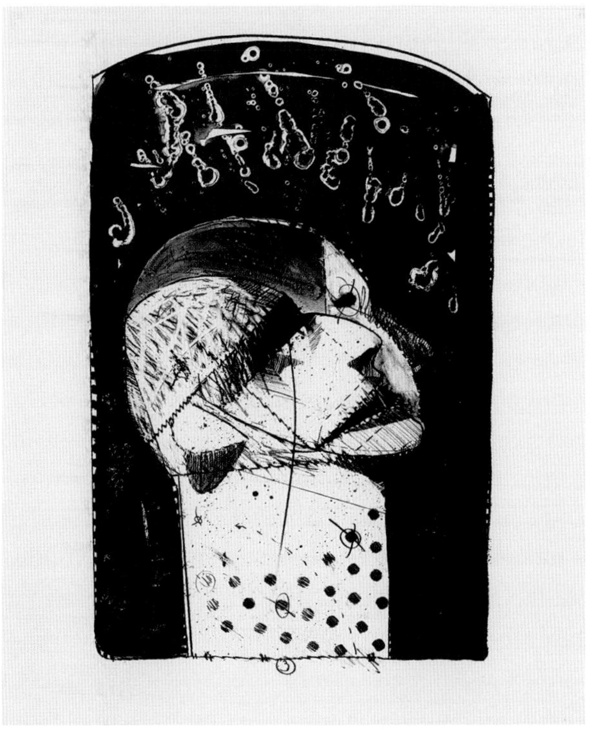

FIGURE 15 Rick Bartow (Yurok/Wiyot), *The Change*, Edition 36/80, 1989, offset lithograph on paper, 30 in. × 22 in., MoCNA Collection, CAL-4 (photo by Jason S. Ordaz).

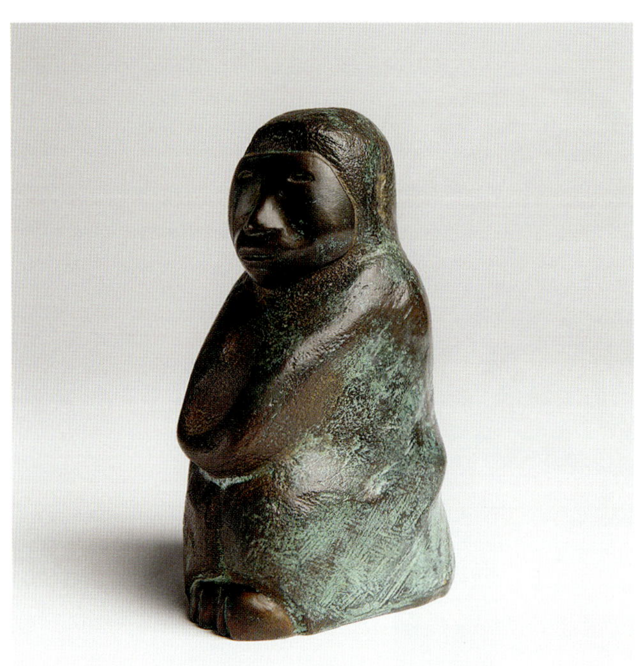

FIGURE 16 Clara LaRose Gaseoma (Shoshone/Ute), *Watcher*, 1985, bronze, 5.38 in. × 3.38 in., MoCNA Collection, SS-22 (photo by Addison Doty).

encing the work, with no biographical or historic record available at present), but we can comprehend the brave and bold impulses of the artist to make the phenomenon of violence evident. The expressions of horror are undeniable, but the execution of the works leaves room for interpretation of who is the victimizer and who the victim. These nudes do not celebrate: they mourn.

Rick Bartow's two 1985 lithographs on paper likewise address human suffering using a stark palette and profiled heads that beg for the viewer's attention. In *Cry 1* (figure 14), a masked head sits atop a square geometric pedestal that serves as a type of neck. An open mouth and tongue jutting out seem to summon the voice of this silent subject. Geometric forms in the arch hovering above the head suggest thought bubbles of fear or anxiety, while the uneven rectangular frame of the piece adds tension and uncertainty.

Bartow's work *The Change* (figure 15) suggests resolution: the geometric base seems less commanding and the head turns slightly to look upward. The thought bubbles are no longer encased and appear to float effortlessly above the profiled head as if offering instructions or a way forward. These mature renderings are consistent in their approach and materials, a result of the artist's prolific career and subsequent identifiable style. Bartow's military service in Vietnam and his resultant post-traumatic stress disorder behaviors have an impact on the mood and the content of his work; however, he was

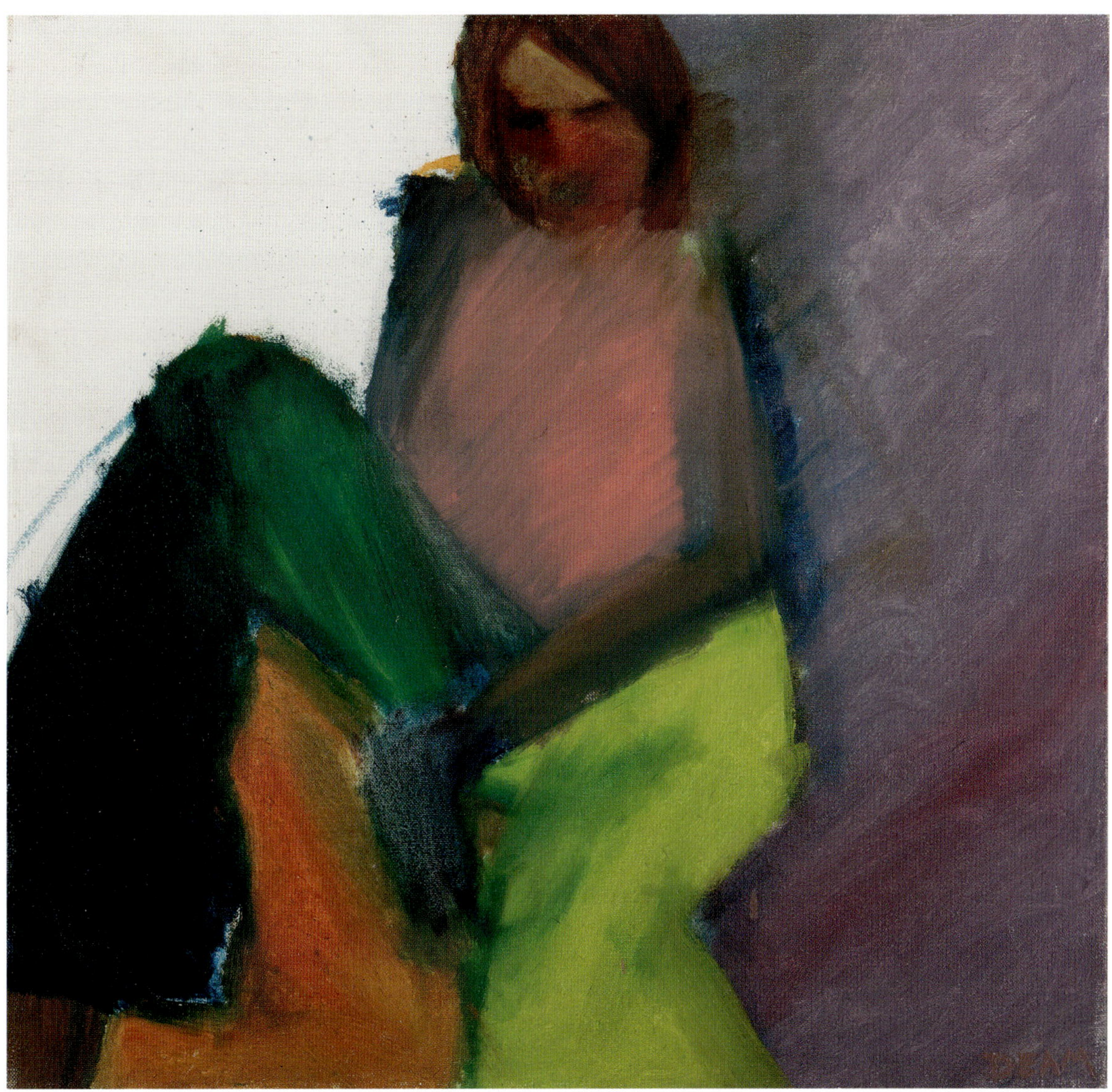

FIGURE 17 Peggy Deam (Suquamish), *My Backyard Larry*, 1969, acrylic on canvas, 18 in. × 18 in., MoCNA Collection, SUQ-17 (photo by Addison Doty).

also influenced by European artists, Northwest Coast carving traditions, and human/animal iconography.[10]

A work from the same 1980s time period, *Watcher* by Clara LaRose Gaseoma (figure 16), is a compact seated form in bronze only five by three inches in size. Viewers cannot discern if the figure is male or female, but its solid resting presence speaks of certainty and care. The face is solemn, the posture erect, with small feet protruding from under a folded wrap. Like Bartow's *The Change*, viewers gain a sense of a forceful presence and hopeful resilience.

Peggy Deam's 1969 acrylic on canvas *My Backyard Larry* (figure 17) achieves some of this same sense of place and security, but through the color choices and the body's posture rather than by weighty material and mass. A lone figure bisects the center line of the canvas, with the face turned to confront the viewer. An assertive stance of legs parted and a hand limply resting on one knee suggest self-possession, while the colorful hues—a pink shirt and lime-green pants—deny a serious tone. It is noteworthy that this work rendered by a woman of a man features a fully clothed individual in complete possession of his dignity and with no evident possibility of victimization. Deam is working within a genre of American Indian painting that became notable in this era of the late 1960s, although we rarely associate her with the movement that became aligned primarily with male practitioners.

The works featured above allow the reader examples of how to "read" selections from the IAIA collection using the variables of materials, composition, content, and technique. We have discussed questions regarding the significance of the gaze, nudity, tribal affiliation, the era the work was produced, gender, age, and potential sensuality or materialism in the female nude. Given these roadmaps, let us now turn to a deeper discussion of these concepts, looking specifically at key artists making contributions in abstraction and Indigenous knowledge production.

"ABSTRACTION SERVES INDIGENEITY"

I wrote the quote above for a 2012 article in which I argued, "Form becomes a way to shield the viewer and the subject from exposing information that is too personal. Abstraction serves indigeneity."[11] I want to explore this concept further by discussing in more depth the works of five artists (two male and three female) whose works I know personally. I will attend to the variable of Indigenous methodologies and how subjectivity, or my own positioning as a researcher and writer, informs what I write and how I write it.

Bill Soza War Soldier's 1969 oil painting *Ghost Dance II* (figure 18), part of a triptych, is a subdued composition of stars and half-moons arranged around a prominent central blue crescent moon. Sometimes referred to as the Ghost Dance of 1890, the multitribal religious revival it references was led by Wovoka, a prominent Paiute spiritualist. Is Soza's reference to the Ghost Dance representative of the Institute of American Indian Arts as a revival of Native resistance and resilience? A belief in renewal holds common appeal throughout American Indian histories, and one can imagine Soza's experience as a young man in the newly established arts school as empowering and inspired.

Soza's canvas uses abstraction to represent what appear to be masses moving in a parallel fashion against smaller groupings. Is this the American Indian Movement on the rise against smaller impotent forces? Or should one read the small clusters as American Indian peoples working against a larger bureaucratic government system? In either case, these abstracted icons are dramatically interrelated in a constellation of signs and meanings. What is important to note is that Soza has strategically chosen not to paint actual bodies in a figurative form, but substituted stars for what appear to be human beings, given the title of the work. In this action, has he chosen to avoid directly addressing the terrible horrors of the 1890 Wounded Knee Massacre (which is unavoidably associated with the Ghost Dance) by utilizing geometric icons?[12] My reading of this work is that he has given dignity to those slaughtered by relying upon abstracted stars to stand in for the physicality

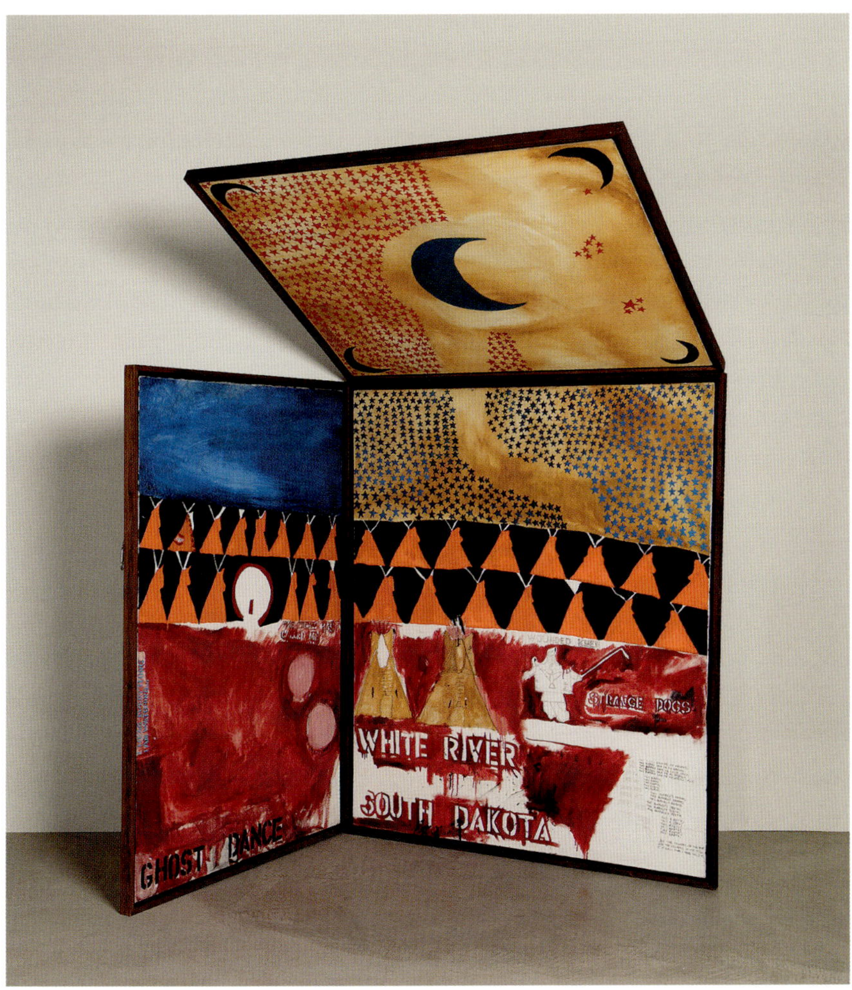

FIGURE 18 Bill Soza War Soldier (Cahuilla/White Mountain Apache), *Ghost Dance II*, Triptych, 1969, oil on canvas, 64 in. × 54 in. × 42 in. MoCNA Collection, MS-8, MS-9, and MS-10 (photo by Addison Doty).

of the body. He has utilized indigeneity as an artistic strategy for refusing to render the graphic violence against Native communities.[13] This refusal is a powerful indication of agency, the ability to control one's own image.

Given this excellent use of abstraction, why then does Soza utilize representative figures in *Self Portrait* (1968, figure 19) and *John Wesley Hardin, Killer of Men* (1969, figure 20)? The earlier *Self Portrait* is a masterpiece of classic technique, color, proportion, and composition that defined what has become known as the golden era of the IAIA. Soza was a student of Fritz Scholder, the IAIA painting instructor whose name would become synonymous with the "ugly Indian" style apparent in this early Soza canvas. As Alex Jacobs relates, it is a classic story of "who-influenced-who," as both men excelled in this genre of colorful, energetic, and distorted figurative works.[14] Scholder would go on to become wildly successful commercially and define the new Indian arts movement. Soza's life was nonconformist, as his entanglements with Indian activism and the legal system (along with his own cultivated sense of style and bravado) would come to define him as an outlaw figure, unpredictable and, in some quarters, feared. His self-portrait is distorted, while his *John Wesley Hardin* is controlled. Hardin, a notorious Texas gunslinger in the late 1800s, was known for killing twenty men in a ten-year period, the first murder when he was sixteen years old. This canvas is drawn from a famous photograph of the young outlaw. What is Soza telling the viewer with this association? Was Hardin a type of icon to be emulated? Readers should note that many, if not most of the artworks from the IAIA collection of the late 1960s were made by young artists in their teens and early twenties. Their identities were still being formed and their personalities emerging. Numerous self-portraits exist in the collection, attesting to the fact that the students were searching, experimenting, and trying on new narratives as they matured.

Up until this point in my narrative, I have remained fairly impartial or even impassionate in my appraisal of artworks discussed, but I knew Bill or "Billy" as a friend who was part of the Santa Fe arts world that I inhabited for over twenty years. While some people were intimidated by Soza's "rugged" persona, I experienced Bill as someone who was sensitive and sentimental, especially at the time that my youngest daughter was born. He carried a baby picture of her with him and considered her one of his own. Our friendship was based in the fact that I could see this part of him, the best of what he strove for in himself—a protective leader who only wanted good for the People.

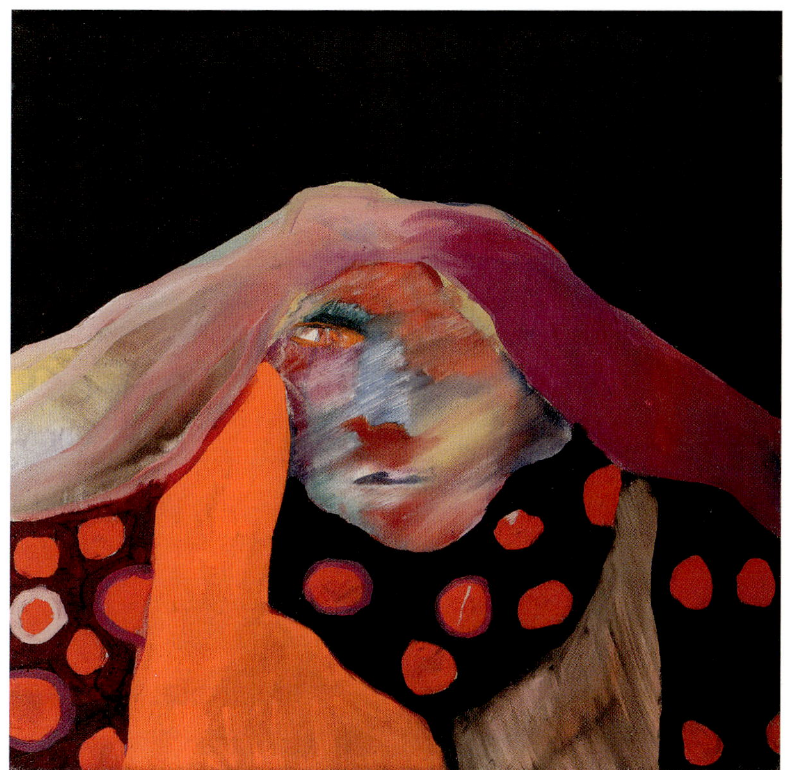

FIGURE 19 Bill Soza War Soldier (Cahuilla/White Mountain Apache), *Self-Portrait*, 1968, oil on canvas, 21 in. × 21 in., MoCNA Collection, MS-22 (photo by Addison Doty).

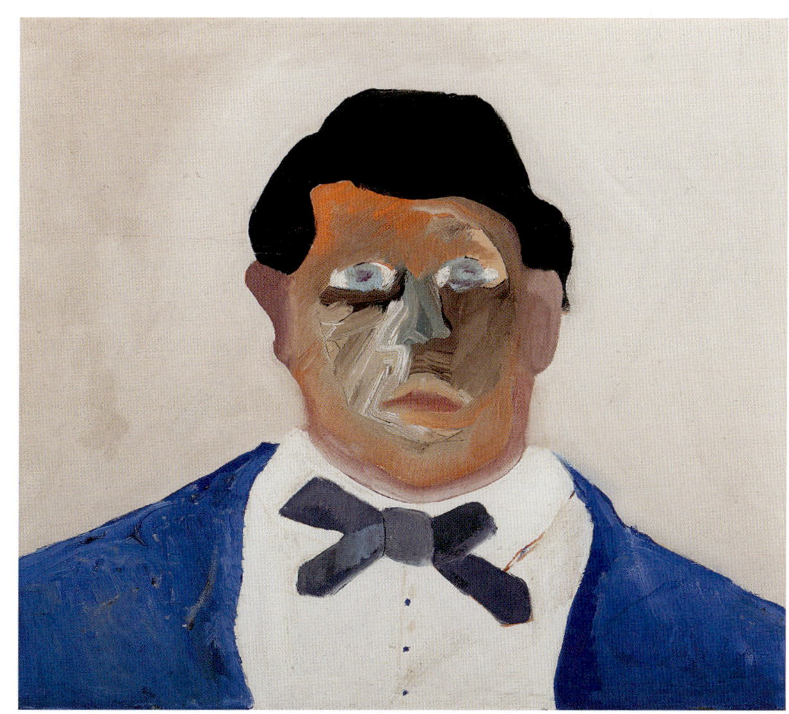

FIGURE 20 Bill Soza War Soldier (Cahuilla/White Mountain Apache), *John Wesley Hardin, Killer of Men . . .*, ca. 1969, oil on canvas, 16.75 in. × 18.75 in., MoCNA Collection, MS-17 (photo by Addison Doty).

I would write letters to Bill when he was periodically incarcerated, not fully knowing what charges had been brought against him, although I believed they were gun-related. He would write back with lavishly illustrated sketches on the envelopes. His letters were a combination of long tirades criticizing the system and poetic musings about life. I cared for this person, but I also understood that he was capable of aggressive behavior, as I had once nurtured his distraught ex-girlfriend after a breakup. In his own life, Bill made some hard choices that aligned somewhat with the John Wesley Hardin historical figure, an outlaw. But at the time he painted these canvases in 1969, he could not have known that. He was just twenty years old and, by all accounts, full of life and inquisitive, although at times shy. How could he know then that he would pass on by the age of sixty-five? The last time I saw Bill at the Santa Fe Indian Market, I teased him for his "wild ways" and he seemed genuinely hurt. We shot a quick selfie photo, me all smiles, him stoic behind his shades, but I should have known then that he was aware of himself fading. Ultimately, he only wanted me to know him as the kind uncle—the Billy who had hope for the future.

I share this story with the reader because each of the works that I discuss has layers of meaning attached to it. We can interpret art in its formal qualities, relate it to the social period in which it was created, but, to my mind, the most potent appraisal is in the intersections of lived experience and personal contact. Art historians may discuss hundreds of artists, but I have always felt uncomfortable speaking about people I did not know, or whose works I could not relate to personally. When I lecture about artists, I make an effort to let them know I am using their work and how. While this is not always possible, for me it is a "best practices" approach to an Indigenous methodology of working. It is also why I chose to be trained as a visual anthropologist rather than an art historian.

I write about an American Indian Curatorial Practice as work that is long-term, mutually meaningful, reciprocal, and with mentorship. I cannot employ this methodology if I am lecturing on hundreds of artists in what appears to me as a mechanical approach. Writing about the artists in the MoCNA IAIA collection seems more familial because I was a student at the IAIA and I continue to be supportive of the school. IAIA is truly a unique social world of which I have been fortunate to be a part. This positioning as a cultural insider necessarily has an impact on my approach to the work and my sensitivity to how it is presented. I believe in the concept of service for a higher good and I strive for my work to reflect that. I was asked recently about how I make my curatorial choices and found myself saying that I do not choose: I am in the hands of the creator and simply being of service. While I know this may sound corny or perhaps, like Billy, sentimental in nature, it also seems the right way to be.

It would be impossible for me to write about Allan Houser dispassionately. He was a member of my tribe, grandfather to my daughter, and father to my husband of ten years, the noted sculptor Bob Haozous. Standard art criticism would not allow me to divulge this information. As one of my colleagues once told me (paraphrasing art critique Clement Greenberg), "You can buy an artist a drink, but you cannot buy him dinner." I received this advice when I was an emerging writer and had confronted my colleague about why I was not included in a published volume he edited. The answer was that I was too close to the material, being married to a well-known artist. The value of objectivity has long been discredited in a number of fields. It is associated with the values of science. The premise of objectivity holds that, to be real scholarship, the findings of research cannot have any relation to a social context—cannot have subjectivity, or the presence and influence of the researcher. This value is still often at play in Native arts criticism today, but it is masked, as many developments in the field are, under the rubric of quality.

I want to include methodology and these masked values here in my discussion because I think it is important to reveal the inner workings of the art field. Scholar Scott Lauria Morgensen states, "Indigenous methodologies do not merely model Indigenous research. By exposing normative knowledge production as being not only non-Indigenous but colonial, they denaturalize power within settler societies and ground knowledge production in decolonization."[15] This more assertive stance of not only engaging in Native ways of doing but also calling out the colonial nature of standard knowledge production in higher education is an essential step in making the Native arts field more equitable for Natives and their collaborators to make positive strides toward legibility and education.[16]

One's subjectivity as a researcher should always be present, if not in the body of the work, then in the footnotes or endnotes. Even more so, a close, familial association with an artist should be divulged to avoid the charge of conflict of interest. (A conflict of interest is largely tied to the receipt of direct benefits: for example, financial compensation or award of a contract.) I argue that it is unethical and counter to Indigenous methodologies to prevent a researcher from engaging in work simply because there are social ties between the scholar and her subject. If applied consistently, the value of objectivity would necessitate that only non-Native scholars could write about Native arts. Intimate knowledge of a person, place, or thing does not distort, but increases accuracy.

Allan Houser was the first child of our tribe born free from our prisoner of war status in 1914. He was noted in both Native and non-Native worlds as a successful artist and educator. Allan's narrative became a universal symbol of freedom and accomplishment. His path from rural Oklahoma to Santa Fe demonstrated the American Dream—a rags-to-riches story in a classical sense.[17] What many people may not recognize is that he was a supporter of our tribe, the Fort Sill Apache (he paid the light bills on the tribal complex when the tribe could not), and a holder of Chiricahua Apache knowledge through song, history, and story. His many years as an educator at the IAIA, as well as his immense talent and skill, ensured that his legacy would continue for many generations.

I include two pieces here that Allan produced in the 1980s, *By the Water's Edge* (1987) and *Dawn* (1989). My interest in selecting these works is to discuss the meaning of abstraction in relationship to nudity and Indigenous knowledge. One of the questions asked at the beginning of this essay was whether Indian artists, and therefore Indian communities, had adopted a more European view of sexuality in the arts. *By the Water's Edge* (figure 21) depicts a naturalistic woman reclining easily on one elbow. She appears relaxed and self-possessed in attitude, with her head looking almost upward and the edges of her mouth turned slightly down. Her long fingers touch at the front of her body, which is solid and muscular. The bronze material of this cast piece adds to the sense of weight, with the patina on the surface casting a sensuous glow. Nothing about this work makes me worried for this individual's safety or welfare. Her power is almost palpable.

What makes *By the Water's Edge* a piece that is women-affirming and life-affirming? Is it the trust we have in the artist, a well-known and respected figure in both Native and non-Native communities? Is it the way the work has been rendered in smooth lines? Is it the facial expression of the individual, her sense of confidence and ease? In referencing the concept of the gaze, we as viewers are clearly in the position of a voyeur; even the title gives one the impression that we have somehow surreptitiously encountered this person by a body of water after she bathed. Apache women, like many Native women, are notoriously conservative in their dress and demeanor. I recall once cooking at our dance ground and having one of my aunties chastise me for having one too many buttons of my shirt undone at the neckline. To enter the dance ground, women are expected to have shawls covering their backs, yet this has never struck me as anything other than appropriate for a

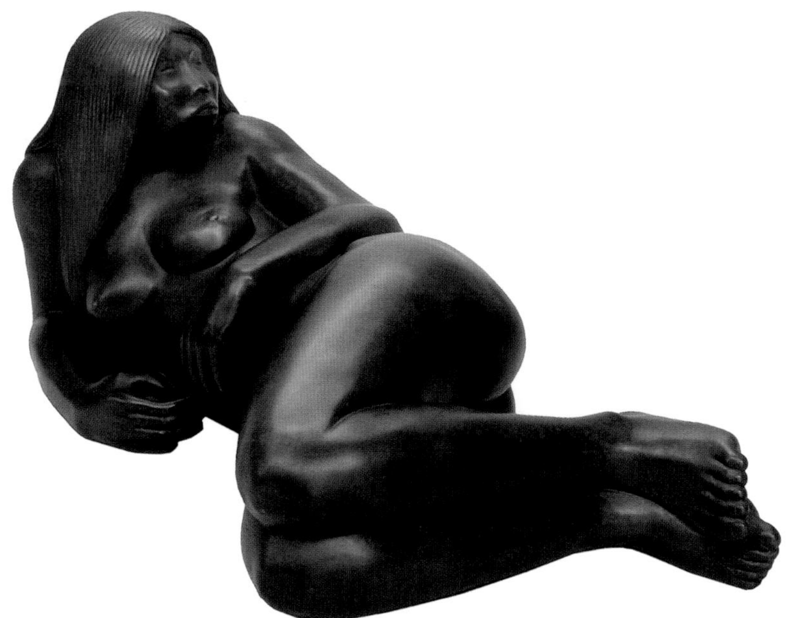

FIGURE 21
Allan Houser (Chiricahua Apache), *By the Water's Edge*, 1987, bronze, 17 in. × 38 in. × 16 in., edition of 12, © Chiinde LLC (photo courtesy of Allan Houser).

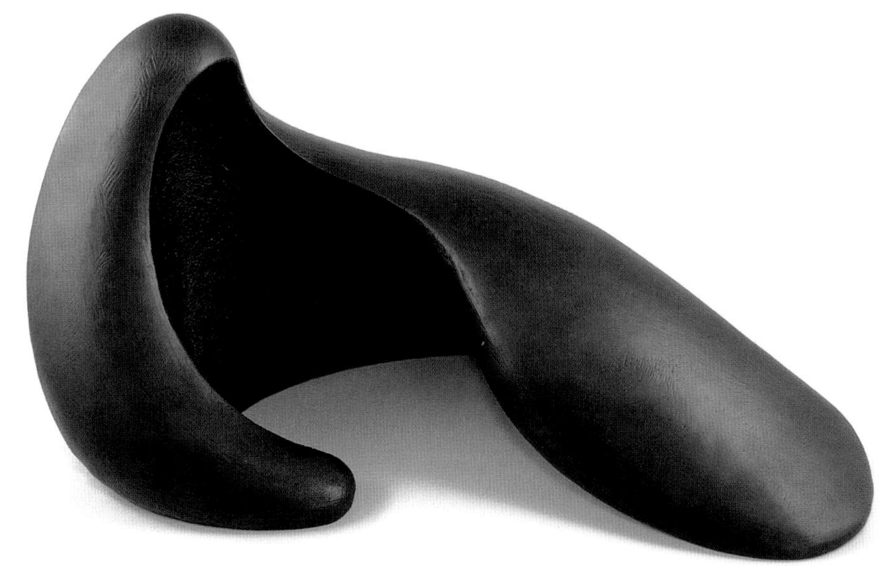

FIGURE 22
Allan Houser (Chiricahua Apache), *Dawn*, 1989, bronze, 19 in. × 38 in. × 20 in., edition of 10, © Chiinde LLC (photo courtesy of Allan Houser).

religious ceremonial. Why would I be less concerned about a full nude, and why would Allan have so confidently produced such a work?

Alex Jacobs' pastel work discussed earlier, *Thursday Blues*, also features a reclining nude, yet her body is prone, with her hand draped over her head. We, as viewers, cannot make eye contact with her, and the bright colors and strokes add a sense of raw action. In Allan's pieces, I am confident that he understood how posture, material, and the visibility of the figure's face added a strong sense of presence and agency to his nudes. Like Jacobs, he also would have been exposed to the Western value of being able to render a human figure in a realistic manner. This technical achievement, when executed expertly as this work is, brings recognition and respect to an artist. Allan may also have enjoyed the ability to produce such a bold piece, given his age and status in the community. No peer could criticize or fault him for depicting an indecent exposure of a female nude, and if they did, I doubt that he would have cared. He was beyond these concerns at this point in his life, or he appeared to be.

The piece *Dawn* (figure 22), dated two years later, in 1989, has a similar shape to *By the Water's Edge*; both are relining nudes, yet *Dawn* is entirely abstracted. The artist's gallery describes this work as a "culmination of Houser's exploration of the reclining female form."[18] All details, including arms, legs, and head, are removed, leaving a completely fluid form with a void interior. Why is abstraction a culmination? Was the execution more difficult? Did the artist wish to make works in a more Modernist vein? Did he simply want a new challenge?

The artistic movement known as Modernism is a problematic concept in relation to Native arts, because it is often employed to discern the difference between traditional and more contemporary forms (modern). The reader will note that this chapter avoids the characterizations of traditional and modern, as these concepts do not reflect the realities of Native arts production.[19] Instead, we are addressing the physicality and intended purpose of arts-making over the past sixty years in reference to abstraction and figurative forms. If we, as viewers, seek an Indigenous reading of abstraction, what kinds of knowledge would we be seeking? Is Houser's *Dawn* more relatable to a universal audience, now that the visible markings of a Native physicality are gone? Or, instead of wishing to reach a broader audience (universal), is abstraction a way to hide sensitive knowledge?

Allan was quoted as stating, "What I'm trying to do, is to make the Indian image look more contemporary and beautiful."[20] To me, this assertion speaks of how Native peoples were imagined in his own lifetime, a span that knew intimately of colonial injustices, including the forced imprisonment of his parents and his tribe for twenty-eight years. This treatment of being political prisoners, held indefinitely, must have had an impact on his motivations as an artist. As Indigenous Studies writers Jarrett Martineau and Eric Ritskes state, "Art creates experiences of potentiality that inspire and sustain our collective struggles for freedom."[21] The ability to execute works in representational norms as well as total abstraction are both exercises in Houser's freedom to create counternarratives to popular imagery and thought that sought to destroy Native cultures. Houser, like many others, including his students, became a survivor and thriver by simple self-representation.

I turn next to the artist Shan Goshorn in relation to the notion that abstraction serves Indigeneity. In this discussion, I am expanding on the more common definition of abstraction as a Modernist norm to consider it in what we typically think of as more traditional mediums, in this case basketry. I was honored to work with Shan for the 2017 Venice Biennale exhibit *Wah.shka*. Her contribution to the exhibit, which sought to explore the Osage tribal philosophy of forward movement, included the work *Feminine Sacred*. I will discuss this piece in relationship to the work *Vessel*, which depicts a nude pregnant female. Both works were executed in 2015.

Shan described to me the way in which she entered into making three-dimensional baskets rather than the two-dimensional photographs, drawings, and paintings for which she was known earlier in her career. As she described it, the political messages inescapably inscribed in her works were difficult for a non-Native audience to engage with. The motion was to physically and mentally move away from stories that documented Indian boarding school abuse, violence against Native women, and disparaging stereotypes. In an effort to engage in a new approach, Shan started stripping her photographs into long vertical forms that she then wove into a form of basketry based on traditional Cherokee weaving styles. In this manner, her audience was disarmed—they moved in closer to see the works and were then able to hear the message she was intent on conveying. These forms and patterns are complex and challenging to execute, and Goshorn's excursions into mastery of this technique served as a decolonizing strategy to reactivate the Indigenous knowledge of these artistic works for a new generation. In doing so, she has accomplished a monumental task, that of disrupting the dichotomous categories of traditional and modern. In the words of photographic scholar and artist Shawn Smith, Goshorn has succeeded in "destabilizing their oppositional paradigms" by incorporating medium and message in a unique fashion.[22]

FIGURE 23 Shan Goshorn (Eastern Band Cherokee), *Vessel*, 2015, Arches watercolor paper splints printed with archival inks, acrylic paint, 8.25 in. × 8.25 in. × 19.5 in., set of 3, © Shan Goshorn Studio (photo courtesy of Shan Goshorn Studio). Denver Art Museum.

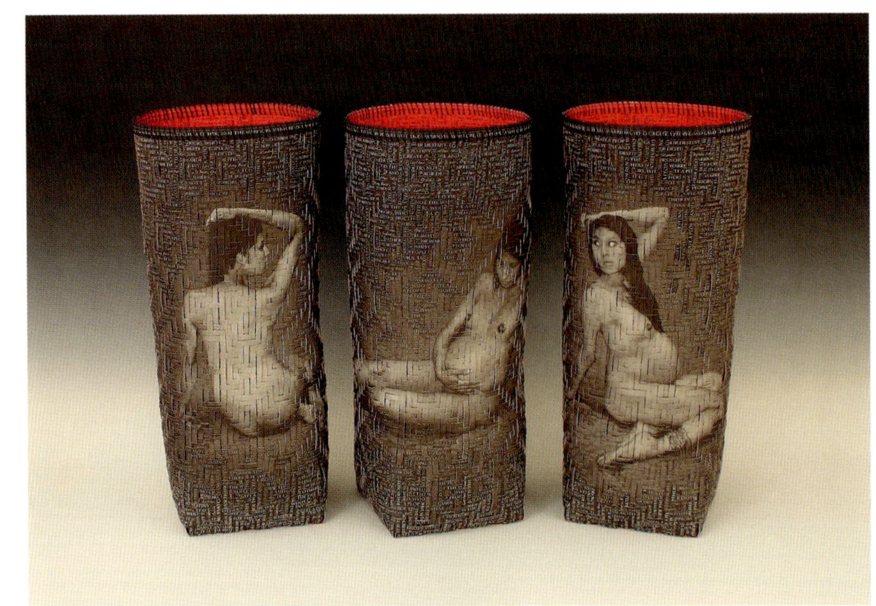

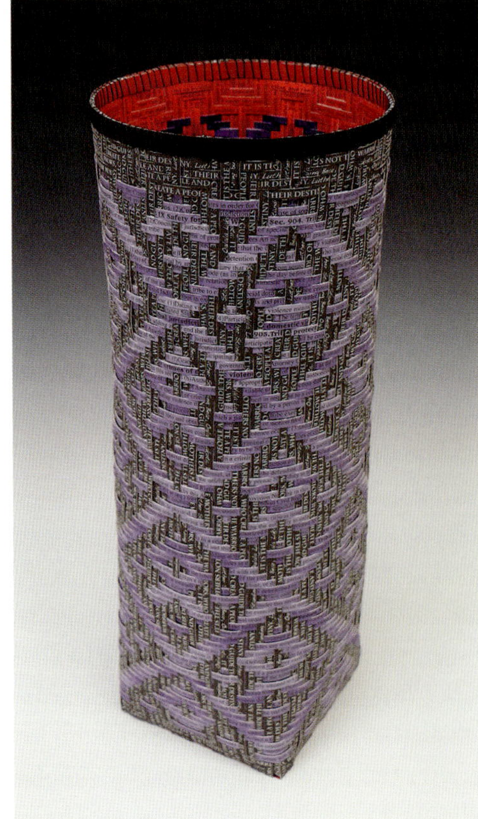

FIGURE 24 Shan Goshorn (Eastern Band Cherokee), *Feminine Sacred*, 2015, Arches watercolor paper splints printed with archival inks, acrylic paint, 8.25 in. × 8.25 in. × 21 in., © Shan Goshorn Studio (photo courtesy of Shan Goshorn Studio). Private Collection.

Vessel (figure 23), a triptych set of Cherokee-style single-weave baskets, was conceived of in relationship to a quote by Oglala Lakota Luther Standing Bear: "It is the mothers, not the warriors, who create a people and guide their destiny." Shan has bravely depicted a nude Native woman, but, like Allan's, her figure is boldly captured. In one instance, the figure looks downward, cradling her full belly. The other images depict her looking away from the camera, resting on one arm, the other arm against her head serving to balance her seated posture. These representational images are complemented by the internal weaving, which contains conversations between the subject and the artist in which the expectant mother conveys "how beautiful and powerful motherhood makes her feel."[23] The cumulative effect is of a personal narrative that honors the life-giving nature of a woman's body.

The work *Feminine Sacred* (figure 24) is similar in size and form to *Vessel*, but it does not feature a representative image, only evocative wording. The quote by Luther Standing Bear is joined with the wording from the 2003 reauthorization of the Violence Against Women Act that was amended to protect Native women from abuse on tribal reservation lands. Prior to this legislation, a Native woman could not prosecute a non-Native man in the tribal court system who had abused her on reservation lands.[24] The basket's exterior purple face is complimented by a red interior with the same dialogues from *Vessel* with the expectant mother. The content of this work, then, balances the legal mandate with the personal narrative, the tone of the act on the exterior contrasting with the sensitive testimony within.

I want to connect these two artists—Houser and Goshorn—in terms of their generational standing and their professional strategies and impulses. Houser, in the twentieth century, demonstrated complete ease in engaging in figurative and abstract Modernist iconic forms and influences (including Arp, Zuniga, and Brancusi). Goshorn, in the twenty-first century, likewise exercises freedom of movement, but by engaging in a medium—basketry—that has been firmly identified with craft and the work of women and thus often nullified in fine art terms.[25] These demonstrations of the will and ingenuity of both artists reveal how Indigenous thought is not primarily reactive or engaged in a linear development that solely parallels Western fine arts premises, but moves back and forth in time and spirals with engagement of trauma and resilience. This resourcefulness and integrity, demonstrated in simultaneous fields and directions, is an indication of how Native arts dynamically enact Indigenous knowledge.

> The process of describing the body is never innocent.
> One must always ask who is doing the describing, and why?
> JOHN PULTZ / *The Body and the Lens*

Do Indigenous artists have something unique to contribute to the dialogue of human nudity and images of the body in art? This chapter has described the strategies of Native artists from the 1960s to the present using collections primarily from the Museum of Contemporary Native Arts. Up until this point in our narrative, we have discussed the terminology, strategies, and diverse intents of artists to try and understand how the body informs Native epistemologies, or patterns of thinking. I want to turn now to the proposition that the body does not need to be limited to the conventional aspect of figurative painting, drawing, and sculpture, but can also be thought of in a more expansive sense, as reflected in narratives of land and territories.

In the wake of the water protector movement stirred by the 2016–2017 Dakota Access Pipeline controversy of Standing Rock, South Dakota, and nationally, interest in Native peoples as guardians of the earth has been reborn. By "guardians of the earth," I do not mean a stereotypical attachment to ecological concerns in the sense of land and water conservation alone, but a deeper engagement with Indigenous knowledge that the earth is inseparable from human beings, that our destinies are tied in a reciprocal exchange. An excellent example of how this understanding might be visualized is in the work of Keli Mashburn and Marcella Ernest in the films *Wah.shka* and *Nibiin Water Song*, both featured in the 2017 Venice Biennale exhibition that I co-curated with Mary Bordeaux.[26]

Wah.shka references the Osage philosophy of regeneration after chaos and disorder. Following our 2015 Venice Biennale *Ga.ni.tha* exhibit, wahshka as a concept is a reminder that, for all of the genocidal policies of the United States, Indigenous peoples—in this case specifically the Osage tribe—have drawn from deep collective knowledge to survive and thrive. The video *Wah.shka* features archival film from Osage sources, intermixed with the stirring voice of artist Mashburn relating a prayer in the Osage language. Mashburn's evocative landscape photographs (figure 25) are featured in a dynamic intermingling with abstracted figures dancing in traditional regalia as well as ordinary dress in the public setting of community events. These interspersed images of land, when presented with the strong audio component and images of community members moving in unison, suggest to the viewer a symmetry and the notion that these two seemingly disparate events—the movement of

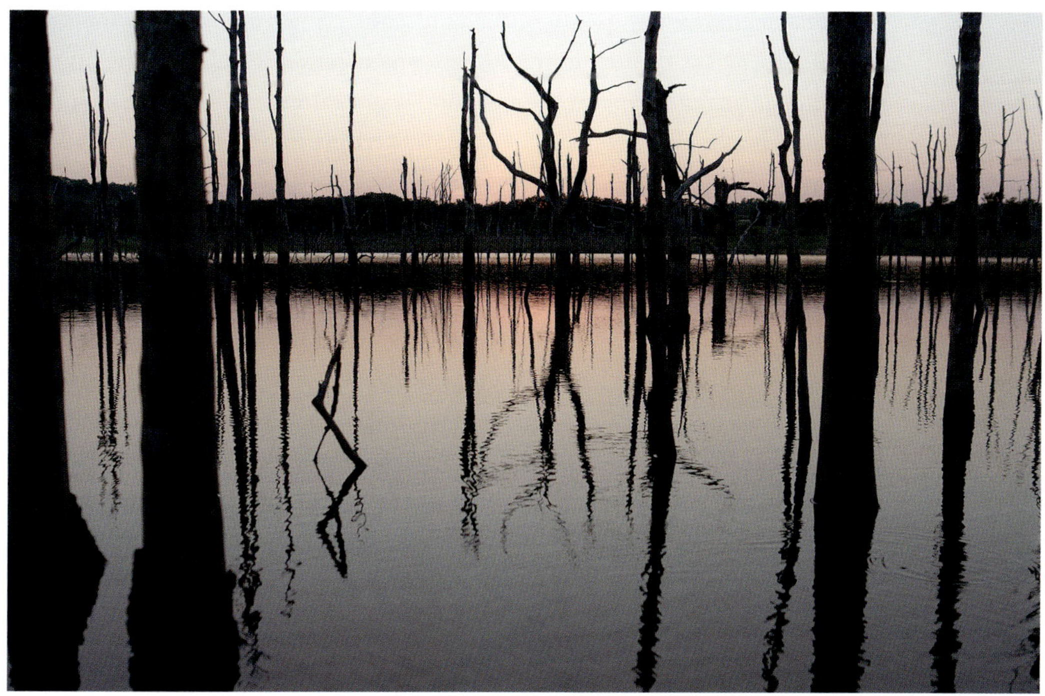

FIGURE 25 Keli Mashburn (Osage), *Water Study #1*, 2016, archival ink jet, 16 in. × 20 in., artist's collection.

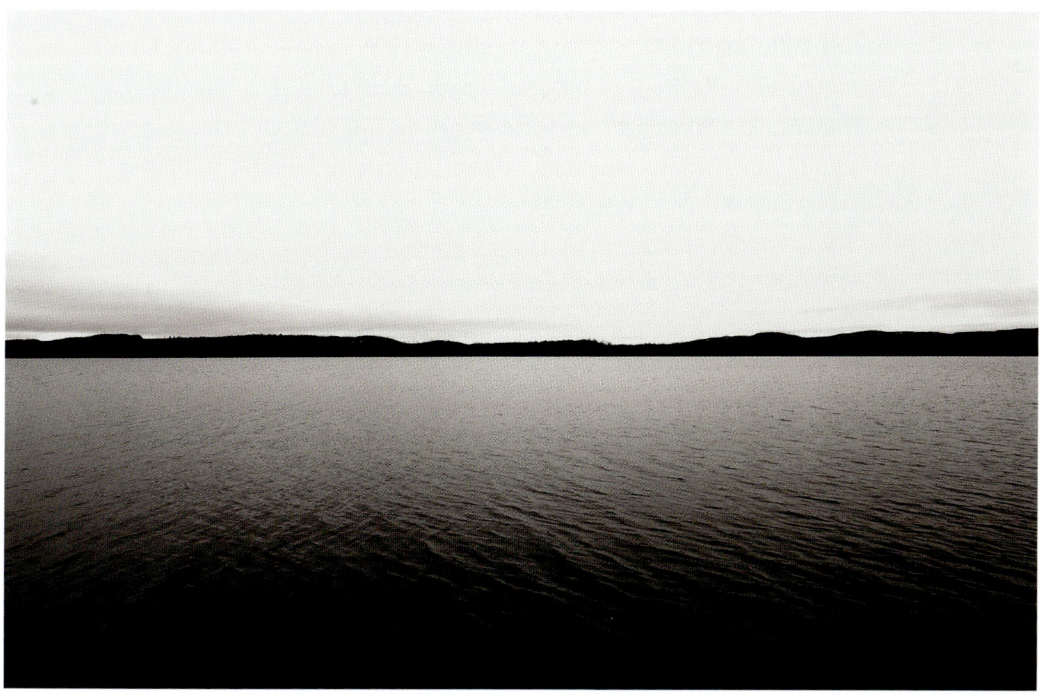

FIGURE 26 Marcella Ernest (Ojibwe), *Nibiin Water Song*, still, 2017, artist's collection.

dancers and the tranquility of the landscape photos animated in their presentation across the film horizon—are dynamically interrelated. The humans animate the landscape as the land and water reflect the movements of the groups' harmonic movements. People and nature interact in meaningful and complex ways, forming a union.

The *Nibiin Water Song* video by Marcella Ernest depicts water features from around the globe with the amazing vocals of Mary Maytwayashing, an *Anishinaabe* singer and religious leader. *Nibiin Water Song* powerfully evokes the unity of humans and the water sources that enable our survival. Ernest placed a call over the social media site Facebook for individuals to submit cell phone-generated videos of water from their territories (figure 26). She then edited submissions from California to Hawaii to the Great Lakes into one evocative poem, a prayer really, for viewers to sit with and contemplate. The fact that *Nibiin Water Song* was shared with an international audience in the year that the water protectors at Standing Rock and their supporters made Native agency visible to the world is vitally significant. Native women and their allies demonstrated with song and image that the inner strength of resiliency and power is always available, always with us as we go forward (wahshka) collectively.

An examination of Native arts in several mediums (sculpture, pastel, print, painting, and film) across the past fifty years demonstrates that Indigenous arts employ a variety of methods in incorporating, questioning, and reaffirming cultural practices in conversation with Western traditions. Depictions of nudity in Indigenous creative endeavors do not simply mimic the mainstream traditions of "the gaze," but often work in ways that say something altogether different—sending a message of self-empowerment and resiliency.

PROMPTS

1. Explain what heteronormative looking is and provide a visual example. Compare the different examples that other students have identified. What qualities are similar?
2. What are the four components of American Indian Curatorial Practices? Work in small groups to discuss what this approach to art may look like in practice.
3. The value of the "seen face" would appear to be counter to the use of the web for communication. Discuss with a classmate or friend the difference in quality of dialogue when you are talking in person as contrasted with an email communication.

4. Choose one of the following terms and define it using an illustration from this book: agency, essentialism, duality, abstraction, realism, sexuality, universal, eye contact, androgynous, victimization, subjectivity/objectivity, decolonization.

NOTES

1. Nancy Marie Mithlo, *Our Indian Princess: Subverting the Stereotype* (Santa Fe: School for Advanced Research, 2009).

2. I wish to express my gratitude to Richard Hill, former director of the Institute of American Indian Arts Museum and his curated exhibit *The Human Figure in American Indian Art: Cultural Reality or Sexual Fantasy?* (May 24–June 30, 1991). This exhibit at 1369 Cerrillos Road on the Santa Fe Indian School campus was the last show to be mounted at the old Institute of American Indian Arts Museum, where I was trained as a museum professional under Charles Dailey from 1985–1990. The museum moved to its current location on 109 Cathedral Place in 1992 and was subsequently renamed the Museum of Contemporary Native Arts. *The Human Figure in American Indian Art* posited that the female nude is representative of an Earth Mother figure and frequently used as "a metaphor for the vulnerability of the environment, showing that what we are doing to the land is the same thing that we in a male-dominated society are doing to women." Dave Steinberg, "Museum's Show Focuses on Human Figure in American Indian Art," *Albuquerque Journal*, May 24, 1991: C8, C12.

3. For examples, see Elizabeth Edwards, "Looking at Photographs: Between Contemplation, Curiosity, and Gaze," in *Distance and Desire: Encounters with the African Archive: African Photography from the Walther Collection, Göttingen* (Göttingen, Germany: Steidl, 2013), 48–54. Also see Catherine Lutz and Jane Collins, "The Photograph as an Intersection of Gazes: The Example of *National Geographic*," *Visual Anthropology Review* 7, no. 1 (1991): 134–49.

4. Linda Tuhiwai Smith, *Decolonizing Methodologies: Research and Indigenous Peoples* (New York: Zed Books, 1999).

5. Nancy Marie Mithlo, "No Word for Art in Our Language?—Old Questions, New Paradigms," *Wičazo Ša Review* 27, no. 1 (2012): 111–26.

6. Richard Hill, "The Human Figure in American Indian Art: Cultural Reality or Sexual Fantasy?" in *The Human Figure in American Indian Art*, exhibition catalogue (Santa Fe: MoCNA, 1991), n.p., Institute of American Indian Arts archives.

7. Hill, "The Human Figure in American Indian Art," n.p.

8. "Maze of Injustice: The Failure to Protect Indigenous Women from Sexual Violence in the USA," Amnesty International website, https://www.amnestyusa.org/wp-content/uploads/2017/05/mazeofinjustice.pdf.

9. For more information on the high rates of sexual violence against Native women, see Sarah Deer, *The Beginning and End of Rape: Confronting Sexual Violence in Native America* (Minneapolis: University of Minnesota Press, 2015).

10. Rebecca J. Dobkins, "Tears and Rain: One Artist's View from Sea Level," *Oregon Historical Quarterly* 107, no. 3 (2006): 445–53.

11. Nancy Marie Mithlo, "Blood Memory and the Arts: Indigenous Genealogies and Imagined Truths," *American Indian Culture and Research Journal* 35, no. 4 (2012): 112.

12. Patti Jo King, "The Truth about the Wounded Knee Massacre," *Indian Country Today* website, published December 30, 2016, https://newsmaven.io/indiancountrytoday/archive/the-truth-about-the-wounded-knee-massacre-PIQqUKeCEEmnLeQn0Q5SOQ.

13. Audra Simpson, "On Ethnographic Refusal: Indigeneity, 'Voice' and Colonial Citizenship," *Junctures* 9 (2007): 67–80.

14. Alex Jacobs, "Painter, Provocateur and AIM Activist Bill 'War Soldier' Soza Walks On," *Indian Country Today*, January 22, 2014, https://newsmaven.io/indiancountrytoday/archive/painter-provocateur-and-aim-activist-bill-war-soldier-soza-walks-on-GxISbqKlD06bfoH_VFUVNQ.

15. Scott Lauria Morgensen, "Destabilizing the Settler Academy: The Decolonial Effects of Indigenous Methodologies," *American Quarterly* 64, no. 4 (2012): 805–8.

16. I want to be clear, however, that there are ethical and legal standards articulated in many professional organizations such as the American Alliance of Museums and the International Council of Museums that should be noted and followed. These notices apply more directly to museum workers than to art writers. The problem with many of the institutions that fall subject to these national and international guidelines is that they often do not consider American Indian populations as the public to whom they are accountable.

17. See Barbara Perlman, *Allan Houser (Haozous)* (Santa Fe: Glen Green Galleries, 1992).

18. "Dawn," Allan Houser website, https://allanhouser.com/work/dawn-1.

19. See "Art Terms," Tate Modern website, http://www.tate.org.uk/art/art-terms/m/modernism.

20. "Art of Allan Houser," Allan Houser website, https://allanhouser.com/.

21. Jarrett Martineau and Eric Ritskes, "Fugitive Indigeneity: Reclaiming the Terrain of Decolonial Struggle through Indigenous Art," *Decolonization, Indigeneity, Education & Society* 3, no. 1 (2014): i–xii.

22. Shawn Michelle Smith, "'Looking at One's Self through the Eyes of Others': W. E. B. Du Bois's Photographs for the 1900 Paris Exposition," *African American Review* 34, no. 4 (2000): 276.

23. Shan Goshorn, "Vessel," Shan Goshorn website, http://www.shangoshorn.net/vessel.

24. "Violence Against Women Act (VAWA) Reauthorization 2013," United States Department of Justice website, https://www.justice.gov/tribal/violence-against-women-act-vawa-reauthorization-2013-0.

25. Camille Gajewski, "A Brief History of Women in Art," Khan Academy website, https://www.khanacademy.org/humanities/art-history-basics/tools-understanding-art/a/a-brief-history-of-women-in-art.

26. "Wah.shka," Nancy Marie Mithlo website, www.nancymariemithlo.com.

Mapping Indigenous Space and Place

JOHN PAUL RANGEL

Indigenous aesthetics take into account Native American perspectives, ways of knowing, cultural values and beliefs, and also conceptions of space or place; these are reflected in contemporary Native art. Continuity is an important consideration, as Native people are currently and have continuously produced art that reflects their cross-cultural influences, experiences, and cultural expressions.[1] By looking at Indigenous concepts of place or space, one can begin to understand the complex context of the work. This chapter focuses on the works of nine artists who employ Indigenous concepts of place or space in their art. Whether referencing an actual place or a conceptual space, these artists create work from their cultural perspectives as Indigenous persons.

"Indigenous place" often refers to actual geography that holds importance to the artist, such as their home or ancestral lands. These connections permeate Indigenous culture, traditions, stories, histories, language, and modes of communication. The land serves as a container and marker of culture. Indigenous peoples, whether sedentary or migratory, have maintained an ecological engagement with the land for many generations by developing relationships to their surroundings, including the plants, animals, growing seasons, migration patterns, and sources for water. Through the act of naming, certain aspects of the landscape become important or activated as they reference oral histories, spirituality, and origin stories. Native people living near their landmarks build a visible visual reference to their traditions, ancestors, and spiritual practices and beliefs. The land, a Native person's homelands, becomes the container for culture through these references and relationships. It also becomes a marker of culture when used as hunting grounds or for ceremony. Returning to these specific places reaffirms relationships and connections to culture. These interactions are forms of Indigenous mapping that are intrinsically tied to creative expression and Indigenous aesthetics.

Indigenization of space happens when Native people activate a space for a ceremonial or cultural purpose with language, songs, dance, regalia, and prayer. Activation, in this sense, is bringing together people, intention, purpose, and often food. It is about building community and inclusion, affirmation of core values and identity, sharing knowledge and mentoring, recognizing and honoring elders, and building on traditions. Modern iterations of this include social gatherings such as powwows, but also tribally specific gatherings for prayer or ceremony. It is important to note that while some of these occurrences are open to the public, there are other instances where participation requires membership in or initiation into a specific community or nation. Native artists may reclaim a location through cultural signifiers, performance, song, dance, or installation to convey the existence and presence of Native peoples and cultures.[2] Public works of Native American art, performance, or installation demonstrate this reclamation. Any time there is Native art in a public space, that art is an example of Indigenizing that space by virtue of the Native artist who created the work.

Native cultures are not static or immutable: they are living and dynamic. Native people adapt and incorporate new ideas, influences, and materials into their lexicon of cultural expression. I refer to this reconceptualizing and reframing as "Indigenizing of materials," an act both physical and discursive. One of the earliest examples of this concept was the introduction of small glass beads to Plains cultures. Porcupine quills were used prior to beads for embellishment on personal items such as clothing, footwear, regalia, and ceremonial pieces. As Europeans moved across the continent, they brought beads from Italy and the Slavic nations and traded them with Native peoples. The bright colors and small sizes of the beads allowed for expanded color palettes and tighter designs. Another example was the introduction of silversmithing to the Southwest around 1850. Atsidi Sani (Navajo), formerly a blacksmith, is credited as the first Native person to have learned the craft. He transposed his skills to a new metal, experimenting with silver that was accessible through trade with the Spanish and Mexicans. This resulted in the proliferation of silver ornamentation (horse gear, belts, buckles, and necklaces) in the Southwest.[3]

Native artists working in two-dimensional mediums such as paintings, photography, and prints illustrate adaption to new materials from prior artistic traditions of carving on rock (petroglyphs) or painting on natural land formations (pictographs). Native artists Indigenize materials and art processes by using them to claim discursive space and assert cultural stories, values, languages, knowledge systems, traditions, and histories. ("Discursive space" or "discourse" refers to systems of knowledge and how knowledge about a topic is organized.) It is important for Native artists and scholars to take command of their own representations and build understanding for Indigenous knowledge, including histories, culture, aesthetics, and the creative process.

JASON GARCIA—OKUU PÍN

Turtle Mountain / K'ha Po Owingeh —Santa Clara Pueblo

Some Native artists directly reference their heritage and homelands—actual places and also the conceptual space of their particular culture—in their art. A good example of this is Jason Garcia's *Feast Day Selfie* (2016, figure 27), a serigraph print or silkscreen that depicts a Snapchat "selfie" of two Native women in traditional Pueblo ceremonial attire.[4] The woman in the foreground appears partially in view with her arm extended, presumably holding a cell phone and capturing the woman standing behind her with two structures in the background, along with a telephone or power-line pole. The words "Feast Day Selfie" appear in the foreground, following the typical titling format of a Snapchat selfie.

Jason Garcia is from K'ha Po Owingeh ("Rose Path Village" in Tewa), also known as Santa Clara Pueblo, one of the nineteen Native American Pueblo nations located in New Mexico. The term "Pueblo" in Spanish means town or village. When the Spanish moved across the Southwest, they found Native Americans living in adobe structures and referred to these peoples as Pueblo Indians. Members of these nations have continuously occupied these villages for hundreds of years.[5] Garcia, an accomplished artist known primarily for his illustrations on ceramic tiles, comes from a family of artists, including his parents, Santa Clara Pueblo potters John and Gloria Garcia (known as Goldenrod), and his great-grandmother, Severa Tafoya. He is a graduate of the University of New Mexico and the Master of Fine Arts program in printmaking at the University of Wisconsin. Garcia has twice earned the "Best of" classification in paintings, drawings, graphics, and photography at the Santa Fe Indian Market, most recently for *Tewa Tales of Suspense!*, a suite of seven serigraph prints depicting a Native perspective on historical events from the Pueblo Revolt.[6]

Garcia is known for his use of popular culture references and often utilizes the comic book or graphic novel genre as an illustration style. The imagery he focuses on is based on his desire to portray facets of his culture that include historical events as well as current aspects of Native life. The two women in *Feast Day Selfie* are dressed in the traditional attire typical for female members of Santa Clara Pueblo participating in Feast Day dances and activities celebrated annually on the twelfth of August. Their headpieces or *tablitas*,

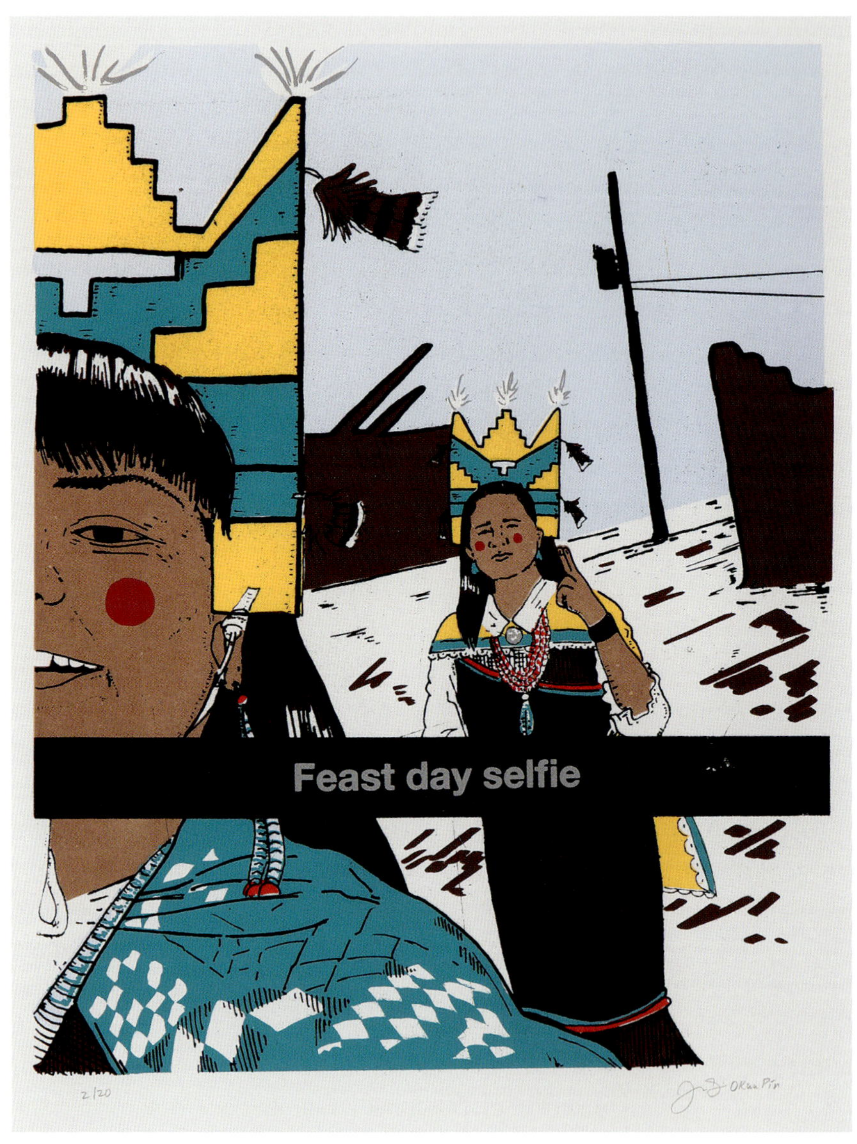

FIGURE 27 Jason Garcia (K'ha Po Owingeh-Santa Clara Pueblo), *Feast Day Selfie*, Edition 2/20, 2016, silkscreen on paper, 19 in. × 12 in., MoCNA Collection, SC-171 (photo by Addison Doty).

face paint, dresses, shawls, and jewelry indicate that these women are either coming from or on their way to participate in the dances.

The buildings in the background have architecture typical of Santa Clara Pueblo, with the building on the left referencing a kiva or spiritual gathering place. Garcia places this scene in the present, referencing technology not just with the selfie but also the telephone/electric pole in the background. He uses technology such as the cell phone, TV antennas, and utility poles as symbols for his Pueblo, its location, and the People's spirituality. This is actual space and conceptual space conveyed together. Garcia's use of contemporary technology becomes a metaphor for Tewa spirituality and prayer: the cell phones and utility pole reference what the artist describes as a "receiver/transmitter," capable of sending and receiving information or energy. He suggests that Tewa spirituality, enacted through prayer, song, and dance, functions in a similar manner. The telephones and TV antenna are also a reference to St. Claire of Assisi, the patron saint of the blind, embroiderers, television, and Santa Clara Pueblo.[7] In this lighthearted approach, Garcia is making commentary on the current conditions in his pueblo—that his culture is alive and thriving, that young people are using technology to express their culture, and that Native people don't live in an enigmatic, romanticized past devoid of technology or modernity.

Garcia's reference to photography cannot be overlooked, as his subject matter is a "selfie" snapshot taken during a feast day. Ethnographic documentation and photography by non-Native people are often intrusive and have served to either relegate Native culture and peoples to the past or perpetuate romanticized or stereotypical one-dimensional characterizations. In *Feast Day Selfie*, the ethnographic gaze is self-referential, with the subject and the artist taking responsibility for the framing and telling of the story. Garcia is at once tying to the past and generations of his people who gathered at certain times of the year to pray and dance while also taking into account the way that younger generations share and develop their culture through the sharing of photos electronically. In many Native American cultures, and Pueblo cultures specifically in this context, the use of photography is restricted or not allowed. According to cultural protocols (which vary with individual tribal nations), some cultural, ceremonial, or spiritual activities are meant only for those who are initiated, have an awareness of and respect for those protocols, or are members of the particular Indigenous nation. These are not open to the public or to any type of recording. The proliferation of information disseminated to the general public by anthropologists and ethnographers over many years led to the closing of Pueblos for religious events.

Feast Day Selfie does bring up the topic of which aspects of culture are considered appropriate or inappropriate to display or share with the public. However, this particular scene does not depict any aspect of ceremony that would not be visible to the general public on any given feast day. The topic of recording and sharing Native culture is very complex and requires careful attention to and respect for the guidelines and boundaries of each Native American nation. As with photography and ethnographic documentation, there are many problematic examples of appropriation or misrepresentation of Native American culture in mainstream art, history, fashion, movies, and popular culture.

An abundance of cultural appropriation is easily visible in popular culture with the use of Plains-style clothing and headdresses on mascots, fashion models, and Halloween costumes or of tribal names as branding for products such as clothing or vehicles or to identify cities and streets.[8] These examples take an aspect or symbol of specific Native culture for use in a way that does not reference the originating peoples or cultures. This is, at a very basic level, disrespectful to Native peoples and their cultures, knowledge systems, and beliefs. Cultural appropriation will remain a subject or subtext of contemporary Native art and scholarship as long as it is pervasive and continuously visible. Native artists who respond to cultural appropriation or stereotype in their art are, in part, Indigenizing or reclaiming that space.

MATEO ROMERO *Cochiti Pueblo*

Mateo Romero is from Cochiti Pueblo, another of the nineteen Native American Pueblo nations in New Mexico. He lives and participates in his wife's community at the Pueblo of Pojoaque. He is from a family of artists spanning many generations: his grandmother, Teresita Chavez Romero, was a notable Cochiti Pueblo polychrome potter and his father, Santiago Romero, a Dorothy Dunn School–trained watercolorist, while his older brother, Diego Romero, is a prominent ceramicist. Romero received a Bachelor of Arts degree in studio art and an MFA in printmaking from the University of New Mexico. His work is in the collections of the Hood Museum of Art, the Smithsonian Institution's National Museum of the American Indian, the Institute of American Indian Arts, the Denver Art Museum, and the Peabody Essex Museum. He was also the recipient of the Native Arts and Cultures Foundation 2016 National Artist Fellowship.[9]

In his book *Painting the Underworld Sky* (2006), Romero describes his conceptual, ideological, and cultural framework, along with his art-making

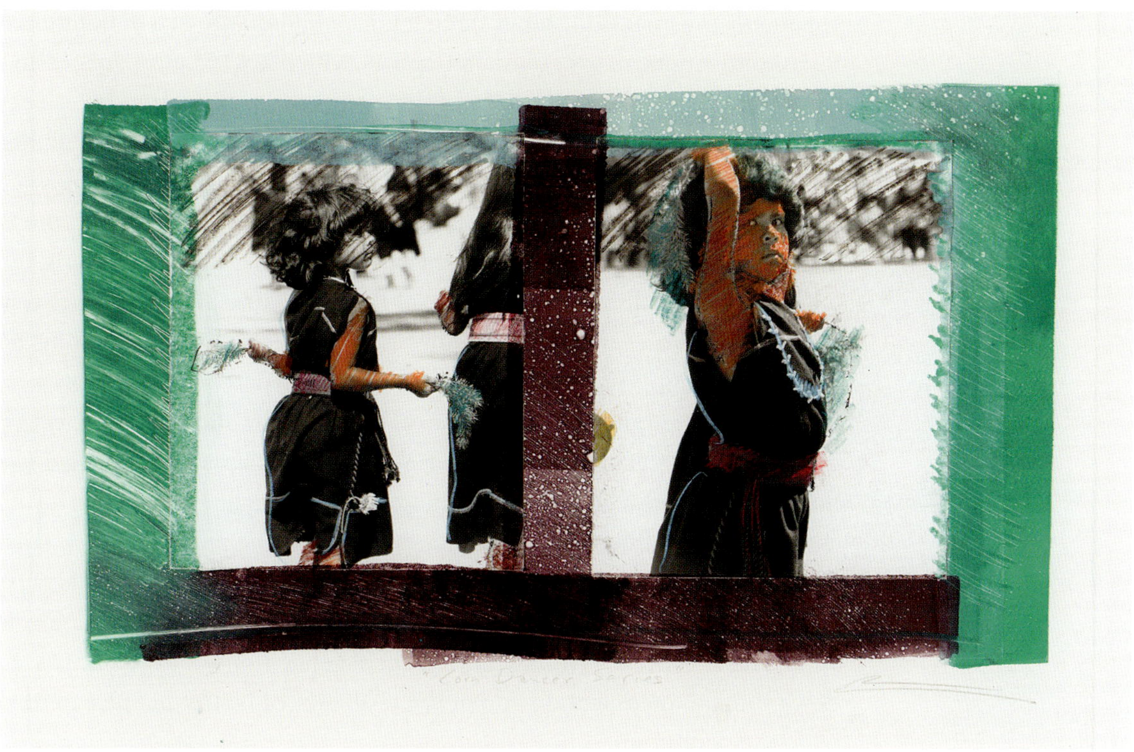

FIGURE 28 Mateo Romero (Cochiti Pueblo), *Corn Dance Series*, 1991, monotype, photograph, chine-collé, 22 in. × 30 in., MoCNA Collection, CO-37 (photo by Jason S. Ordaz).

process: "My metaphor for the Pueblo world, both past and present, is a stream. . . . Some people, villages, artwork, dances might seem at first glance to be more central, essential, or forceful within the flow of the stream . . . If my metaphor for the Pueblo world is a stream, then painting could be a metaphor for the act of making art out of this experience."[10] His *Corn Dance Series* is part of a larger series on Pueblo culture that spans more than three decades. This series is meditative and reflective, with its repetition and suggestion of the cyclical seasonal prayers, dances, and ceremonies that embody the Rio Grande Pueblo cultural way of life. The example shown in figure 28 draws on Romero's use of both conceptual space (the Rio Grande Pueblo cultures) and actual place (the lands connected to these people and cultures).

Corn Dance Series (1991) is a mixed-media piece with monotype, photography, and chine-collé. Chine-collé is a special printmaking technique in which paper of a different color or texture is adhered to the overall piece. The paper, usually in precut shapes, is not just glued to the print as a collage element, but bonded to the heavier support paper of the print in the printmaking process.[11] The space that this piece inhabits is cultural: Romero conveys an aspect of his culture that is intrinsically tied to place. This particular place is San Ildefonso Pueblo during a Corn Dance/Tablita dance. Romero's photo, apparently taken in situ, shows three female children dressed in traditional Pueblo attire typical for ceremonial dances, with black "Manta" dresses and woven sashes. Two of the young girls are carrying pine boughs. The subject matter is simple and direct and richly conveys an aspect of Pueblo culture, the Corn Dance, which is held in various forms at many of the Pueblos.

The framing of the photograph highlights the girl on the right, who is facing the camera. As with Garcia's *Feast Day Selfie*, Romero is using the ethnographic lens to express an aspect of Pueblo culture. As a person actively participating cross- and interculturally in Pueblo culture and ceremony, he necessarily complicates this lens or gaze. He is also part of Pueblo culture(s) that have restrictions and limitations on photography and recording, yet he has been able to gain the proper permissions to take photographs and use them in public art. Like Garcia, Romero is not taking liberties by conveying aspects of the culture that would not be visible to the public during a feast day. Unlike other ethnographic photographers such as Edward Curtis, who staged his subjects, Romero has captured a real moment with the subjects appearing in context.[12] His artwork speaks of generational knowledge passed down through participation and of the resiliency of Native peoples to hold on to their cultures.

EDGAR HEAP OF BIRDS *Cheyenne / Arapaho*

Cheyenne/Arapaho artist and educator Edgar Heap of Birds uses words to reference place, Native American histories, resistance, and cultural signifiers in paintings, prints, large-scale drawings, glasswork, public art signage, and outdoor monumental sculpture. He is a BFA graduate of the University of Kansas, earned a Master of Fine Arts from the Tyler School of Art, and was awarded an Honorary Doctor of Fine Arts by the Massachusetts College of Art and Design. Heap of Birds is a professor emeritus at the University of Oklahoma. His work is included in the collections of the Metropolitan Museum of Art, the Denver Art Museum, and the Walker Art Center. The Smithsonian's National Museum of the American Indian exhibited his *Most Serene Republics* as a collateral public art project at the 2007 Venice Biennale.[13] Heap of Birds Indigenizes actual places and reclaims conceptual space with his work.[14] He uses the English language to confront racism, stereotype, histories of violence, and the erasure of Native peoples and their cultures. This is most apparent with his text pieces or signage.

Heap of Birds' *Telling Many Magpies, Telling Black Wolf, Telling Hachivi* (36/90 1989, figure 29) is a silkscreen print on paper with words and abstract

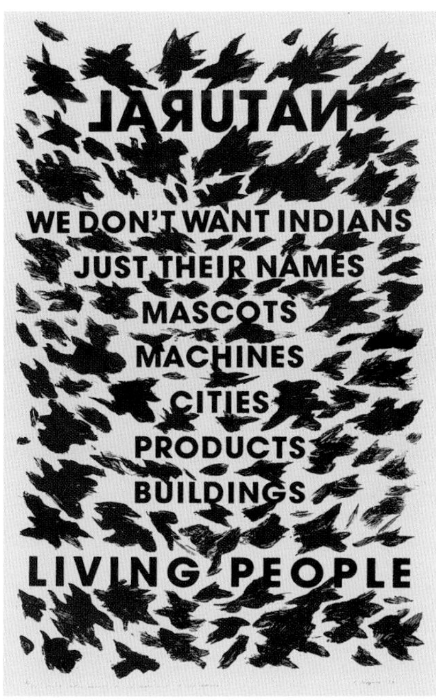

FIGURE 29 Edgar Heap of Birds (Cheyenne/Arapaho), *Telling Many Magpies, Telling Black Wolf, Telling Hachivi*, Diptych, Edition 36/90, 1989, silkscreen on paper, 35 in. × 45 in. each, MoCNA Collection, CHY-66.1 and CHY-66.2 (photo by Jason S. Ordaz).

featherlike shapes. It is a large-scale print comprising two sheets of paper 72 inches tall by 45 inches wide. The first word at the top, "NATURAL," is spelled backward. The following phrases appear in the center: "WE DON'T WANT INDIANS, JUST THEIR NAMES, MASCOTS, MACHINES, CITIES, PRODUCTS, BUILDINGS." At the bottom are the words "LIVING PEOPLE." Heap of Birds surrounds the text with abstract shapes that are reminiscent of his *Neuf Paintings*,[15] an ongoing series of large-scale acrylics on canvas. These paintings use color and abstract shapes to reference his tribal reservation lands near Oklahoma City, Oklahoma. They connect the artist to his home, tribe, and community, and in doing so make it possible for the viewer to experience the Cheyenne/Arapaho landscape through Heap of Birds' lens. He states that "From this rural yet invigorating landscape a painted language began," by which he refers to the colors and shapes in the abstract landscapes that he uses to signify place, people, and the histories of dominance and survival.[16]

Heap of Birds' use of text is often politically charged and meant to promote or even provoke thought and dialogue. The piece shown in figure 29 is no different. The word "NATURAL" is spelled backward to suggest that the erasure and assimilation of Native peoples is unnatural. The phrases in the middle are an indictment of the commodification of Native culture and the reduction of tribal names and images to symbols used without any reference to actual Native people. The term "LIVING PEOPLE" calls attention to the fact that Native people and their cultures are thriving and persistent.

The title of the work has a succession of names ending in the artist's own, "Hachivi,"[17] which connotes the way that oral histories, cultural mythology, and even spiritual practices are handed down through generations in many Native traditions. Black Wolf is the artist's great-grandfather. Many Magpies (Heap of Birds) is the artist's great-great-grandfather, a Cheyenne chief. The abstract feather/bird shapes that cover the piece are also meant to represent him.[18]

Heap of Birds has said that he wants his works to be accessible, so, like street signs, they are large enough to read from a distance. This print is six feet tall, which would give it dominant presence in an exhibition space. "Basically, if they can read English they can enter the piece," he explains. "And they can enter it before they can run away from it. They have already read it, so they already got it."[19] This work challenges the viewer to examine his or her preconceived notions about Native Americans. Through it, Heap of Birds reclaims discursive space and challenges the use of Native names out of context.

JESUS BARRAZA *Mexico / Xicano*

Jesus Barraza, an interdisciplinary Mexican/Xicano artist, is a graduate of San Francisco State University with a degree in Raza Studies. He is a cofounder of Dignidad Rebelde, a graphic arts collaboration that produces screen prints, political posters, and multimedia projects, and a member of Just Seeds Artists Cooperative, a decentralized group of political artists based in Canada, the United States, and Mexico. Barraza's exhibits, installations, public art, and lectures are platforms for retelling history, discussion of social justice issues, and advocacy for minoritized groups.[20] He uses references to actual place and enacts a form of Indigenous mapping to reclaim discursive and actual space.

Barraza's poster titled *Indian Land* (2004, figure 30) shows a silhouette map of North and South America. The words "Indian Land" follow the left curvature of the continents from north to south. The message is simple and direct: Barraza is stating that Indians or Indigenous peoples occupy both continents and that the land is theirs. There are no borders or demarcation of states or countries. Native Americans or American Indians have often been relegated to the boundaries of the United States. Barraza reminds the viewer that Indigenous people occupy and have occupied both continents. He cre-

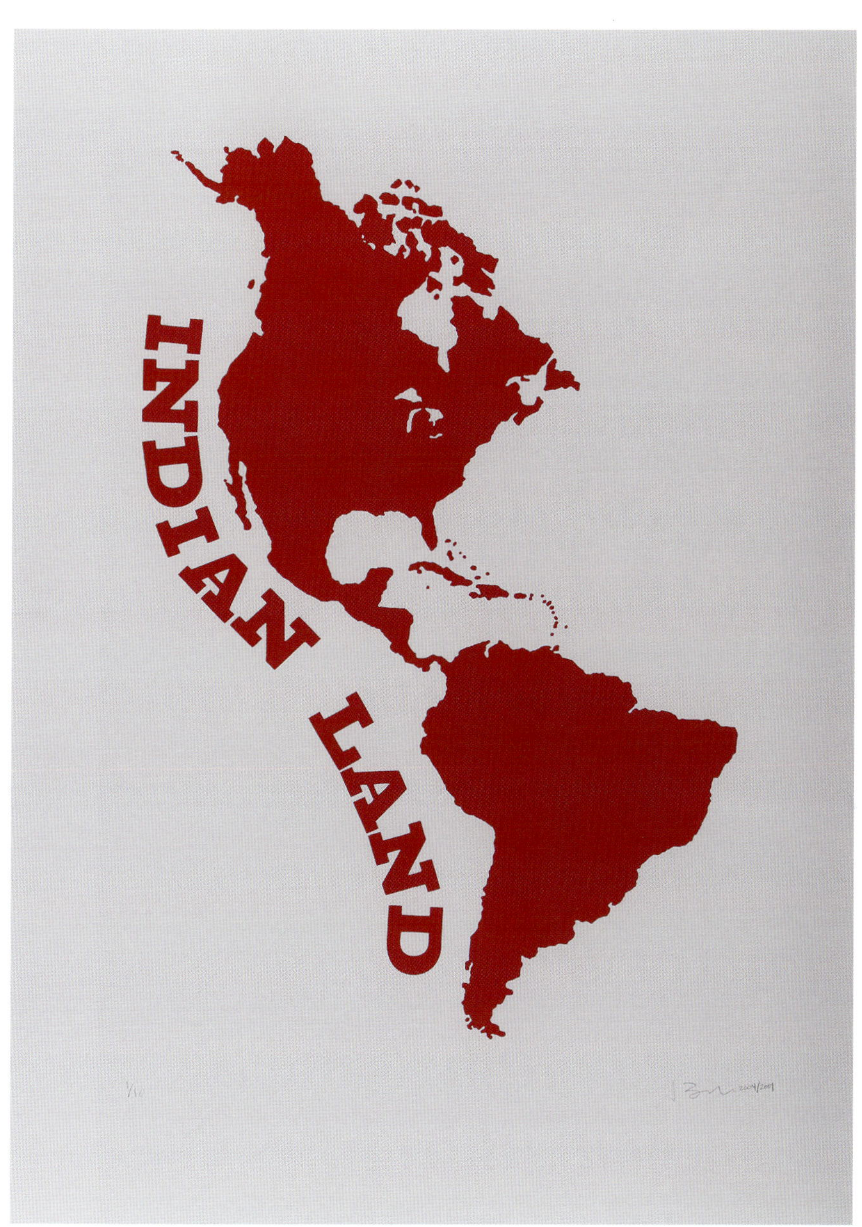

FIGURE 30 Jesus Barraza (Mexico/Xicano), *Indian Land*, Edition 1/10, 2004, poster, 30 in. × 20 in., MoCNA Collection, MEX-36 (photo by Addison Doty).

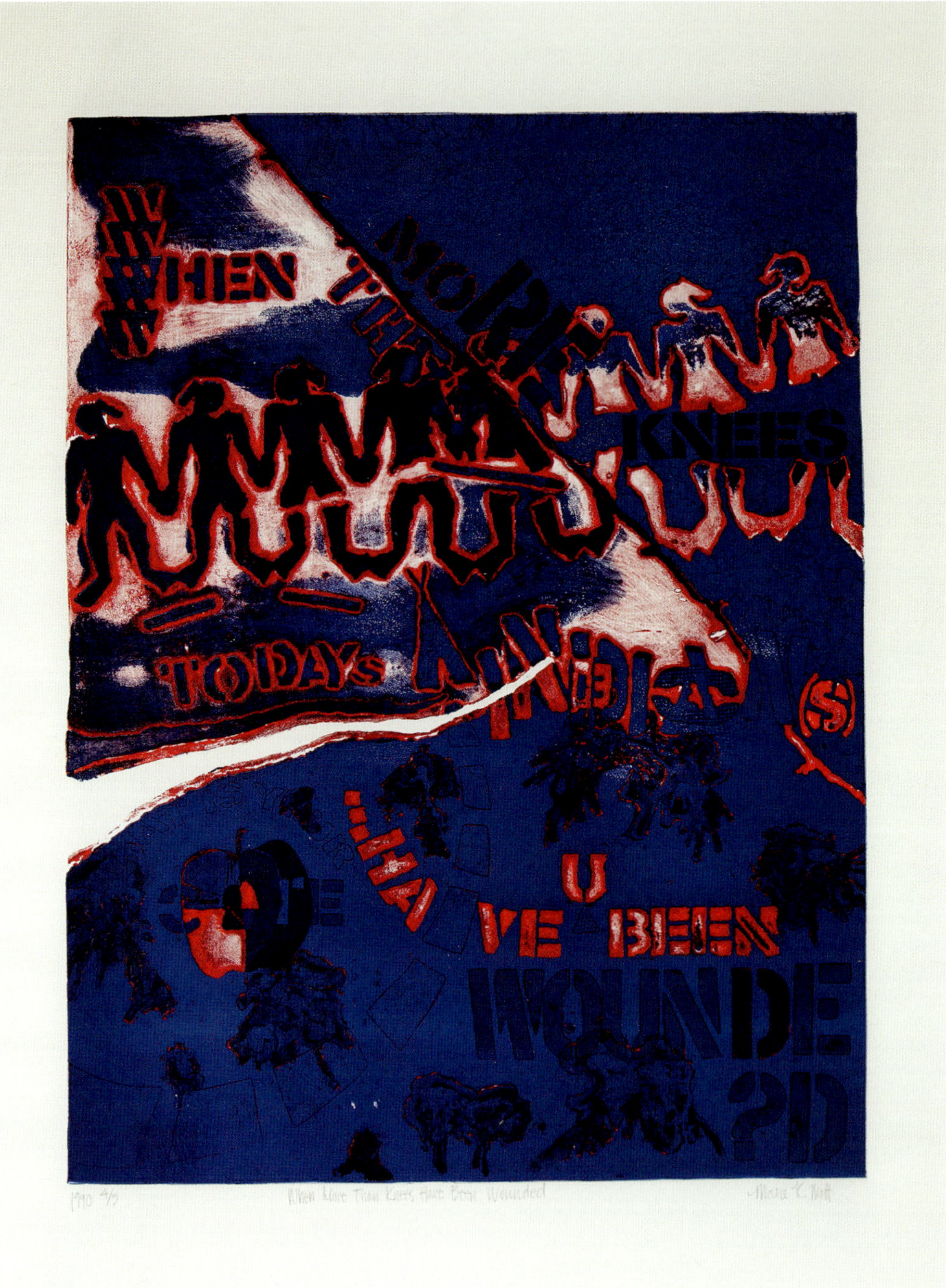

FIGURE 31 Marie K. Watt (Seneca), *When More Than Knees Have Been Wounded*, Edition 4/5, 1990, lithograph on paper, 29.75 in. × 22 in., MoCNA Collection, SEN-36 (photo by Jason S. Ordaz).

ated the *Indian Land* poster as a fundraising effort for Peace and Dignity Journeys. His use of the Turtle Island imagery came out of this group's goal to reunite the Eagle/North and Condor/South Indigenous nations through a spiritual run across the continents. Barraza stated that the poster's "message references the history of Alcatraz and the struggle to regain a land base, so we adapted the welcome graffiti one sees when arriving—'You are on Indian Land.' This message is true everywhere on these continents, wherever we stand is and will always be Indigenous land."[21] The artist is provocative, but his intention is to promote consideration and dialogue. Barraza questions the territorial naming of Canada, the United States, Mexico, and the countries in South and Central America, and reminds the viewer that regardless of colonial demarcation, this is still Indigenous land. He also implies that Indigenous people are still there and occupying the land.

Like Heap of Birds' *Telling Many Magpies . . .*, this work is accessible. The words are easily read and the shapes of the North and South American continents are also clearly recognizable. Jesus Barraza intends to engage with an English-speaking and -reading audience to get his message across quickly. This is an example of Indigenization of place and the discursive space of cartography. While Barraza is not conveying aspects of his particular culture, he is making a statement about hemispheric and even global Indigenous concepts of place.

MARIE WATT *Seneca*

Marie Watt is a multimedia artist based in Portland, Oregon. Her most well-known works explore narratives connected with commonplace woolen blankets, cedar wood, and iron. (The use of narrative refers to making connections through stories and their contextual association to the materials incorporated into art.) Watt draws her aesthetic and creative inspiration from history, biography, and Indigenous principles. She asserts that her work "addresses the interaction of the arc of history with the intimacy of memory."[22] Watt has a Bachelor of Science degree from Willamette University and a Master of Fine Arts in painting and printmaking from Yale University. Her work is included in the collections of the National Gallery of Canada, the Smithsonian Institution's National Museum of the American Indian, the Tacoma Art Museum, the Fabric Workshop and Museum, the Seattle Art Museum, and the US Library of Congress.

In *When More Than Knees Have Been Wounded* (1990, figure 31), Watt connects to conceptual space by retelling history through an Indigenous perspective. While her work has shifted to become more community-based, this lithograph seems more personal, based on its content. Its figural cutouts and words outlined in red on a blue background address dark moments in Native history while calling into focus the ongoing effects of assimilation and racism toward and among Native people. The words are in phrases from top to bottom: "WHEN MORE THAN KNEES," "ONE LITTLE . . . ," "TWO LITTLE . . . ," "THREE LITTLE INDIANS . . . ," "TODAY'S INDIAN(S)," "WHAT IS YOUR CORE," and ". . . HAVE U BEEN WOUNDED?." The images of the cutout figures are holding hands and have feathers in their hair. "One little, two little, three little Indians" references "Ten Little Indians," a children's counting song that has racist and violent origins.[23]

The words "TODAY'S INDIANS" in the center of the lithograph are separated by a symbol for a tipi. In popular culture and media, all of Native American culture is often relegated to Plains Indian culture, with its use of feather bonnet headdresses, war paint on the face, Indians on horseback, and tipis. This overgeneralization negates the hundreds of Native nations with distinct languages, cultures, aesthetics, and worldviews. In her artwork, Watt calls into question what and who Native people really are today. On the lower left is an image of an apple with the words "WHAT IS YOUR CORE" above and over it. This refers to a derogatory term for a Native American who is "red on the outside but white in the middle," that is, who looks phenotypically Native but acts and thinks like a white person. Watt brings into focus how this term can be harmful and promote internal racism among Native people. Her concluding thought and question " . . .HAVE U BEEN WOUNDED?," coupled with the statement about knees, calls attention to the treatment of Native people and specifically two incidents at Wounded Knee, South Dakota. The massacre that occurred there in 1890 solidified the reservation era and signified a loss of freedom and rights for Native Americans, including the right to practice their religions. The occupation of Wounded Knee in 1973 made the world aware of Native peoples struggling for their freedom and equality. Her question ". . .HAVE U BEEN WOUNDED?" is rhetorical in the context of this piece. Watt uses the actual place of Wounded Knee as a metaphor for conceptual space of human rights and specifically Indigenous rights.

ANTHONY GAUTHIER *Menominee / Ho-Chunk*

Like Marie Watt, Anthony Gauthier uses images and words to connect to a conceptual space. Gauthier is a Menominee/Ho-Chunk artist who attended the Institute of American Indian Arts (IAIA) in the late 1970s. Unlike other artists in this chapter, he does not have many exhibitions on record. He created his painting *Freedom* (1976, figure 32) during his time as a student at IAIA and it is part of the permanent collection. The artwork incorporates portraits of Chief Joseph and Martin Luther King, Jr. on either side of an American flag. Superimposed over the flag are a number of symbols, including a dove over a stylized Native American water bird, MLK's famous statement, "I HAVE A DREAM!," a Native storm cloud, fire, tipis, and cotton buds. Below Chief Joseph are a dancing skeleton with a headdress, silhouette figures, the words "DON'T SELL THE BONES OF YOUR MOTHER AND FATHER," a buffalo skull, and a skeleton lying in a red rounded rectangular box.

In this painting, Gauthier is clearly making a comparison of the struggles of Native Americans and African Americans. The painting is full of symbolism and metaphor. On the left side, Chief Joseph stands in as a leader and advocate for Native peoples, much as Martin Luther King, Jr. was a figurehead for the civil rights movement. Gauthier's admonition "DON'T SELL THE BONES OF YOUR MOTHER AND FATHER" actually comes from an account of

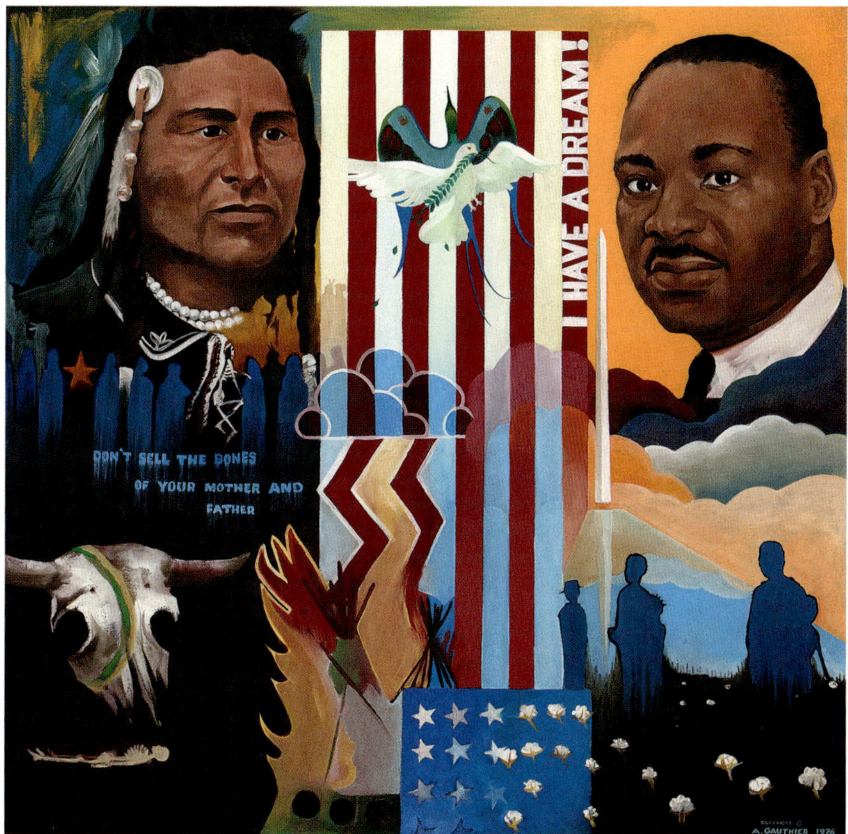

FIGURE 32 Anthony Gauthier (Menominee/Ho-Chunk), *Freedom*, 1976, acrylic on canvas, 52.25 in. × 52.25 in., MoCNA Collection, WIN-14 (photo by Walter BigBee).

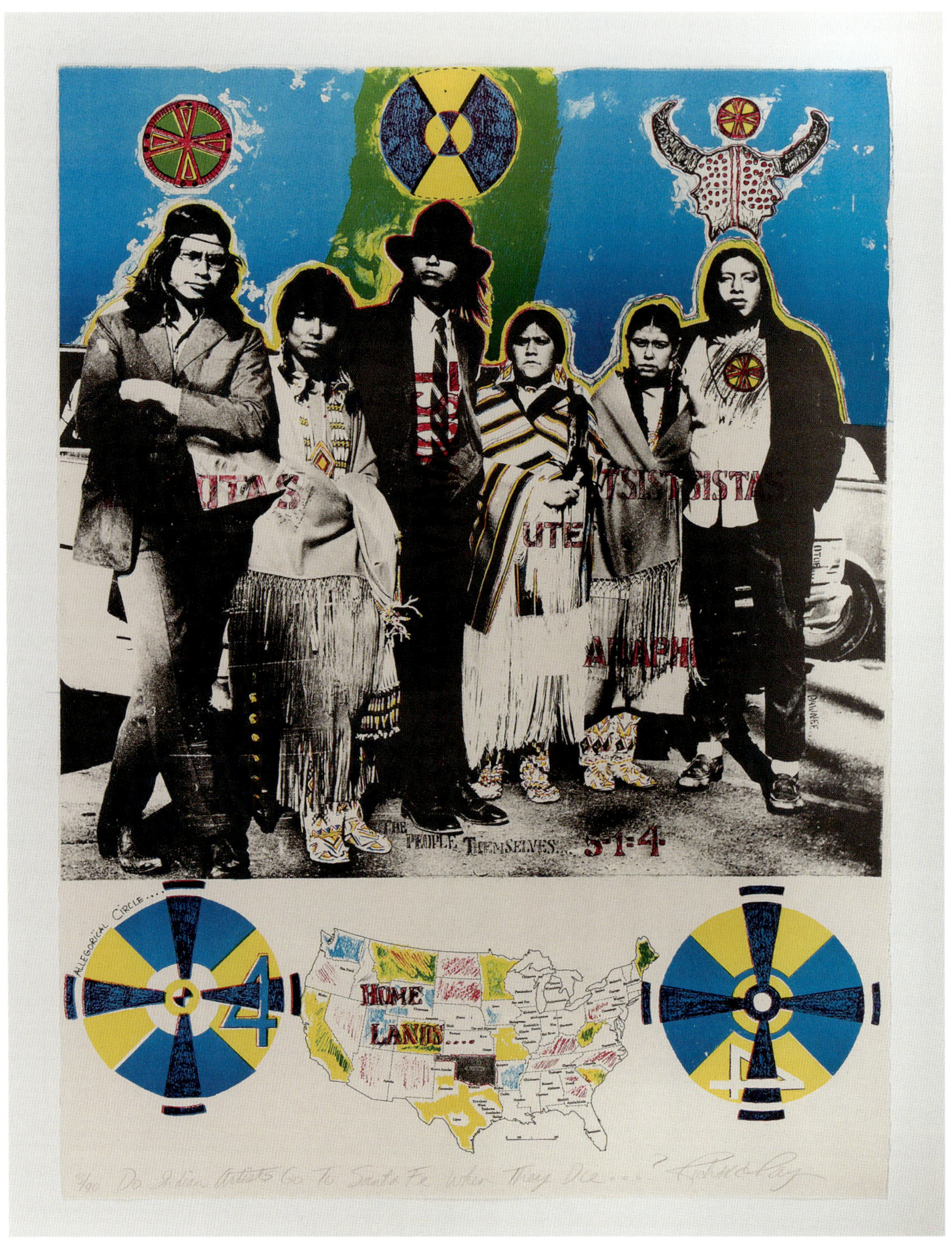

FIGURE 33 Richard Ray Whitman (Yuchi/Muscogee Creek), *Do Indian Artists Go to Santa Fe When They Die . . . ?*, Edition 3/90, 1989, offset lithograph on paper, 30 in. × 22 in., MoCNA Collection, YC-13 (photo by Jason S. Ordaz).

the deathbed words of Chief Joseph's father.[24] His final directives were for his son not to sign treaties or sell the homelands where his father would be buried. The dancing skeleton and silhouetted figures are apparitions of the ancestors. The buffalo skull serves as a reminder of the importance of that animal to Native peoples and the settling of the West, which included the mass slaughter of buffalo across the plains. The silhouetted figures and the cotton on the right below Martin Luther King, Jr. symbolize the oppression of African Americans and their struggle for racial equality. The imagery in the middle signifies hope, redemption, and even, as the title suggests, freedom and "equality for all," as symbolized by the American flag. Gauthier places "I HAVE A DREAM!" directly over the flag. These famous words were spoken by a member of an oppressed race imagining and calling for equality and an end to racism. The dove is a universal symbol for peace. The water bird, storm cloud, tipis, and fire serve as metaphor for Native culture and spirituality—things passed down through generations that would sustain Native people. Gauthier emphasizes the convergence of inequities and also redemption or restitution for people of both oppressed groups.

This 1976 artwork was created in the bicentennial year—the 200th anniversary of the founding of the United States—which was a time of turmoil for Native and African American people. Martin Luther King, Jr. had been assassinated in 1968, less than ten years earlier. Racial tensions were prevalent while the nation was nearing the end of the Vietnam War. The occupation of Wounded Knee occurred in 1973 and Native American religious freedom would not be constituted formally into law until 1978.[25] Given these considerations, Gauthier was using his artwork to express current conditions and social issues relevant to the time. He uses the conceptual space of freedom and civil rights to suggest that the struggles of Native Americans are no less important than those of African Americans. The overlapping of symbols indicates his idea of the shared values coexisting and implicit with the American flag and what it stands for all US citizens.

RICHARD RAY WHITMAN *Yuchi / Muscogee Creek*

Richard Ray Whitman is a Yuchi/Muscogee Creek artist, photographer, poet, actor, and activist whose work has been exhibited widely, including by the Smithsonian's National Museum of the American Indian and La Biennale di Venezia in Italy. An Institute of American Indian Arts graduate, he later attended the California Institute of the Arts. Whitman acknowledges that his people and his family shape his understanding of the world and inform his aesthetic. He states about his art-making, "I was born of the Yuchi people (TsoYaHa) and my perceptions and expressions emerged from the core of this identity. My mother, grandmother and extended family were my most immediate teachers, informing my basic knowledge of the world and shaping my aesthetic sensibilities . . . My work is a layering of cultural, political and aesthetic ideas which are always changing and evolving, just as my own identity and the identity/identities of Indian people have always evolved and changed."[26] Like other artists in this chapter, Whitman operates from an aesthetic that is grounded in his cultural frame first and includes reflections on contemporary issues and influences. His statement conveys that Native people and their cultures are not static or immutable, but dynamic. Native people are adaptable and able to maintain their cultural continuity regardless of change or influence. This belief counters popular understandings of Native people having intact and insular cultures prior to European contact and little or no cultures afterward.

Whitman's lithograph *Do Indian Artists Go to Santa Fe When They Die . . .?* (1989) features a group photograph of Native men and women standing in front of a row of cars with individual tribal names superimposed in block letters. The men are dressed in typical Western clothing and shoes, while the women are in dresses with shawls and beaded moccasins. Whitman explains, "The central image is taken from a black-and-white photograph I took of myself and other students at the Institute of American Indian Arts in Santa Fe in 1969."[27] Above the people are Native symbols often found in beadwork or quillwork and a drawing of a painted buffalo skull in the upper right corner. Directly below the people are the words "THE PEOPLE THEMSELVES." Across the bottom in the white space are a United States map and TV airwaves symbols below. The map has the words "HOME LANDS" and tribal names written across the states. The state of Oklahoma is filled in with black in what Whitman referred to as "a mingling of colors for a place where people from tribes throughout the country were forced to relocate, away from their home lands. Even so, tribal identities remain strong, as evidenced by the individuals who came to study art in Santa Fe." [28] Whitman uses tribal names to identify his subjects, including himself, and juxtaposes them with the map of the United States and the implication that the colors and tribal names represent concentrations of Native people on their own lands and those to which they were relocated.

The Indian Relocation Act of 1956 was a United States law intended to encourage Native Americans to leave reservations, acquire vocational skills, and assimilate into the general US population.[29] Whitman's piece reflects on his time at the Institute of American Indian Arts and in Santa Fe, where there is a long history of Native art production and commerce at the Santa Fe Indian Market. The IAIA has provided a means for both students and instructors to put forward progressive ideas and examples of contemporary Native art. The Santa Fe Indian Market was created to provide economic opportunity and visibility for Native artists primarily in the Southwest, but later extended to Native and First Nations artists from across the United States and Canada. Whitman suggests that there are social and cultural implications to Native artists' going to Santa Fe, offering a critique of the impact of the Indian Market and the proliferation of patron- or market-driven art. His suggestion in the title is that Native artists go to Santa Fe to gain recognition, but he questions that by suggesting that in doing so, they lose themselves, their connection to their people or culture. Whitman at once levels the critique while reaffirming tribal identities and their connections to place.

ANITA FIELDS *Osage / Muskogee Creek*

Anita Fields is an award-winning multimedia artist and educator working in ceramics, traditional Osage ribbonwork, sculpture, painting, and installation. Her work is in the collections of the Museum of Art and Design, the Institute of American Indian Arts Museum of Contemporary Native Arts, the Heard Museum, and the Smithsonian Institution's National Museum of the American Indian. She is a BFA graduate of Oklahoma State University. Fields creates from an aesthetic that is rooted in her Osage culture. As she describes it, "Osage worldview is based on the division of the earth and sky; it represents the order, balance, and duality found in life, nature, and the universe. I use this as metaphor in my work." [30] This aesthetic connects her art to not only her culture as a discursive space but also to her tribal homelands in Oklahoma.

Untitled (Osage Woman with Landscape) (1973, figure 34) is a mixed-media painting on canvas showing a female figure with her back to the viewer. She is ostensibly a Native woman and Osage as indicated in the title. The layers of cloth and clothing, along with the ribbonwork design on her skirt and floral fringed shawl, are typical of Osage women's attire. The woman appears at the far left of the frame, facing a mountain landscape. Fields creates a stark background so that the focus is on the figure in the foreground. She engages the viewer to consider the finer details of the figure: her long braided hair, her clothing, her brown skin. This is a celebration and honoring of the women in the artist's culture. Because the face is obscured, the woman

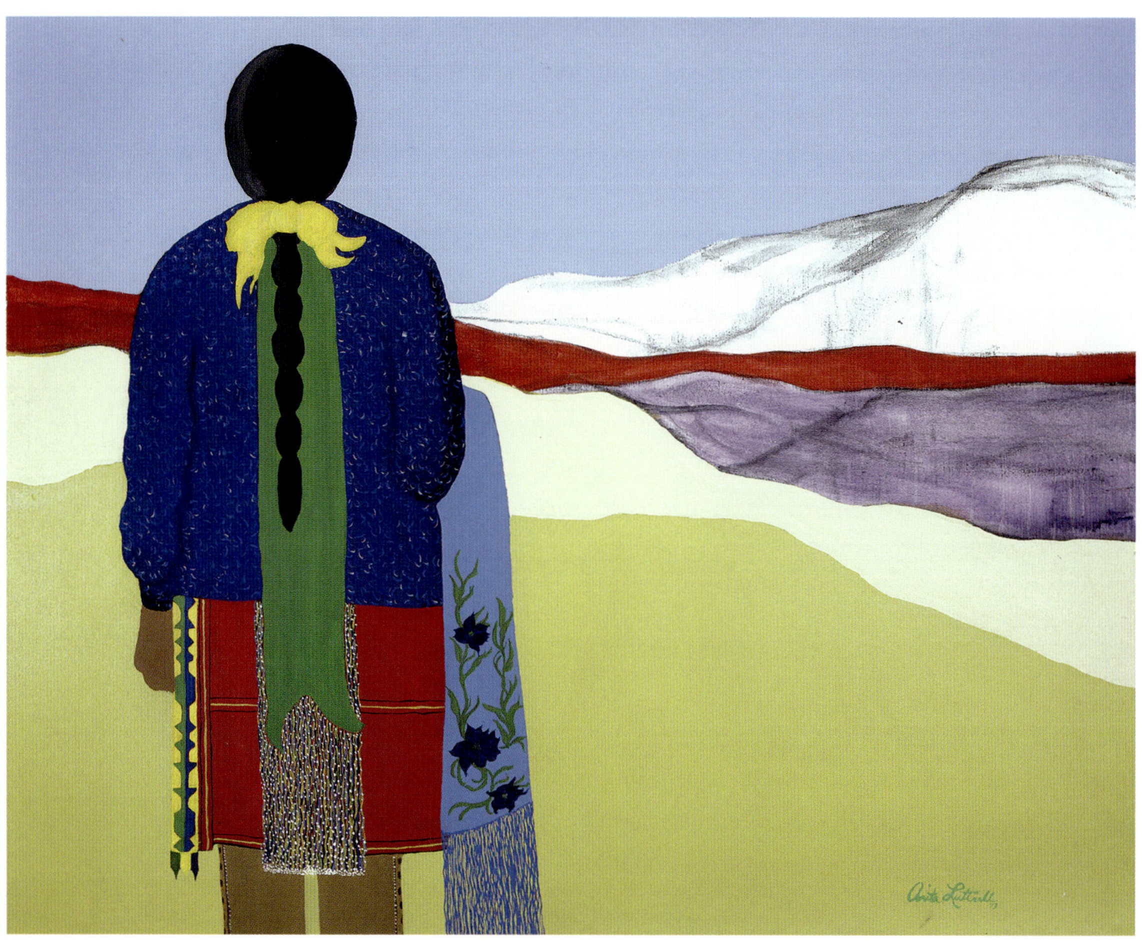

FIGURE 34 Anita Fields (née Luttrell) (Osage/ Muskogee Creek), *Untitled*, 1973, mixed media on canvas, 60 in. × 72.25 in., MoCNA Collection, OS-40 (photo by Walter BigBee).

represents generations of women, her mothers, aunts, grandmothers, and also her children and their children.

This artwork has a certain timeless quality to it in that many aspects of the Osage woman's dress are seen today and could also have been seen in the early 1900s. When looking at Native art, it is important to consider the continuity of aspects of culture, in this context forms of dress. This is not to say that Native culture is static or immutable; in fact, it is dynamic and adaptable. This piece speaks to the resiliency of Osage culture, but is also a reflection of the survival and resiliency of all Native peoples. Fields describes her use of figures and landscapes as signifying "a continuum of thought, knowledge and the essence of who we are as indigenous human beings living in a modern, chaotic, and challenging world. In works reflecting land and nature, I am interested in creating symbolic representations of the spiritual and cultural memory found throughout the terrain of our original homelands and sacred places."[31] This statement would suggest that, in this piece, the Osage woman stands firmly connected to her culture and tribal identity. Her presence is an Indigenization of place. Fields is at once connecting to a physical and a cultural space. The landscape is symbolic of Osage culture and the ecological knowledge contained there—songs, dances, families, cyclical prayers, language, and histories. This work communicates reciprocity, as this piece is a tribute to her family, homeland, and culture.

NORMAN AKERS *Osage Nation*

Painter and educator Norman Akers, a BFA graduate of the Kansas City Art Institute and an MFA graduate of the University of Illinois, Urbana-Champaign, has exhibited and lectured nationally for over two decades. He is an associate professor in the Department of Visual Art at the University of Kansas.

Akers uses the medium of painting as a form of visual storytelling and has developed a number of symbols and visual metaphors to convey stories, narratives from his culture, personal life experiences, and connection to place. He explains, "The underlying principles that inform my art include tribal oral histories, maps, art historical references, and nature. Through visual narrative, I explore how my point of view relates to a historical, political and cultural sense of place in contemporary society. The use of narrative in my work acts as a continuation of the Native American storytelling tradition. Ancestral tribal stories and sayings have served to explain the world in which we lived. New and emerging stories serve as allegories of transformation in an ever-changing world."[32] Akers uses metaphor and symbolism to express an Osage Indigenous aesthetic that necessarily references culture and his connection to place: what he terms the "Native American storytelling tradition."

In Akers' painting *Sorting Out Blind Sensations* (1998, figure 35), the land and landscape become a container for references to the artist's culture and homelands and commentary on personal experiences and transformation. In the foreground, a figure partially covered by a red cloth, his arms and legs outstretched, sits in a barren field next to a pond with catfish. The figure, who appears to be male, has black empty sockets where his eyes should be and is holding a pair of binoculars. His right arm reaches out toward a white figure emerging from the water. Black butterflies circle thin white outlines of acorn caps with a tornado in the distant field. To his left is the outline of a lunch box; above him are a sun symbol and dove. Directly behind him, new growth emerges from below the cutline of a tree stump. In the distance is a satellite dish up on the grassy hill.

FIGURE 35 Norman Akers (Osage Nation), *Sorting Out Blind Sensations*, 1998, oil on canvas, 75 in. × 70 in., MoCNA Collection, OS-79 (photo by Jason S. Ordaz).

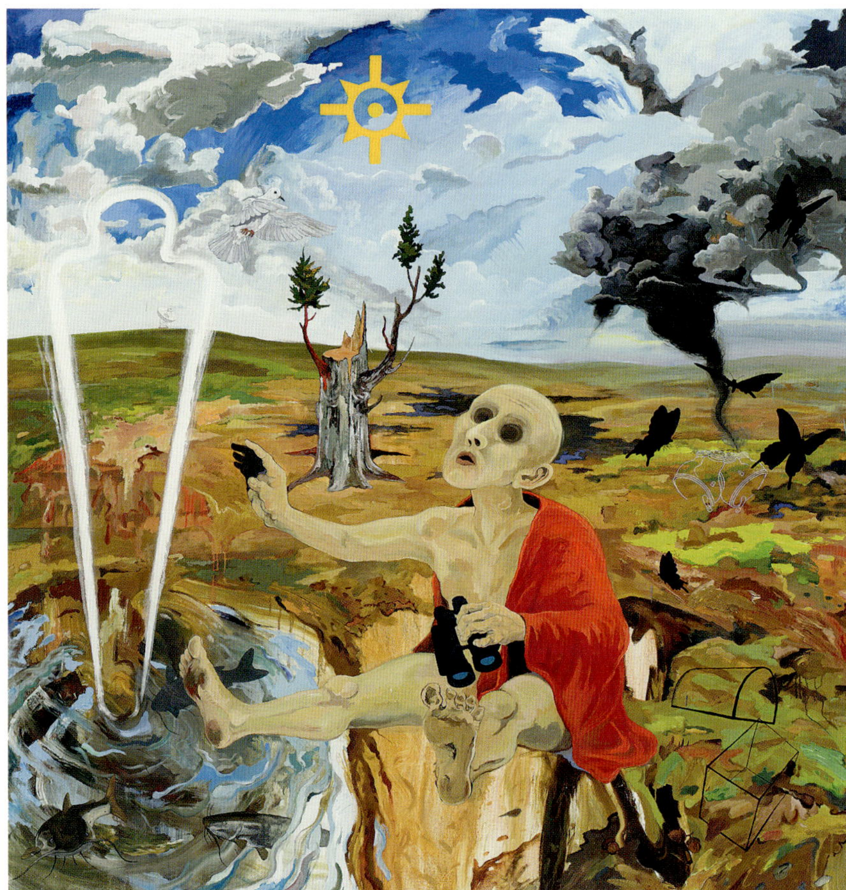

Akers draws his imagery from his homelands in Oklahoma. While some of it is metaphorical in nature, other elements come from and signify aspects of his home and culture. The sun symbol is a prominent aspect of many Native cultures and spiritual systems. The cut tree appears as a symbol for renewal and shows that life can emerge out of destruction. There is an ecology to living in a particular place. The tornado he pictures, a common occurrence in the plains, symbolizes the destructive force of nature. This reference to Akers' homelands is fairly direct, but there is also the inherent caution and respect associated with the elements. In many Native American cultures, associations to spirituality are reflected in the relationships to these forces. In this instance, however, the tornado represents chaos and a ravaged landscape, also indicated by the tree stump. Butterflies are often meant to symbolize transformation, but here they are dark like the storm clouds and tornado behind them, tying them to the barren and forbidding landscape.

According to Akers, the doves in his painting are a symbol for the Holy Spirit; this brings a Christian spiritual element into the work. The dove and the sun image express the interconnectedness of Western and Native spiritual beliefs.[33] The catfish are also a direct reference to the land. The lunchbox is a personal reference to Akers himself, which he includes in many of his artworks. Because this is a reflection of his worldview and he is relating aspects of Osage culture, this symbol represents the storyteller. It places the artist within the narrative of the painting and is something like a signature, but it is also a vessel or container that is slightly broken. Akers leaves its meaning open for interpretation. The satellite dish in the distance places the context in modern times with an indication that there are transmissions and reception. Akers explains, "The radio telescope is a scientific device that collects data from faraway places. It is a technological instrument that assists us in our attempt to understand the invisible nature of the universe."[34] The enigmatic old blind man sits holding a pair of binoculars, but can't see. He is reaching for something that he knows is right in front of him. Given Akers' themes of exploring identity and culture, this figure represents the struggles of trying to find one's nature and place within one's self and culture, and discovering that the answers are not without, but within.

Both Fields and Akers approach conveying aspects of their Osage aesthetic in different ways but are both reinforcing connections to land and culture. They each use symbol and metaphor to reaffirm and honor their Osage nation, culture, and homelands. Akers' use of the radio telescope is reminiscent of the telephone lines Garcia uses. While the symbols similarly point to technology, each artist is interpreting those symbols through his own cultural lens.

CONCLUSION

In this chapter, Watt, Gauthier, Heap of Birds, and Barraza offer accessible pieces from which a person with little or no knowledge about Native people or their cultures can gather meaning. It is more apparent that the work would speak directly or indirectly to a large audience. Gauthier uses well-known and -documented leaders, Nez Perce Chief Joseph and Martin Luther King, Jr., along with descriptive text. The use of text and the English language by these four artists gives the viewer an entry point into the artworks. Garcia's and Romero's pieces require a little more knowledge, awareness, or understanding of Native cultures, as they speak to Pueblo aesthetics and have overt cultural signifiers such as the attire and references to dances and feast days.

Both Fields and Akers utilize Osage aesthetics with references to traditional forms of dress and visual metaphors and symbols for the land and culture. Whitman refers to Santa Fe in his work's title and uses tribal names. His references are a little more obscure unless a person knows that the tribal names are in their respective languages. It is very clear that audience perception and reception is very important to Heap of Birds and Barraza, while this is possibly less so with Romero and Akers. The artists who are addressing a particular social or political issue seem to be more accessible because of their use of textual elements. The question of audience and accessibility is a variable that is dependent on the artist and their body of work. This can be said for any art. It can be argued that a lot of contemporary Native art has sociopolitical elements and themes. Each of these artworks has layers of information with some universalizing elements. What is integral to this discussion is trying to understand the motivations, aesthetics, and perspectives of the Native artist through his or her work.

Throughout this chapter, the primary organizing concept has been connections to place or Indigenization of space or materials. The artworks were selected for their suitability to interpretation using an Indigenous epistemological methodology with an Indigenous aesthetic analytical framework based on materiality and design, metaphor and symbolism, reciprocity, and connections to place or Indigenization of space or materials. This framework is intended to promote the consideration and prioritization of Indigenous epistemologies, the perspectives and knowledge that emerge from an artist's cultural heritage. Using Indigenous aesthetics creates the opportunity to gain a better understanding of the artist's creative process and, more broadly, how Native culture and identity figure into his or her creative expression.

USING INDIGENOUS AESTHETICS

Indigenous aesthetics are an expression of cultural continuity and reciprocity that includes conceptions of space or place. They and Native perspectives—and, in some cases, the Indigenization of space or materials—are necessary concepts for understanding Native art and culture. Indigenous aesthetics are best understood through an Indigenous epistemological framework that centers on Indigenous cultural values, beliefs, ways of knowing, and knowledge systems.[35] Indigenous scholar Margaret Kovach's *Indigenous Methodologies: Characteristics, Conversations and Contexts* (2009) and Shawn Wilson's *Research Is Ceremony* (2008) identify the need for centering research on Indigenous epistemologies and local bodies of culturally based knowledge. These provide research methodologies that, when utilized, become more meaningful, ethical, and respectful of Indigenous artists, their cultures and communities.[36]

Choctaw/Chickasaw scholar heather ahtone theorizes about Indigenous aesthetics and proposes a methodology that includes materiality, metaphor/symbolism, and reciprocity. According to ahtone, the materiality and design of an object created by a Native artist reflect ideas about and extend local Indigenous bodies of knowledge.[37] When Native artists use natural materials, they often obtain them following cultural protocols for gathering. The materiality, in the context of a cultural art form such as a basket, pottery, or leatherwork, ties the work to the legacy of generational knowledge in those forms and points to tribal and even family-specific designs. An artist's use of metaphor and symbolism in an Indigenous aesthetic will often reference semiotics directly relevant to his or her culture and tribal specificity. ("Semiotics," in this context, refers to the study of the designs, symbols, and visual metaphors used to make meaning and reference culture or place.)

Reciprocity is an exchange with mutual benefit. Enacting reciprocity is a form of gratitude. Reciprocity acknowledges in a very visceral way the deep continuity to which Indigenous people have access through their connections to place, community, and cultural expression. I agree with ahtone that by continuing to use the signs, symbols, and metaphors of one's culture and ontology, Indigenous artists honor and respect their histories, their legacies, and the perseverance and continuation of their cultures and traditions.[38] The above works by Norman Akers, Anita Fields, Jason Garcia, and Mateo Romero are clear examples of this concept of reciprocity.

These concepts are meant to be not the definitive measure of Indigenous aesthetics, but a starting point for an analytical model. What is important to remember is that Native artists create from their unique cultural perspectives, personal experiences, influences, and cultural understanding. Some make overt references to their culture through the use of designs and materials that are tribally specific. Some embed their cultural references into metaphor or symbolism or abstraction. Native artists will reference place or reclaim a discursive space in order to convey an aspect of their cultural understanding and identity, reframe a historical event, or redress a social issue such as water rights or racism. While these concepts are meant to guide a viewer's analytical framework, they are not meant as concrete, static boundaries.

In this chapter, consider the use of Indigenous aesthetics as an analytical framework for each of the artists and their work. How does materiality or the use of metaphor and symbolism function within the piece? How are these

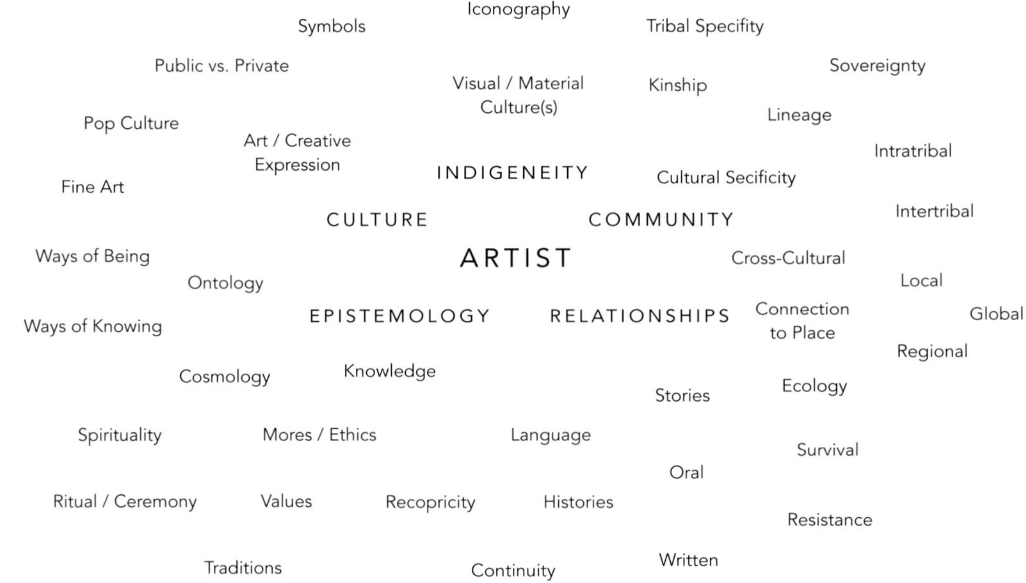

RANGEL'S MODEL FOR INDIGENOUS AESTHETICS ANALYTICAL FRAMEWORK.

works connecting to place, physical or discursive? Are these works relating aspects of the artist's own culture or are they retelling aspects of history from a Native perspective?

I developed my own conceptual model of a visual representation for an Indigenous aesthetic analytical framework as a way of thinking about art beyond Western conceptions by including Indigenous aesthetics and perspectives.[39] It includes overlapping circles of information, with the center being the bodies of knowledge that emerge from the artist's home community, elders, and specific tribal nation(s). It can be helpful in considering how these different concepts relate to the creation of artworks.

The way I imagine people using this conceptual model is to identify an object of art and its artist, then move outward, asking questions in relationship to the surrounding variables. Rather than a linear process, I see it as a method for gathering information, understanding the artist's intentionality, and reading the work through Indigenous aesthetics. A simplified approach would be to start with a piece of art and take the following steps:

1. Identify the artist.
2. Identify the artist's tribal affiliation.
3. Research the tribal nation's geographic location and historical or cultural information.
4. Examine the materiality of the artwork.
5. Determine whether it is a cultural art form that is particular to the

tribal nation or similar to other Western traditions of art (painting, sculpture, photography, etc.).

Once this information is known, the viewer should consider the following questions. Doing so will aid in understanding more about the artwork, the artist, Indigenous aesthetics, and the distinctiveness and diversity of Native art and culture:

1. If the piece is a cultural art form, it likely communicates something about tribal specificity. Are there discernable symbols or iconography? Do these say something about the artist's tribal culture, spirituality, stories, or histories? If the piece is not a cultural art form, is it using themes that are secular or spiritual?
2. Some Native art draws on popular culture influences or references. How do these relate to the artist's connection to family/lineage, Native communities, tribal nation, or tribal homelands?
3. Is the work conceptual or using ideas, themes, and symbols that speak cross-culturally or universally? Does this focus place emphasis on perspectives, material conditions, and current issues relevant to Indigenous peoples and their communities?
4. Is the work directed toward a general audience or a specific audience?
5. Can you determine if the piece is referencing a particular place or a conceptual space?
6. Is the work an example of Indigenizing materials or space?

In national and international museums and institutions, Native art is often relegated to non-Western art categorization and displayed in ethnographic groupings with other art that is not considered European or Euro-American fine art. These works are commonly perceived as relics and artifacts of lost or ancient primitive cultures instead of from living, thriving peoples and cultures. Native art is more than artifacts or cultural art forms and includes Western traditions of art such as painting, sculpture, photography, and installation/performance. These works build on Indigenous cultures, traditions, and creative expressions while also innovating and developing new traditions.

NATIVE ART 101 QUESTIONS

1. What are examples of appropriation of Native art or culture going on today? Do these examples contribute to a better understanding of Native art or culture?
2. How is land a container for culture? Why is this reference to place or connection to place important to the reading of the art?

3. What is "Indigenizing of materials and space"?

4. What are ethical considerations for recording Native art or culture?

5. Did you learn something new about Native art or a Native artist? Did this change your perceptions about Native art?

VOCABULARY

activation of space—In a Native context, bringing together people, intention, purpose, and often food. This type of activation is about building community and inclusion, affirming core values and identity, sharing knowledge and mentoring, recognizing and honoring elders, and building on traditions. Within art specifically, it is anything that indicates Native presence.

conceptual space—the nonphysical space of theories, ideas, themes and abstractions, such as art that is political or communicates reciprocity.

discursive space—systems of knowledge and how knowledge about a topic is organized.

ethnographic gaze—the recording of a cultural subject by someone who is not of the same culture. In the case of Native American peoples, the recorder is often a person from the dominant Western Euro-American culture.

Indigenizing of materials—adapting and incorporating new ideas, influences, and materials into the lexicon of Indigenous cultural expression.

Indigenizing of space—activating a space for a ceremonial or cultural purpose with language, songs, dance, regalia, and prayer. Native artists who Indigenize space reclaim a location through cultural signifiers, performance, song, dance, or installation to convey the existence and presence of Native peoples and cultures. Indigenization takes place any time there is Native art in a public space.

Indigenous epistemologies—theories of Indigenous knowledge and ways of knowing, especially with regard to its methods, validity, and scope.

Indigenous mapping—the act of naming places, geography, or landmarks and connecting them to ecological engagement with the land, oral histories, mythology, spiritual practice, families, language, and traditions.

land as a container of culture—Indigenous mapping of and ecological engagement with the land, which solidifies relationships and builds on cultural foundations and creative expression.

NOTES

1. John Paul Rangel, "Indigenous Perspectives on Contemporary Native Art, Indigenous Aesthetics, and Representation" (dissertation, University of New Mexico, 2012), 11, http://digitalrepository.unm.edu/educ_llss_etds/37/.

2. John Paul Rangel, "Contemporary Native (NDN) Art and Representation" (master's thesis, University of New Mexico, 2006).

3. Janet C. Berlo and Ruth B. Phillips, *Native North American Art* (Oxford: Oxford University Press, 1998), 68.

4. Snapchat is a popular mobile application that allows the user to share quick, often candid images, video, or multimedia. The term "selfie" has become ubiquitous worldwide with sharing a self-portrait photograph through social media networks.

5. For more on the nineteen Pueblo nations, visit the Indian Pueblo Cultural Center website: www.indianpueblo.org.

6. Jason Garcia, "Biography/Resume," Okuu Pín website, http://www.okuupin.com/biographyresume.

7. Jason Garcia, "Jason Garcia Exhibit Preview & Artist Panel." (Artist panel discussion at the Poeh Cultural Center, Santa Fe, NM, August 16, 2017).

8. Native Appropriations (http://nativeappropriations.com) is an online forum for discussing representations of Native peoples, including stereotypes, cultural appropriation, news, and activism. Adrienne Keene (Cherokee) is an educator and this website's author.

9. Mateo Romero, "Bio," Mateo Romero Studio website, https://www.mateoromerostudio.com/bio.

10. Mateo Romero, *Painting the Underworld Sky: Cultural Expression and Subversion in Art* (Santa Fe: School of American Research, 2006), 9.

11. Steve Grant, "What is Chine-Collé?," 15th Street Gallery website, https://15thstreetgalleryboulder.com/blog/faqs/chine-colle.

12. Christopher M. Lyman and Edward S. Curtis, *The Vanishing Race and Other Illusions: Photographs of Indians by Edward S. Curtis* (Washington, DC: Smithsonian Institution Press, 1982).

13. Edgar Heap of Birds website, http://heapofbirds.ou.edu/.

14. Edgar Heap of Birds has displayed public works using signage across the United States and internationally. There are many examples on the artist's website.

15. "Neuf" is the Cheyenne word for the number four. In many Native cultures, four is a sacred number and representative of many things, such as the cardinal directions, the seasons, and the stages of life.

16. Edgar Heap of Birds, "Thoughts on Artistic Practice." There are examples of the *Neuf* paintings on the Edgar Heap of Birds website.

17. He often uses the phonetic version, "Hock E Aye Vi."

18. Euan Kerr, "Edgar Heap of Birds' Enigmatic Simplicity," Minnesota Public Radio website, https://www.mprnews.org/story/2017/09/12/edgar-heap-of-birds-enigmatic-simplicity.

19. Kerr, "Edgar Heap of Birds' Enigmatic Simplicity."

20. "Jesus Barraza," Dignidad Rebelde website, http://dignidadrebelde.com/?page_id=748.

21. Jesus Barraza, e-mail message to author, September 16, 2017.

22. "About," Marie Watt website, http://www.mariewattstudio.com.

23. Iona Opie and Peter Opie, *The Oxford Dictionary of Nursery Rhymes* (Oxford: Oxford University Press, 1951, 2nd ed., 1997), 333–34. Julianne Jennings, "The History of 'Ten Little Indians'—How Did the Genocidal Nursery Rhyme Come About?" *Indian Country Today* website, published October 11, 2012, https://indiancountrymedianetwork.com/culture/social-issues/the-history-of-ten-little-indians/

24. Brian Schofield, *Selling Your Father's Bones: America's 140-Year War against the Nez Perce Tribe* (New York: Simon & Schuster, 2009), 49.

25. American Indian Religious Freedom Act (AIRFA), Public Law 95-341, National Park Service website, https://www.nps.gov/subjects/historicpreservation/laws.htm.

26. Richard Ray Whitman, "About," Richard Ray Whitman website, http://richardraywhitman.wordpress.com.

27. Richard Ray Whitman, "About the Artists," University of Puget Sound Collins Memorial Library website, https://www.pugetsound.edu/academics/academic-resources/collins-memorial-library/about-collins/artwork-exhibits-in-the-library/brandywine-workshop/about-the-artists/. "Do Indian Artists Go to Santa Fe When They Die . . .?" (1989) was part of the 2014 exhibit for the Brandywine Workshop at the University of Puget Sound in Tacoma, Washington.

28. Whitman, "About the Artists."

29. Indian Affairs: Laws and Treaties database, Oklahoma State University Library website.

30. Anita Fields, "About Anita Fields," Robert Nichols Gallery website, https://tinyurl.com/yx3toh93.

31. Fields, "About Anita Fields."

32. Norman Akers, Norman Akers website, http://normanakers.com.

33. Norman Akers in discussion with the author, September 2017.

34. Norman Akers in discussion with the author, September 2017.

35. heather ahtone, "Reading Beneath the Surface: Joe Feddersen's Parking Lot," *Wíčazo Ša Review* 27, no. 1 (Spring 2012): 73–74. John Paul Rangel, "Indigenous Perspectives on Contemporary Native Art," *Wíčazo Ša Review* 27, no. 1 (Spring 2012): 11. Steven Leuthold's *Indigenous Aesthetics: Native Art, Media and Identity* (Austin: University of Texas Press, 1998) theorizes about using a more culturally appropriate methodology for analyzing Indigenous aesthetics, focusing primarily on media and film. This approach does not fully address how or what Indigenous aesthetics would be when applied to Native art.

36. Margaret Kovach, *Indigenous Methodologies: Characteristics, Conversations and Contexts* (Toronto: University of Toronto Press, 2009). Shawn Wilson, *Research Is Ceremony: Indigenous Research Methods* (Halifax: Fernwood, 2008).

37. ahtone, "Reading Beneath the Surface," 73–84.

38. ahtone, "Reading Beneath the Surface," 81.

39. John Paul Rangel, "Indigenous Perspectives on Contemporary Native Art" (dissertation), 231.

GALLERY TWO

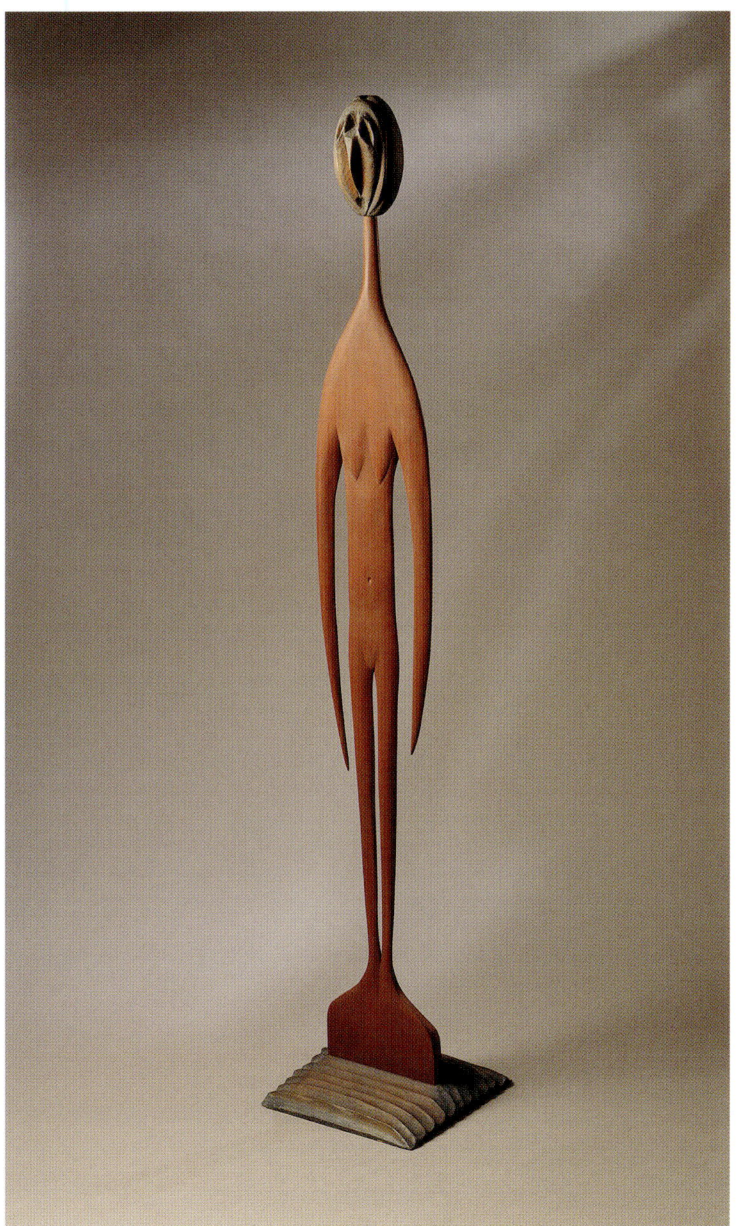

PLATE 23 John Hoover (Aleut), *Hawk Woman*, 1970, cedar, paint, 54.25 in. × 10 in., MoCNA Collection, AT-32 (photo by Walter BigBee).

PLATE 24 Carol Frazier Aikens (Paiute), *Untitled*, 1963, watercolor, felt-tip pen on paper, 27 in. × 33 in., MoCNA Collection, PU-8 (photo by Jason S. Ordaz).

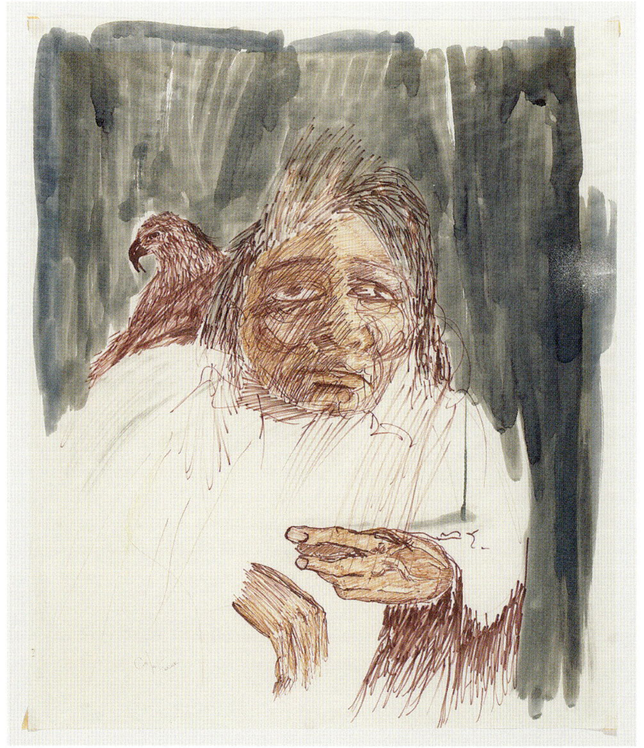

PLATE 25 Helen Hardin (Santa Clara Pueblo), *Changing Woman*, Edition 35/65, 1980, metal etching on paper, 30 in. × 21.75 in., MoCNA Collection, SC-109 (photo by Jason S. Ordaz).

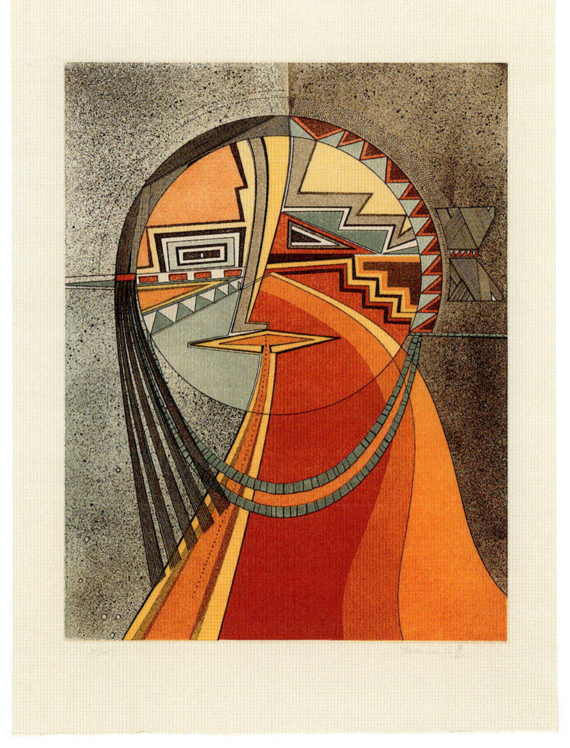

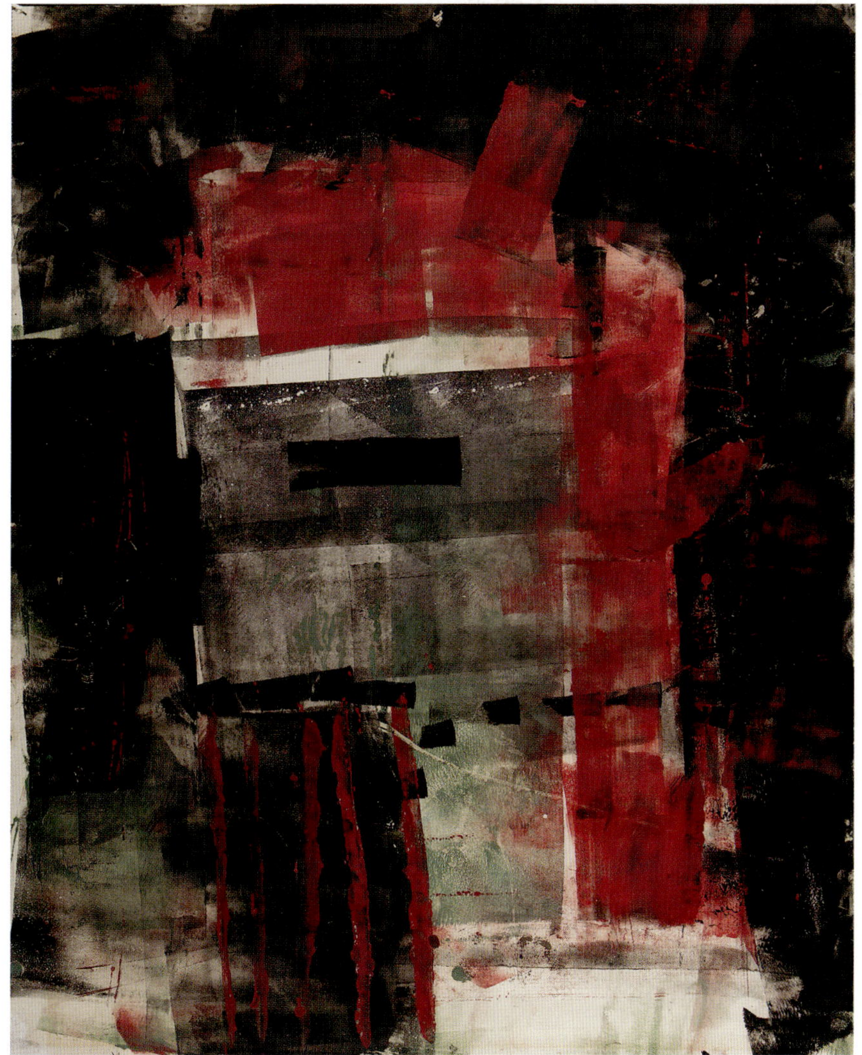

PLATE 26 Robert Tsabetsaye (Zuni Pueblo), *Katchina No. 1*, ca. 1965, oil, casein on canvas, 28 in. × 22.13 in., MoCNA Collection, ZU-31 (photo by Addison Doty).

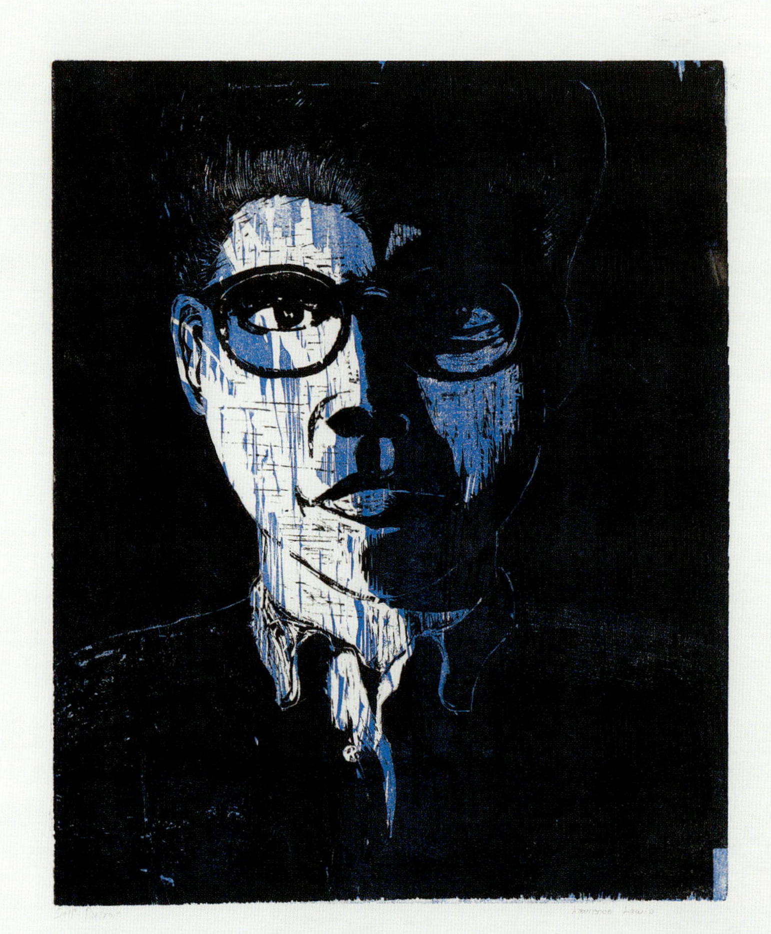

PLATE 27 Lawrence Lewis (Akimel O'odham), *Self-Portrait*, n.d., woodcut, ink on paper, 26 in. × 21.5 in., MoCNA Collection, P-43 (photo by Jason S. Ordaz).

PLATE 28 Anita Fields (née Luttrell) (Osage/Muskogee Creek), *Gina Gray*, n.d., black-and-white photograph on board, 20 in. × 16 in., MoCNA Collection, OS-53 (photo by Walter BigBee).

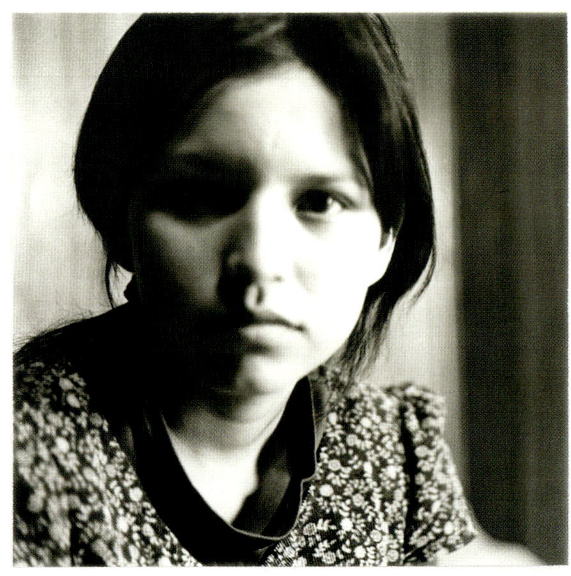

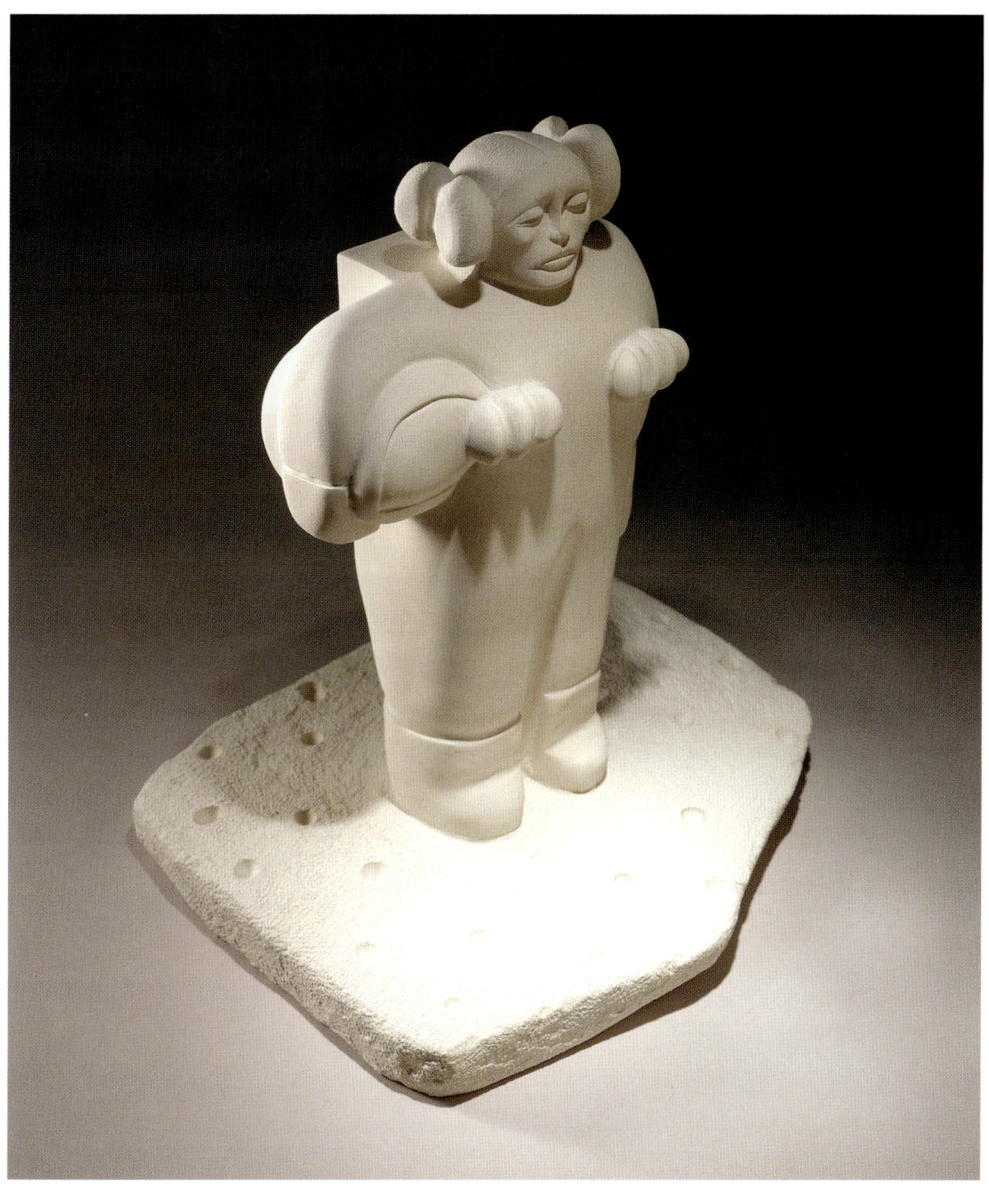

PLATE 29 Ken Tohee (Otoe/Ioway), *Maiden Voyager*, 1999, limestone, 17 in. × 15 in. × 12.5 in., MoCNA Collection, O-5 (photo by Walter BigBee).

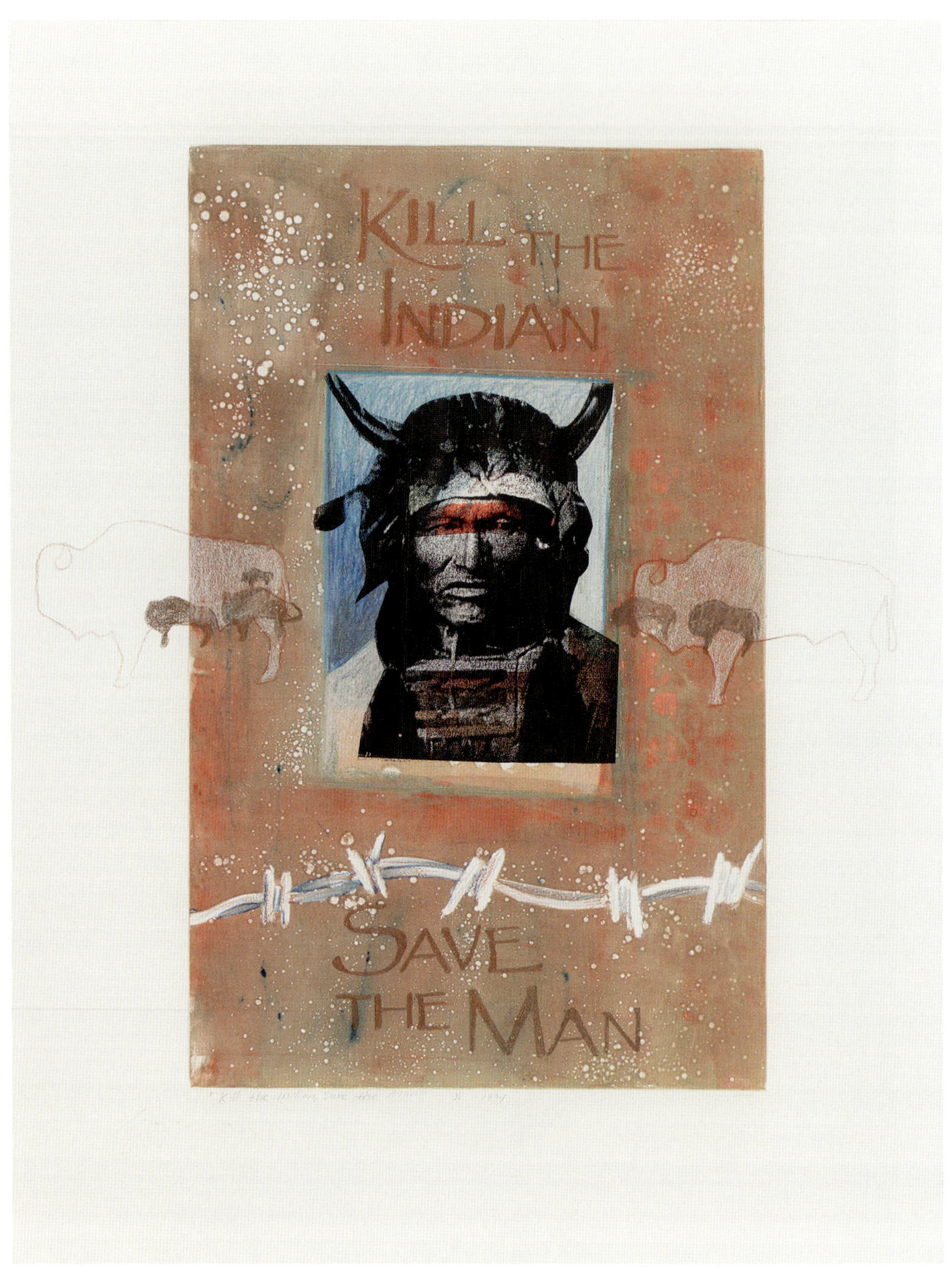

PLATE 30 Marwin Begaye (Diné-Navajo), *Kill the Indian Save the Man*, 1992, monotype, chine-collé, mixed media on paper, 30 in. × 22 in., MoCNA Collection, N-1138 (photo by Jason S. Ordaz).

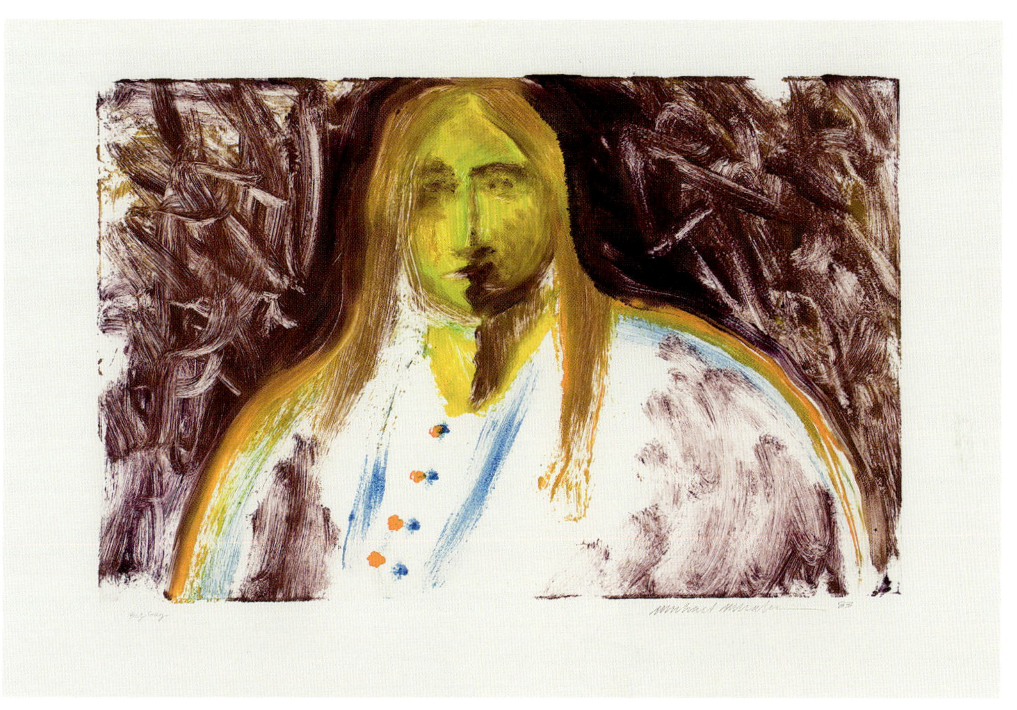

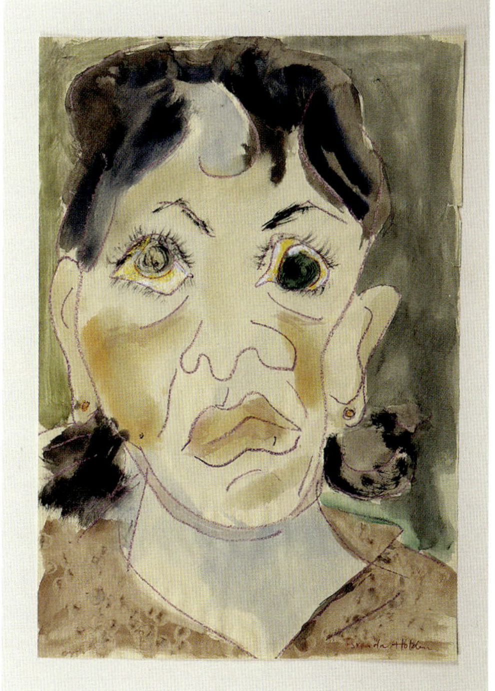

PLATE 31 *above* Michael McCabe (Navajo), *Big Guy*, Edition 1/1, 1983, monotype on paper, 16 in. × 23 in., MoCNA Collection, N-951 (photo by Jason S. Ordaz).

PLATE 32 *left* Brenda Holden (Miwok), *Untitled*, 1969, watercolor on paper, 21 in. × 14.75 in., MoCNA Collection, MIW-34 (photo by Jason S. Ordaz).

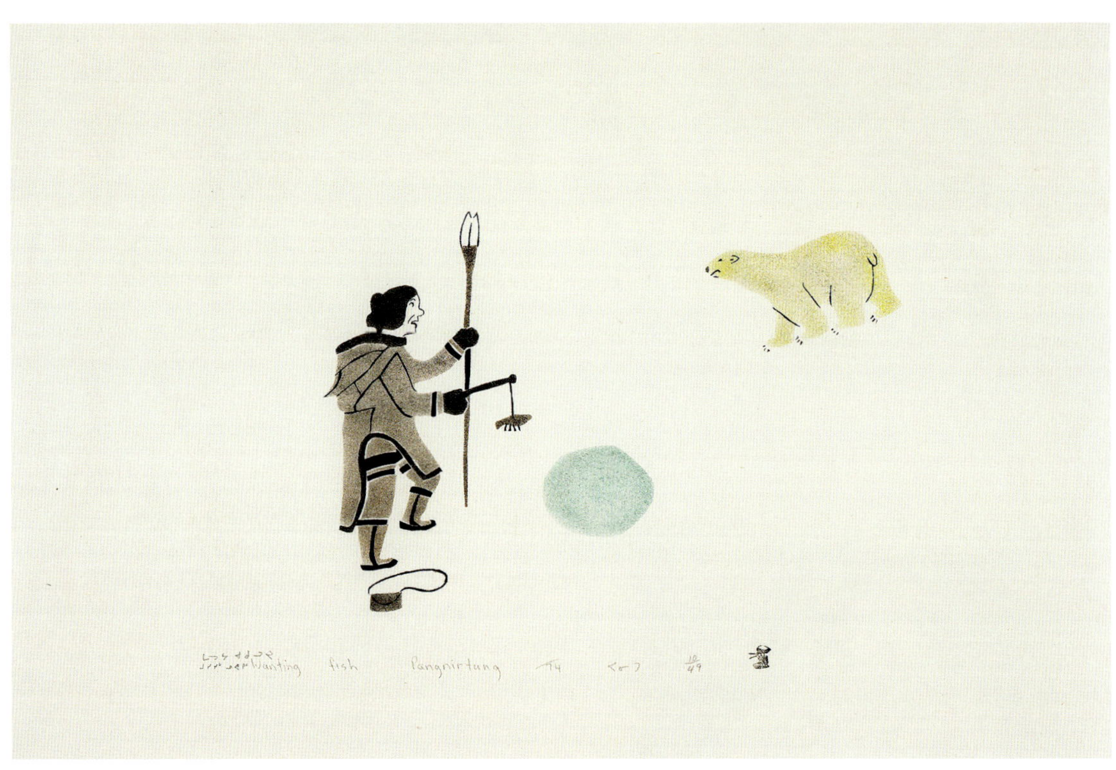

PLATE 33 Tronto Malaya Akulukjuk (Canadian), *Wanting Fish*, Edition 10/49, 1974, lithograph on paper, 19 in. × 10.5 in., MoCNA Collection, CAN-75 (photo by Jason S. Ordaz).

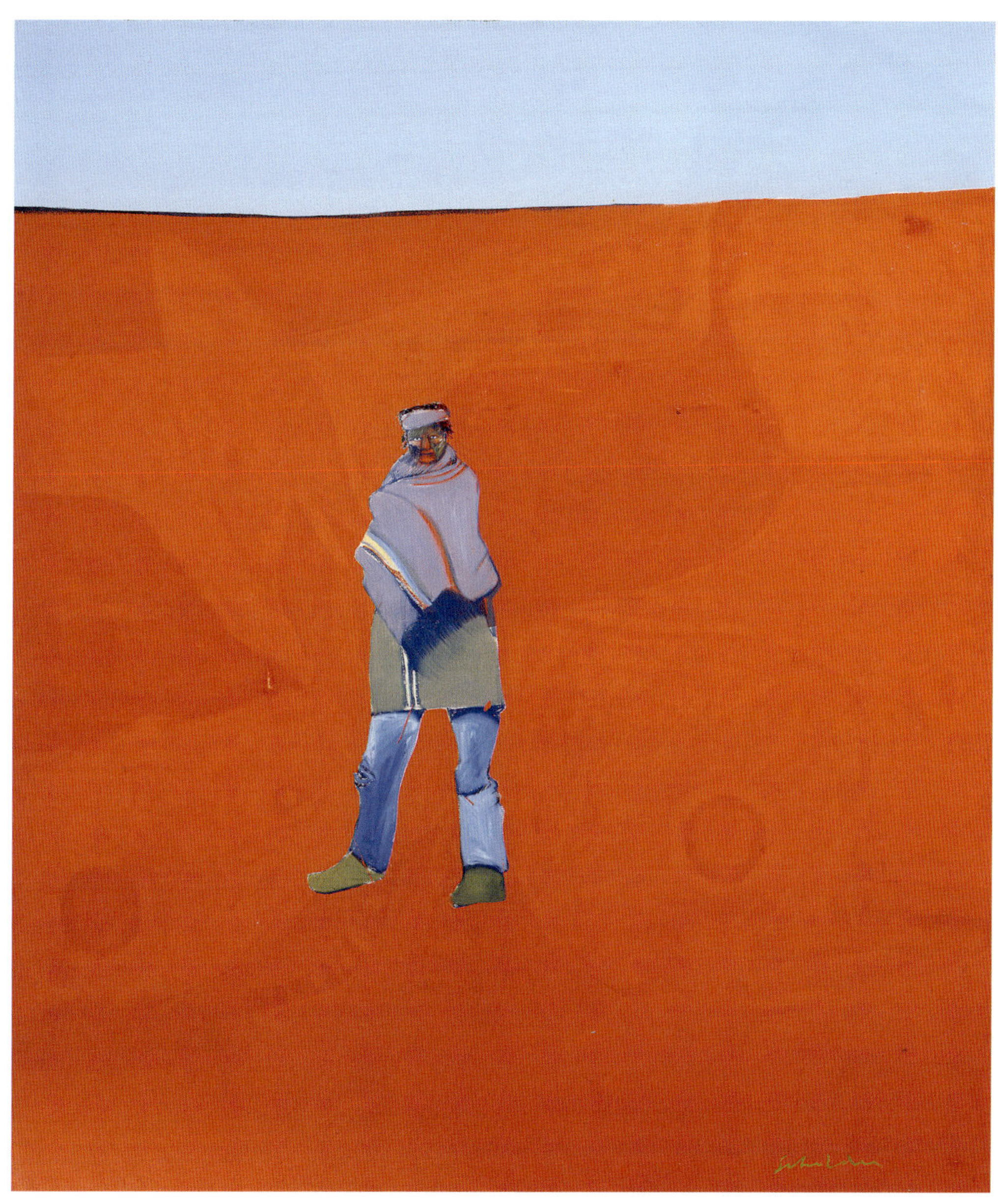

PLATE 34 Fritz Scholder (Luiseño), *One Navajo*, 1968, oil on canvas, 74.25 in. × 62 in., MoCNA Collection, MS-28 (photo by Walter BigBee).

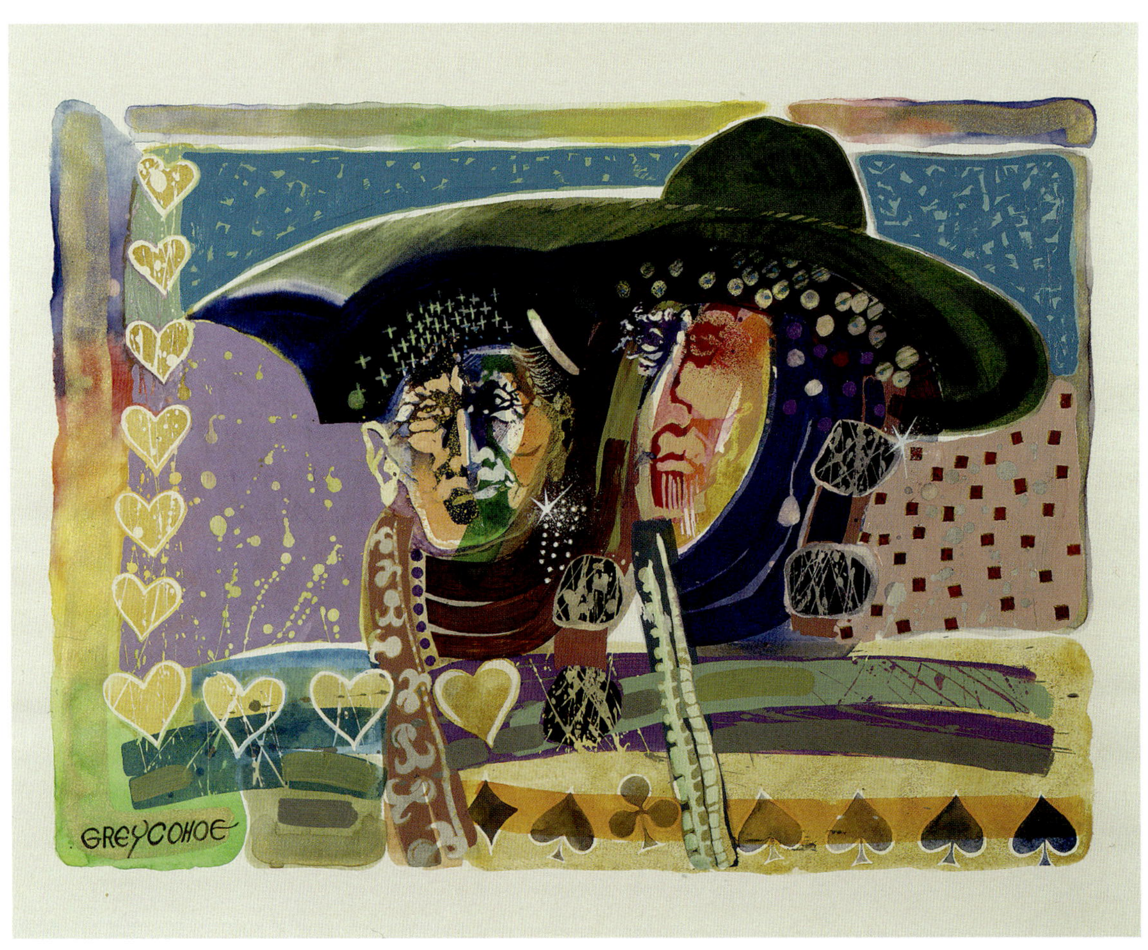

PLATE 35 Grey Cohoe (Navajo), *Mesa Mirage from Tocito Rain*, 1983, acrylic on paper, 19.5 in. × 23.63 in., MoCNA Collection, N-1146 (photo by Walter BigBee).

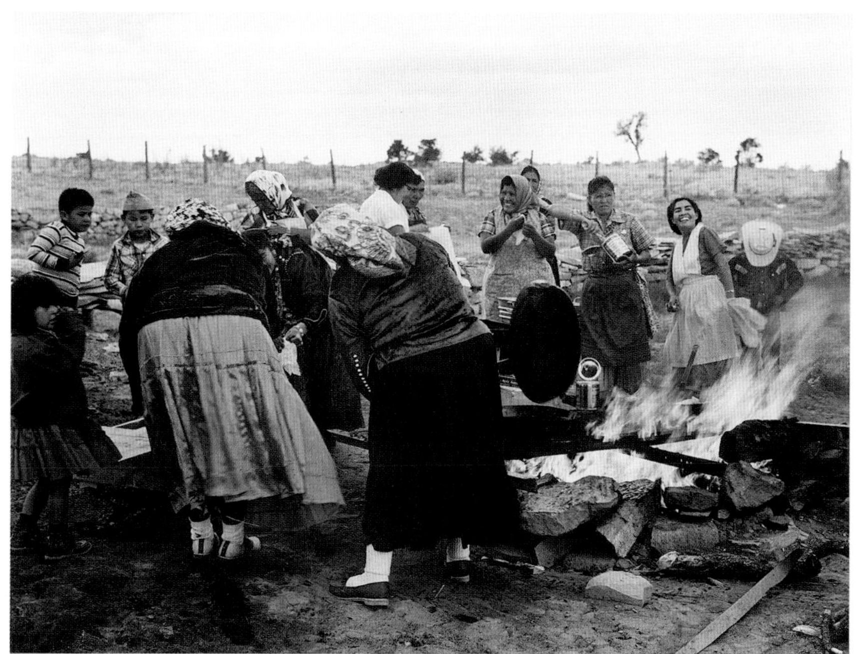

PLATE 36 Laura Gilpin (Non-Native), *17 Navajos Gathered*, ca. 1968, black-and-white photograph on paper, 20 in. × 28.25 in., MoCNA Collection, INST-130 (photo by Jason S. Ordaz).

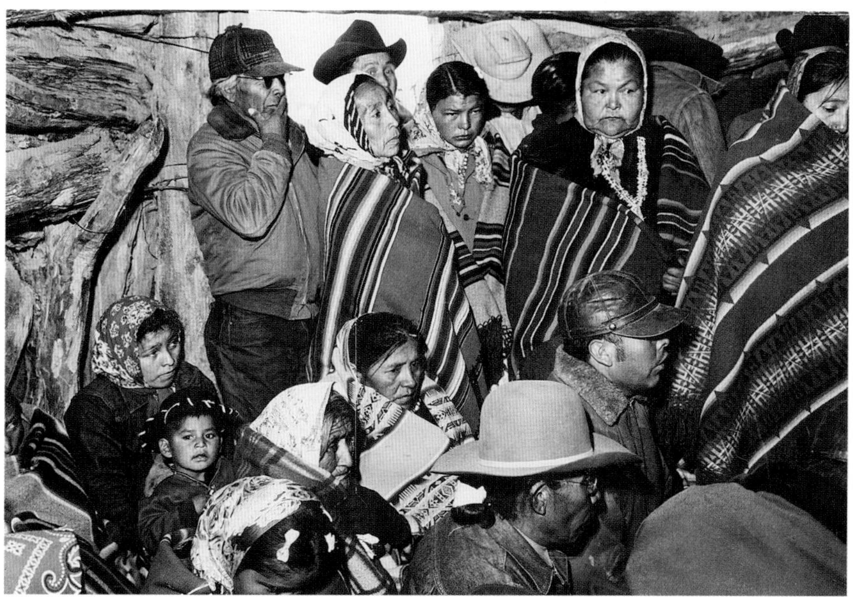

PLATE 37 Laura Gilpin (Non-Native), *Making Frybread at Crownpoint School 1960*, 1960, black-and-white photograph on board, 10.38 in. × 13.38 in., MoCNA Collection, INST-142 (photo by Jason S. Ordaz).

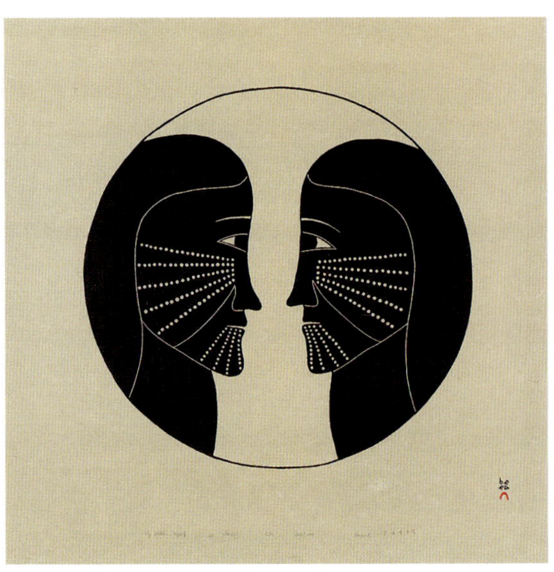

PLATE 38 Kenojuak Ashevak (Nunavut, Cape Dorset), *My Mother, Myself*, Edition 2/50, 1995, stonecut on paper, 24.5 in. × 23.5 in., MoCNA Collection, CAN-40 (photo by Jason S. Ordaz).

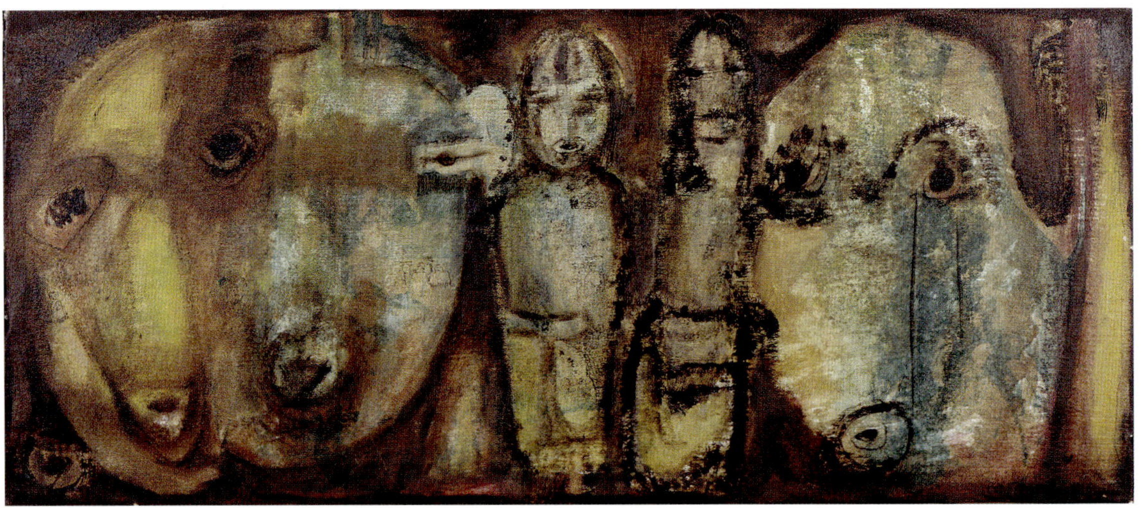

PLATE 39 Otellie Loloma (Hopi), *We Come as Clouds*, n.d., oil on canvas, 15.75 in. × 36.25 in., MoCNA Collection, H-67 (photo by Walter BigBee).

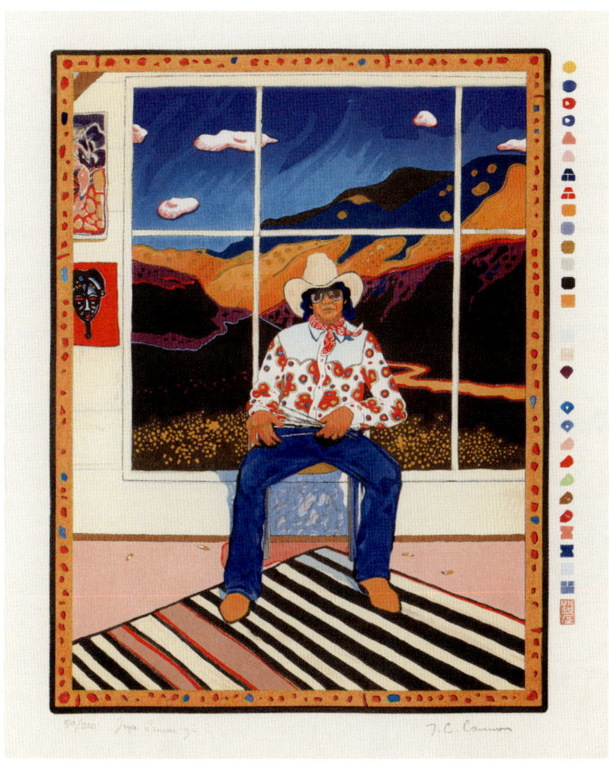

PLATE 40 T. C. Cannon (Caddo/Kiowa), *Self Portrait in the Studio* (1975), Edition 50/200, ca. 2006, woodblock on paper, 25 in. × 19.5 in., MoCNA Collection, CD-35 (photo by Jason S. Ordaz).

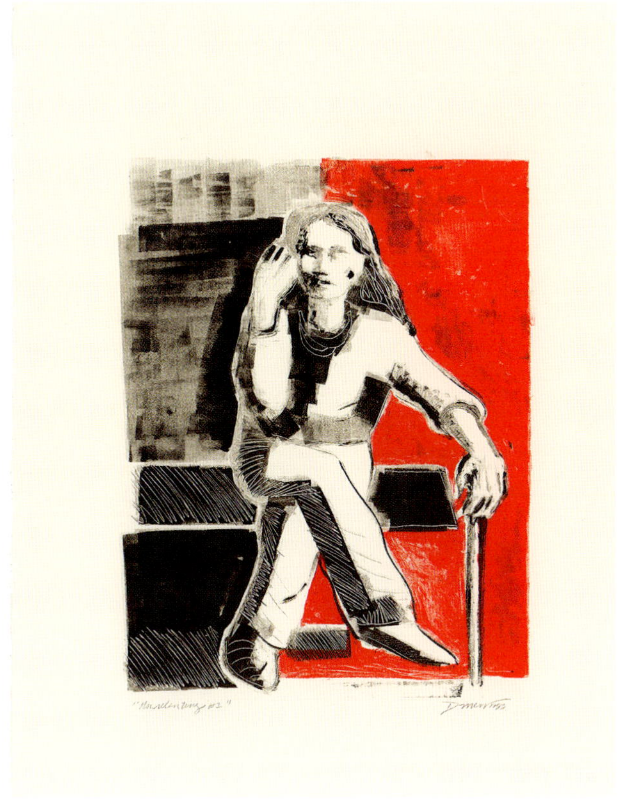

PLATE 41 Darren Vigil Gray (Jicarilla Apache/Kiowa Apache), *Unrelenting-Number 1*, 1983, monotype on arches paper, 28.75 in. × 22.5 in., MoCNA Collection, A-148 (photo by Jason S. Ordaz).

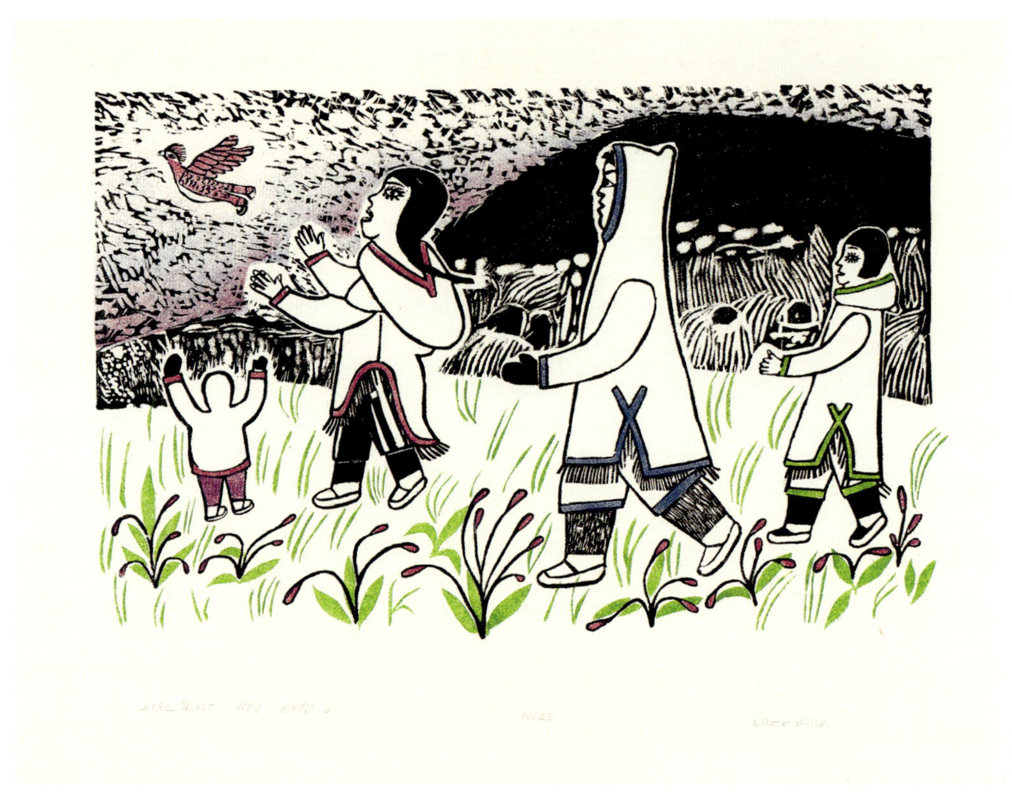

PLATE 42 Magdelene Ukpatiku (Nunavut), *Frightened Baby Becomes a Ptarmigan*, Edition 10/25, 1997, woodcut on paper, 20 in. × 24.75 in., MoCNA Collection, CAN-30 (photo by Jason S. Ordaz).

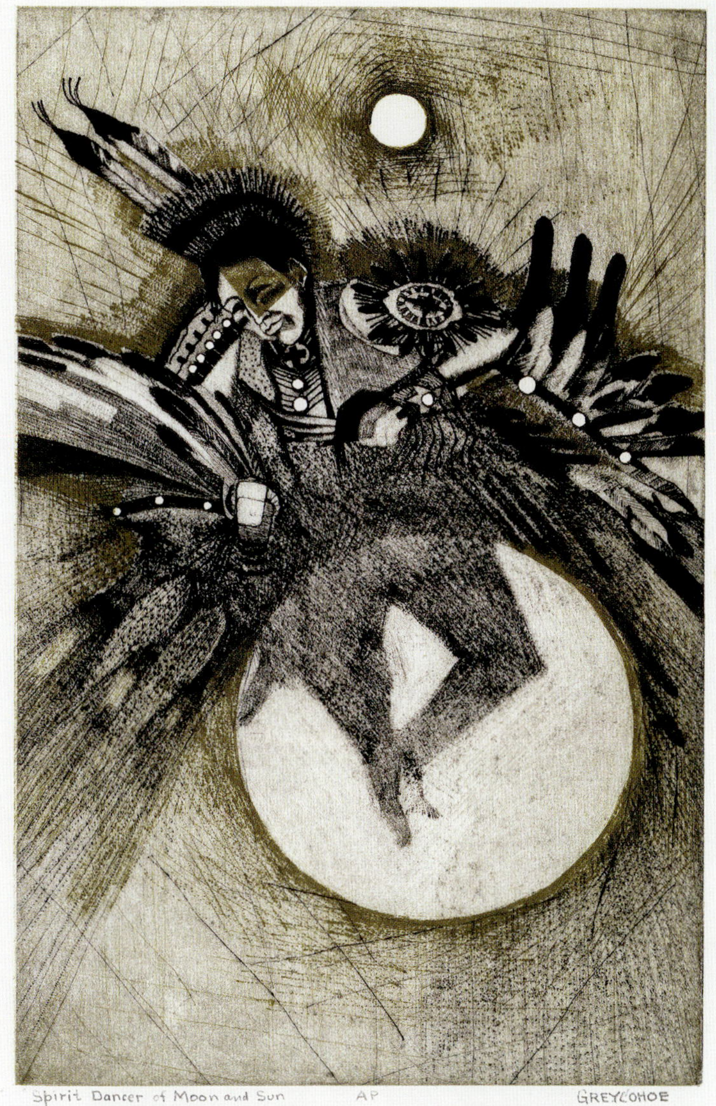

PLATE 43 Grey Cohoe (Navajo), *Spirit Dance of the Moon and Sun*, Edition A/P, 1967, dry point on paper, 14.38 in. × 10 in., MoCNA Collection, N-296 (photo by Walter BigBee).

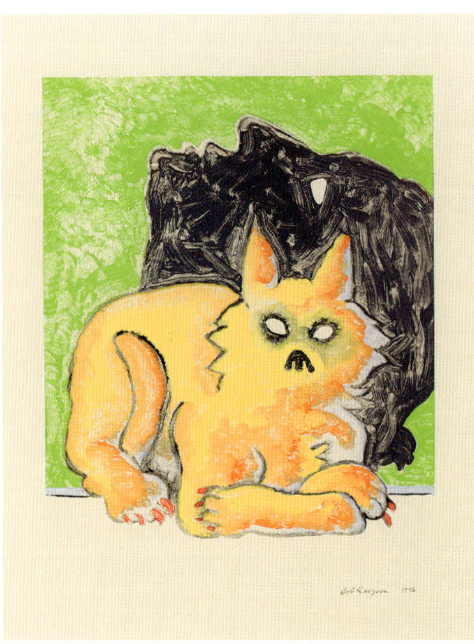

PLATE 44 Bob Haozous (Chiricahua Apache), *Yellow Cat*, 1995, monotype on paper, 30 in. × 22.25 in., MoCNA Collection, A-226 (photo by Jason S. Ordaz).

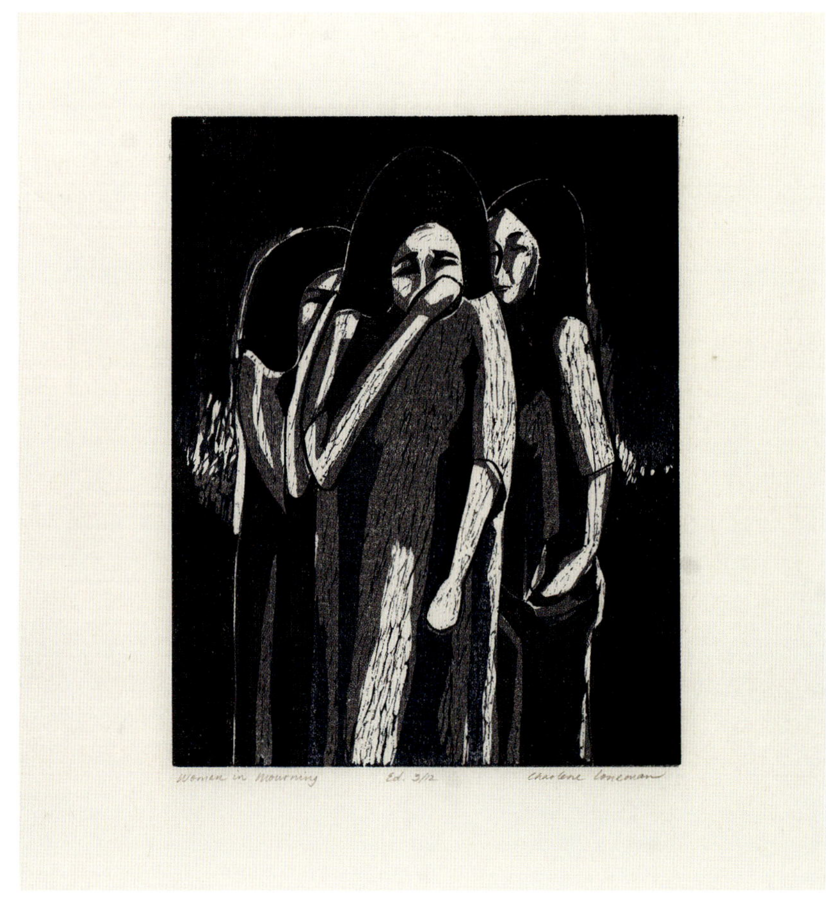

PLATE 45 Charlene Loneman (Arapahoe), *Women in Mourning*, Edition 3/12, ca. 1966–1969, linocut on paper, 17 in. × 13.75 in., MoCNA Collection, AR-1 (photo by Jason S. Ordaz).

Presentations & Representations

IMAGES OF DANCES FROM THE SOUTHWEST AND WEST

SUZANNE NEWMAN FRICKE

In 1980, Harry Fonseca (Nissan Maidu, Hawaiian, and Portuguese) painted *Dance Land #2* (figure 36) with Coyote, in his signature zippered black leather jacket, dancing with his companion, Rose, who wears a pink dress with red hearts and has two hibiscus flowers behind her left ear. He began his Coyote series with *Coyote Leaves the Rez* in 1979, featuring an anthropomorphized coyote in his jacket standing in front of a brick wall.[1] The artist noted, “Coyote is often up against a brick wall as are so many Native peoples and artists.”[2] Fonseca was referencing Coyote’s role as a trickster figure within many Native American cultures who, during ceremonies, acts improperly to teach children proper behavior; in many stories his mischief brings rewards.[3] Coyote’s disregard for social conventions and his ability to survive challenges and changes appealed to Fonseca. He stated, “Coyote gave me a chance to confront the world” in both his art and in his life.[4]

Patsy Phillips, director of the Institute of American Indian Arts’ (IAIA) Museum of Contemporary Native Arts (MoCNA) and an author in this collection, was friends with Fonseca for many years. She wrote that in his series, “Coyote represents human contradictions such as truth and deception, joy and sadness, life and death.”[5] For the artist, Coyote also represented freedom. With Coyote, Fonseca gained the freedom to express himself more openly, accepting himself as a gay man despite the social norms that forced him to hide and moving out into the world more openly. A few years into the series, Fonseca gave Coyote an ally for his adventures based on his own glamorous aunt, with whom the artist was close. Like her, Rose in *Dance Land #2* is sophisticated and colorful, with flowers in her hair. As Coyote moved from ceremonies and dances on the reservation to other stages, his performative skills increased. He and Rose shuffled off to Buffalo on a vaudeville stage, performed a pas de deux in *Swan Lake*, and sang opera in *La Bohème*.

By showing the pair performing on different stages, Fonseca reflects the importance of performance in twentieth- and twenty-first-century Native

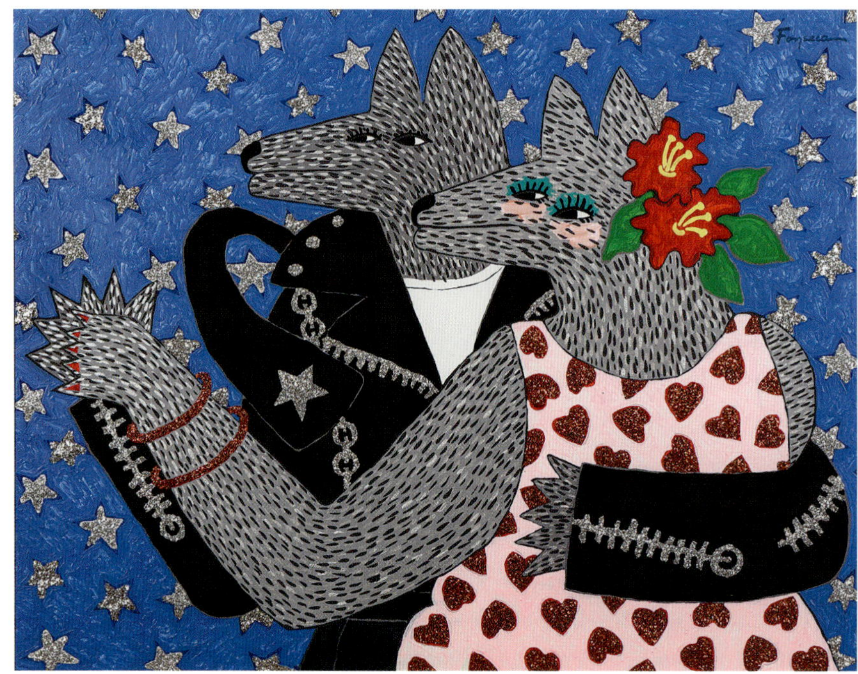

FIGURE 36 Harry Fonseca (Nissan Maidu/Hawaiian/Portuguese), *Dance Land #2*, ca. 1980, acrylic paint and glitter on Masonite, 24 in. × 30 in., Gift of Suzanne C. Wengel. Eiteljorg Museum of the American Indians and Western Art. © 2016 Harry Fonseca Collection, Autry Museum of the American West.

American paintings from the Southwest, the West, and California, which often feature images of dance. As art historian Sasha Scott notes, "Pueblo ceremonials were among the most frequently represented subject matter in New Mexico from the early to mid-1920s" and are rooted "in nature, rhythmic qualities, and transformative powers."[6] Art historian J. J. Brody observes that the dances that "provided the subject matter for most pictures made by the first watercolorists . . . are of vital importance" to Native communities. He continues, "Layered with profound meaning, these communal events promote group harmony, health, the coexistence of the human and natural worlds, and favorable weather, and they benefit all of humanity."[7] With their elaborate, brightly colored outfits and energetic choreography, dances make ideal images, but they also tie in to strong cultural values. Art historian Aaron Fry connected the images of dances from San Ildefonso Pueblo in New Mexico to social and political changes happening at the time, demonstrating how the paintings reflect both timely and timeless ideas.[8]

Within Native American culture, especially in the Southwest and California, dances themselves are representations of Native ideology, articulating the relationship between the physical and spiritual worlds: the natural forces in the world, such as the changes of seasons, the cycle of growth, and the importance of water. When the dance is then translated into a two- or three-dimensional art form as a painting or a sculpture, it becomes a representation of a representation. Rather than becoming a simulacrum, or a copy of a copy, this new representation takes on more meaning given by the artist and expressed through his or her individual approach. As seen in the drawings, paintings, prints, and sculptures presented here, each offers a different perspective on the dances, reflecting the artist's personal aesthetics and experiences. The images include the stylized yet energetic Studio Style seen in Allan Houser's early painting, a jarring and pensive treatment by Fritz Scholder, more spiritual and humorous in Harry Fonseca, and more layered and complex in Melanie Yazzie and Mateo Romero. This chapter will consider how Native American artists use images of dance to show the relationship between earthly and otherworldly forces. The examples discussed are primarily by Native artists from the Southwest and California rather than the Northwest Coast, Northeast, or Southeast.

Within Native communities, dances, ceremonials, feasts, and powwows tie the dancers and the viewers to the history of the society. When translated into two-dimensional images, they provide a diagram for understanding the complex relationships between the physical and metaphysical worlds.[9] As a non-Native scholar who focuses on Native American art, I try to be respectful and only research images already in the public rather than trying to expose aspects of Native culture that were intended to be private.[10] Too often, non-Native scholars have shown a lack of respect in their investigations, transgressing important social and religious customs by looking at images that are private, even sacred. Moving forward as a scholar or as someone interested in Native American art and history, it is important to be aware of these lines and how they might be different from culture to culture to avoid the mistakes of the past. In this vein, looking at images created for a public audience usually—though not always—helps avoid transgressions.

The importance of dance as an expression of Native culture and values cannot be overstated. Every time a dance is done, it reinforces the connection to culture, brings the past into the present, and articulates a Native worldview. During the nineteenth century, the governments of the United States and Canada outlawed dancing in Native communities, considering it a threat to assimilationist efforts. In a 2016 article, professor of American Indian Studies at Bacone College Patti Jo King wrote that an 1889 investigator of the "Ghost Dance phenomenon among the Plains tribes issued a warning that if the practice was not stopped, it could lead to an all-out Indian war. In response, the War Department deployed 7,000 troops to maintain control over the Lakota."[11] The violent reaction by the US government underscores

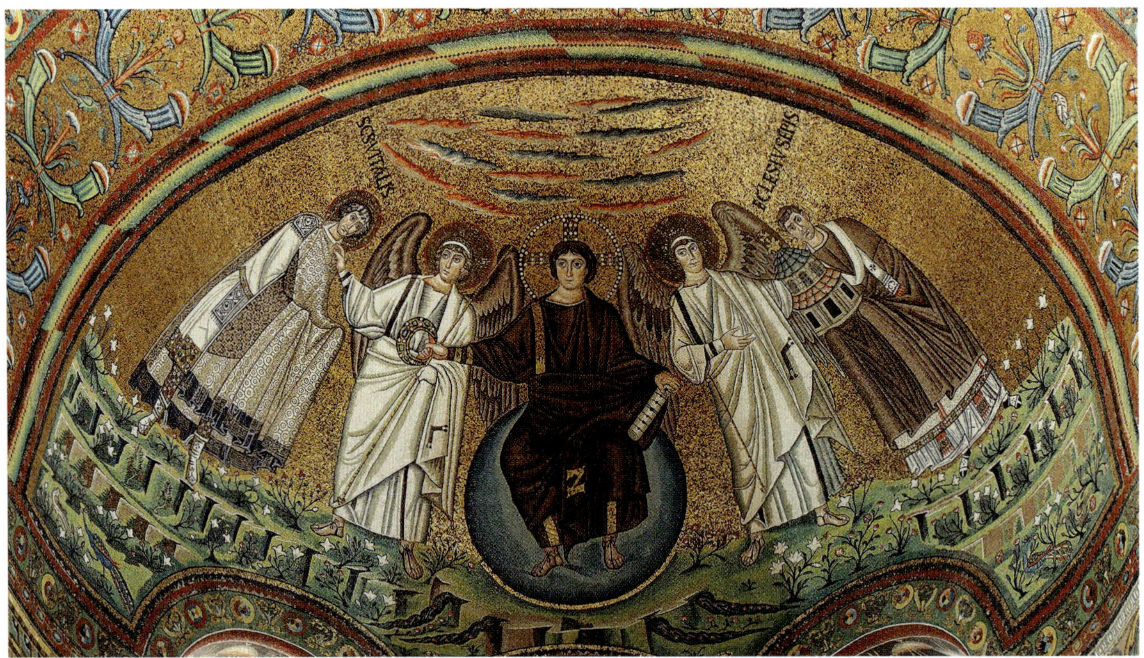

FIGURE 37 *Christ, St. Vitalis, Bishop of Ravenna, and Archangels*, San Vitale, 547, Byzantine, Ravenna, Italy, mosaic (Photo courtesy of Petar Milošević / CC BY-SA 4.0).

the importance of dance within Native communities as a demonstration of social cohesion.

The dances, then, present Native cultural structures and values through movement, costume, and music, and images of dances are representations of presentations—or representations of representations. As described by the Postmodern theorists Jean Baudrillard and Gilles Deleuze, the simulacrum replaces reality with representation until the artificial becomes indistinguishable from reality, forming a hyperreality. While Baudrillard defined hyperreality as a representation without an original idea, Deleuze argued that simulacra do not just copy, but retain the power of the originals, without a privileged perspective on either. Similarly, the representations of the dances have become something new and unique, imbued with meaning and ideology of their own.

Returning to Fonseca's *Dance Land #2*, the artist calls attention to the artificiality of his representation by employing a distinctive style that emphasizes the flatness of the bodies, exaggerating their two-dimensionality by eliminating all modeling so they are like cardboard cutouts. Throughout the series, Fonseca depicts both Coyote and Rose with the same facial features, combining different perspectives. He paints the muzzle in profile, then sets both eyes next to each other as though seen from the front, similar to the Old Kingdom depictions of figures. Space is compressed, as seen in the nightclub's checkered floor, which is shown without perspective or depth as though from above. The figures do not move inward, as with images shown in linear perspective, but instead are pushed outside of the surface of the painting. Fonseca's figures are trying to leave the picture plane and join the viewer. It is a movement not only in space but in time as well. With no background or perspective to pull the figures into space or into the past, they exist in an idealized future, moving easily between ceremonials and theatrical stages, allowing the artist to envision an existence in which all stages can be home to the Indigenous population.

Fonseca's use of flatness references two distinct influences. He cherished the sixth-century mosaics in the Byzantine churches of Ravenna, Italy, which he visited.[12] The ones like those of San Vitale, illustrated in figure 37, depict saints and holy figures without modeling or using light and shadow to create three dimensions. Instead, the bodies hover in a gold background that becomes otherworldly. They are both human and spiritual, as though they exist in both places at the same time. For the artist, Byzantine art offers "a totally different means of representation. The figures just soar, floating in the gold. Their bodies are both in the world and not."[13] Fonseca's characters could transcend worlds, thriving both on and off the reservation. Just as the flatness of the bodies in Byzantine mosaics allowed the figures to move freely between different realms, Coyote and Rose could dance in ceremonies but also waltz in a blue sky full of shimmering silver stars made with glitter, a nod to the Byzantine use of gold and semiprecious stones to make a shiny reflective surface.

Another reason for Fonseca to paint his figures as flat and plain reflects historic models from the Southwest. The use of strong outlines, flat planes, a lack of background, and an emphasis on clothing design dates to the late nineteenth and early twentieth centuries, when paper, pencils, and paints first became more widely available in the western states.[14] This led to more drawing and painting on paper by Native artists, including images of *katsinim*[15] from Hopi Pueblo from around 1900 and of dance from San Ildefonso Pueblo Day School from 1900 to 1915.[16] These representations share certain formal qualities, including a lack of perspective or depth, background, and modeling of the bodies. This approach took on further prominence when the Santa Fe Indian School began teaching art in 1932 under Dorothy Dunn, who taught her students to draw and paint in what came to be known as the Studio Style. During her five years teaching at the school, Dunn insisted that her students use opaque paints to represent specific topics she believed represented Native life, such as ceremonials, dances, and pottery-making.

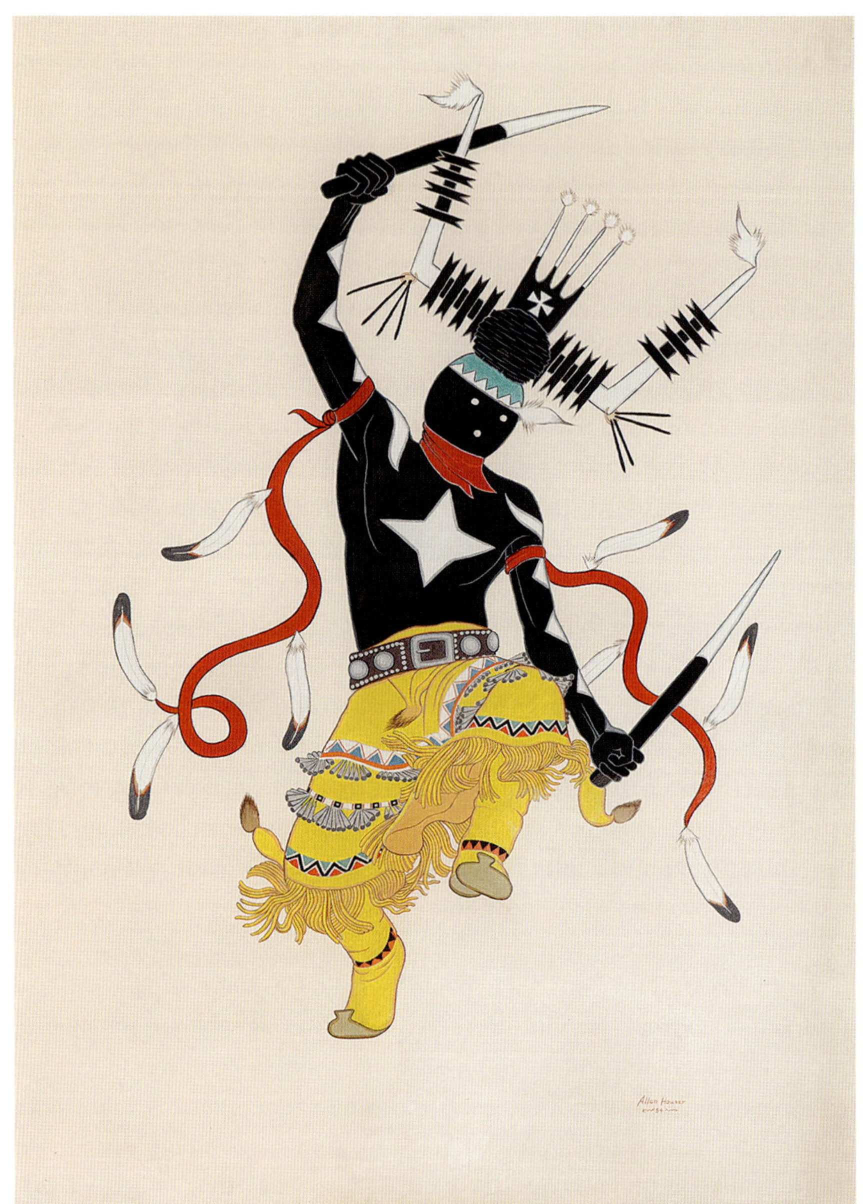

FIGURE 38 Allan Houser (Chiricahua Apache), *Crown Dancer*, 1954, casein on masonite, 66.5 in. × 47.5 in., MoCNA Collection, A-166 (photo by Addison Doty).

The Studio Style held considerable sway for several decades and many well-known artists trained using the technique, including Allan Houser (1914–1994), Pop Chalee (1906–1993), and Pablita Velarde (1918–2006). The work was bright, pretty, and popular, but many artists, notably Houser, complained about its limitations.

Houser, an artist from the Warm Springs Chiricahua Apache tribe, created many paintings and sculptures throughout his long career. Born in 1914 in Oklahoma, he was twenty years old when he arrived in Santa Fe to study at the Santa Fe Indian School. He created hundreds of images in the Studio Style, including *Crown Dancer* from 1954 (figure 38). These figures, today more commonly known as Mountain Spirit Dancers, accompany coming-of-age and healing ceremonies, in which Houser participated. The artist helped to paint the dancers' bodies, describing the process as "very religious" and adding, "I like the seriousness with which the medicine men treat the subject, it is a healing subject."[17] Painted with casein on Masonite, *Crown Dancer* fits the Studio Style, with strong outlines, flat blocks of color, and no background. Despite these limitations, Houser captures the energy of the figure, who is vital and active, with legs stomping and arms waving. Even without shadows or highlights, it has a strong physical presence. Houser shows a sensitivity to lines, creating an S-curve through the arms and legs to form serpentine lines, which, according to Baroque theories, embody beauty.[18] He also gives a sense of visual solidity by using a pyramidal composition, a hallmark of High Renaissance art. The triangular shape formed by the dancer, with the knees forming the base and the headdress at the top, anchors it in place even as the curved lines of the limbs allow it to move. This contradiction between stillness and movements add to the image's energy.

The artist continued to paint images of Apache dances. He was invited to paint a series of murals for the Department of the Interior Building in Washington, DC, as part of the Works Progress Administration (WPA), founded by President Franklin D. Roosevelt to offer work to stimulate the economy during the Great Depression. During World War II, Houser moved to Los Angeles, where he saw the works of abstract British sculptors in Unit One, including Henry Moore and Barbara Hepworth, and those of Jean Arp and Constantin Brancusi. These artists were attuned to the nature of their materials, whether wood, stone, or bronze, and they all focused on both the positive space, where the material was left, and negative space—the shapes created where the material was removed. As Houser began to work more in sculpture, he also showed a sensitivity to the materials he used and to the shapes he created, consciously forming the figures and the voids in between.

Following the war, Houser's work received more and more attention and accolades. In 1948, he was awarded a Guggenheim Fellowship, which is given to talented artists in different fields. He was offered teaching positions, including at the Intermountain Indian School in Utah. In 1962, he was asked to head the sculpture department of the newly opened Institute of American Indian Arts (IAIA) in Santa Fe, New Mexico, the first college-level art school dedicated to teaching Native American students.

While in New Mexico, Houser had access to a bronze foundry, where he created his bronze *Fire Dancer* from 1990 (figure 39). The figure is almost a three-dimensional version of *Crown Dancer*, a dancer in motion with deeply bent legs lunging to the side, arms bent and twisting.[19] It has the same attention to the details of energy, costume, and posture, seen in the headdress, dance staffs, and fringed skirt. In this piece, Houser combines two important elements: the serpentine line and the pyramidal composition. Like the S-curves in the two-dimensional dancer, the arms and legs in the sculptural figure form serpentine lines that can be traced from all directions: from the front, side, and back. These lines give the sculpture a sense of motion and dynamism; it is a body depicted in the act of dancing. As in his painting, Houser contrasts the pyramidal composition for a sense of stability and strength with serpentine lines for movement, adding an inherent opposition that energizes the piece.

Toward the end of his career, Houser had established a strong reputation as an artist, especially in 1992, when he became the first Native American awarded the National Medal of Arts. Houser had the opportunity to create a series of large-scale fabricated-steel sculptures, including *Evolution* or, as it was originally titled, *Cerrillos*, named after the village in New Mexico (figure 40). In this piece, the artist offers an entirely abstract vision of geometric shapes. More than six feet high, it is built of a series of polygonals set on top of each other. Houser stated that he was inspired by working in a larger scale: "Size is no problem. Working in a larger scale, I can express myself much better."[20] He uses the mass to redefine the space, making triangles in the negative spaces and in the facets. With part balanced on a point and the other on small edges, this piece seems to float above the ground. Though it is entirely abstract and rectilinear, Houser captures the essence of his dance images, full of energy and the sense of movement with the serpentine lines that run through the piece, while at the same time anchored by the pyramidal composition. It is both delicate and massive, stable and active. The inherent contradictions in Houser's art balance the piece and add to its power.

If Houser illustrates dances as a balance between vitality and stillness,

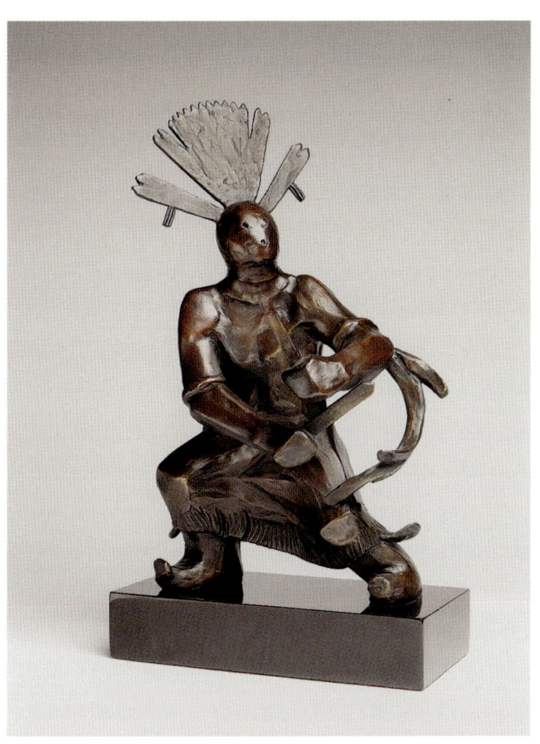

FIGURE 39 *left* Allan Houser (Chiricahua Apache), *Fire Dancer*, Edition 10/15, 1990, bronze, 17.75 in. × 10 in., MoCNA Collection, A-230 (photo by Addison Doty).

FIGURE 40 *below* Allan Houser (Chiricahua Apache), *Evolution*, Edition Dedicated Copy, 1993, bronze, 114 in. × 50 in. × 141.5 in., MoCNA Collection, A-234 (photo by Jason S. Ordaz).

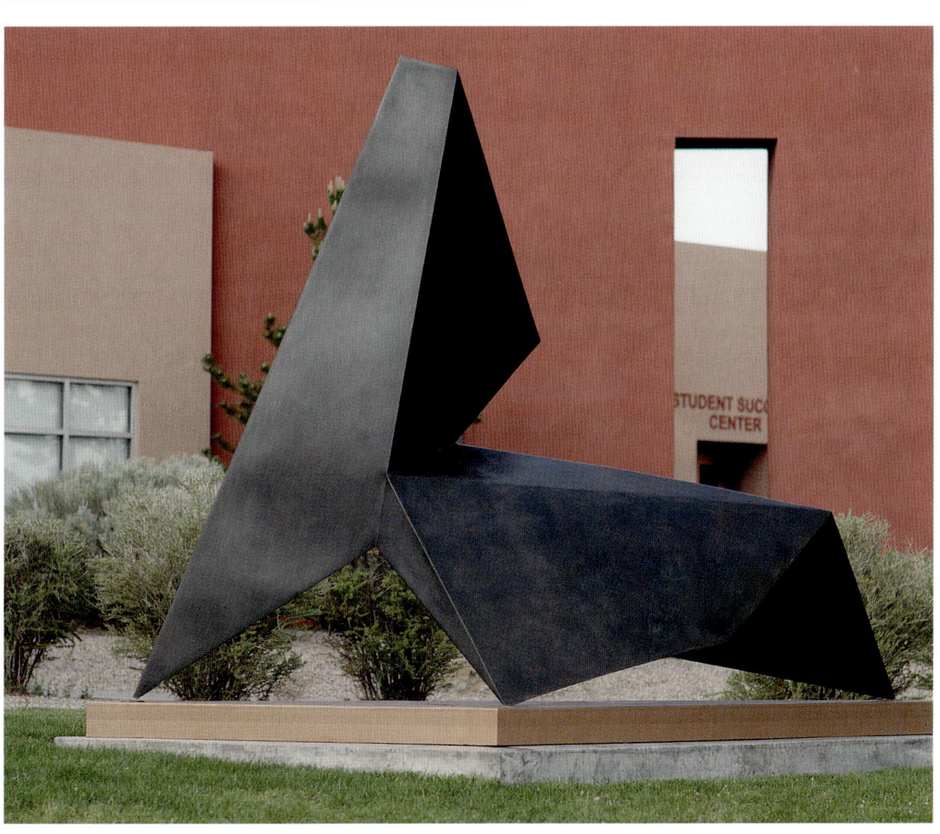

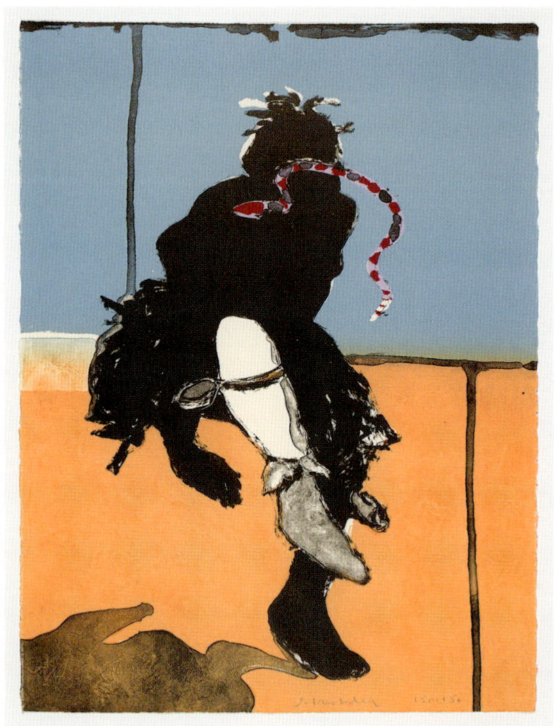

FIGURE 41 Fritz Scholder (Mission/Luiseño), *Snake Dancer*, Edition 150/150, 1979, lithograph on arches paper, 30 in. × 22.5 in., MoCNA Collection, MS-52 (photo by Jason S. Ordaz).

painter and printmaker Fritz Scholder enjoys frenetic energy and imbalance in his work, as seen in his 1979 lithograph *Snake Dancer* (figure 41). Scholder, who is of Luiseño and Cupeño heritage, two Native American tribes from southern California, was born in 1937, and his father worked for the Bureau of Indian Affairs in Pierre, South Dakota. The artist avoided addressing his heritage in his work for many years, famously saying that he was an "Artist first, Indian second"[21] and describing himself as "a non-Indian Indian."[22] After completing a Master of Fine Arts degree at the University of Arizona, Scholder, like Houser, was invited to IAIA, where he taught from 1964 to 1969. Those years were transformative for Scholder. He began to consider Native American culture, collecting photographs, artifacts, postcards, and books, and studying how Native Americans were represented. The willingness of his students to experiment with new styles and stated representations of Native life inspired Scholder to reconsider his vow to never paint Native Americans.[23] As he later stated, "When I first came to Santa Fe . . . I vowed I'd never paint the Indian because everybody else was doing it. But at the Institute, I realized that the subject had always been placed in a certain context, and I thought . . . that somebody ought to do it differently.[24]

Scholder approached his images of Native life from a contemporary perspective, one that included both Native and non-Native influences. In *Snake Dancer*, he offers a nod to Studio Style. It is similar in subject matter, that of a single dancer in full regalia. The lack of a background and the use of strong outlines also reflects Studio Style. Scholder diverged from this influence in the medium—lithography, a printing technique—the color scheme, and the lighting. While Houser's painting, like most works done in Studio Style, features primary colors and bright, even lighting, Scholder's image is dark. The figure stands off-center, not solidly in the middle, giving a sense of being off-balance. The shadows suggest a figure outside the picture frame, giving an ominous sense to the print. His use of blue and green inks adds a dissonant, or inharmonious tone to the piece, since analogous colors, or those that are next to each other on the color wheel, are harder for the eye to distinguish as opposed to complementary colors, which are across from each other. Scholder also shows the dancer while not dancing, ready but not yet engaged. It is a touching but uncertain moment as the performer is ready to begin.

In the 1992 *Picture Tour of Arizona*, Diné (Navajo Nation) master printer Melanie Yazzie considers how images of Native peoples, especially Native dancers, are often appropriated by non-Native advertisers without permission. Born in Ganado, Arizona, in Dinétah, Yazzie earned a Master of Fine Arts from the University of Colorado at Boulder, where she is a professor and head of printmaking. She plays with different printing techniques, sometimes challenging the accepted practices for the media, as seen here where she printed on a piece of floral wrapping paper rather than archival printing paper because she "felt like people see regalia as a stereotype, a way to gift-wrap Native American people for the public."[25] Yazzie printed a souvenir map of Arizona next to a photo of a toddler in full regalia with cartoon versions of a cowboy and Indian underneath. The cartoon figures relate to items with Native images that are sold as souvenirs, like dream catchers and faux dance paraphernalia mass-produced in factories overseas. With the passage of the 1990 Indian Arts and Crafts Law, it became illegal to sell objects as Native-made unless the artist can legally prove ancestry, yet the

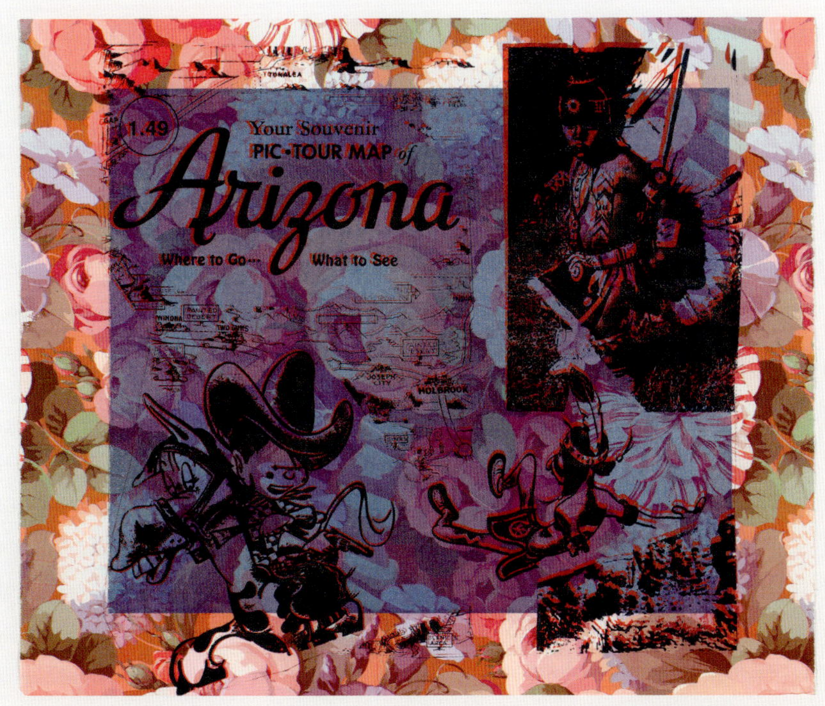

FIGURE 42 Melanie Yazzie (Diné/Navajo), *Picture Tour Map of Arizona*, 1992, silkscreen on wrapping paper, 15 in. × 17.5 in., MoCNA Collection, N-846 (photo by Jason S. Ordaz).

law does not prevent factories in China, Vietnam, and other foreign nations from producing inexpensive items that resemble Native-made objects.[26]

The image is intentionally difficult to read due to the flowers underneath. Parts of the printing are blurred and printed slightly off, which the artist did intentionally to suggest that things are not right. Yazzie is concerned about the lack of respect for the dancers: "At a pow-wow, everyone is photographing the dances, but people don't understand that it's important to ask for permission to photograph people. People don't know the protocol. Some of these dances are sacred and at certain times people are asked not to photograph. Yet, as a dancer, you could find your image in the newspaper for everyone to see." Yazzie notes that photos of dancers in regalia, especially children like the one included in *Picture Tour*, are especially popular in magazines and newspapers.

Picture Tour also reflects the need to obscure certain parts of Native culture in order to show respect. Yazzie sees "underlying my work . . . the need to question that and to hide these stories and things that are sacred, things that are special. When I was growing up, my mom's mother, Grandma Baldwin, would see fabric like curtains that had Navajo designs that were special. And she'd say, 'They're not supposed to use that,' or 'Those things are only for certain times,' or 'These things shouldn't be out there.' In my own work, I do not use things that are sacred. I create my own imagery to tell a story." For Yazzie, the layering of these images, all associated with her homeland as a tourist destination, questions the commercialization of dance.

In Mateo Romero's mixed-media image *Red Meridian* from 2012, the representation of dance serves as a link between different times and different worlds. Romero, an artist from Cochiti Pueblo, was born in Berkeley, California, and has a Master of Fine Arts degree in printmaking from the University of New Mexico. For the artist, the image is a "discourse with the past, with the ancestors, and the world as it exists now, . . . an underworld projection, that creates a metaphysical and ritualistic, ceremonial experience."[27] Romero combines past, present, and even future by mixing an old photograph of a Pueblo dance with mid-twentieth-century comic book images. In *Red Meridian*, a line of dancers across the middle, which represents the terrestrial world, connects to the underworld with paint dripping down. In the cosmic world above, the dark sky is populated with World War I–era airplanes flying in a V-formation in a sky filled with planets and lightning, drawn in the style of noted comic-book illustrator Jack Kirby known as the "Kirby Krackle." Romero has been a fan of comic books since he was young and his use of the stylized sky suggests cosmic energy, the natural forces that cannot be controlled.

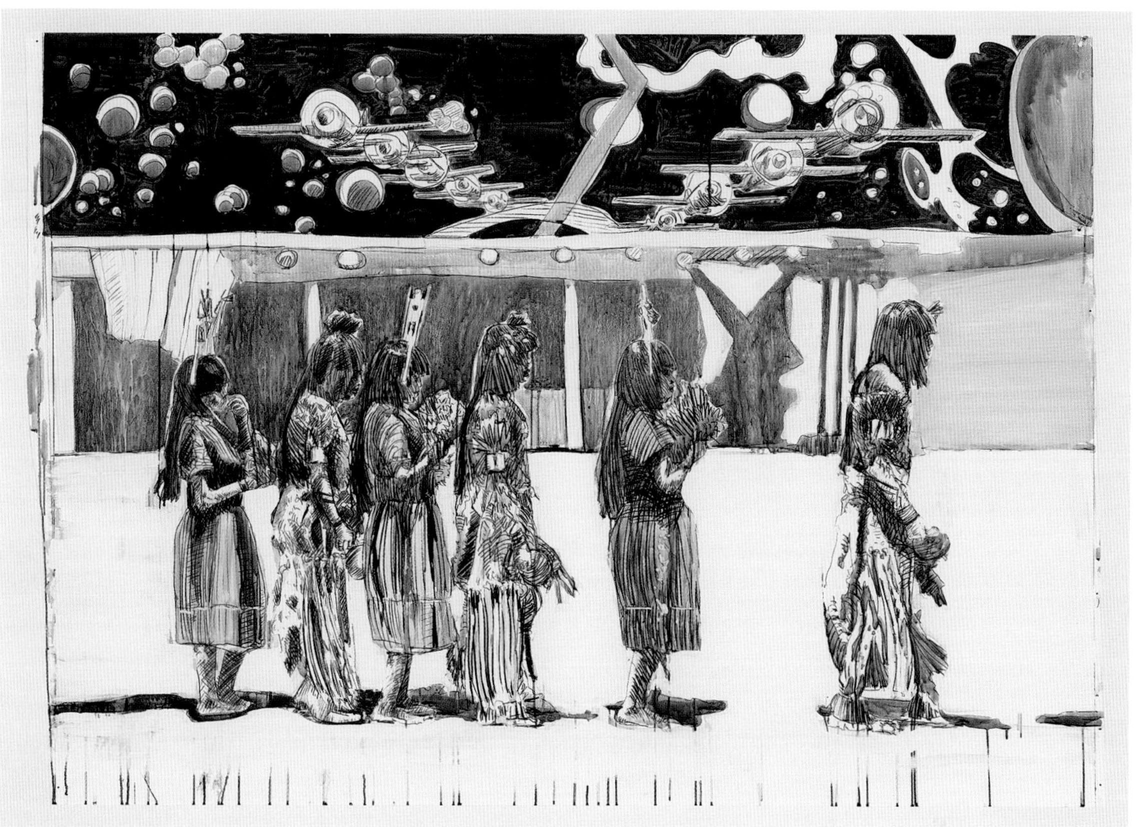

FIGURE 43 Mateo Romero (Cochiti Pueblo), *Red Meridian*, 2012, acrylic, india ink, china marker on polystyrene, 60 in. × 82.5 in., MoCNA Collection, CO-45 (photo by Jason S. Ordaz).

The title refers to a meridian line, or a virtual line that links important sites; the red meridian connects places across the Southwest, from Mexico to Chaco Canyon, an Ancestral Pueblo site in northern New Mexico era from AD 850 to 1250. Romero chose the title to suggest "connection between Native peoples, a sharing of ideas and thought and art and ideology" and to show a continuity of Native experience. He also considered the almost-daily confrontation between the past and the present found at the pueblos because the "time we live in is a complicated, complex time and these kinds of symbols coexist in the world right now, a multiple layering of these images and signifiers that are all mixed together now."[28]

Red Meridian depicts the Corn Dance from Santo Domingo Pueblo (also known as Kewa Pueblo), a ceremony held every August 4 to celebrate the feast day of St. Dominic, its patron saint. Lasting from morning to sunset, it includes singing and dancing, as well as a procession of the statue of St. Dominic from the church to the main plaza. Romero chose a photograph from the late nineteenth century, in which he saw a "nostalgic moment frozen in time" where the community joins with each other to express their understanding of the world in which "all people are connected to the underworld, to prayer and to sacrifice. Their bodies experience religious epiphanies as part of a discourse with the underworld and the spirit world."[29] By appropriating elements in *Red Meridian*, Romero widens his references. The "Kirby Krackle" lightning embraces the power of nature even as the sky is overrun with enemy planes. The image of the dance connects to the past, a reminder that these dances have been held for centuries and continue to be, tying the present to the past.

As ceremonials, the dances themselves enact unseen elements, showing the spiritual forces that shape the world, from rain and wind to the movement of the sun, the moon, and the stars. Through movement and music, the dances both celebrate and express gratitude toward nature, and they also demonstrate the relationship between the land and those who live on it. These dances reshape the physical space from a Native perspective. As John Paul Rangel describes it, "The Indigenization of space occurs when Native people reclaim a location through cultural signifiers, performance, ceremony, song, dance, or installation that convey the existence and presence of Native peoples and cultures."[30] Similarly, the images of dances capture the idea of an indigenized perspective on the world, creating a portable sense of Native spaces where they are, wherever they are. These paintings, prints, and sculptures carry the spirit of the dances, allowing viewers the opportunity to share this worldview as seen through the perspective of individual artists. Houser, Scholder, Fonseca, Yazzie, and Romero, as well as many other Native American artists, all offer their strong personal aesthetic to share a glimpse of a world that is both literal and spiritual, linking the past to the future through the present.

USING INDIGENOUS METHODOLOGIES

Vocabulary

ambiguity—uncertainty, lack of clarity.

appropriation—using an existing image in a new work, such as sampling in music. Popular in Postmodern art.

casein—an opaque, water-soluble paint with a binding agent made from milk proteins.

Chaco Canyon—an archaeological site in northern New Mexico that was the home of the Ancestral Pueblo people from AD 850 to 1250. It was a major site for trade and art.

dissonant—lacking in harmony, jarring.

Ghost Dance—ceremonial dance introduced in 1890 on the Plains by Wovoka, a Northern Paiute spiritual leader, as part of a movement to return to a pre-Contact time.

hyperreality—when a representation becomes indistinguishable from reality. For Postmodern theorist Jean Baudrillard, hyperreality was a representation without an original idea.

lithography—a form of print-making in which the artist draws and/or paints directly on a stone.

meridian—a virtual line across the earth linking two sites.

modeling—In two-dimensional images, when the artist adds darker tones to create shadows and lighter tones to create highlights, adding a three-dimensional quality to the figures.

mosaic—using small pieces of stone, tile, and/or glass to form a two-dimensional image.

negative space—the area shaped by the empty spaces around the material in a sculpture.

nostalgia—a sentimental affection for the past.

pyramidal composition—when a two- and three-dimensional artwork forms a triangle and suggests solidity. Popular during the High Renaissance.

sacred/otherworldly—connected with the divine, having a religious meaning.

serpentine line/S-curve—curved lines suggesting movement and beauty. Popular during the Baroque era.

simulacrum—A term used by Postmodern theorists Jean Baudrillard and Gilles Deleuze to describe when representation replaces reality.

terrestrial—of the earth.

Trickster—an animal figure from Native American narratives, such as Coyote and Raven, who plays tricks and breaks or bends the rules.

Unit One—a group of British sculptors active from 1933 to 1935 who were known for their abstraction, among them Henry Moore and Barbara Hepworth.

US Assimilation Policy—efforts by the US government from 1790 to the early twentieth century to force Native American tribes to change by giving up their own languages, religious practices, arts, ways of dressing, etc.

Questions from the Chapter

1. From a visual perspective, why would images of dances be popular?
2. How do the dancers in Harry Fonseca's *Dance Land #2* reflect a sacred perspective?

3. Comparing Allan Houser's *Crown Dancer* and Mateo Romero's *Red Meridian*, how does the lack or inclusion of background details have an impact on the viewer's perception of the dancers?

4. How does the figure in Fritz Scholder's *Snake Dancer* express a dissonant or inharmonious sensibility?

5. How does Melanie Yazzie appropriate imagery to consider cultural boundaries?

NOTES

1. Harry Fonseca's official website, http://www.harryfonseca.com/news/index.htm.

2. Patsy Phillips, "Sundays with Harry: An Essay on a Contemporary Native Artist of Our Time," *Wíčazo Ša Review* 27, no. 1 (Spring 2012): 65.

3. The role of the coyote as a trickster figure in Native American culture has been discussed by many scholars, including Anne Doueihi, "Inhabiting the Space between Discourse and Story in Trickster Narratives," in *Mythical Trickster Figures: Contours, Contexts, and Criticisms*, ed. William J. Hynes and William G. Doty (Tuscaloosa: University of Alabama Press, 2009), 193–201; Kimberly M. Blaeser, "Trickster: A Compendium," in *Buried Roots and Indestructible Seeds: The Survival of American Indian Life in Story, History and Spirit*, ed. Mark A. Lindquist and Martin Zanger (Madison: University of Wisconsin Press, 1993), 47–66; Barbara Babcock, "'A Tolerated Margin of Mess': The Trickster and His Tales Reconsidered," *Journal of the American Folklore Institute* 9 (1975): 147–86; William Bright, *A Coyote Reader* (Berkeley: University of California Press, 1993); and Jarold Ramsey, *Coyote Was Going There* (Seattle: University of Washington Press, 1977).

4. Quoted in Frank LaPena, "Contemporary Northern California Native American Art," *California History* 71, no. 3 (Fall 1992): 398.

5. Phillips, "Sundays with Harry," 63–72.

6. Sasha T. Scott, *A Strange Mixture: The Art and Politics of Painting Pueblo Indians* (Norman: University of Oklahoma Press, 2015), 185.

7. J. J. Brody, *Pueblo Indian Painting: Tradition and Modernism in New Mexico, 1900–1930* (Santa Fe: School of American Research Press, 1997), 40. The popularity of dance as a topic can be seen in several collections and shows. For example, in the collection of more than two hundred 1900–1930 paintings from New Mexico housed at the School of Advanced Research (formerly the School of American Research), more than half of the works depict dances.

8. Aaron Fry, "Local Knowledge and Art Historical Methodology: A New Perspective on Awa Tsireh and the San Ildefonso Easel Painting Movement," *Hemispheres: Visual Cultures of the Americas* 1 (Spring 2008): 46–61.

9. Jessica Horton introduced the diagrammatic interpretation of Native dance paintings. She notes that it "bridges a division between embodied memory and objectified

history." Jessica Horton, "A Cloudburst in Venice: Fred Kabotie and the U.S. Pavilion of 1932," *American Art* 29, no. 1 (Spring 2015): 58.

10. Perhaps the best example of this is the work by Elsie Clews Parsons, an anthropologist and sociologist in the early twentieth century. She wanted to see the murals inside a kiva, a sacred structure in the Southwest, although she knew the images were not for public view. She preyed on the weakest men at Isleta Pueblo, alcoholics who were desperate for money, and bribed them to copy the images for her. This story is related in Bill Anthes, *Native Moderns: American Indian Painting, 1940–1960* (Durham, NC: Duke University Press, 2006).

11. Patti Jo King, "The Truth about the Wounded Knee Massacre," *Indian Country Today* website, published December 30, 2016, https://newsmaven.io/indiancountrytoday/archive/the-truth-about-the-wounded-knee-massacre-PIQqUKeCEEmnLeQn0Q5SOQ.

12. Personal interview with the artist, 1991.

13. Personal interview with the artist, 1991.

14. With the construction of the transcontinental railroad in the nineteenth century, drawing and painting materials became more widely available. See Barbara Babcock and Marta Weigle, editors, *The Great Southwest of the Fred Harvey Company and the Santa Fe Railway* (Tucson: University of Arizona Press, 1996).

15. *Katsinas* or *katsinim* (pl.), formally known as *katchina* or *katchinas*, are physical manifestations of the spirit messengers of the universe. For more information, see Zena Pearlston, *Katsina: Commodified and Appropriated Images of Hopi Supernaturals* (Los Angeles: University of California Press, 2002); Polly Schaafsma, *Kachinas in the Pueblo World* (Albuquerque: University of New Mexico Press, 1994); and E. Charles Adams, *The Origin and Development of the Pueblo Katsina Cult* (Tucson: University of Arizona Press, 1992).

16. Despite the small size of the San Ildefonso Pueblo, which at the time had only 138 full-time residents, a number of noted painters emerged, including Crescencio Martinez, Julian Martinez (Pocano), Tonita Peña (Quah Ah), Awa Tsireh (Alfonso Roybal), and Oqwa Pi (Abel Sanchez). Brody, *Pueblo Indian Painting.*

17. W. Jackson Rushing and Allan Houser, *Allan Houser: An American Master (Chiricahua Apache, 1914–1994)* (New York: H. N. Abrams, 2004): 45–46.

18. In his *Analysis of Beauty* (1772), Baroque painter and theorist William Hogarth (1697–1764) was the first person to describe serpentine lines as the most aesthetically pleasing because they signify liveliness and activity, while straight lines signify stasis or death.

19. Rushing and Houser, *Allan Houser: An American Master*.

20. Quoted in Rushing and Houser, *Allan Houser: An American Master*, 84.

21. Cited in many sources, including Kevin Gover, "A New Kind of Indian Art," in *Fritz Scholder: Indian, Not Indian*, ed. L. Stokes Sims (Washington, DC: Smithsonian Press, 2008), 9; and Nancy Marie Mithlo, "No Word for Art in Our Language?: Old Questions, New Paradigms," *Wíčazo Ša Review* 27, no. 1 (2012): 111.

22. Fritz Scholder, *Indian Kitsch: The Use and Misuse of Indian Images* (Santa Fe: Northland Press, 1979).

23. The impact of Scholder's students on his work is explored in Leslie Wasserberg, "An American Expressionist," in Stokes Sims, *Fritz Scholder: Indian, Not Indian*, 36–75, and in Lawrence Abbott, "Interview with Alfred Young Man," *The Canadian Journal of Native Studies* 16, no. 2 (1996): 322–23.

24. Piri Halasz, "Fritz Scholder's Indian Paradoxes," *ARTnews* 78, no. 8 (August 1974): 94.

25. All quotes from Melanie Yazzie come from a personal interview between the author and the artist, 2015.

26. For more information about the Indian Arts and Crafts Act of 1990, see Gail Sheffield, *The Arbitrary Indian: The Indian Arts and Crafts Act of 1990* (Norman: University of Oklahoma Press, 1997).

27. Personal interview with the artist, 2015.

28. Personal interview with the artist, 2015.

29. Personal interview with the artist, 2015.

30. John Paul Rangel, "Indigenous Perspectives on Contemporary Native Art, Indigenous Aesthetics and Representation" (dissertation, University of New Mexico, 2012), 34, http://digitalrepository.unm.edu/educ_llss_etds/37/.

SELECT BIBLIOGRAPHY

Abbot, Lawrence. *I Stand At the Center of the Good: Interviews with Contemporary Native American Artists*. Lincoln, Nebraska: University of Nebraska Press, 1994.

Allan Houser: Apache Sculptor. Documentary film. Directed by Films for the Humanities & Sciences, Films Media Group, 2006. https://www.visionmakermedia.org/watch/allan-houser-apache-legacy.

Anthes, Bill. *Native Moderns: American Indian Painting, 1940–1960*. Durham, North Carolina: Duke University Press, 2006.

Archuleta, Margaret. *Coyote, A Myth in the Making*. New York: National History Museum Foundation, 1986.

———. "Tap Dancing on the Stars: Reflections on Harry E. Fonseca, 1946–2006." In *Diversity and Dialogue: The Eiteljorg Fellowship for Native American Fine Art, 2007*, edited by James H. Nottage, 6–7. Indianapolis: Eiteljorg Museum of American Indians and Western Art, 2007.

Archuleta, Margaret, and Rennard Strickland. *Shared Visions: Native American Painters and Sculptors in the Twentieth Century*. New York: The New Press, 1993.

Babcock, Barbara, and Marta Weigle, eds. *The Great Southwest of the Fred Harvey Company and the Santa Fe Railway*. Tucson: University of Arizona Press, 1996.

Berman, Tressa, ed. *No Deal!: Indigenous Arts and the Politics of Possession*. Santa Fe: School for Advanced Research, 2012.

Bernstein, Bruce. *Santa Fe Indian Market: A History of Native Arts and the Market*. Santa Fe: Museum of New Mexico Press, 2012.

Bernstein, Bruce, and W. Jackson Rushing. *Modern by Tradition: American Indian Painting in the Studio Style*. Santa Fe: Museum of New Mexico Press, 1995.

Brody, J. J. *Anasazi and Pueblo Painting*. Albuquerque: University of New Mexico Press, 1991.

———. *Pueblo Indian Painting: Tradition and Modernism in New Mexico, 1900–1930*. Santa Fe: School of American Research Press, 1997.

Brown, Tracy L. *Pueblo Indians and Spanish Colonial Authority in Eighteenth-Century New Mexico*. Tucson: University of Arizona Press, 2013.

Chase, Katherin L. *Indian Painters of the Southwest: The Deep Remembering*. Santa Fe: School of Advanced Research, 2002.

Cooper, Karen Coody. *Spirited Encounters: American Indians Protest Museum Policies and Practices*. Lanham, MD: AltaMira Press, 2013.

Doueihi, Anne. "Inhabiting the Space between Discourse and Story in Trickster Narratives." In *Mythical Trickster Figures: Contours, Contexts, and Criticisms*, edited by William J. Hynes and William G. Doty, 193–201. Tuscaloosa: University of Alabama Press, 1993.

———. "Trickster: On Inhabiting the Space between Discourse and Story." *Soundings: An Interdisciplinary Journal* 67, no. 3 (Fall 1984): 283–311.

Emmons, Sally L. A. "A Disarming Laughter: The Role of Humor in Tribal Cultures: An Examination of Humor in Contemporary Native American Literature and Art." PhD diss., University of Oklahoma, 2000.

Fry, Aaron. "Local Knowledge and Art Historical Methodology: A New Perspective on Awa Tsireh and the San Ildefonso Easel Painting Movement." *Hemispheres: Visual Cultures of the Americas* 1 (Spring 2008): 46–61.

Garmhausen, Winona. *History of Indian Arts Education in Santa Fe: The Institute of American Indian Arts with Historical Background 1890 to 1962*. Santa Fe: Sunstone Press, 1988.

Gritton, Joy L. *The Institute of American Indian Arts: Modernism and US Indian Policy*. Albuquerque: University of New Mexico Press, 2000.

Halasz, Piri. "Fritz Scholder's Indian Paradoxes." *ARTnews* 78, no. 8 (August 1974): 90–96.

Holm, Bill. "The Dancing Headdress Frontlet: Aesthetic Context on the Northwest Coast." In *The Arts of the North American Indian*, edited by Edwin Wade, 134–40. Tulsa: Philbrook Art Center, 1986.

Horton, Jessica, and Janet Catherine Berlo. "Pueblo Painting in 1932: Folding Narratives of Native Art into American Art History." In *A Companion to American Art*, edited by John Davis, Jennifer A. Greenhill, and Jason D. LaFountain, 264–80. Chichester, UK: John Wiley and Sons, 2015.

Houser, Allan, et al. *Allan Houser, a Life in Art: (Ha-O-Zous)*. Santa Fe: Museum of New Mexico, 1991.

Lamar, Cynthia Chavez, and Sherry Farrell Racette with Lara Evans. *Art in Our Lives: Native Women Artists in Dialogue*. Santa Fe: School of Advanced Research, 2010.

LaPena, Frank. "Contemporary Northern California Native American Art." *California History* 71, no. 3 (Fall 1992): 386–401.

———. "Coyote: A Myth in the Making. An Interview with Harry Fonseca." *News from Native California* 1, no. 5 (1987): 18–19.

Lincoln, Kenneth. *Indi'n Humor: Bicultural Play in Native America*. New York: Oxford University Press, 1993.

Lukavic, John P., and Laura Caruso, eds. *Art in Motion: Native American Explorations of Time, Place, and Thought*. Denver: Denver Art Museum, 2016.

Mithlo, Nancy M. "'Give, Give, Giving': Cultural Translations." *Vision, Space, Desire: Global Perspectives and Cultural Hybridity*. Washington, DC: National Museum of the American Indian, 2006: 85–97.

———. *Manifestations: New Native Art Criticism*. Santa Fe: Museum of Contemporary Native American Art, 2012.

Nuttage, James H., ed. *Into the Fray: The Eiteljorg Fellowship for Native American Fine Art*. Indianapolis: Eiteljorg Museum of American Indians and Western Art, 2005.

Penney, David W., and Lisa Roberts. "America's Pueblo Artists: Encounters on the Borderlands." In *Native American Art in the Twentieth Century*, edited by W. Jackson Rushing III. London: Routledge, 1999.

Phillips, Patsy. "Sundays with Harry: An Essay on a Contemporary Native Artist of Our Time." *Wíčazo Ša Review* 27, no. 1 (Spring 2012): 63–72.

Rangel, John Paul, "Indigenous Perspectives on Contemporary Native Art, Indigenous Aesthetics and Representation." PhD diss., University of New Mexico, 2012.

Ringlero, Aleta. "Harry Fonseca: In Your Face, In His Element." In Nuttage, *Into the Fray*, 59–72.

Rushing, W. Jackson. *Native American Art in the Twentieth Century: Makers, Meanings, Histories*. Florence, KY: Routledge, 1999.

Rushing, W. Jackson, and Allan Houser. *Allan Houser: An American Master (Chiricahua Apache, 1914–1994)*. New York: H. N. Abrams, 2004.

Ryan, Allan J. *The Trickster Shift: Humor and Irony in Contemporary Native Art*. Vancouver: University of British Columbia Press, 1999.

Sando, Joe S. *Pueblo Nations: Eight Centuries of Pueblo Nations*. Santa Fe: Clear Light Publishers, 1992.

———. *Pueblo Profiles: Cultural Identity through Centuries of Change*. Santa Fe: Clear Light Publishers, 1998.

Scott, Amy. "Coyote as Clown, Cowboy, and Creator." *The Iris: Behind the Scenes at the Getty*. Blog post. August 9, 2016. http://blogs.getty.edu/iris/coyote-as-clown-cowboy-and-creator/.

Scott, Sasha T. *A Strange Mixture: The Art and Politics of Painting Pueblo Indians*. Norman: University of Oklahoma Press, 2015.

Sheffield, Gail. *The Arbitrary Indian: The Indian Arts and Crafts Act of 1990*. Norman: University of Oklahoma Press, 1997.

Spivey, Richard. *The Legacy of Maria Poveka Martinez*. Santa Fe: Museum of New Mexico Press, 2003.

Sweet, Jill D. *Dances of the Tewa Pueblo Indians*. Santa Fe: School of American Research, 1985.

Wade, Edwin, ed. *The Arts of the North American Indian*. Tulsa: Philbrook Art Center, 1986.

Transforming Art History in the Classroom

LARA M. EVANS

Art history involves the use of many tools. There is a variety of scientific equipment for measurements, scanning, and testing. Then there are the analyses of social movements, economic influences and impacts, connoisseurship, and systems of symbolic references; the use of personal biography and psychology, semiotics, and reception theory; the study of institutional relationships; historical research using publications, archives, museums, and private collections; and interviews with knowledgeable experts. When working with living artists and artists of the recent past, interviews with artists and people with personal connections to the artists are important resources, too. And, of course, looking at the art itself and experiencing it in person provide a very specific set of data. This is not an exhaustive list—there are many different tools and approaches to choose from.

The field of art history developed during a period of European ethnocentrism called positivism. It had contradictions built into it from the beginning. Non-European civilizations and their cultural lenses were only considered in relationship to their ability to illustrate the superiority of European culture or to actively appropriate concepts that might lead to "progress" in the skilled hands of European artists, scholars, philosophers, and theologians (and later, those of Euro-Americans). This is a simplistic overview, and competing tensions nearly always exist. Each social movement aimed at equalizing gender rights, shifting colonial and decolonial practices, or changing the systematic oppression of people of color caused incremental shifts that led cumulatively to slow changes in academia, including art history. Late-twentieth-century events such as the civil rights movement and the American Indian Movement had a particularly strong impact.

Like history, art history has "story" at its heart. I do not use the word "story" in a pejorative sense, as in an untruth, but to describe narrative. Regardless of what scientific methodologies and tools of measurement we might use when examining a work of art, when we speak about that artwork or write about it, we put scientific results and the facts together into a narrative. There are some fairly common narratives in art history that are easy to recognize. Think of the genius who demonstrated precocious artistic ability at a very young age and worked with single-minded dedication and made unique achievements. What about the tortured soul who experienced such anguish that their work broke with the conventions of the time and they died too soon, their genius unappreciated until later? Have you ever heard about the master artist who took credit for the skills and creativity of students, or the student who eclipsed the master, or the woman whose groundbreaking work was overlooked in favor of her husband's work? Perhaps you know about the outsider artist, untrained, whose work came to signify events of the time, a break with social convention, a rebellion against expectations, or maybe the deft ability to network with those in positions of power. Sometimes the story is about how art drives social change, or how it works heroically to preserve or reinstate the best qualities of the past, leading to a revival or a renaissance. Some narratives seek to raise one artist's reputation at the expense of another's, placing them in a hierarchy rather than recognizing their artistic production as part of a dialogue. Some stories are borrowed from realms that have nothing to do with art, but force art narratives into structures developed to describe other systems, such as organizing artists into "movements" the way plants and animals are organized into evolutionary trees. In fact, plant metaphors are frequent in writing about art: seeds, flowering, growth, maturity, decay. Some of the narratives are so commonly found in art history that it can be difficult to see other possible narratives. Metaphors and similes are often used to describe and interpret works of art: they can help convey the subjective experiences involved in encountering artworks and provide a familiar context to describe the unfamiliar or the new.[1]

If we consider connoisseurship, the ability to view works of art and attribute them to a particular artist or a particular style or movement, we uncover some contradictory impulses that affect the field of Native art history. The collision of anthropology, archaeology, and art history is specifically where the problem can be located. Anthropology and archaeology as applied to Native Americans prior to the 1970s sought to identify normative features of cultural experiences, including material culture. Art history, particularly connoisseurship, emphasized the identification of exemplary artists, their artworks, and their entire body of work, and tended toward hierarchical classifications of which works were the most important and consequently the most valuable. Identifications of normative examples of material culture were performed by non-Native scholars, largely using methods from the fields of anthropology, archaeology, and ethnography. Throughout the late nineteenth and early twentieth centuries, individual identity was not significant to their research goals and patterns of collecting, whether of examples of material culture for private collections and museums or archaeological and anthropological scholarship; attribution to a particular tribal culture and geographic area was the priority. Aesthetic objects made by Native peoples of the Americas entered into curiosity cabinets—collections of unusual natural and human-made objects—then into institutional collections. Many still remain in institutions dedicated to natural history, such as the Field Museum in Chicago. Art history's emphasis on the individuality and identity of the singular artist means that the discipline has come late to the processes of examining art by Native peoples. And in the case of many works, the basic information that art history especially values is unknown, having never been recorded.[2]

The formation of collections of Native American material culture was based on decisions by and the value systems of non-Native collectors, who were often guided by non-Native scholars. An unfortunate side effect is a narrowly defined concept of authenticity that is applied to Native-made art in a different manner than that applied to other kinds of art. I will use a passage from philosopher Denis Dutton to identify some distinctions in the use of the term "authenticity":

> Despite the widely different contexts in which the authentic/inauthentic is applied in aesthetics, the distinction nevertheless tends to form around two broad categories of sense. First, works of art can possess what we may call nominal authenticity, defined simply as the correct identification of the origins, authorship, or provenance of an object, ensuring, as the term implies, that an object of aesthetic experience is properly named. However, the concept of authenticity often connotes something else, having to do with an object's character as a true expression of an individual's or a society's values and beliefs. This second sense of authenticity can be called expressive authenticity.[3]

"Nominal authenticity" therefore involves verifying the identity of the artist and, in the case of Native American art, the artist's tribal affiliations. "Expressive authenticity" includes consideration of cultural authenticity, though interest in this has potentially negative ramifications when analysis of cultural authenticity is influenced by racism, nationalist narratives, and/or cross-cultural misunderstandings.

From the point of view of artists, we might consider the assertion that artistic value is dependent upon whether or not an artwork expresses the authentic values of its maker, especially when those values are also shared by the artist's immediate community.[4] How "immediate community" is defined is absolutely crucial for Native artists. Nancy Blomberg, former curator of Native arts for the Denver Art Museum, wrote in her introduction for the book *[Re]inventing the Wheel*,

> If we accept American Indian art as a valid category for scholarly study, then it must no longer be studied solely in isolation--for it was never created in isolation. American Indian art did not develop in a vacuum. There were many, many influences among different tribes--and from non-Indians. We have all been complicit in a false narrative of purity, immutable tradition, and isolation. We must acknowledge and celebrate the complexities of cross-cultural exchange, because the Taos School, the Hudson River School, and the Santa Fe Studio School of artists did not develop in isolation. Our segregation of American Indian art has not raised awareness; instead we have unwittingly fragmented a common narrative to the detriment of the narrative.[5]

Native art scholarship does not move in a clean, predictable, or easily classifiable fashion. The collision of preservation, revival, and connoisseurship still affects Native art in messy ways. All of these approaches to considering objects created by Native peoples were created by people outside of those cultures and, moreover, were practiced by individuals who, even when their research was entered into with the best of intentions, were part of a colonialist endeavor with power over those they studied. In fact, by the nineteenth century the practice of connoisseurship had already divorced the consideration of the values, priorities, and intentions of the *makers* of objects from the appreciation of the *viewer*.[6]

When students begin researching Native art and first encounter publications from the early twentieth century and earlier, there is often a sense of shock at the openly racist language, the casual dehumanization, permeating the scholarship. For Native American researchers, the language used is not so surprising because most of us still encounter it on a regular basis, but it is still infuriating and alienating. It takes a personal toll. Omitting such readings from the curriculum is not a solution. As soon as a student starts researching something like pottery or quillwork, hide painting, or architecture, they will encounter this early research, likely when alone at a computer or in the quiet shelving at the library, without anyone on hand to explain why such dehumanizing language is no longer appropriate, or without a safe outlet for their frustration and anger.

Any art history course introduces students to formal analysis as a useful tool in helping guide observations about the physical artwork. While this is still considered a fundamental means of understanding and interpretation, formal analysis historically assumed the existence of universal references, meanings, and symbolic vocabulary in art. It assumed a shared canon of references based on knowledge of history, literature, religious practice, philosophical theory, and classed and gendered socialization—in short, a shared educational standard. In-depth education about the diversity of Native American cultural perspectives has not been part of that shared educational standard. Therefore, formal analysis is only helpful if the artwork being analyzed was created by an artist intentionally making use of the mainstream conventions, or if the student is knowledgeable about the Native artist's cultural background and influences. Most Native artists customarily work with multiple layers of coded references, knowing that different kinds of interpretations will be made by different viewers based on their own knowledge. Formal analysis can still be a starting point, a tool to help students develop observational skills, but it also should be used to help them think about *how they know what they think they know*.

The canon of art history is diversifying, but slowly. The examination of the processes by which objects become part of the canon has become a research subject in itself. Joyce Szabo examined canon formation in relationship to Native American art in an essay worth reading, "Native American Art History: Questions of the Canon" (2006).[7] She identifies exhibitions, auctions, marketing, institutional investments, publishing, and government support as key factors in canon formation for Native American art history itself, as well as the slow expansion of the general canon of art history. A crucial component of Indigenous art scholarship as it is being practiced by scholars who are themselves Indigenous is a reconnection to the intent, aesthetics, and judgement of the *makers* of art. For Native American and First Nations artists, this is combined with efforts to broaden mainstream ideas about the functions of art, not simply as a means of passive contemplation, but as a method of producing meaning in a participatory, community-based manner. It is possible to make an argument that "socially engaged art" and other cutting-edge developments have been longstanding practices in Indigenous communities. The problem is merging specialized vocabulary from the rarified art world with Indigenous concepts and practices.

Studying art history in the context of a college class usually involves a lot of reading, listening to lectures, and looking at projected images in a dark room.

I experienced a sense of bafflement in my first art history survey classes. I would read a section of my textbook and look at the artwork and find myself thinking that I must be absolutely ignorant for not seeing the work the way the art historian saw it. The authors of my first textbooks were largely male and thought of themselves as being very cultured, with a wide experience of the world, but their world was defined by upper-class experiences and travel throughout Europe and the major art centers, with very limited experience with people from different cultures and other economic realities. Of course, my own experience was limited in the opposite sense: a semirural upbringing in an oil-and-agriculture center, with travel throughout the rural areas and cities of the western United States. I was alienated and disempowered by something that was supposed to connect me to the "universal" human condition. I understood at an early age that knowing something about art and literature was absolutely crucial to improving my economic opportunities, but the process of gaining that learning pointedly educated me in how much my family's socioeconomic status and interracial marriage made me an outsider. I persisted anyway. The field of art history has changed substantially since my early experiences in the 1980s and '90s. Now art history incorporates the study of material culture, visual studies, pop culture, performativity, and more. It examines the meanings of the everyday objects around us, in addition to objects from the canon of art.

A substantial amount of my energy as a college professor has gone into working out ways to teach art history that recognize the knowledge each person brings to looking at art and include encouragement for original research and interpretation. So much work could be done about Native American art. It seems a shame that there are so few monographs about individual Native artists and so little in-depth analysis of individual artworks. What is published covers very limited time periods and uses narrow categories of work based on materials or geography. Memorization of lists of images and identifying information, having students write papers that rehash the narrow range of published works, is insufficient. Guiding them through the process of looking at artworks and finding questions they want to ask and helping them figure out how their questions might be answered—not what the answer is, but what steps could or should be taken to find answers—is what a good art history course in Native American art should do.

Under everyday circumstances, only a few methods are available or appropriate for any given research undertaking. Available time and available funding also play a role in the tools and methodological choices. Every instructor, scholar, and student must make choices about the approaches he or she will use in research. In a college setting, the instructor sets parameters around assignments to guide students, which provide some helpful and practical limitations.

But what to do in class, other than lecture and show art in the dark? Most undergraduate art history is still taught via lecture courses with little active participation by students beyond taking notes and asking or answering a question or two posed by the instructor. Moving students from rote memorization of information to independent critical thinking and discussion requires a drastic change in what takes place during class. This can feel terribly risky for an instructor if the college or university does not have a history of experimentation in classroom methods. It can be very helpful to have the support of a department chair or other faculty and administrators.

Lectures do not need to be completely abandoned, but should be shortened and interspersed with exercises that actively engage students. For a fifty-minute class session, I recommend a ten-minute lecture with direct relationship to the upcoming activity, five minutes of instructions and setup time, thirty-five minutes for students to work in groups and report their findings, and five minutes at the end for summary and reminder of what to prepare for the next class session. For eighty-minute class sessions, there are more options, including adding a second short lecture, multistage group activities, student presentations, or more extensive reports from groups. General rules to incorporate into group activities are that each person in the group be required to say something in the report, and that group composition be changed frequently, rather than allowing habitual cliques to develop. Weekly three-hour seminar class formats provide even more options for varying structures, but fifteen to twenty minutes should still be the maximum length of time for uninterrupted lecture components. Select readings carefully and devise in-class activities around them. Giving a lecture that is a repeat of material from the readings provides no incentive to actually do the homework. If the readings are full of errors that need to be corrected, devise group discussion prompts that help students figure out those errors themselves.

USING INDIGENOUS AESTHETICS

The types of assignments below can be adapted and experimented with. They are a provided as a jumping-off point for creating assignments that provide active and creative learning opportunities.

Activities around Readings

GROUP SUMMARIES OF PORTIONS OF A READING Each group of students is assigned a section of the reading and given the task of summarizing the most important concepts and information. The instructor circulates among the groups, helping only if a group requests it. Students who are struggling with the reading have a chance to work through comprehension issues with other students and pick up on ways to discern what is important. Reporting aloud to other students causes them to organize their thinking on the reading, and hearing other students provide summaries of important points can be more memorable because students listen actively to their peers, rather than being safely in the dark, invisible, while the professor lectures.

Activities using in-class readings might be very simple, such as giving a short exhibition review, artist interview, or artist statement to each group to discuss and report on. The report phase can lead to free-flowing discussions about relationships and patterns students see in the set of readings. Instructions for this work can be given in class verbally.

TERMINOLOGY ASSIGNMENT AND DISCUSSION This is a low-stakes assignment that can be done quickly by students outside of class and then used as a discussion prompt during class. Each student writes key words of their choice from the readings on the board so the instructor can get an idea of the range of reading comprehension, vocabulary, and discipline-specific knowledge in the class and adjust classroom activities to assist students who need help developing their academic skills while also providing scope for the development of those operating at advanced levels. The practice of sharing definitions in class means that students can tackle the reading without feeling as though every unfamiliar term is a stumbling block: They know they will learn some terms from other students. This is an activity that also works very well for online or hybrid courses using discussion boards.

TERMINOLOGY ASSIGNMENT Have students pick three terms or concepts that are new or confusing to them, look up the definitions, and copy and paste the terms and definitions into a word-processing document, citing sources and page numbers for each. Ask them to follow each definition with an explanation of how it applies to the way the word was used in the reading. Have them bring enough copies to share with their class members and another to turn in.

LETTER TO THE AUTHOR ASSIGNMENT Have the students imagine they are writing a letter to the author of a selected reading, following the conventions of formal letter writing. They should briefly identify themselves and the piece of writing to which they are responding. Require students to include a quotation from the reading (with page number), respond to the quotation, and pose at least one question that might lead to further correspondence/conversation with the author.

LETTER TO THE ARTIST ASSIGNMENT Have students write a letter in response to a specific work of art, describing the artwork and providing its title, date, medium, dimensions, etc. The letter should include a statement about why this artwork was chosen and how the student relates to the work's content and context. Students should incorporate a quote from a reading or other relevant critical or historical text and a full citation. Including a question that could possibly serve as the opener to a continued correspondence or conversation with the artist is recommended.

Activities around Canon Formation

Examination of the process of canon formation can be a recurring theme in any art history course. Providing students with opportunities to engage actively in identifying works they think should become part of the canon helps them build a sense of their own agency. It also encourages independent research, analysis, and practice with argumentation. For students who have never taken art history, a physical set of images that can be used like flashcards is invaluable, especially if they can be taped to the wall of the classroom or in the hallway outside. For years, I have been printing out postcard-sized color reproductions and laminating them so they are sturdy and reusable. I make a generic timeline on a wall using removable painter's tape. I randomly distribute the laminated cards and wet-erase markers during class. During the short fifteen-minute lecture, students are watching to see if I talk about the card they have in front of them. If I do, they flip the card upside-down and write the artist, tribal affiliation, title, date, and materials on the back. At the end of the lecture session, the lucky students tape their images up on the wall with the others in appropriate relationship to the timeline, and the cards not discussed go back into a box for use in the next lecture session.

STUDENT ADDITIONS TO THE SLIDE LIST This process is easy with a course management system, but can be done via email, too. Every other week, students upload a JPEG image of an artwork they think should be added to the course's slide list. An electronic discussion-board format makes it possible for the whole class to view each other's image files and the arguments for why their particular artwork should be part of the canon/exam slide list. Many learning management systems also have ways for students to vote or "like" or show agreement with entries. Once the class has responded to the proposals, the instructor prints the selected image files and laminates them to match the other cards. They can be added to the timeline in class the following week. Alternatively, assign students to do short presentations about a work they propose for the canon. After everyone has presented, have the class discuss which works they learned enough about from the presentations to add to the slide list/timeline. The instructor has laminated cards made for those works and they go on the wall for the next class session.

Weekly activities using these physical flashcards posted on the wall are very helpful for students, especially in the lead-up to exams. Because a chronological timeline is often the default, exercises during class that have students regroup the artworks according to different organizational structures is very valuable. Returning them to a time-based order later also helps them better recall chronology. The physicality of the cards and students' ability to physically manipulate them in space helps add body-memory to abstract concepts. Some class activity sessions can involve groups of students doing entirely different types of tasks, reporting, and then taking a turn at the other task(s). For example, a group of students can be assigned to reorganize the physical placement of the timeline works according to some system other than chronologically. They have to devise categories into which every work on the timeline must fit. One by one, the groups report to the class what categories they used and why.

Once students have learned how to write comparison essays, having students select two works from the timeline, take them back to their seats, and hand-write a comparison essay in class in fifteen minutes is an excellent follow-up activity. Students then work in groups, reading their peers' essays and discussing them. The short essays are turned in to the instructor and graded. This exercise can be repeated as often as necessary for students to become comfortable with selecting comparison choices and writing a good short essay on the spot. During midterm examinations, I always remove the works that are actually on the exam. The remaining works are available for students to use for the final question, a comparison essay based on two of the remaining artworks. Students have an incentive to be on time for the exam, too, because the first action before the exams are passed out is the chance to pick two cards off the timeline wall to use for their comparison essay. Students tape the cards onto the essay itself. For a large class, it might be necessary to have two sets of images so that students have enough variety to choose from.

Including the study of canon formation and a process for developing class consensus on the slide list actively engages students in decision-making and critical thinking. Students have better recall of information because they usually associate the artworks selected by the class with the students who proposed them, and they certainly recall the works they themselves proposed. They also probably remember the works they thought about proposing but ultimately decided against.

Activities around Research

LIBRARY RESOURCE SCAVENGER HUNT ASSIGNMENT AND DISCUSSION For the introduction to this assignment, the instructor explains the citation system required for the course, usually Chicago or MLA, and explains what an annotated bibliography is and how it can be useful for students when they are working on their papers. For first-year students or students new to art history, this is particularly important. I also suggest bringing a selection of different types of art books and have students work in pairs to flip through a book and answer some basic questions about it.

The following questions can be used on the same handout with citation format information:

1. What is the disciplinary background or authority of the author(s)?
2. Who do you think their audience is? In other words, who did the author write the book for?
3. Who published the book and why do you think they published it?
4. How could this book be useful to someone? Could it be useful to you?
5. Can you find all the pieces of information you would need to write a bibliographic entry for this book?

I bring a mix of types of books: an exhibition catalog with substantive essays,[8] a coffee-table book with high-quality art images, a *catalogue raisonné*, a monograph, a museum collection catalog, a collection of essays by multiple authors, a book of essays by an art critic, an instructional book about artistic techniques, books from anthropological, ethnographic, and archaeological fields, a book for young adults or children, an encyclopedia or reference book, etc. I also select books from different decades. The students discuss the questions for about five minutes and then report briefly to the class about their chosen book.

Once students are familiar with the different types of art-related books and have a handout showing them the bibliographic format, they are ready to go to the library for the scavenger hunt. Doing this early on in the term makes students familiar with the physical locations of books related to the course. Compose a list of relevant subjects, taking care that the physical locations of the books are not all in the same aisle and that the library has multiple books related to the topic. Students pick a slip with a topic randomly out of a container, then the whole class proceeds to the campus library to do the assignment. A list of appropriate topics from an introductory survey course on Native North American art might include Navajo weaving, Salish weaving, Plains Indian clothing, Pueblo pottery, Native American origin stories, Federal Indian policy, Pueblo architecture, longhouse, Indigenous mapping, birch bark, Indigenous humor, Naskapi, Native performance art, Indigenous aesthetics, ledger drawings, Chilkat blanket, Cohokia, Cape Dorset Inuit art, totem pole, and petroglyph.

Allow at least thirty minutes of class time in the library. Have students use the computer system to find two books on their subject and complete a handwritten annotated bibliographic entry for each, with the annotation including brief answers to the questions listed above. The library staff—who should be notified in advance about the exercise—can help students unfamiliar with the database or the Library of Congress / Dewey decimal system, and the instructor can work with those who need assistance with the bibliography. If time permits, each student should have another class member double-check the formatting of his or her handwritten bibliographic entries and sign off on them before they are submitted.

It is one thing to tell students to go use books in the library. Taking them there as part of class and giving them a simple but relevant assignment like this makes sure that everyone knows how to do a bibliography and can recognize the different types of books that might be useful for studying Native American art history. The casual milling about gives students who are reluctant to ask questions in front of their peers the chance to get help without drawing attention to themselves. Many students continue to explore in the library after the class session ends, and some will check out a book to take away with them.

This entire assignment is best repeated in conjunction with training from library staff about searching for *journal articles* using the library's databases, accompanied by instructions on creating citations for periodicals and websites.

INTERVIEWS Students can conduct interviews as assignments and have very rewarding experiences doing so, but it requires some substantial setup by the instructor. In the 1980s and early 1990s, interviews with Native artists were more common than any kind of critical analysis. The interview format is a fairly easy way for a writer who is somewhat new to considering Native American art to publish something. Local and regional periodicals often carried such pieces, of varying quality. The problem with them was often a narrow set of questions that put a hefty burden on the artists themselves, especially if the writers were asking politically volatile questions that might put the artists at risk with their own community, or with institutions supporting their work. This is something to be cautious about if assigning students to do an interview.

Assign students to search for published interviews with artists and share them with the class, identifying an interview they think is "good" and one they think is "bad." They should look closely at the questions. Are they specific to the artist's work? Do they prompt the artist to tell a story? Does the reader come away with a better understanding of the artist's work? Then ask students to draft questions they would like to ask of a particular artist and have them read and discuss each other's questions and vet them before actual interviews take place. Interviews can be conducted by phone or video call or in person. E-mail is not ideal for most artists, who would rather not spend hours typing answers to questions they could answer more quickly with a conversation. Gaining a little experience in transcribing conversation is helpful for thinking about voice and even mechanics such as punctuation. (See Patsy Phillips' chapter in this book for more about conducting interviews.)

In a time period when many documents can wind up in the public eye, I add the suggestion that the final assignment be approved in writing by the artist interviewed. It is easy to get something factually incorrect by accident, but it is also possible that an artist may reconsider the effect of a particular statement on his or her own community. The artist should have the chance to redact too-sensitive information before the assignment is turned in. It usually takes a month for students to identify and contact an artist, vet questions, conduct an interview, and transcribe sections into a reasonable narrative. If this is too time-consuming, an interview assignment can also consist of having a student devise several questions for a particular artist and go through the stages of editing and vetting them with peers. The interview would not be required to take place, but could be an option for a final course assignment. Providing students with a choice of type of final assignment—a conventional research paper, an interview, an exhibition review, or an exhibition proposal—is an excellent way of accommodating a wide range of skills and encouraging some personal agency.

Activities around Art Experiences:

FIELD TRIP RESPONSE PAPER INSTRUCTIONS *(gallery or museum field trip)* Have students respond to the following prompts: Which work in the exhibition can you imagine making/doing yourself? Which work can you *not* imagine making/doing? Describe each work and why you would/could or couldn't/wouldn't create such a work. 300–500 words.

EXHIBITION REVIEW ASSIGNMENT If field trips to exhibitions of Native American art are an option, an exhibition review assignment is useful. The worksheet below can be adapted to fit different types of exhibitions. Students use it to guide their observations while they are visiting the exhibition. In the case of group exhibitions, the tallying of information about the artists and works can be used for classroom analysis of exhibition statistics, if combining quantitative and qualitative reasoning is desirable.

Exhibition Review Worksheet

Title of the exhibition:

Name of the curator:

What type of exhibit is it?

Who owns the works of art, and does that information seem to be important for this exhibit?

Is there a curator's statement available? (If so, get a copy as a gallery handout or by taking a picture or writing it down.)

Fill in the table below—if it is useful. Alter the headers if you need to. (This is only relevant if it's a group show. Use your best judgment.) It may also be useful to graph the range of years the artworks were made (or add "year made" to the table):

ARTIST	WORK 1	WORK 2	WORK 3	WORK 4	WORK 5	WORK 6	GENDER	TRIBE

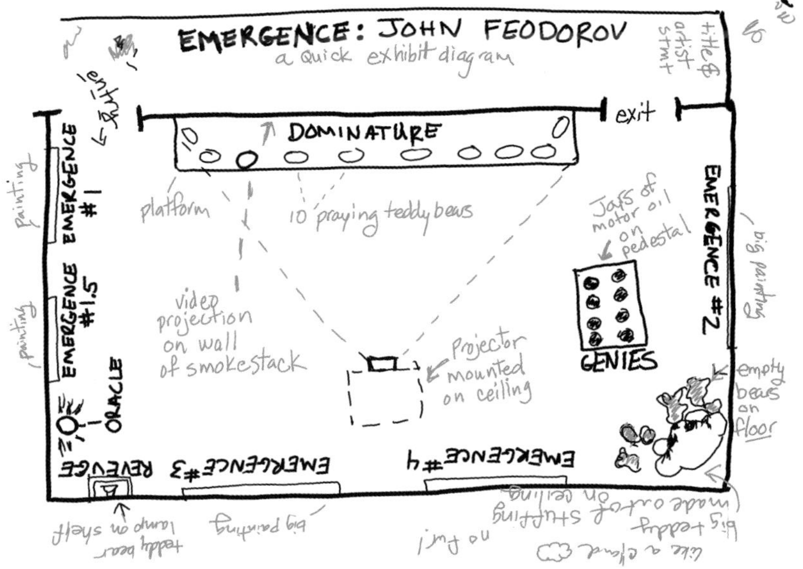

Making a diagram of an exhibition helps you think about the arrangement of space and the physical context of the arrangement of artworks. This is *very* useful when you are writing about the exhibit at home. Digital photos help with remembering artworks and can record the label information, but the diagram helps evoke directions, scale, etc., that get lost, even in a video sweep of the gallery.

Overall impressions upon entering the space:

Lighting:

Color scheme(s):

Amount of text:

Types of objects:

Spatial arrangement:

Audio ambiance:

A/V components:

Thematic divisions:

Who do you think is the intended audience for the exhibition?

How do other visitors interact in the space?

Can you identify the curator/institutional goals of the exhibit? Are those goals achieved?

How, or how not?

Do the goals seem appropriate for the institution? For the audience?

Is the exhibition worth seeing? Why or why not? And by whom?

How did you feel while viewing the exhibit? Is that how most people would feel, in your opinion?

As you made closer observations in the exhibit, did it change the nature of your experience? How?

Incorporating Hands-on Experiences: Involving artists in class as speakers, demonstrators, or workshop leaders is an important way to bridge the distance between considering art as a consumer or connoisseur and considering art from the point of view of a maker. Institute of American Indian Art (IAIA) art history courses change constantly in response to varying opportunities to connect students with participants in the artist-in-residence programs on the campus and at the museum, as well as artists who live in the area. When hands-on art activities are taught, they make the abstract concepts in books into a tactile experience. Students might learn to thigh-spin a z-twist, for example, a technique for combining plant or animal fibers into a sturdy string that can then be used as the basis for several types of weaving and basketry. Or they might learn how to remove porcupine quills and clean, sort, and dye them with a quillworker.

Focusing on early steps of complicated processes provides students with knowledge about the materials and first-hand experiences with them in ways that do not promote a problematic emulation of art forms that have specialized cultural and ceremonial knowledge. These are important considerations at IAIA because our role is not to replace the existing modes of knowledge transmission that still exist within our students' more than ninety tribal communities. Our role is to guide them in exploring the intersections between cultures, Native and non-Native. Drawing exercises, workshops in color mixing with different types of paints, printmaking workshops, performance art exercises, and many more short activities can be incorporated into art history courses.

Alternative to a Conventional Research Paper: An Exhibition Proposal and Didactic Panels: Long research papers are an important part of college, but are not particularly creative. Not every library has sufficient resources to support students writing about Native American art, and with many older sources being of limited usefulness, such research papers often replicate mistakes in earlier scholarship. In fact, the stumbling block for students' research papers about Native American art is often the selection of work. It takes a substantial amount of time to look at a number of artworks, find connections among a handful of them, and then construct an essay with facts, theory, and a sound approach. (This book's chapters by John Paul Rangel, Suzanne Newman Fricke, and Nancy Marie Mithlo are large-scale examples of this thematic approach.) A very basic exhibition proposal, on the other hand, gets art history students to imagine themselves as curators and communicators with a public audience.

An exhibition proposal provides a structure within which students can think about how their perception of the meanings of a particular artwork can shift when thinking about it in relationship to other artworks. The proposal assignment can vary in complexity. A simple version like the sample that follows would be a collection of images (with artist, title, date, and dimensions), a short curatorial statement, and one or two didactic panels of two hundred to three hundred words each. A more complex assignment for more advanced students could require a floorplan of the imaginary exhibition space, placement of works, color schemes, identification of where the artworks would need to be borrowed, and consideration of the aesthetics of display.

Art exhibitions and their documentation can be used as a basis for in-class activities and group discussions. The exhibition documented here raises questions for discussion and provides beginning points for student research.

WAR DEPARTMENT: SELECTIONS FROM MoCNA'S PERMANENT COLLECTION

An exhibition curated by Lara Evans
January 24 to December 31, 2015
Institute of American Indian Arts Museum of Contemporary Native Arts

Curator's Statement

All of the works in this exhibition have something to do with war, but depict very little gore or physical violence. The armed conflicts referenced in these artworks span five hundred years, from the Spanish and Pueblo conquest to World War II, Vietnam, Wounded Knee, the Mohawk and Oka Crisis, and present-day conflicts. This selection of works from the permanent collection examines the nuanced depictions of war and civil unrest in contemporary Native art.

We tend to think of war as a separate category, a separate "department." Most of these works break the artificial separations between war and not-war. Soldiers are embedded in daily life, with family and friends, ceremony, policies, and politics. These artists show us ways in which wars spill outside war-zone boundaries, decades and even hundreds of years later. The lasting impacts of war and civil unrest are not decided by government officials in offices, but by the stories we tell and how we tell them, long after the War Department is disbanded.

—Lara Evans

Ceremony and Celebration

Contemporary Native ceremonial dances are fascinating to visitors, but they also have a long history of being interpreted as a military threat. Every culture and nation has traditions for preparing combatants and noncombatants for violent conflict. Ceremonies and rituals can maintain balance and help make sense of past conflicts, not just prepare for a new one.

Heidi BigKnife's installation *The Night after Columbus* (figure 44) uses celebratory Christmas traditions to analyze colonial impacts on everyday

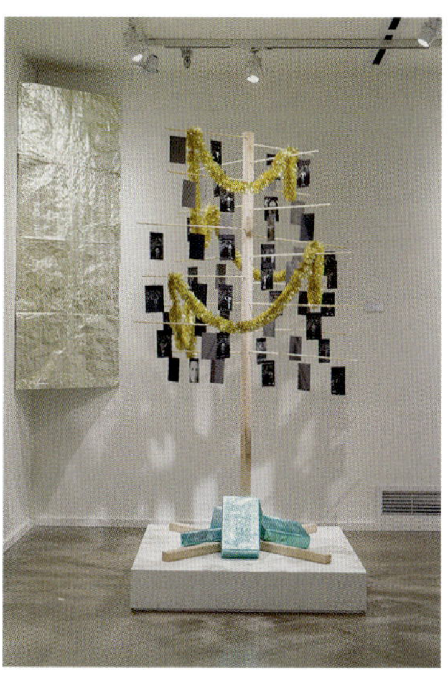

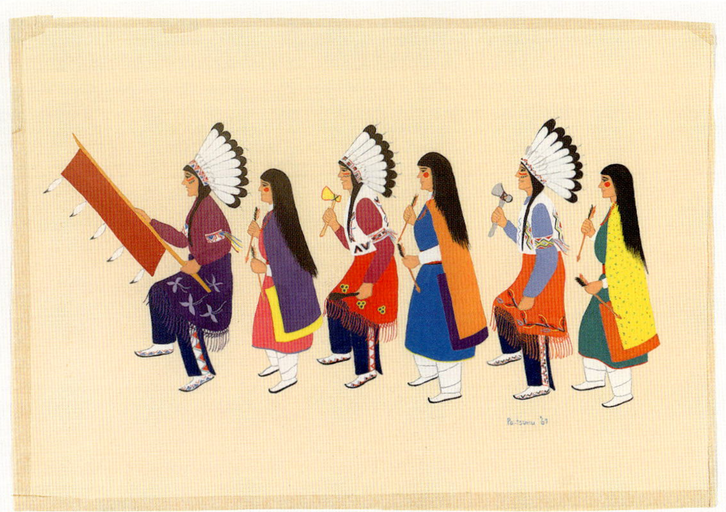

FIGURE 44 *left* Heidi BigKnife (Shawnee), *The Night after Columbus*, 1991, mixed-media installation, 48 in. × 64 in., MoCNA Collection, SH-2 (photo by John Joe).

FIGURE 45 *right* Geronima Cruz Montoya (Ohkay Owingeh), *War Dance*, 1967, tempera on paper, 14 in. × 19.5 in., MoCNA Collection, SJ-62 (photo by Jason Ordaz).

life. BigKnife created this piece during the lead-up to the Columbian Quincentennial in 1992, a controversial celebration of Christopher Columbus's journey to North America.

In the case of Geronima Cruz Montoya's *War Dance* (figure 45), the artist presents a dance commemorating historical conflicts between her pueblo and the Comanche, who alternately raided and traded with the pueblos. This dance continues to be observed even though the raiding ended in the 1800s.

Rituals and ceremonies are an important part of everyone's lives, and they continue even in the midst of upheaval. Some of the works in this exhibition address the tensions between everyday experiences and the extraordinary experiences of war.

Symbols

Some of the same visual symbols appear in several works in this exhibition. The artists are using a visual vocabulary. What do the symbols communicate? Do they hold the same meaning in each work? How is the context of the symbol meaningful?

MUSHROOM CLOUD Explosive devices are a feature of modern warfare. Any large explosion can produce a mushroom-shaped cloud. The most famous mushroom clouds resulted from testing nuclear bombs and from their use by the United States against Japan in World War II.

A mushroom cloud can symbolize modern tactics of warfare but may also refer to the horrors of the use of large explosive devices against civilian

FIGURE 46 Melanie Yazzie (Navajo), *Education*, Edition 1/1, Set 1/2, 1992, monotype on paper, 22.25 in. × 29.875 in., MoCNA Collection, N-843 (photo by Jason Ordaz).

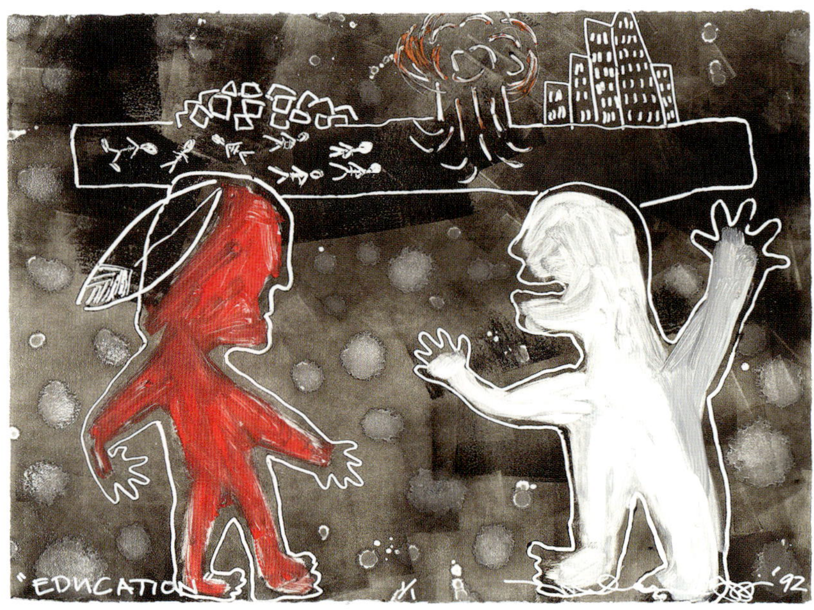

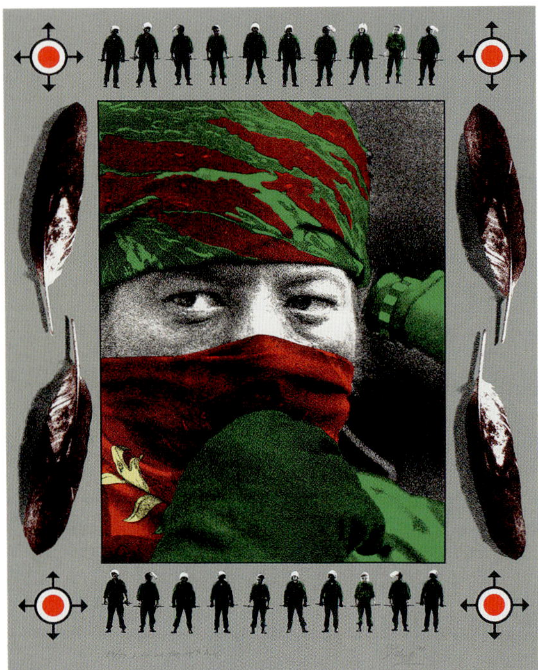

FIGURE 47 David Neel (Kwakiutl), *Life on the 18th Hole*, Edition 69/75, 1990, serigraph on paper, 37 in. × 31.5 in., MoCNA Collection, CAN-18 (photo by Jason Ordaz).

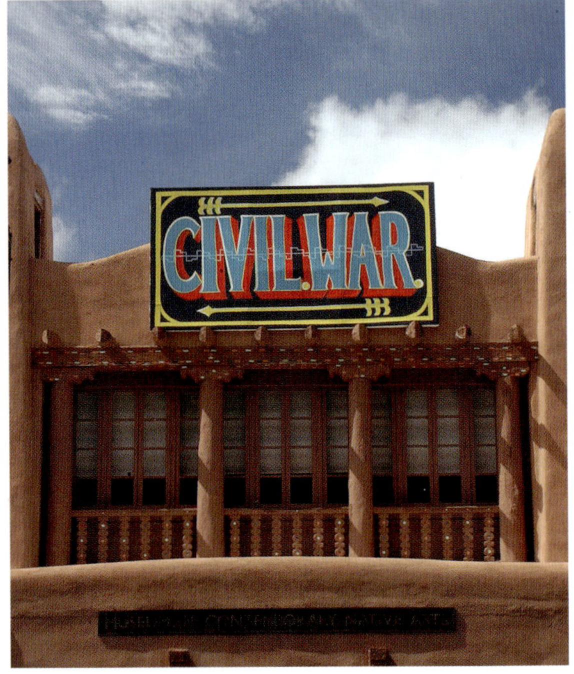

FIGURE 48 Nani Chacon (Diné/Navajo and Chicana) and Jaque Fragua (Jemez Pueblo), Honor the Treaties Collective members, *Civil. War.*, 2014, acrylic on canvas, site-specific sign installed on the façade of the IAIA MoCNA Museum (photo by Jason Ordaz).

populations. Additionally, radioactive waste from uranium mining has polluted reservation lands and affected the health of Native peoples for the past seventy-five years.

EAGLE FEATHER Eagle feathers are sacred and represent courage and bravery. Eagles and eagle feathers are also part of prayer and healing practices. In common usage, they can symbolize American Indian identity and are a symbol of the United States. How many of the works include an image of an eagle feather or an eagle? Does every eagle feather have exactly the same meaning?

PROTESTS AND CIVIL UNREST How does society make decisions about complex situations that affect large numbers of people? Artistic works form part of the public dialogue, as do public protests, speeches, demonstrations, and media coverage. How and why do civil discourses break down into armed conflicts, or even civil war?

Civil.War. by Nanibah Chacon and Jaque Fragua was displayed on the exterior of the IAIA Museum of Contemporary Native Arts as a component of the *War Department* exhibit. The font and the punctuation prompt us to consider each word separately. What does it mean to be civil? What does it mean to be at war? Both words contain unspoken rules about how to conduct oneself. What is the dividing line between civil protest and civil war? When violence is perpetrated by those in authority or by protestors, is it a form of war?

Works in *War Department* reference some specific protests, including Wounded Knee (1890 and 1973) and the Oka Conflict in Quebec, Canada (1990). Thinking about the works in the exhibition as being either for or against a war oversimplifies some complex relationships. The rate of military service by Native Americans is proportionally much higher than their percentage of the population. Service in the armed forces is viewed with a high degree of respect within Native communities.

Artist Statement

The art activist collective Honor the Treaties creates artworks that offer critical commentary on the current social climate and the issues that revolve around them.

For this piece, Chacon and Fragua have painted the words "Civil.War." This phrase was chosen to call attention to the internal violence presently facing New Mexico as well as the rest of the United States between civilians of color and the police force.

We chose the words Civil War because of their double meaning—as an oxymoron they offer a commentary on the contradictions of our present conflicts. By adding periods at the end of each word we are alluding to the idea of a Civil . . . War. We are also encouraging the idea of non-violent protest, which is supported by the aims of the Honor the Treaties collective.

—Nani Chacon and Jaque Fragua

A Mystery?

There is not complete certainty about the identity of the artist who painted *The Boxer*. It entered the collection in the 1960s with notes that it is probably by artist Alfred Young Man when he was a student at IAIA; however, Young Man is not certain he painted *The Boxer*. We are working to solve this mystery. First steps have included near-Infrared digital scanning and photographing the painting from a side or raking angle with strong light sources.

The painting appears to depict African American boxer Joe Louis, who defeated the Nazi-sponsored boxer Max Schmeling in a 1938 rematch in New York City prior to US involvement in World War II. Nazi soldiers are presented sideways, and the two upside-down figures appear to be President Lyndon B. Johnson and Hubert Humphrey, vice president under Johnson from 1965–1969. Humphrey was instrumental in the creation of the

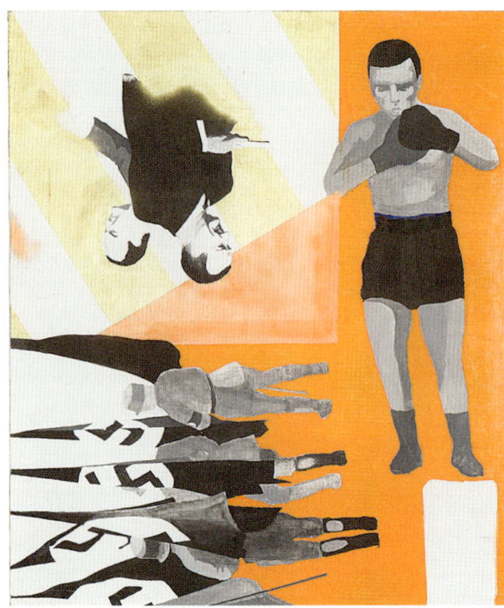

FIGURE 49 Unknown Artist, formerly attributed to Alfred Young Man (Cree), *Untitled* (*The Boxer*), ca. 1962–1968, mixed media on linen, 72.5 in. × 59.5 in., MoCNA Collection, PROP-34 (photo by Jason Ordaz).

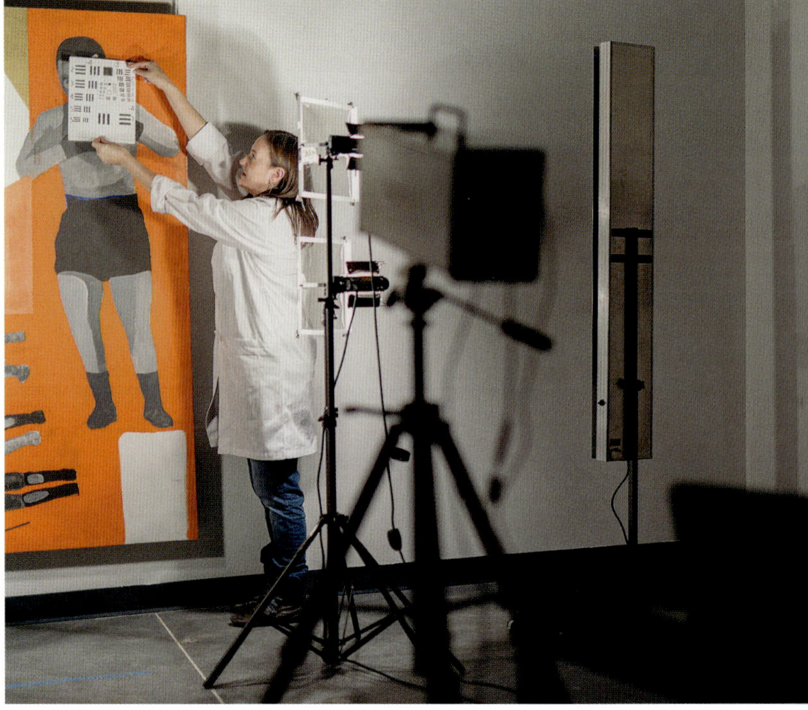

FIGURE 50 Gallery installation: author Lara Evans photographing *The Boxer*, 2014. Near-Infrared scanning in process (photo by Jason Ordaz).

Peace Corps, was an advocate for ending racial segregation, and at times cautioned against the escalation of US involvement in Vietnam.

The artist appears to be using this painting to draw relationships between the two wars, including the dynamics of how race relations and athletic competitions intersected with the politics of war. Alfred Young Man explored similar themes in his paintings from this time period.

ADDITIONAL WORKS FROM THE EXHIBIT

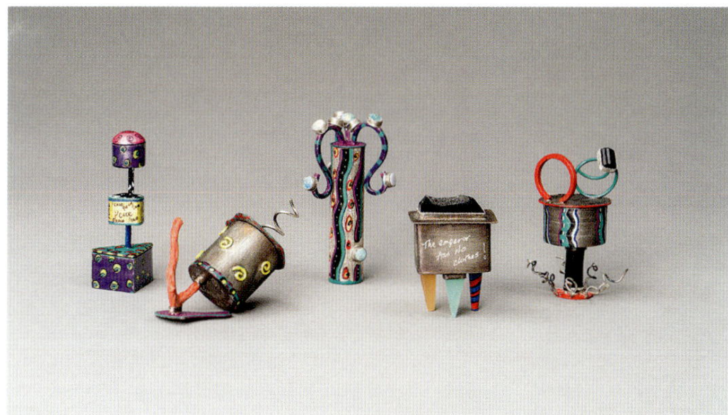

FIGURE 51 *left* Shawn Bluejacket (Shawnee), Combattant de Liberté, 2002, set of 5 containers, mixed media, silver, gem stones, acrylic paint, 4 in. × 3 in. × 9 in., MoCNA Collection, SH-3 (photo by Jason S. Ordaz).

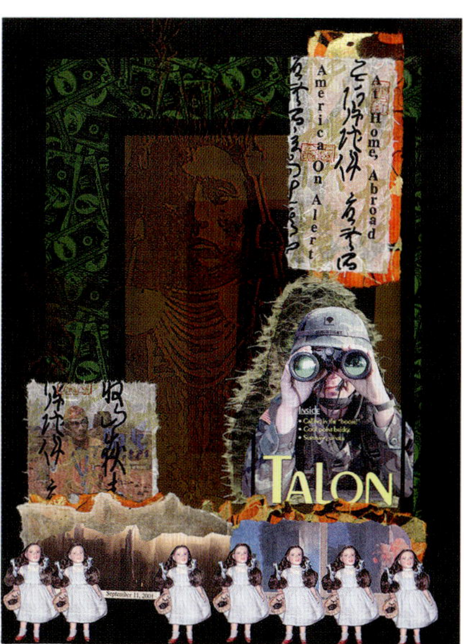

FIGURE 53 Dorothy Grandbois (Turtle Mountain Chippewa), *America on Alert*, 2003, mixed media on paper, 36 in. × 27.75 in., MoCNA Collection, CHP-175 (photo by Jason S. Ordaz).

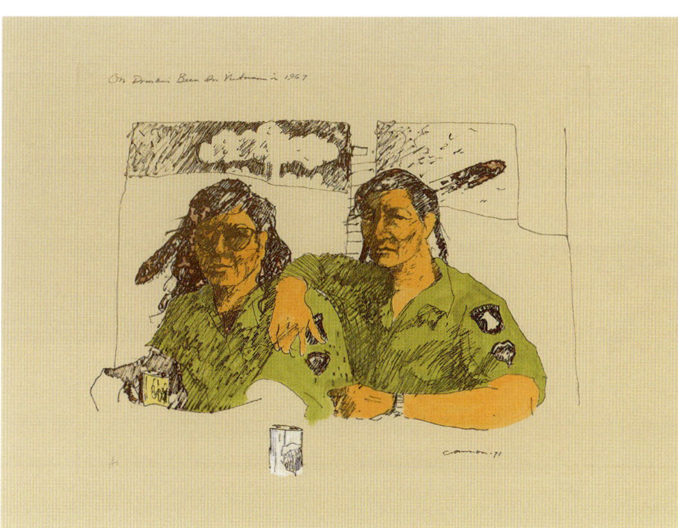

FIGURE 52 T. C. Cannon (Caddo/Kiowa), *On Drinking Beer in Vietnam in 1967*, Edition 6/100, 1971, lithograph on paper, 22 in. × 30 in., MoCNA Collection, CD-33 (photo by Jason Ordaz).

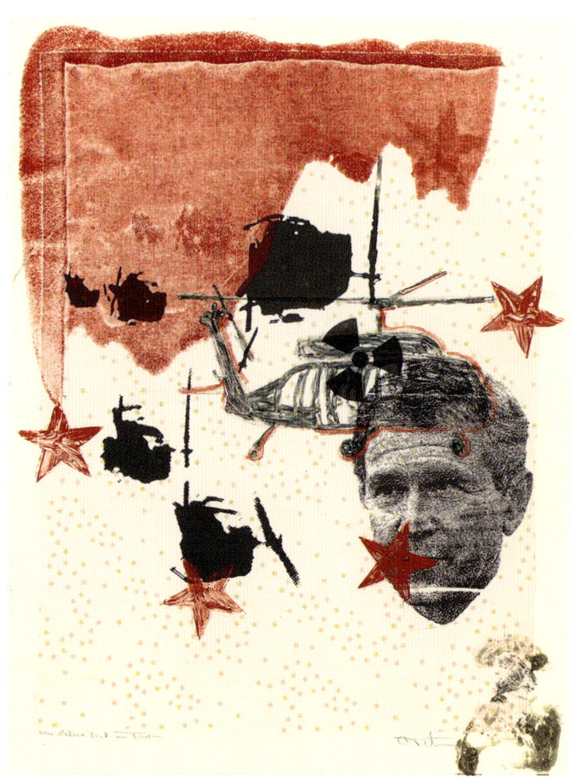

FIGURE 54 Charlene Teters (Spokane), *War Makers Back in Town*, 2003, monotype on paper, 30 in. × 22 in., MoCNA Collection, SPK-52 (photo by Jason S. Ordaz).

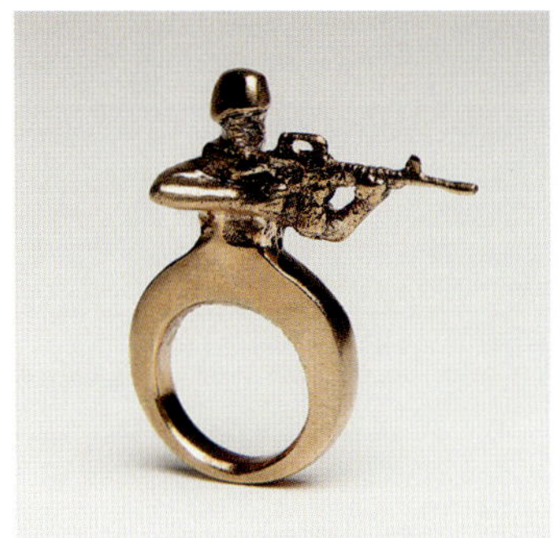

FIGURE 55 Teresa Kaulaity Quintana (Kiowa), *Soldier Boy Ring*, 2013, bronze, 1.88 in. × 0.63 in. × 1.75 in., MoCNA Collection, KI-93 (photo by Addison Doty).

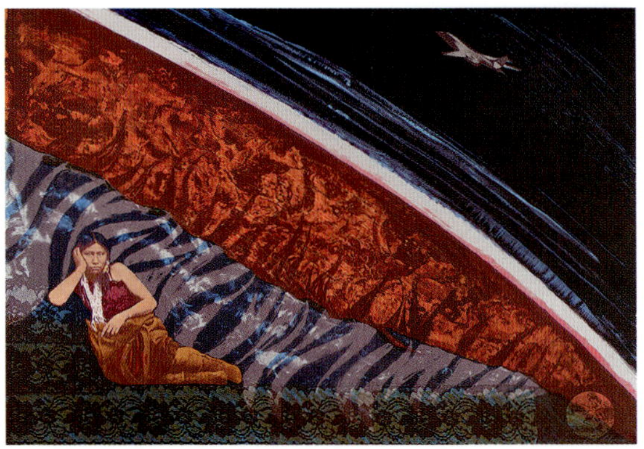

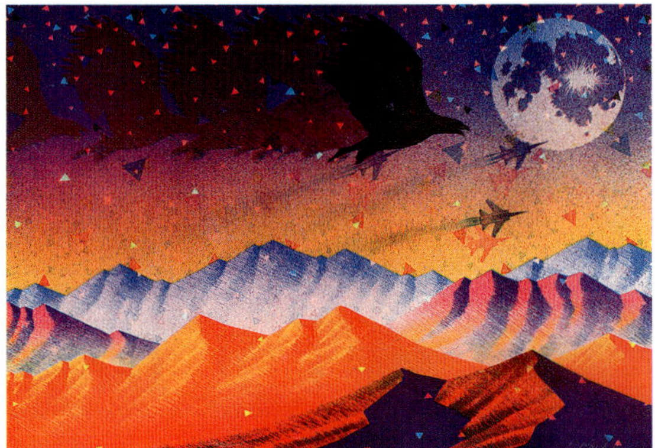

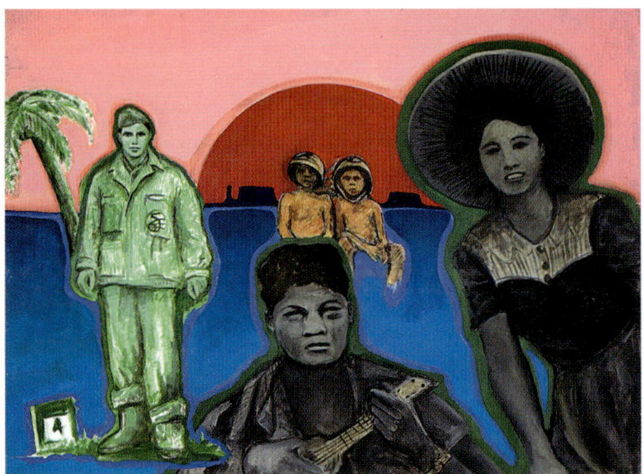

FIGURE 56 *above top* Jean LaMarr (Paiute/Pitt River), *Untitled* (Cover Girl Series), Edition 13/50, 1990, offset lithograph on illustration board, 21 in. × 30 in., MoCNA Collection, PU-75 (photo by Jason S. Ordaz).

FIGURE 57 *above middle* Jack Malotte (Shoshone), *Screaming Eagle Blues*, Edition 38/100, 1990, offset lithograph on paper, 21.5 in. × 30 in., MoCNA Collection, SS-41 (photo by Jason S. Ordaz).

FIGURE 58 *above bottom* Hulleah Tsinhnahjinnie (Navajo/Seminole), *My Father was a World War II Warrior*, 1979, oil on canvas, 37 in. × 49 in., MoCNA Collection, N-452 (photo by Dianne Stromberg).

FIGURE 59 *below left* Floyd Solomon (Laguna Pueblo/Zuni Pueblo), *Deceptus Magnus-October 12, 1492*, Edition A/P, 1990, etching on paper, 22 in. × 30 in., MoCNA Collection, L-46 (photo by Jason S. Ordaz).

FIGURE 60 *below right* Seth Picotte (Cheyenne River Sioux), *Economic Sovereignty*, 2016, graphite on ledger paper, 16.25 in. × 19.25 in., MoCNA Collection, S-319 (photo by Addison Doty).

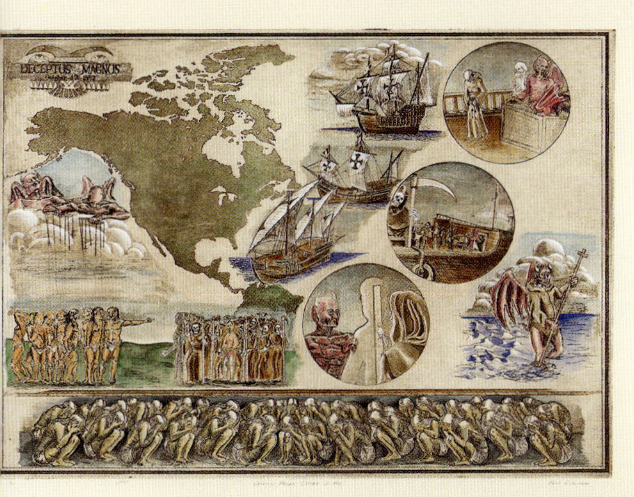

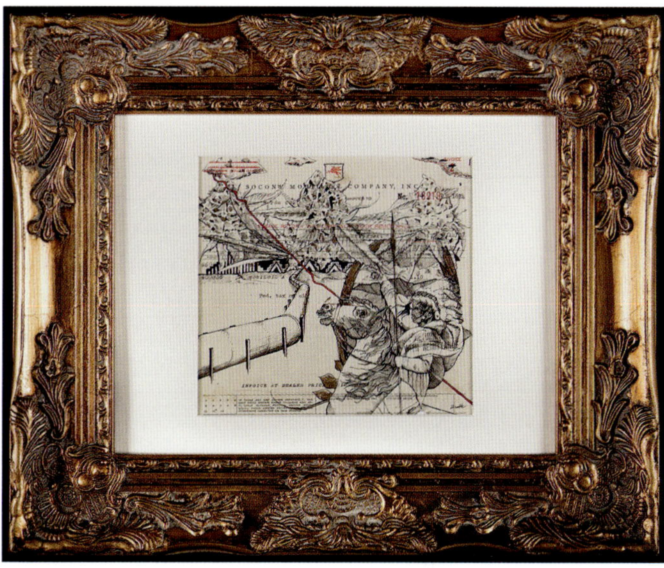

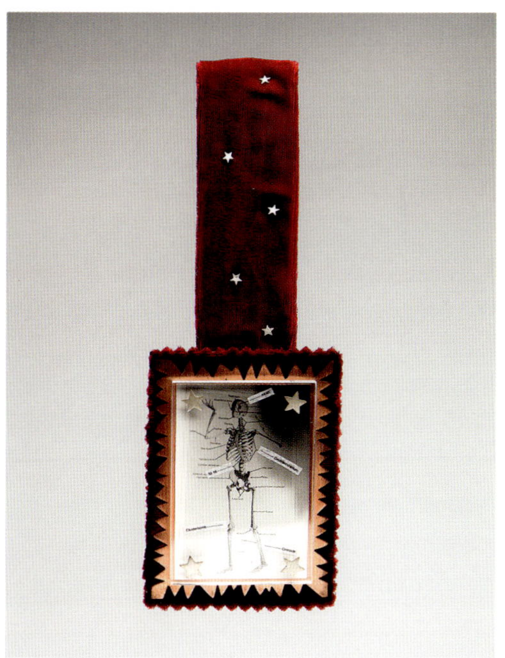

FIGURE 61 Heidi BigKnife (Shawnee), *Medal of Dishonor*, 2003, mixed media on fabric, 8.13 in. × 0.63 in. × 2.81 in., MoCNA Collection, SH-4 (photo by Addison Doty).

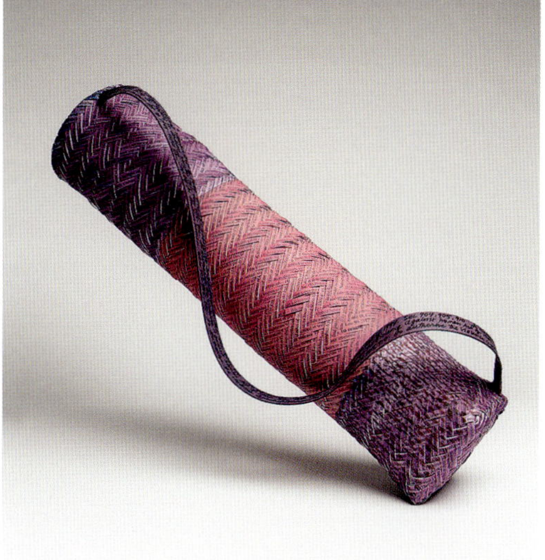

FIGURE 62 Shan Goshorn (East Band Cherokee), *Words Are Our Weapons*, 2015, arches watercolor paper splints, archival inks, acrylic, paint, leather strap on Plexiglas mount, 23.5 in. × 5.5 in. × 5.5 in., MoCNA Collection, CHE-128 (photo by Addison Doty).

NOTES

1. Berys Gaut, "Metaphor and the Understanding of Art," *Proceedings of the Aristotelian Society*, New Series 97 (1997): 223–41.

2. In some cases, that information is recoverable by consulting with the Native community from which the work originated. However, if the method of acquisition was suspect (theft, coercion, confiscation, grave-robbing), some institutions may be reluctant to consult with tribal communities.

3. Denis Dutton, "Authenticity in Art," in *The Oxford Handbook of Aesthetics*, ed. Jerrold Levinson (New York: Oxford University Press, 2003). Also available online at www.denisdutton.com/authenticity.htm.

4. Dutton, "Authenticity in Art."

5. Nancy J. Blomberg, "Advancing the Dialogue," in *[Re]inventing the Wheel: Advancing the Dialogue on Contemporary American Indian Art*, ed. Nancy J. Blomberg (Denver: Denver Art Museum, 2005), 19–24.

6. M. H. Abrams, "Art-as-Such: The Sociology of Modern Aesthetics," from *Bulletin of the American Academy of Arts and Sciences* 38, no. 6 (March 1985): 10.

7. In *Essays on Native Modernism: Complexity and Contradiction in American Indian Art* (New York: National Museum of the American Indian, 2006).

8. Exhibition catalogs are a major source for scholarship about Native American art and are only available as printed books. Internet search engines often steer students to websites for auction houses and commercial galleries. However, the artworks shown on such websites are unlikely to have much research information, which is discouraging for beginning students.

GALLERY THREE

PLATE 46 Kirby Feathers (Ponca/Sioux), *Blue Feathers*, ca. 1966, oil on canvas, 19 in. × 36.75 in., MoCNA Collection, PC-2 (photo by Addison Doty).

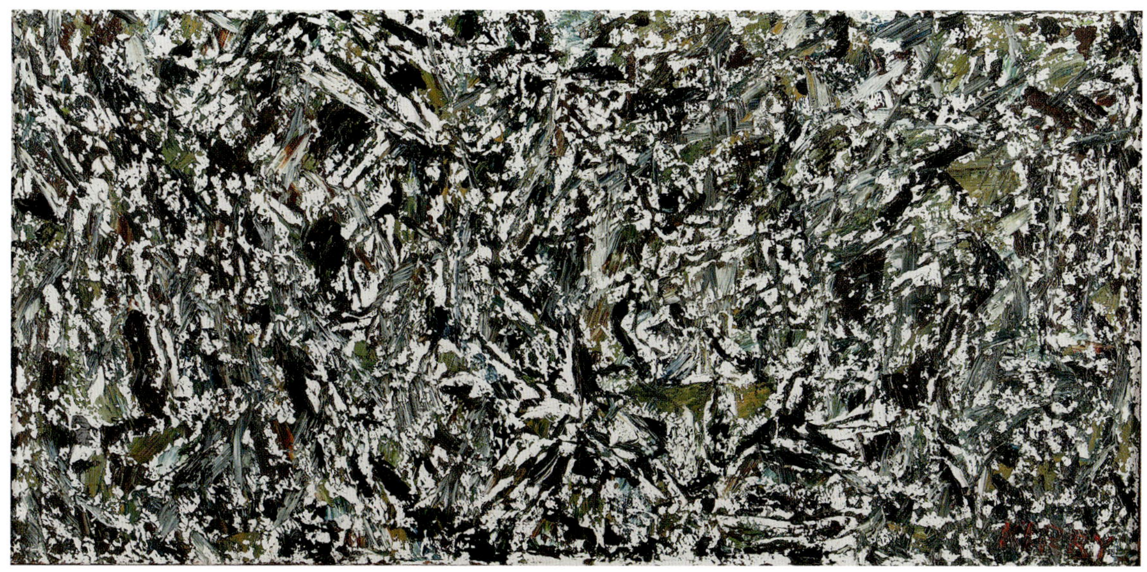

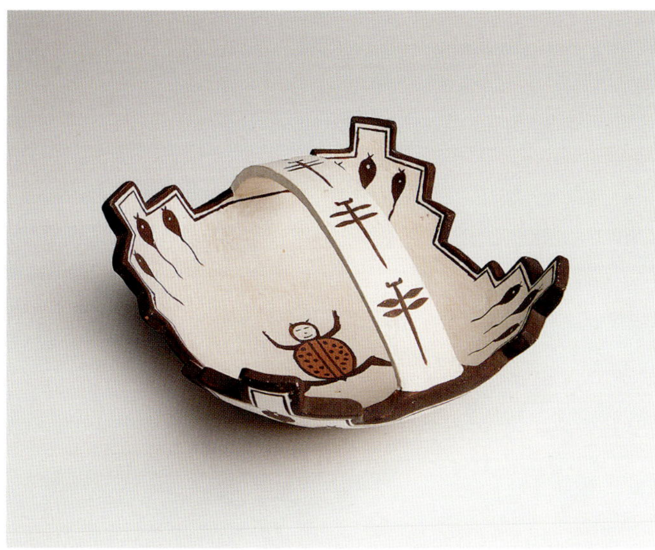

PLATE 47 Ernest Cachini, (Zuni Pueblo) *Untitled*, 1983, clay, 4 in. × 7.5 in., MoCNA Collection, ZU-60 (photo by Addison Doty).

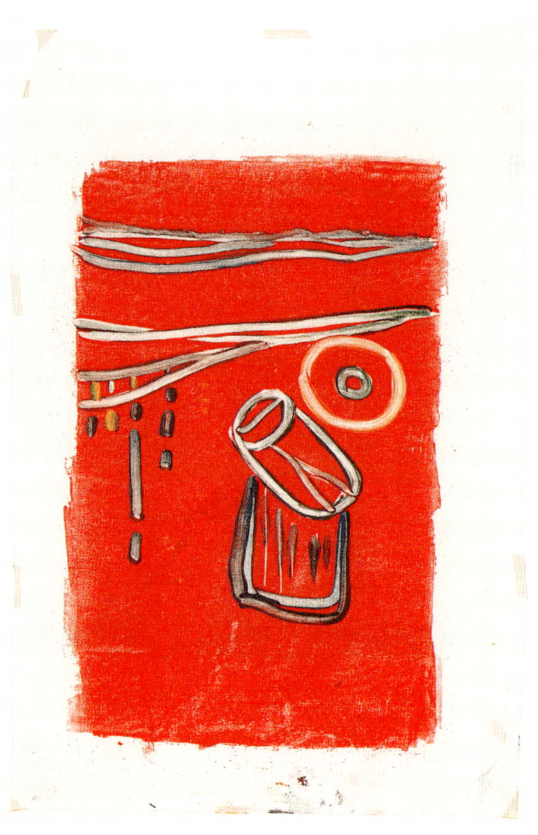

PLATE 48 Henry (Hank) Delano Gobin (Tulalip/ Snohomish), *Red Print II*, 1965, monoprint on paper, 21.25 in. × 33.25 in., MoCNA Collection, SNH-20 (photo by Jason S. Ordaz).

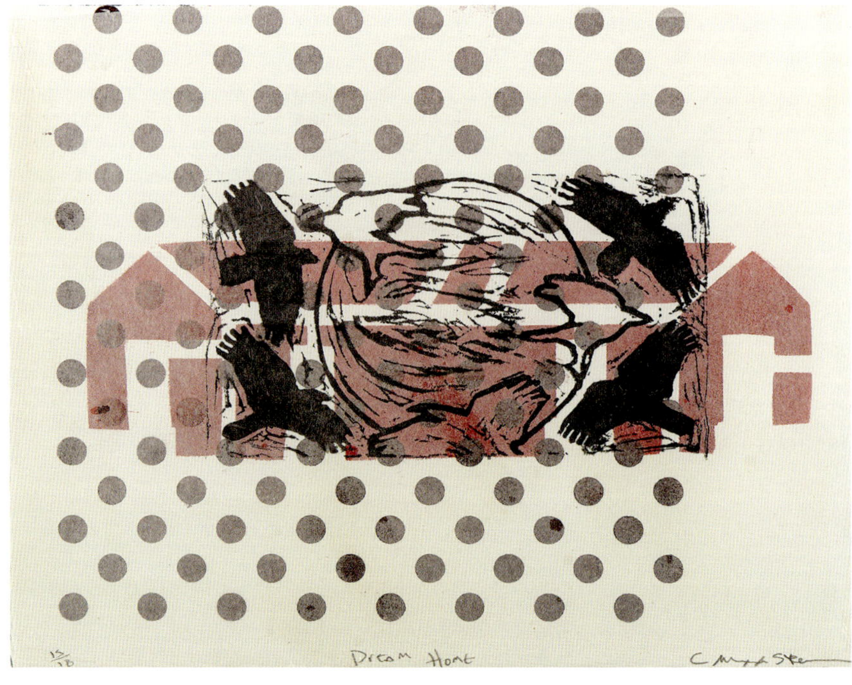

PLATE 49 C. Maxx Stevens (Seminole), *Dream Home*, 2016, monoprint on paper, 15/18 in. × 15 in. × 18.75 in. Courtesy of C. Maxx Stevens.

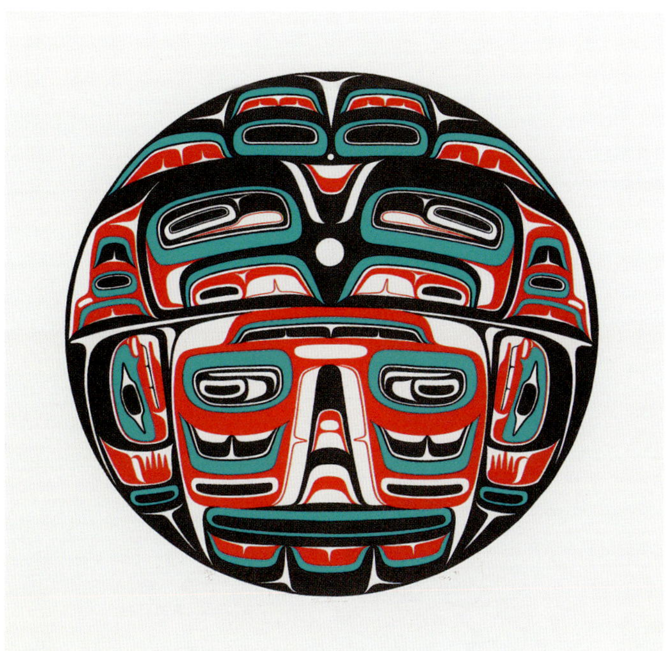

PLATE 50 Reg Davidson (Haida), *Box Drum*, Edition 53/76, 1991, serigraph on paper, 22 in. × 21.88 in., MoCNA Collection, HI-10 (photo by Jason S. Ordaz).

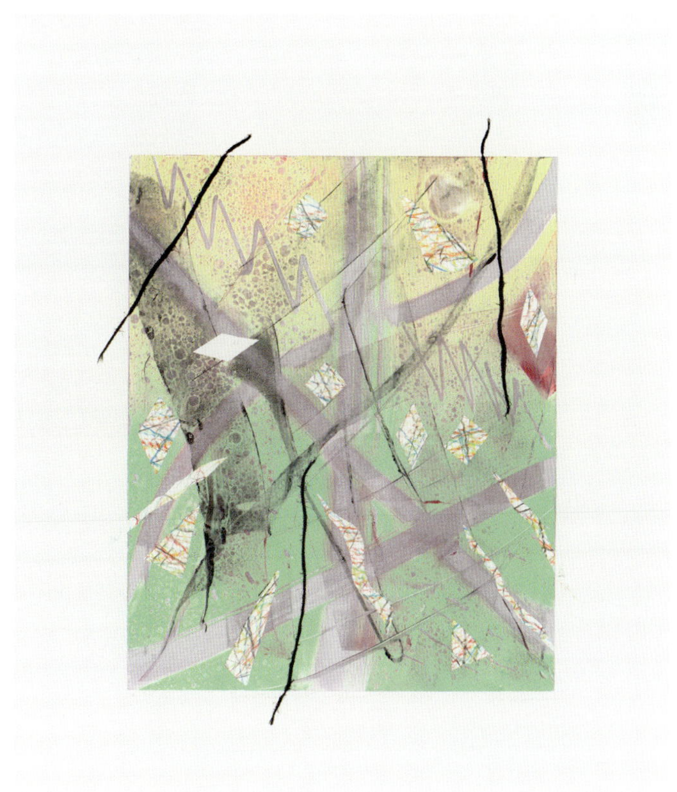

PLATE 51 Jean LaMarr (Paiute/Pitt River), *Sometimes It Happens That Way*, Edition 1/1, 2004, monotype on paper, 30 in. × 22.5 in., MoCNA Collection, PU-82 (photo by Jason S. Ordaz).

PLATE 52 Evans Boone (Zuni Pueblo), *Untitled*, 1969, acrylic on canvas, 24.5 in. × 24.5 in., MoCNA Collection, ZU-32 (photo by Addison Doty).

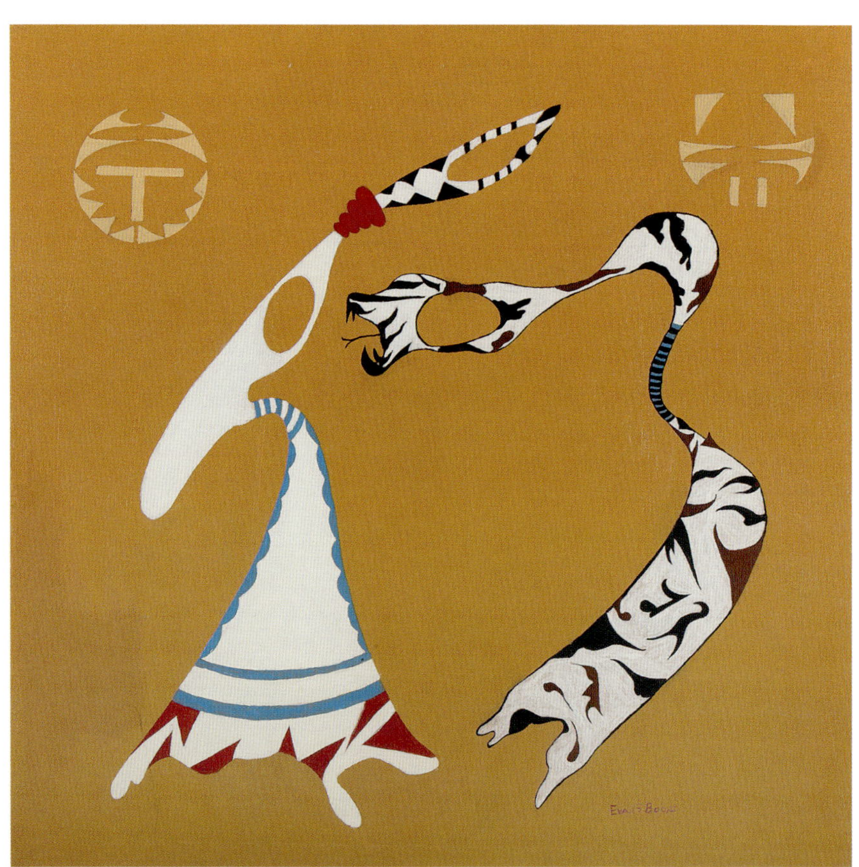

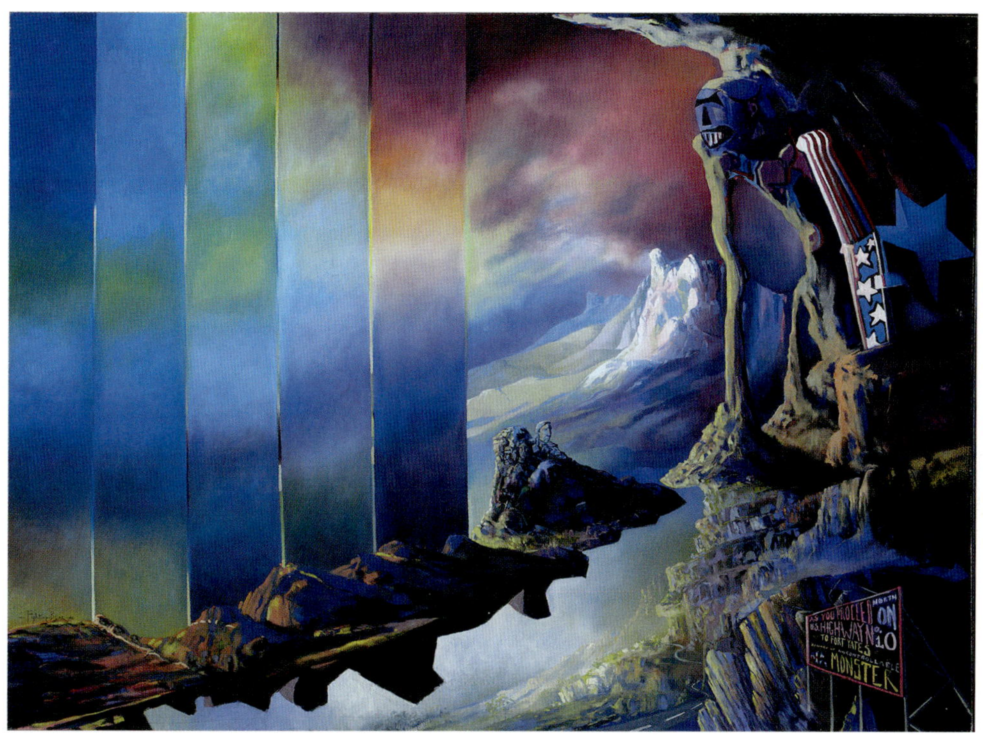

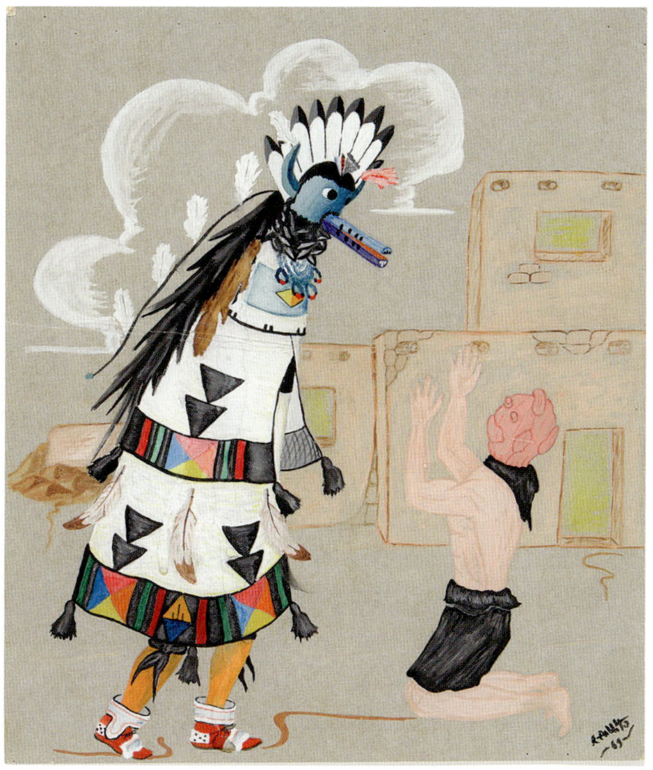

PLATE 53 *above* Raymond Winters (Hunkpapa Sioux), *Somewhere in South Dakota*, 1968, oil on canvas, 74.25 in. × 97.25 in., MoCNA Collection, S-102 (photo by Addison Doty)

PLATE 54 *left* Roy Pablito (A:Shiwi-Zuni Pueblo), *Zuni Shalako Dancer and Mudhead*, 1965, tempera on green cardboard, 9.25 in. × 7.75 in., MoCNA Collection, ZU-100 (photo by Jason S. Ordaz).

PLATE 55 Norman Akers (Osage Nation), *Warning Call*, 2002, monotype on paper, 30 in. × 22.25 in., MoCNA Collection, OS-78 (photo by Jason S. Ordaz).

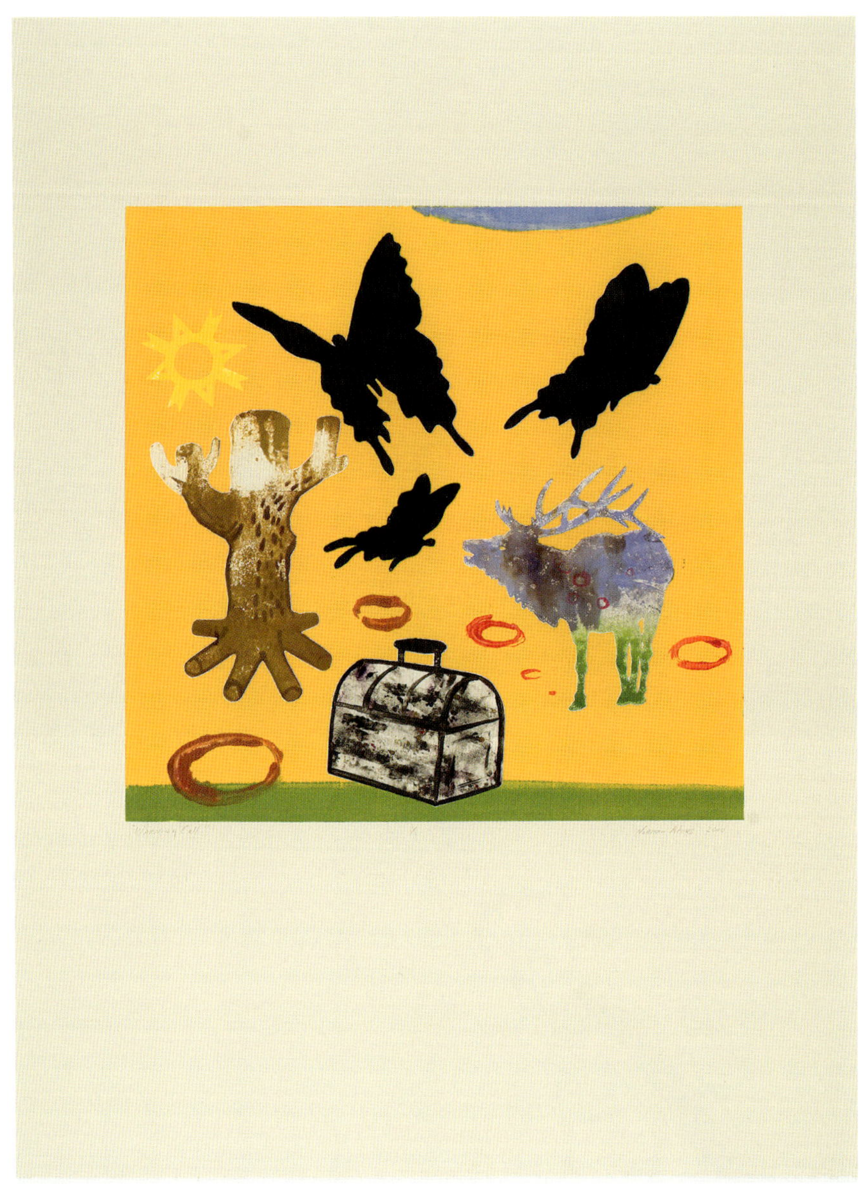

PLATE 57 Margaret Wood (Navajo/ Seminole), *Onyx Mosaic*, 1997, cotton, silk and polyester, 51.5 in. × 46.5 in., MoCNA Collection, N-858 (photo by Walter BigBee).

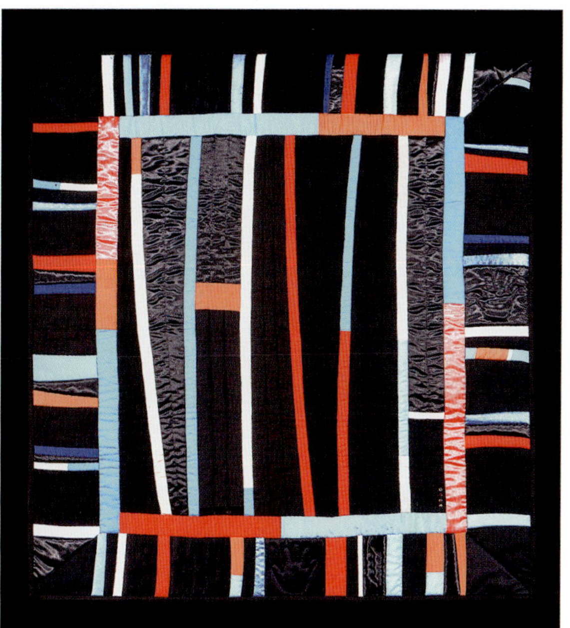

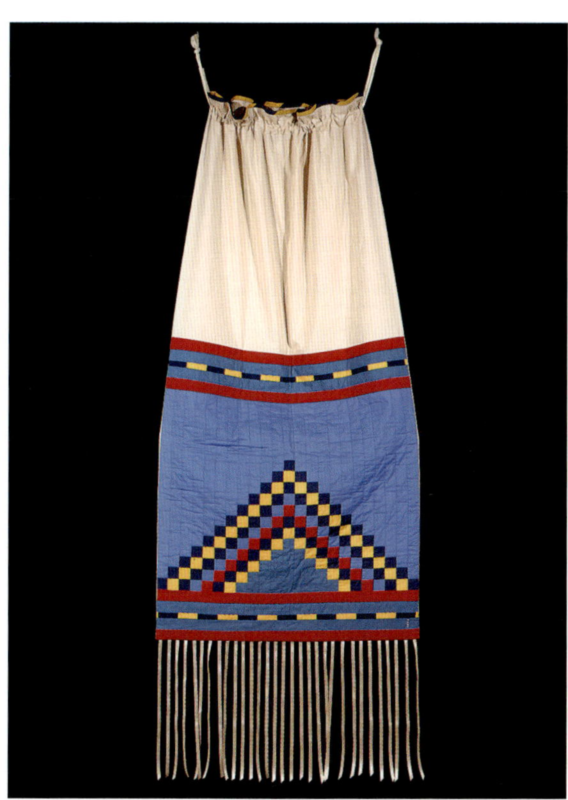

PLATE 56 Margaret Wood (Navajo/ Seminole), *Bag Series #3: Cree Tobacco Pouch*, 1993, cotton, faux suede fabric, 84.5 in. × 32 in., MoCNA Collection, N-859 (photo by Walter BigBee).

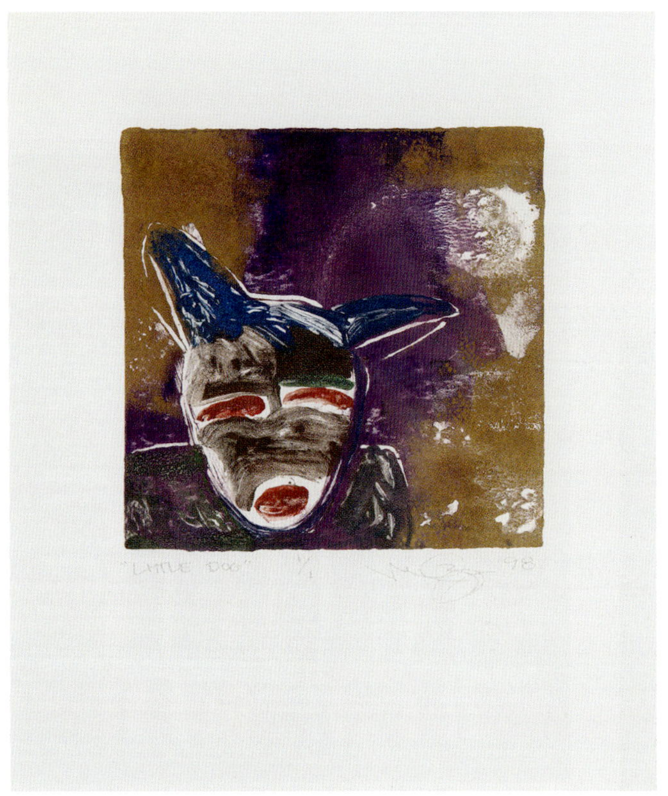

PLATE 58 Melanie Yazzie (Navajo), *Little Dog*, Edition 1/1, 1998, ink on paper, 9.25 in. × 7.25 in., MoCNA Collection, N-1225 (photo by Jason S. Ordaz).

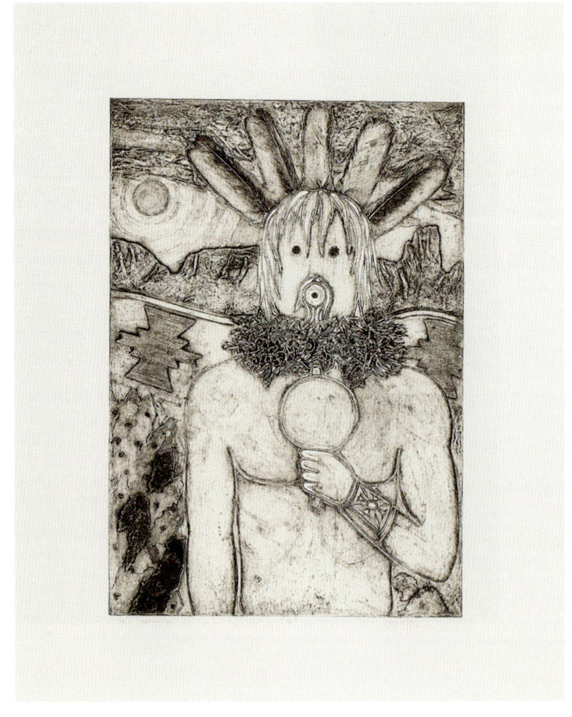

PLATE 59 Larry Yazzie (Navajo), *Ye'ii Impersonator*, Edition 6/8, 1984, collagraph on paper, 22 in. × 29.75 in., MoCNA Collection, N-64 (photo by Jason S. Ordaz).

PLATE 60 Nancy Sevoga (Nunavut, Baker Lake), *Beginning of Winter*, Edition 10/25, 1997, woodcut, stencil on paper, 25 in. × 21 in., MoCNA Collection, CAN-29 (photo by Jason S. Ordaz).

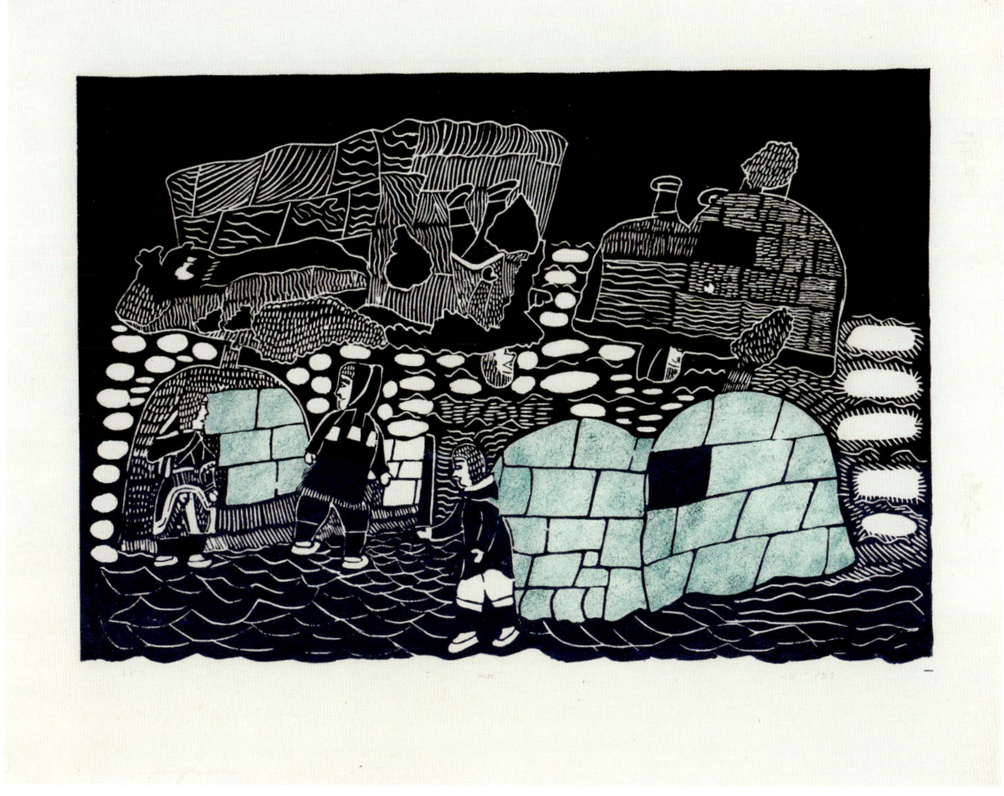

PLATE 61 Linda Lomahaftewa (Hopi/Choctaw), *Circle of Life*, 1990, monotype on paper, 41.25 in. × 29.63 in., MoCNA Collection, 2015-1 (photo by Addison Doty).

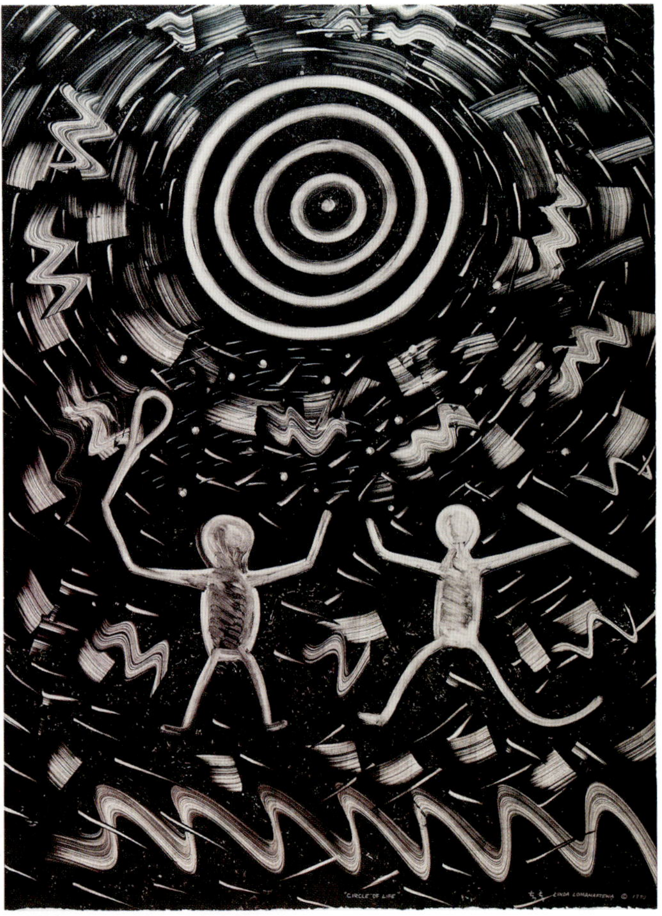

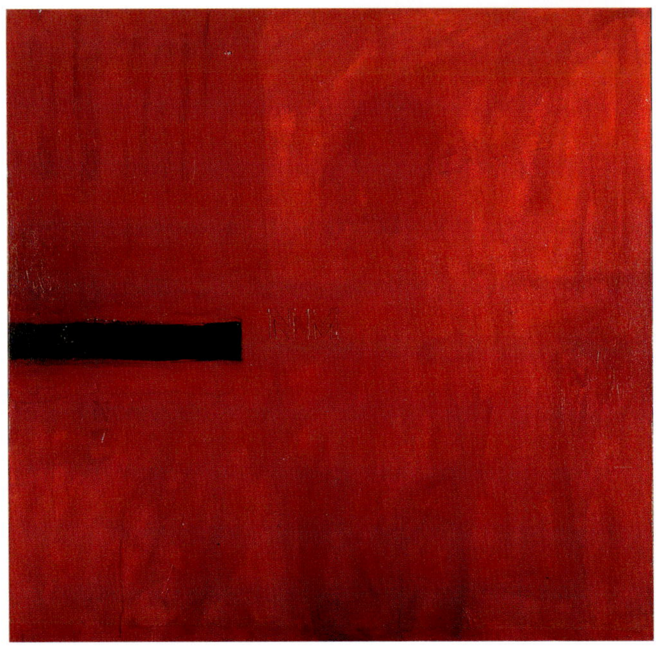

PLATE 62 T. C. Cannon (Caddo/Kiowa), *New Mexico Red*, ca. 1967, acrylic on canvas, 36.75 in. × 36.75 in., MoCNA Collection, CD-14 (photo by Addison Doty).

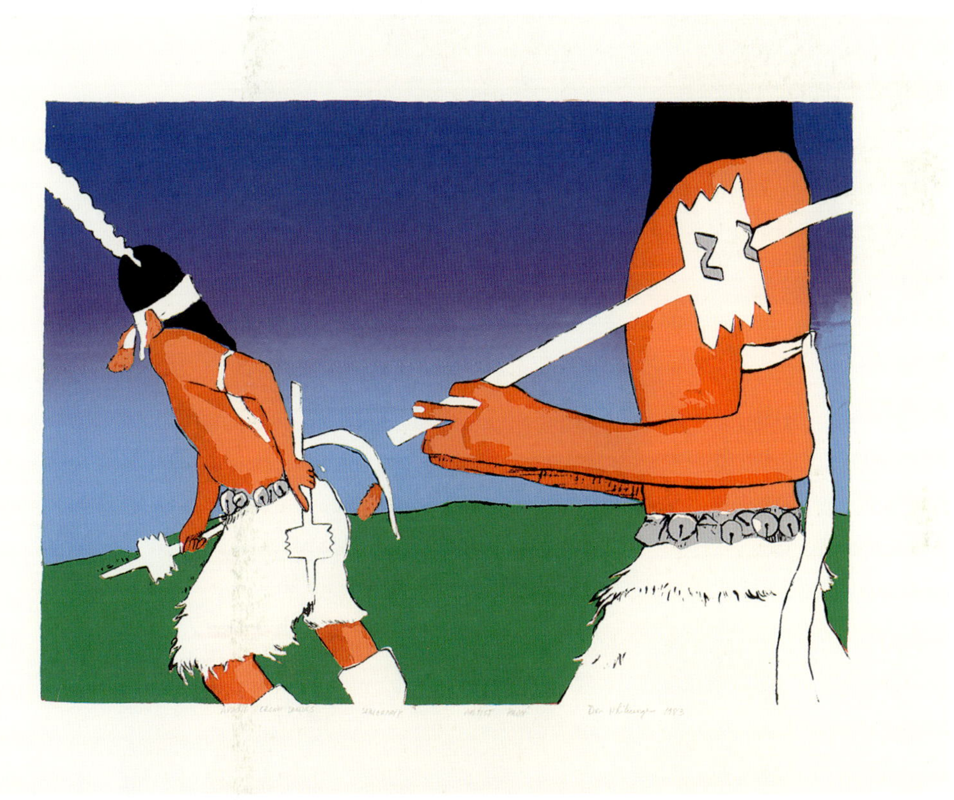

PLATE 63 Don Whitesinger (Navajo), *Apache Crown Dancers*, Edition A/P, 1983, serigraph on paper, 23 in. × 29 in., MoCNA Collection, N-566 (photo by Jason S. Ordaz).

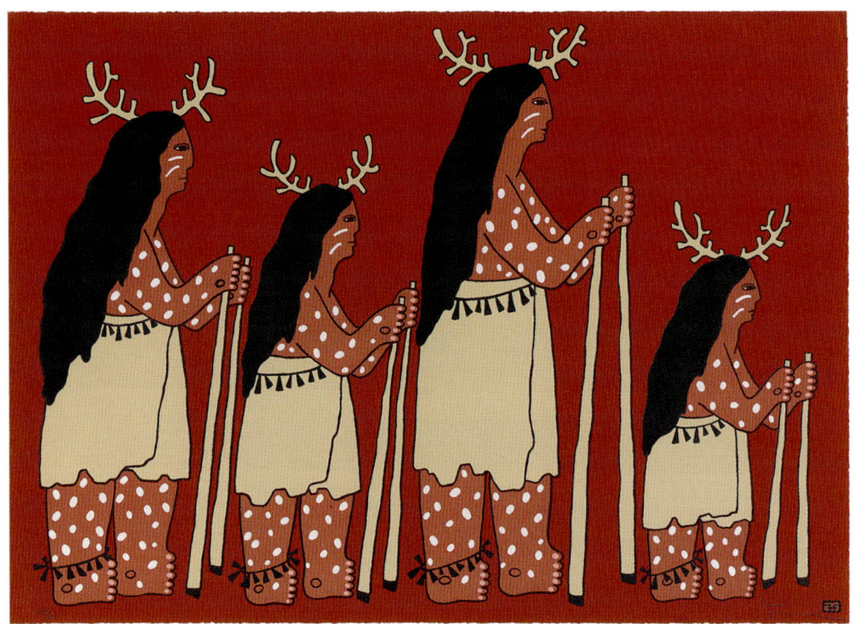

PLATE 64 Harry Fonseca (Nissan Maidu/Hawaiian/Portuguese), *Deer Dancers*, Edition 45/60, ca. 1980, serigraph on paper, 22.75 in. × 31.75 in., MoCNA Collection, MA-25 (photo by Jason S. Ordaz).

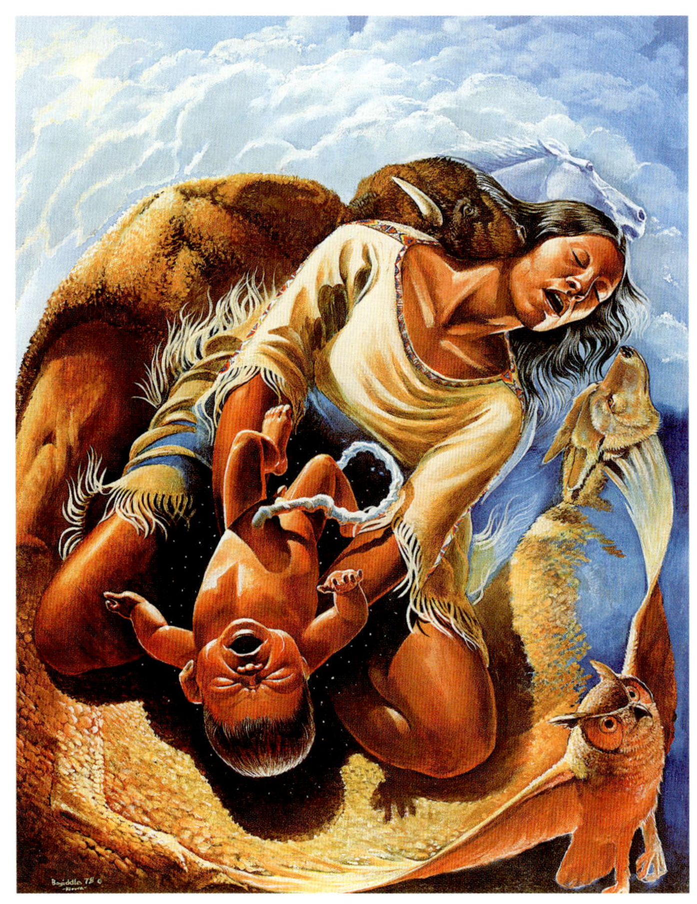

PLATE 65 Parker Boyiddle (Kiowa/Delaware), *Birth (New Life)*, Edition 505/1000, 1978, offset print on paper, 29.38 in. × 22 in., MoCNA Collection, KI-42 (photo by Jason S. Ordaz).

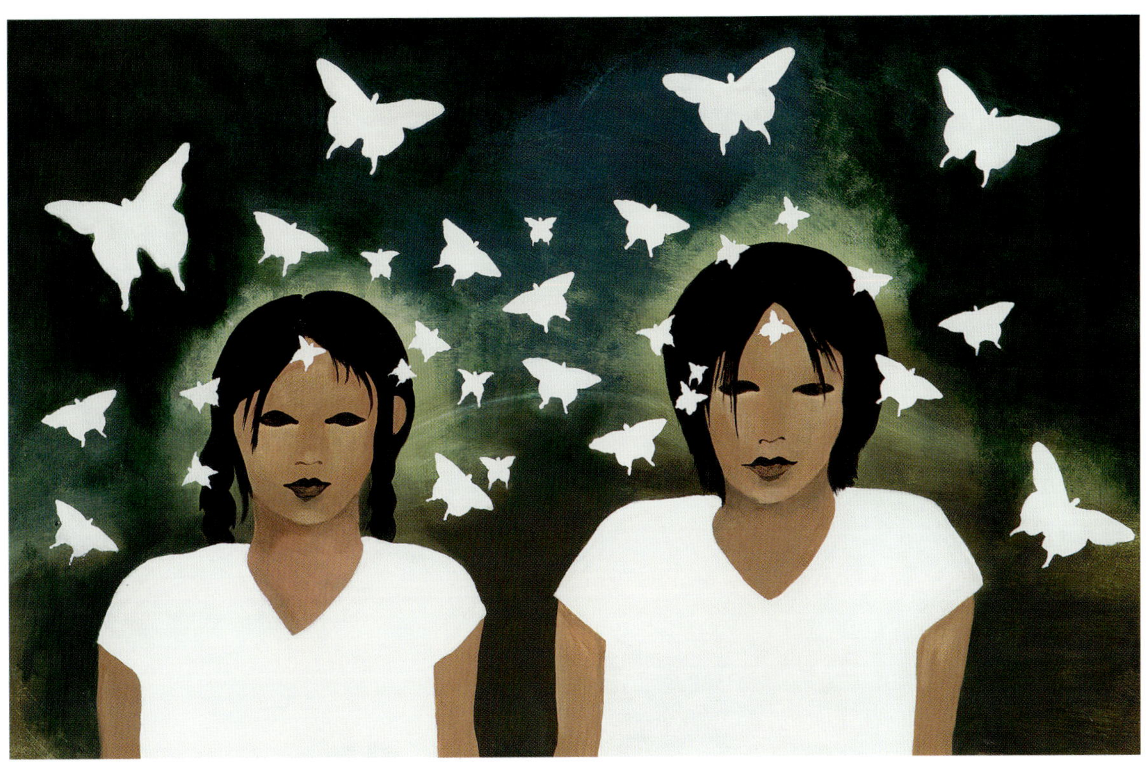

PLATE 66 Selina Farmer (Cherokee), *Butterflies in December*, 1998, acrylic on canvas, 47 in. × 71, 1.5 in., MoCNA Collection, CHE-106 (photo by Jason S. Ordaz).

PLATE 67 Maxine Gachupin (Jemez Pueblo), *Pueblo Dance*, ca. 1964–1968, mixed media on paper, 31 in. × 21.5 in., MoCNA Collection, J-66 (photo by Jason S. Ordaz).

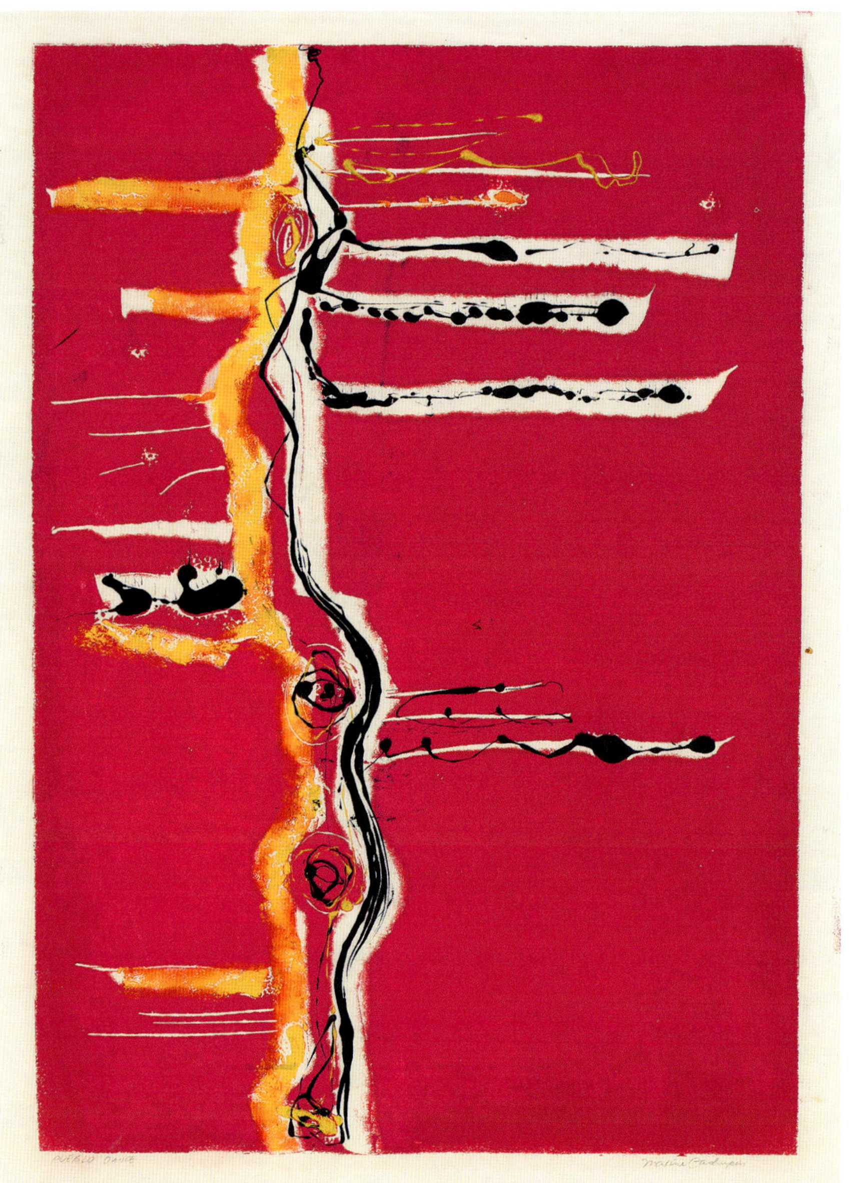

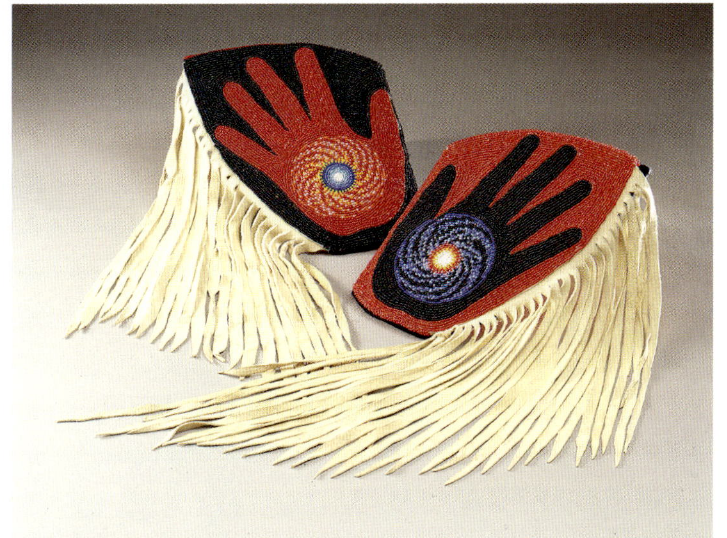

PLATE 68 Marcus Amerman (Choctaw), *Fringed Cuffs*, 1980, beads, wool, buckskin, 20.5 in. × 18.5 in., MoCNA Collection, CHO-33 (photo by Walter BigBee).

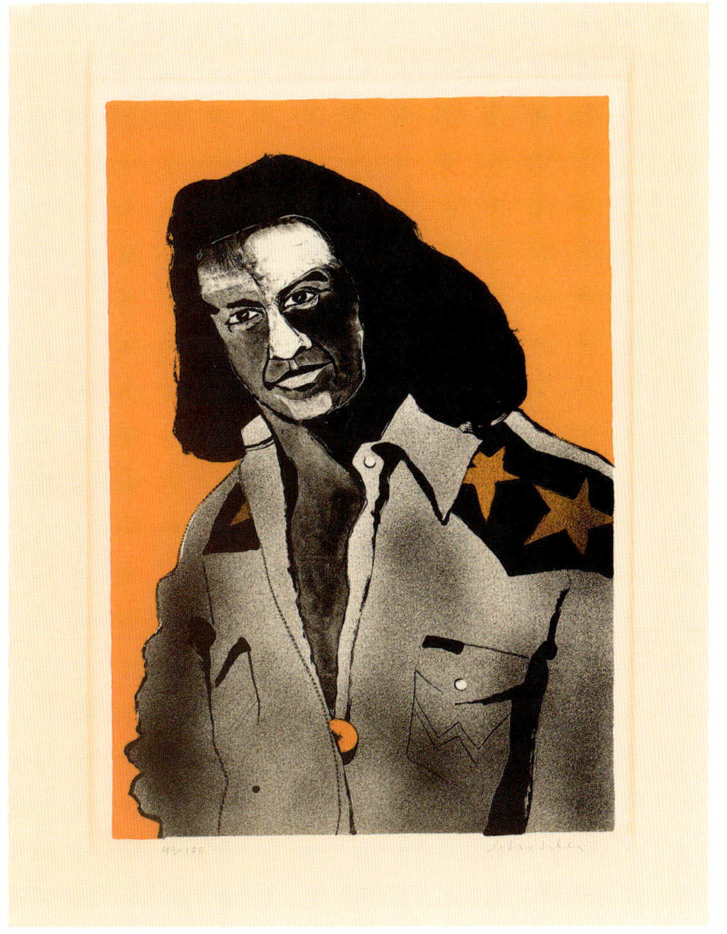

PLATE 69 Fritz Scholder (Luiseño), *Artist at 40 as a Buffalo*, Edition 43/100, 1977, lithograph on paper, 30.25 in. × 22.5 in., MoCNA Collection, MS-58 (photo by Jason S. Ordaz).

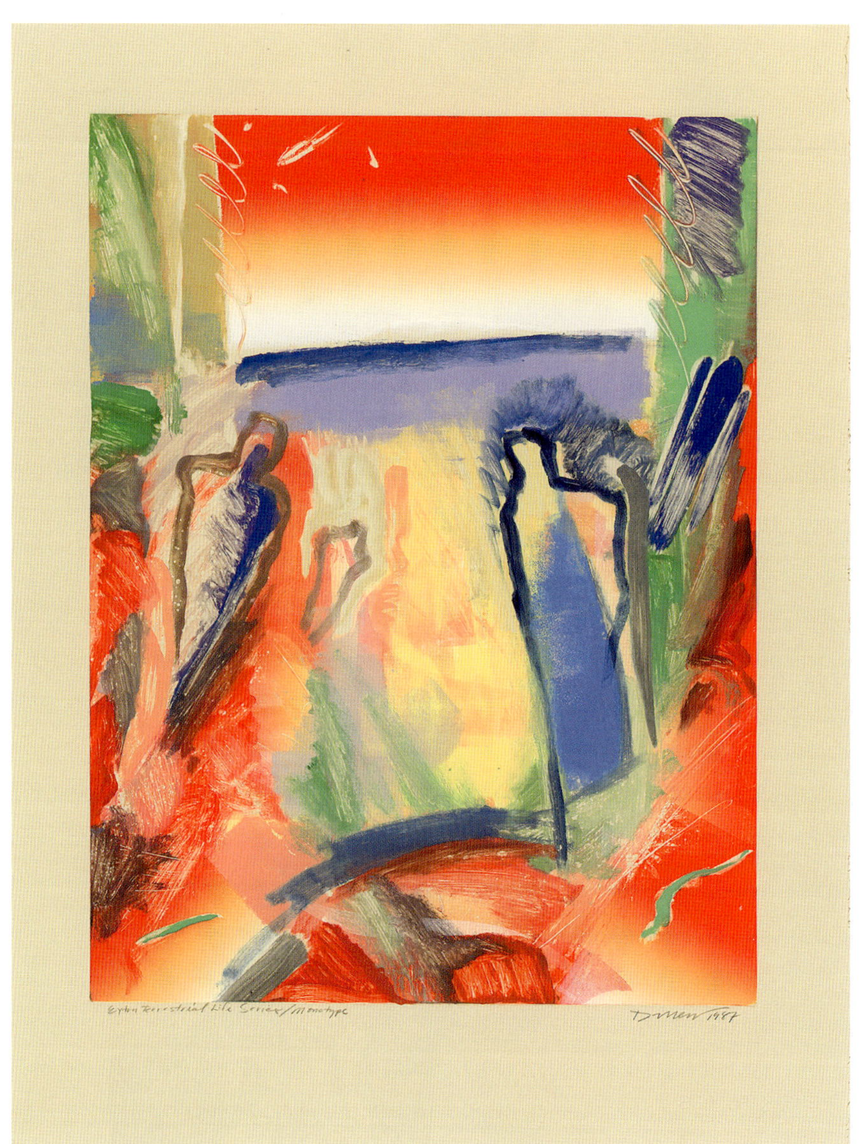

PLATE 70 Darren Vigil Gray (Jicarilla Apache/Kiowa Apache), *Extra-Terrestrial Life Series*, 1987, monotype on paper, 23.5 in. × 17.5 in., MoCNA Collection, A-212 (photo by Jason S. Ordaz).

"No Rules Make Art"

THE WORK OF C. MAXX STEVENS

PATSY PHILLIPS

C. Maxx Stevens was one of the few Native female conceptual artists creating works in the early 1970s. Not many Native women in general were producing art in this genre when it emerged as an art form in the 1960s. In conceptual art all the planning and decisions are made before the work is created. As defined by the Museum of Modern Art, "The idea itself, even if it is not made visual, is as much of a work of art as any finished product."[1] In other words, the idea is as important as the actual work. Conceptual artists often rejected museums and galleries as defining experts and saw themselves as the authority in their art. Although Stevens enjoys the entire creative process—from developing the idea and choosing materials to setting up the installations—the practice of imagining the work in her mind is paramount. She takes a year or more from concept to completion to create a new installation.

This chapter focuses on biography as a means to understand C. Maxx Stevens's art practice and creative life. I will demonstrate how she identifies issues and topics to create artistic installations that are true to her Native life and culture. I will show how Stevens's health and familial relations are integrated throughout her artwork. This essay is intended to encourage students to interview and document the stories of their grandparents, parents, relatives, artists, and friends. Tell their stories. Native peoples' stories need to be told. To illustrate biography, I am writing about Stevens, an important conceptual Native artist who has practiced art for over forty years. I will demonstrate how to write a story and make suggestions on how to interview your subjects. For example, to prepare for my interview with Stevens, I read everything written about her in catalogs and articles, studied her body of art, and drafted a list of questions. I then spent two days in April 2017 interviewing her in person at the IAIA Museum of Contemporary Native Arts in Santa Fe, New Mexico. I recorded the interviews and then transcribed them.[2] I followed up with questions in emails and met with her again when we both

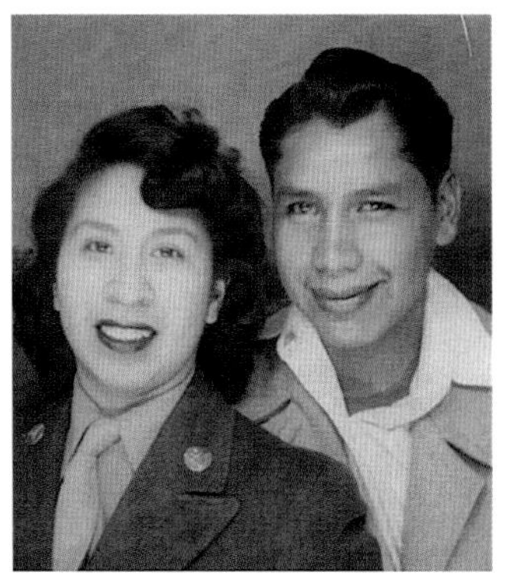

FIGURE 63 Family portrait, late 1940s, C. Maxx Steven's mother Wisey Goat and father Tommy Stevens, artist's collection.

attended a national gathering of Native artists and administrators at the Eiteljorg Museum in Indianapolis in November 2017.

To understand her artwork, it is essential to know her personal story. C. Maxx Stevens was born in Wewoka, Oklahoma in 1951. She is the third oldest of nine children and they are a close family. Her father died in 1982 at the age of sixty-six and her mother died in 2016 at ninety-three years old (figure 63).

When she was five years old, Stevens's family moved to Plainview, Kansas, a small suburb near Wichita, for her father to work as a mechanic at Boeing, an aerospace company. Wichita in the 1950s was an urban center for tribal people of many different backgrounds due to the Indian Relocation Act of 1956.[3] This was not a forced relocation like the Indian Removal Act of 1830.[4] Instead, the Relocation Act encouraged Indians to move voluntarily from their reservations to major cities such as Los Angeles, New York, Chicago, and Wichita for better jobs and housing; however, most Native families found worse conditions in cities far away from their homelands. The relocation program was assimilationist in nature and was intended to separate Indian people from their extended families and their own tribal communities, thus losing their languages and cultures. This program backfired in many respects, as Native people from a variety of cultural backgrounds found solace and relationships in a broader multitribal community. Growing up around many different tribal people, Stevens developed a strong sense of who she was as a Native woman, despite living away from her homelands.

Stevens showed an inclination toward the arts as early as the second grade, when she began creating posters, papier-mâché forms, and drawings. Teachers encouraged her to be an artist and her parents always told her, "Whatever you do is fine." None of Stevens's early work stands out to her, nor did she keep any art from elementary through high school. She believes her creativity began to develop when she studied under Southern Cheyenne artist Richard "Dick" West Sr. at Haskell Indian Junior College (now Haskell Indian Nations University) in Lawrence, Kansas. West is the father of W. Richard West Jr., the founding director (1990 to 2007) of the Smithsonian's National Museum of the American Indian. Stevens attended Haskell from 1970 to 1972 and earned an Associate of Arts degree in Indian Art. She began as a painter, but soon changed with the encouragement of mentor and teacher West, himself a professional artist. He noticed that Stevens struggled at painting and did not enjoy it. Her creativity took a new direction when West assigned her a studio and encouraged her to experiment with three-dimensional art.

West taught students to "Not do the kind of generic Indian art that's taken from different tribes. Look at who you are. Know your own culture," Stevens tells me. He would reprimand some artists who were using images from other tribes, saying, "That's not your tribe, you don't know their customs."[5] She took his advice literally and looked at who she was as a Seminole woman. Stevens quickly learned that she enjoyed creating ideas opposed to painting them. She had entered Haskell as a painter, but graduated working in three-dimensional conceptual and sculptural art. Since those early days at Haskell, she has forged her own direction, always experimenting with new ideas and concepts.

For her entire career, Stevens has examined "issues of identity: her own identity, how it relates to roles within her family and her community and in particular, how it speaks to the role of women."[6] Her work is directly related to all aspects of her life as a Native woman connected to her Seminole culture. To understand the significance of Stevens's art, it is important to know what was going on in the Native art world when she entered it in the 1970s. Established in 1962, the Institute of American Indian Arts (IAIA) is considered one of the most important Native art centers in the nation. At IAIA, Native artists are encouraged to explore new themes and consider new art forms without expectation of, for example, depicting romantic scenes of Great Plains Indians in headdresses on horseback. Artists began painting realistic Natives and showing their conditions of the day.

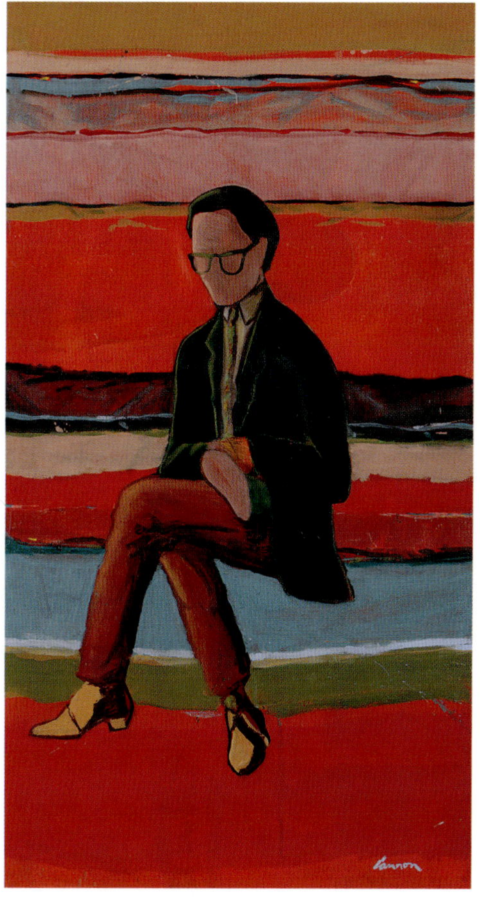

FIGURE 64 T. C. Cannon (Caddo/Kiowa), *Instructor In Green*, ca. 1966, acrylic, oil on canvas, 73.5 in. × 39 in., MoCNA Collection, CD 3, (photo by Addison Doty).

Tommy Wayne ("TC") Cannon (1946–1978), an enrolled member of the Kiowa Tribe, was an IAIA student in the 1970s and an important Native American artist of the twentieth century. One of Cannon's most famous paintings is of his IAIA mentor, Fritz Scholder, titled *Instructor in Green* (1967, figure 64). In this work, Scholder is sporting a modern suit, tie, and pointed shoes. He wears bold eyeglass frames, but his face is blank, with no eyes, nose, or mouth. He could be anyone, Native or non-Native. The background is painted in horizontal vibrant colors of the Southwest such as yellow, green, and orange. If the viewer didn't know the artist and the subject, the painting would not be identifiably by or about a Native person. It may not seem like it today, but in the 1970s this work was cutting-edge. Up to this point in Native art history, artists were not painting such contemporary images or showing realistic Indians of their own day.

When Stevens first began creating conceptual installations, she was not considered an Indian artist. People have said to her over the years when viewing her art, "I don't see Indian in it." She told me that once, a critic wrote, "Stevens doesn't do Native themes."[7] A member of the Seminole Tribe of Oklahoma and a descendant of the Creek Muskogee, Stevens proclaims, "I'm full blood, can't be any more Indian than that."[8] Because she was not pigeonholed as a Native artist, Stevens had the freedom to explore different art forms and themes to find her voice. It was not until she moved to Santa Fe in the 1990s that Natives and non-Natives started to understand and appreciate her work. She thinks audiences in Santa Fe are better educated to understand contemporary Native art. Stevens prefers that audiences who view her work be sensitive to different cultures even if they cannot relate to being Native. Stevens has been able to stay true to her artistic vision because her livelihood does not depend on selling her work. Full-time teaching posts have allowed her to take time to create works and not be bound to selling them to survive. Among other institutions, Stevens has taught at the IAIA, the Rhode Island School of Design, and the University of Colorado at Boulder, from which she retired in 2019 and is now emeritus faculty.

> "The world begins at a kitchen table."
> JOY HARJO / *The Woman Who Fell from the Sky*

Stevens's favorite conceptual installation is a piece she produced in 1994 titled *Aunt Nelly: My Story* (figure 65). This work encompasses many aspects of the artist's ideals. It is a personal and cultural tribute to her favorite aunt and to the Seminole tribe. Aunt Nelly was a strong Native woman who taught her niece "how the Native community was like a family and how sharing times with others was important and spiritually nourishing."[9] Stevens recalls fond memories of sitting around Aunt Nelly's table listening to the elders speak in their language. The installation features a dirt-covered platform with a vacant chair placed next to a square table. Empty chairs typically represent the deceased in Stevens's installations. The table signifies the gathering place for family to talk and make decisions. Wild onions from her tribal homeland in Oklahoma sit in a bowl and are scattered on the table. Placed on the table are four tin cups of coffee. The cups are filled at varying degrees, as if the

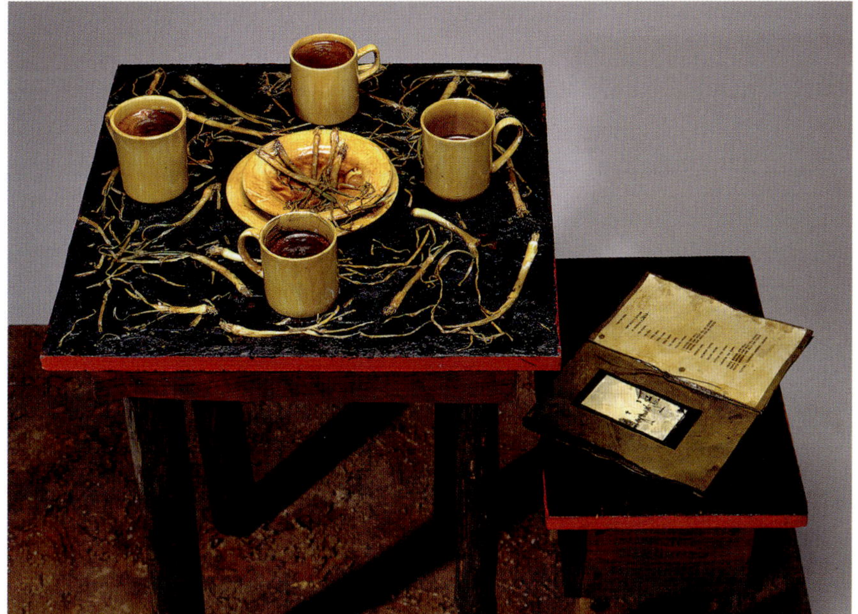

FIGURE 65 C. Maxx Stevens (Seminole/Muscogee Nation of Oklahoma), *Aunt Nelly: My Story*, 1994, Multimedia temporary installation, 5 in. × 8 in. × 8 in., Courtesy of the Heard Museum Billie Jane Baguley Library and Archives RC43(1):23.1 (photo by Craig Smith).

people will come back to finish them. Perhaps they are deceased, but their ideals linger like the coffee in the cups and the wild onions on the table. Resting on a chair is a photo album of her father's family. Stevens laughs when she tells me that when this exhibition was on view at the Heard Museum in Phoenix, Arizona, a curator called to let her know that the wild onions were continuing to grow even though they'd been varnished with shellac. Stevens said, "Let them grow."

Aunt Nelly: My Story symbolizes memories of growing up in the Seminole ways. Stevens respects Aunt Nelly as a warrior for her strength and independence. She believes that one can make the decision to be a warrior or follower. A warrior is a leader. Aunt Nelly was a warrior and Stevens is a warrior like her. Stevens, like Aunt Nelly, is an independent thinker and leader of her day. Aunt Nelly led her Seminole family, while Stevens is a leader in conceptual art.

> "Polio made me who I am, an individual.
> I see things in a different way."
> C. MAXX STEVENS

Stevens contracted polio at the time of her birth. Polio is a crippling and potentially deadly infectious disease caused by the poliomyelitis virus. The virus spreads from person to person and can invade an infected individual's brain

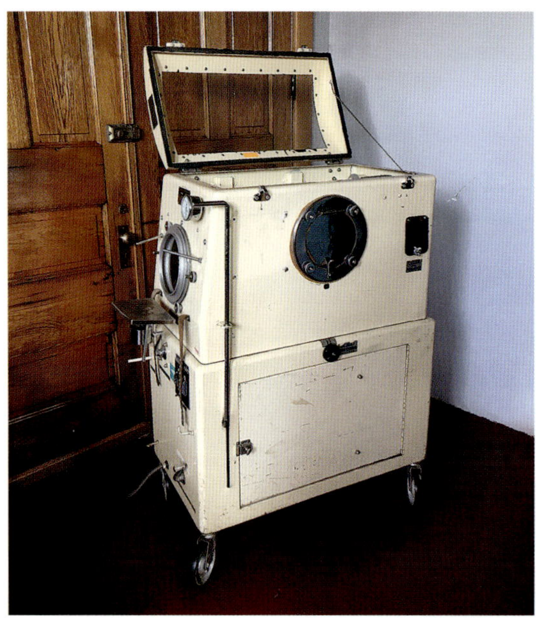

FIGURE 66 Children's Iron Lung, Courtesy of Indiana Medical History Museum.

and spinal cord, causing paralysis.[10] When Stevens was born in 1951, there was no vaccine for polio. Today, the disease is mostly eradicated except in some developing countries. Stevens was *100 percent* paralyzed at six months old and an iron lung machine (figure 66) kept her alive by breathing for her. Polio upset Stevens's parents so much that they wouldn't speak about it, even as she grew older. Only once, she says, her "Mum said how I was a tiny baby in this big machine and all she could see was her baby's head sticking out of the iron lung."[11] Stevens's mother told her the trauma of those years gave her gray hair when she was still a young mother. Although her parents never mentioned how many surgeries she had as a child, Stevens counts three major scars on her body. She believes she is comfortable visiting friends and family members in hospitals today because she spent so much time in them when she was young.

The polio virus left Stevens's right leg shorter and weaker than the left and she walks with a slight limp. She wore a brace until she was twelve years old. The day I interviewed her, she was wearing hot-pink patent-leather high-top Doc Martin boots. She owns these same boots in black and red. She likes to wear bright socks with her colorful boots. Her sisters laugh and ask, "Why do you wear the strangest shoes and socks?" Stevens replies, "If people are going to look at me, they may as well look at something special." In recognition of polio, Stevens created *Childhood* (figure 67). The dress is made of paper, pigment, wood, and electrical components. A crow in flight is backlit at the heart of the dress. Frequently present in Stevens's life and work, the crow is both a messenger and protector. Due to her many childhood surgeries and hospitalizations, Stevens has few memories of when she was young. She uses old photos and fragile materials such as paper to suggest the imperfection of memories. Stevens donated this work to the Minneapolis Institute of Art in 2019. The disease made her stronger, she tells me. Growing up with polio, she found commonality with other Native and non-Native children in her neighborhood who had this condition. She never considered herself different, but always felt accepted. Her parents sent her to the local Shriners polio camp in the summers, where she met and played with other children with this syndrome. "As a polio survivor, this experience shaped the way I think and gave me a sense of gratitude to be alive," Stevens stresses.[12]

“Crows keep me grounded”

C. MAXX STEVENS

Crows are common characters in Stevens’s life and art. To the Seminole, the crow represents both a messenger and an observer. “Wherever I go, crows come around,” she says.[13] The bird reminds Stevens to reconnect to the knowledge of her ancestors and her own past. Crows are both positive and negative agents, and have communicated with Stevens for her entire life. At IAIA, Stevens was a teacher from 1991 to 1996 and an academic dean from 2002 to 2005. In the latter period, she lived near the old IAIA campus located

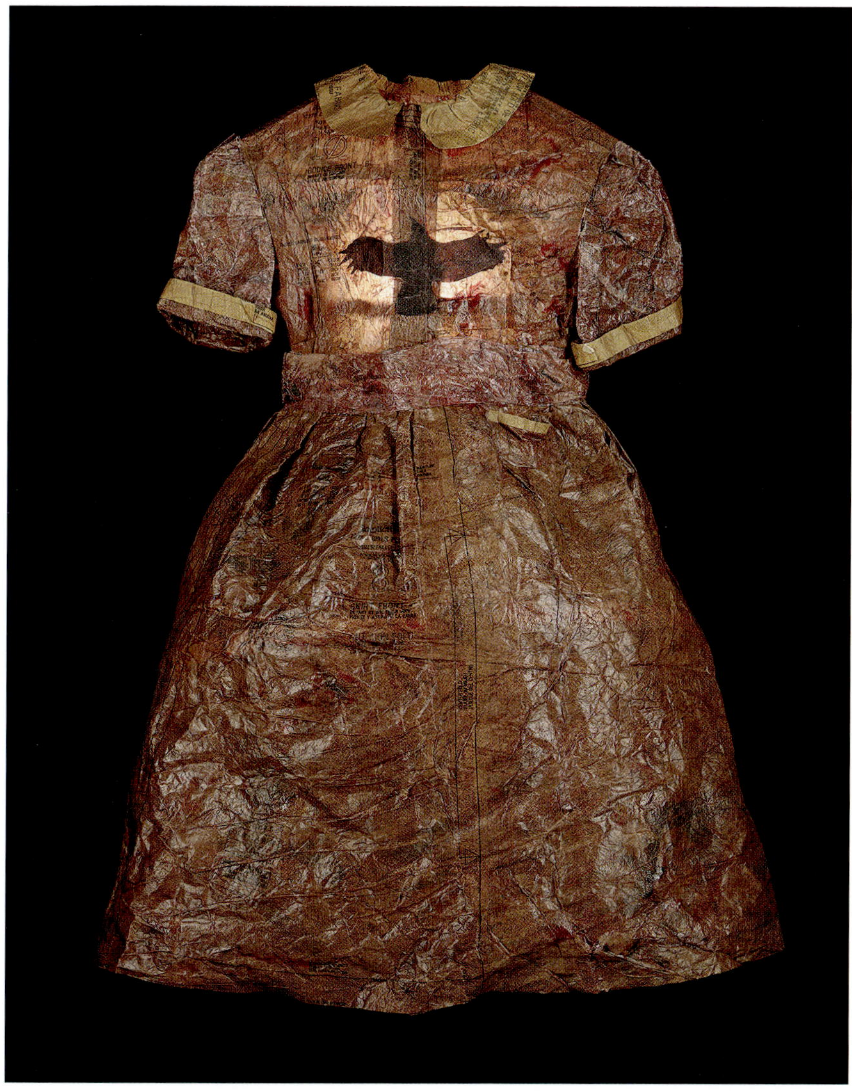

FIGURE 67 C. Maxx Stevens (Seminole/Muscogee Nation of Oklahoma), *Childhood*, 2004, paper, pigment, wood, electrical components, light bulb, 40 in. × 25 in. × 14 in., Minneapolis Institute of Art, Gift of C. Maxx Stevens, 2019.4, © C. Maxx Stevens (photo by Dan Dennehy).

on St. Michael's Road in Santa Fe, New Mexico. She has never learned how to drive a car, but rides a bike or walks everywhere. One day in 2004, when Stevens was on her way to school, she started to take a shortcut across a field, looking down as she walked. The crows began squawking loudly at her—*Caw, Caw, Caw*. The volume of their calls caused her to look up. In the middle of the field, she saw an ominous-looking man. She felt intuitively that he was dangerous, quickly turned around, and did not walk through the field that day. She credits the crows for warning her and possibly saving her from harm. "Crows always know what's going on," she tells me.

> "Objects are my voice."
> C. MAXX STEVENS

Stevens believes that objects can speak the same way people do. She often reveals who she is through her work. She tells me she is a very quiet person and needs objects to be her voice. Stevens selects stories from her own life and experiences. "My family is a major part of who I am," states Stevens. "I'm shy. People don't believe me after you get to know me. When you first meet me, I don't say anything. Just observe." She creates works specifically for Natives because she believes they share her perspectives, such as respect for life and cultures. She considers what is related to being Native before beginning a new work. Sometimes her subjects are universal and non-Natives can connect to them, but her underlying theme is always from a Native perspective. Her work reflects her own life and social realities that hurt deeply. In her own words, "I constantly work to remain true to my cultural heritage and my sense of self. Memories and issues from my personal experience and specifically my life within the Native American culture are always my starting point."[14] She created *House of Constant Rotation* (figure 68) in 2010 to remind herself to stay true to her identity. A bird cage measuring 10' × 4' × 4' symbolizes containment, both physical and emotional. A crow spins on a record player in its center. As it spins, it pecks a photo of Stevens (one side showing her in a traditional Seminole skirt and the other in a black dress). Every time the crow comes around, it touches the photo to remind her that she is a Native woman—a cue to reconnect to the knowledge of her ancestors and her past. She created this work to tell herself to never forget that she is a Seminole woman first. Art and objects speak to and for Stevens.

Ideas for works come to Stevens through her dreams. She typically starts off with a vague idea, draws a little, but doesn't try to figure it out. She says it

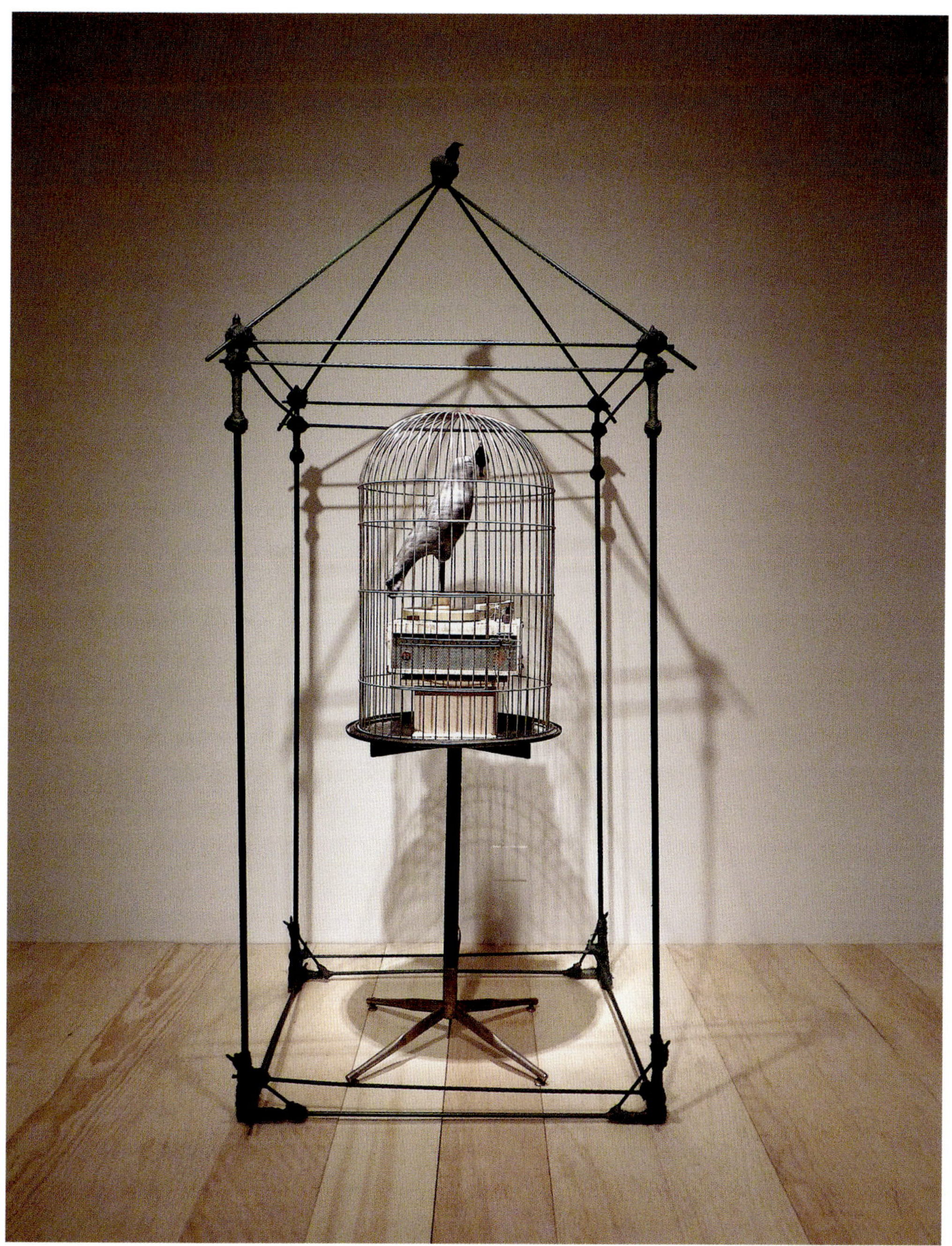

FIGURE 68 C. Maxx Stevens (Seminole/Muscogee Nation of Oklahoma), *House of Constant Rotation*, 2010, decoy, record player, bird cage, plant stake, 10 ft. × 4 ft. × 4 ft., Courtesy of the Smithsonian National Museum of the American Indian.

comes to her eventually and naturally. For her whole life, she has dreamed almost every night, and she remembers details. She accepts her dreams as a second life. "They're just there," she says. In her adult life, she has had a recurring dream where she lives in an apartment on the second floor of an old building in Wichita, Kansas. Crows sit on top of the trees outside her apartment to watch over her. Stevens is shy even in her dreams. Neighbors will come by to visit, but she won't open the door. She can identify them by their shoes from a six-inch gap between the door and the floor. Stevens does not know this apartment or the neighbors in her conscious life, but accepts them as part of her world. Stevens says that by the time she starts a new work, it feels complete because she has dreamed it, imagined it, and identified the materials. She then physically pulls it all together.

Perhaps Stevens's dreams are what sets her apart from other artists. She believes that her ancestors speak to her and give her ideas in her sleep. She doesn't just observe her dreams, but figures them out. Stevens respects, honors and listens to her dreams as if she is listening to her ancestors. She asks herself what their messages are, what she needs to learn. As the crow reminds her to reconnect to the knowledge of her ancestors, dreams remind her to pay attention. Her ancestors ask her, for example, to tell stories that need to be told about Native peoples—stories about diabetes, about Indian boarding schools, about issues of identity, about languages and cultures lost. Listening to her dreams brings about great works of art about Native peoples.

> "Materials speak for me"
> C. MAXX STEVENS

"Art is ephemeral like my life," says Stevens.[15] Her work is not made to last because of the natural biodegradable materials she uses. She makes installations based on time—time in her life and time in terms of materials that won't last forever. Over time, the artworks disintegrate. She collects found objects such as twigs, vines, branches, and horsehair for art installations. She includes old and faded photographs, used clothing, and items she finds at garage sales and secondhand stores. Stevens's favorite material to work with is dirt. Dirt represents Seminole land. She likes to work in the studio at night from 7:00 p.m. until as late as 2:00 a.m. depending on the project. She creates installations in parts and, other than in her mind, never sees them come together until they are installed.

Lighting is another important component to Stevens's work. When she was at Haskell, she worked in the summers at the Wichita Music Theatre and the Lawrence Community Theatre, where she built sets and learned how to light them. Working with choreographers and lighting designers, she learned about space and how light can affect a piece. The right lighting finishes her work, she tells me.

I asked Stevens who inspired her as a young artist and she explained that the Dada artistic movement of the twentieth century had a great effect on her career. Dada was a European artistic and literary movement (ca. 1916–1924) that dismissed conventional aesthetics and produced works that were absurd and nonsensical and/or lacked harmony.[16] Essentially, Dada artists revolted against traditional art and Western society. They rejected conventional concepts of beauty. In other words, artists were free to create without regard to traditions. Stevens likes the way Dadaism opened how art was produced and seen. She appreciates that anything could be art to the Dadaist. Artists during this period lived in the moment. Stevens sees this movement as one where "no rules make art"—a premise she lives by today. When I asked who inspired her in the Native art world, Rebecca Belmore came immediately to her mind.[17] A Canadian Anishinaabe Native and a multidisciplinary artist, Belmore addresses history, place, and identity through the media of sculpture, installation, video, and performance. She confronts stereotypes about First Nations people and highlights unresolved burdens of social justice. Belmore is particularly notable for politically conscious and socially aware performance and installation work.[18] In 2005, Belmore was the first Aboriginal woman to represent Canada at the Venice Biennale. Belmore's work is representational of social realities for all peoples. Stevens appreciates and understands the elements of social issues represented in Belmore's work. Stevens's works also deal with social issues. She, like Belmore, challenges people to reconsider what they know about Aboriginal and Indigenous peoples.

> "My relatives were sick and dying from diabetes."
> C. MAXX STEVENS

The number one health issue in Native communities, next to suicide, is diabetes. As the director of the IAIA Museum of Contemporary Native Arts, I never anticipated buying a shrine to diabetes, although the disease runs in my family. In August 2011, MoCNA opened Stevens's exhibition *Last Supper* (figure 69), a site-specific conceptual installation that points to the negative effect of poor nutrition and how food is having a detrimental impact on Native peoples. The artist builds a visual narrative based on private and public memories and experiences to deal with the devastating effect of diabetes

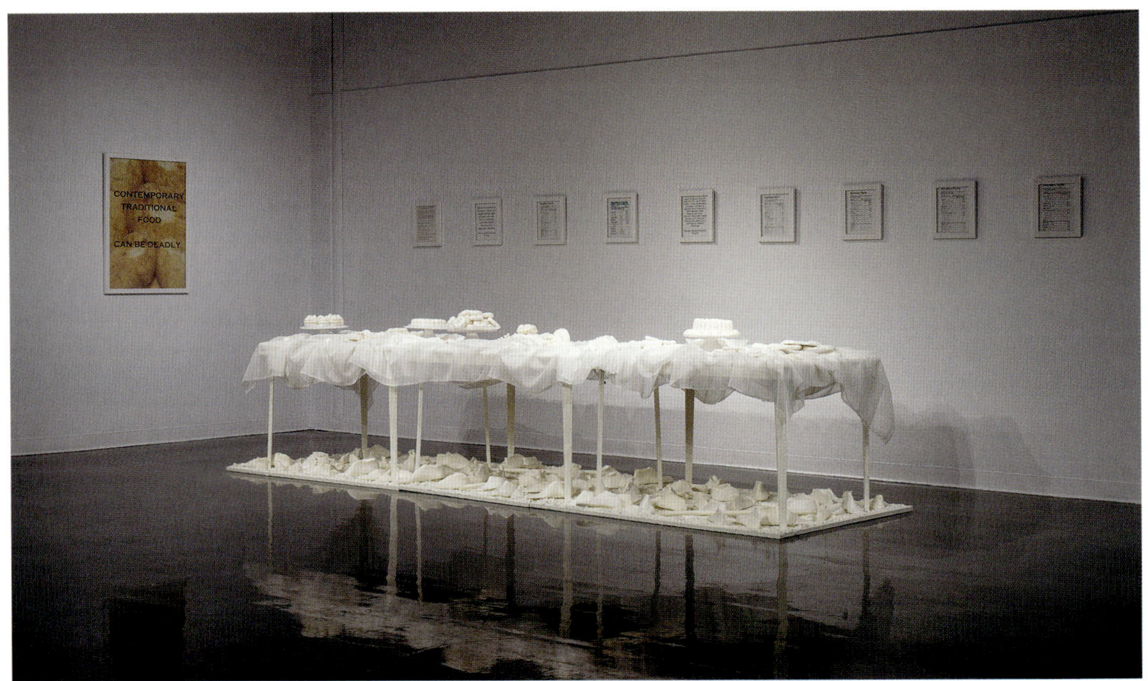

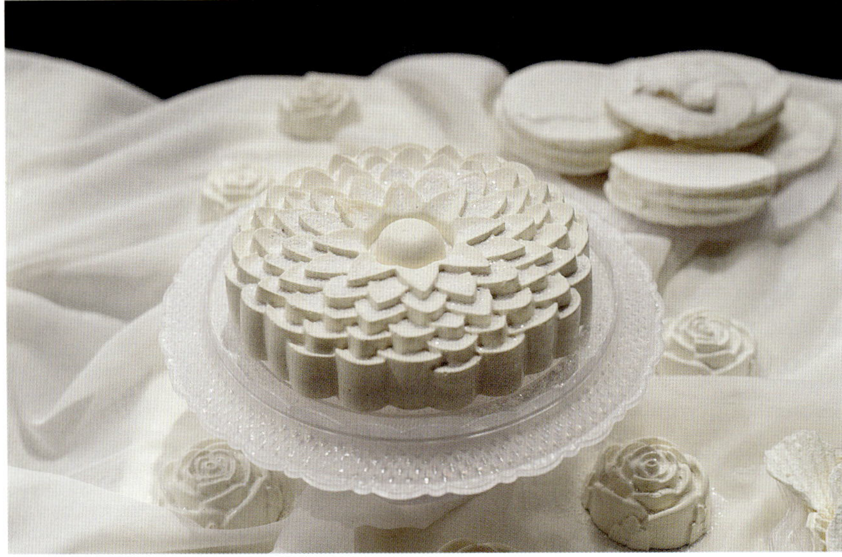

FIGURE 69 C. Maxx Stevens (Seminole/Muscogee Nation of Oklahoma), *Last Supper*, 2011, acrylic resin, glitter, sand, digital prints, wood, tables, canvas, paint, polyester table cloth, cotton curtains, audio, 10 ft. × 20 ft. × 20 ft., MoCNA Collection, SE 94 (photo by John Joe).

FIGURE 70 C. Maxx Stevens (Seminole/Muscogee Nation of Oklahoma), Detail from *Last Supper*, MoCNA Collection, SE 94 (photo by John Joe).

throughout the Native nations. She creates a larger social awareness of the epidemic and its dilemma in the United States. The mixed-media installation includes her family archives and testimonies about the disease and its impact on Native peoples.

As a conceptual work, it was not obvious that *Last Supper* was about diabetes until it was examined closely. As I walked into the gallery that held this work, I saw only the whiteness of the installation. Everything in the room—the floor, the walls, the curtains, the table, the tablecloth, and the framed photos—was white. Molds of pastries, pizzas, pretzels, French fries that lay on the table were white, with shattered glass sprinkled over them that glittered. I heard crows flying overhead—*Caw, Caw, Caw*. As I looked more closely at the platform under the table, I saw canes and amputated feet painted white with glittering glass covering them. Tears came to my eyes the moment I realized this exhibition was about diabetes. I was grateful to be alone in the gallery. I thought of my mother and two sisters who have this disease. I thought of my extended Cherokee family—many who have died from it. My Aunt May's legs were amputated and she lost her eyesight and eventually her life. I cried for my family, for Natives, and for all people who have diabetes.

Stevens created *Last Supper* with the hope of helping people become aware of their diets to avoid diabetes and to live longer. She believes people can relate to the installation because many are addicted to processed food—something she calls "White Death."[19] The food is so treated that there are no healthy ingredients left by the time it ends up on our shelves. Growing up, Stevens says, everyone ate processed foods, nothing healthy. She intentionally placed enticing foods on the table to attract the viewer (see figure 70). To make the small, beautiful, alluring food sculptures, she purchased hamburgers, doughnuts, French fries, cupcakes, and other foods from Walmart, McDonalds, and Burger King to cast molds. Initially, Stevens created the foods out of wax, but to make the components sturdy enough to travel, she re-created them in resin. She also replaced the sparkling shattered glass with a glittering white sand.

Stevens herself developed diabetes in 2014, a few years after she created this installation. She has always taken care of her health by paying attention to food labels and exercising regularly. She says, "When I got diabetes, I realized it's more than eating healthy."[20] She believes the disease is a manifestation of the trauma that Native people have gone through: that diabetes is in the DNA and the body remembers. With all of her family members but one diabetic, she says it was a matter of time before she too would become diabetic, no matter how well she has taken care of herself.

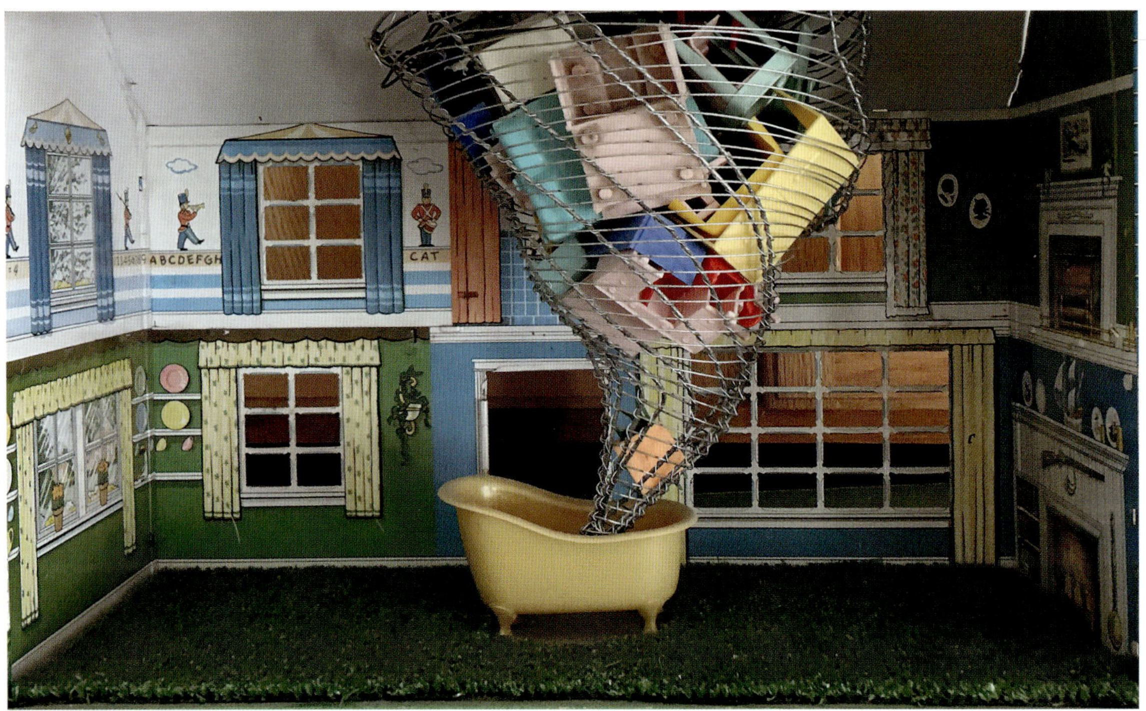

FIGURE 71 C. Maxx Stevens (Seminole/Muscogee Nation of Oklahoma), *Wichita House*, 2019, 14 in. × 18-1/2 in. × 8 in., Collection of Melanie Yazzie (photo by C. Maxx Stevens).

During the time *Last Supper* was on view at the museum, we hosted a reception in honor of Associate Justice of the Supreme Court of the United States Sonia Sotomayor. I personally gave her a tour of this exhibition. As art can do, it inspired a conversation. Justice Sotomayor told me she has diabetes and spoke about how moved she was by this poignant show. On her way out, she exclaimed, "This exhibition needs to travel." She suggested that there was an urgent need to educate Native and non-Native communities about this potentially deadly disease. The museum purchased *Last Supper* with plans to take it to Indian Country—to communities that experience diabetes in high numbers.

C. Maxx Stevens married Randal Julian Stevens in 2019. They live with their pug dog named Nelly Jo-Jo in Wichita, Kansas. At this writing, she is working on a piece that includes dirt from her mother's burial: she took a handful and put it in her pocket. Describing the new work in progress, she says, "Mom's dirt is on the bottom, the second layer is zinc, and on top are rawhide rattles. The three layers symbolize a final resting place, life, and the spiritual realm." She is also making doll houses with small private installations (figure 71). "House is who you are," she believes. They are personal. The doll house series are little worlds with small rooms that make statements with things. As soon as she creates a new doll house, it is sold.

I asked Stevens what advice she has for young artists just starting out. She tells them to "Become unafraid, work, focus, take risks and don't get boxed in. Students get stuck in what traditional sculpture is. If I did I wouldn't be doing what I do." When her students have "crazy" ideas, she examines the concepts with them, but never tells them they can't pursue them. Parents do that, she tells me, but she counsels students, "Do what you want and don't worry about being poor for a while. Play around with ideals until something really works and you feel good about it." Young people now are too busy with their computers, the artist says. She enjoys sitting, talking, and laughing with students. Teaching gets her out of the studio and out of her home. She likes getting students excited about art, telling them to "listen to the crows . . . watch the winds . . . listen to the elders . . . watch for signs . . . honor their past and themselves."[21] Stevens maintains a sense of humor. She still gets nervous at the start of class and once, when she was introducing herself, she said, "Hello. My name is Maxx Stevens and my tribe is Cinnamon Roll." She was, of course, referencing her tribe, Seminole, but it came out like a pastry. Stories like this are endearing and I believe her students appreciate her humor and kindness.

For over four decades, Stevens has followed her ideals as an artist. She was a leader in conceptual installation art at a time when few Native women were working in this genre. She is still creating thoughtful conceptual works of art. Her self-assuredness in her art and in herself is a direct result of a solid and loving support system she received growing up with her Native grandparents, parents, siblings, and extended family. Stevens says her whole family is good and that she could never have asked for more than that. She has always had a strong sense of being Native and where she came from, even as a child. Polio had a profound effect on her life, but it doesn't define her. She began her art studies at a tribal college, where she was supported and gained confidence in her work. When she makes art, she thinks about what is related to being Native. "I constantly work to maintain true to my cultural heritage and my sense of self," she says.[22] Both Natives and non-Natives connect to works like *Last Supper*, where she addresses diabetes—a disease that crosses all boundaries. Stevens's underlying theme is always Native-based. Although she is an introvert, she tells the viewer who she is and about her experiences on earth through her art. Like artists before her, Stevens influences artists today. And, as she learned from Dick West, Stevens creates what she knows. She is an observer and her work speaks for her. Stevens observes like the crow.

Artist Biography Guidelines

1. Choose an artist you want to learn more about—someone who interests you.

2. Set up an appointment. If you have a deadline, it is better to set the appointment early in case the person is busy or not available. Be sure to let the interviewee know the reason for the interview, e.g., a class project.

3. Research. Read everything written about the artist. Look at his or her body of artwork. Be well prepared so that you don't cover material that has already been published about the artist.

4. Develop an interview outline. What are the topics you want to cover with this artist?

5. Draft a list of questions within the topic categories.

6. Have the interviewee sign a letter requesting permission to reproduce text and illustrations (see below).

7. Conduct the interview in person, if possible. If not, set up a teleconference call using a program such as Skype or Zoom.

8. Record the interview and take notes.

9. Interview in a quiet location, perhaps an office, a conference room, or your home.

10. Ask if you may follow up with additional questions later, if necessary.

11. Interview friends of the candidate, if possible.

12. Transcribe the interview. Do not leave anything out.

13. Write your paper based on your notes, the transcription, and your research.

Sample Letter Requesting Permission to Reproduce Text and Illustrations

Date: ....

To: ....

Re: Request Permission to Produce Text and Illustrations

Dear ....,

I request your permission to reprint the following material with nonexclusive world distribution rights and for use in all formats and promotional materials:

List title(s), artist name, dimensions, date, photographer

To make this work easily available to scholars, I would like to reprint this material in a forthcoming book presently entitled .... by ...., which is tentatively scheduled to be published by .... in ....

Thank you for your help. I look forward to your response.
Sincerely,

[Signature]

[Student Name]

Signature of rights holder: ....
Printed name of rights holder: ....
Date: ....

Artist Biography

C. Maxx Stevens earned an Associate of Arts in Indian Art, from Haskell Indian Junior College in 1972, a Bachelor of Fine Arts in Ceramic/Sculpture from Wichita State University in 1979, and a Master of Fine Arts in Sculpture from Indiana University in 1987.

Her solo exhibitions in major museums include *House of Memory*, National Museum of the American Indian (2012); *Sugar Heaven*, Lawrence Art Center (2011); *Last Supper*, IAIA Museum of Contemporary Native Arts (2011); *Figure and Circles*, C. N. Gorman Museum (2005); *UNVEILING*, Gordon Snelgrove Gallery (2003); *can't see the forest through the trees*, Boise Art Museum (2002); *Memories Past and Present*, North Eastern Art Gallery (2002); *Transitional Status*, MOBIUS Gallery (1999); *Crows Carries the Story*, Kansas University Union Gallery (1994); *Bodies and Walls*, Store Front Wickerpark (1989); *Seven Statements*, Alternative Space (1988); and *Fans, Installation No. 1 Exhibition*, Alternative Space (1987). She has participated in over 122 group exhibitions from 1985 to the present.

Stevens's work is in important collections such as the IAIA Museum of Contemporary Native Arts, the Library of Congress, the Brooklyn Art Library, the Smithsonian National Museum of the American Indian, the C. N. Gorman Museum, the Eiteljorg Museum of Indian Art, the Provecto Ace Print Collection (Buenos Aires, Argentina); and the Cork Printmakers Special Collection (Cork, Ireland). Stevens has taught sculpture at the Institute of American Indian Arts, White Mountain Academy of the Arts, Rhode Island School of Design, School of the Art Institute of Chicago, and Indiana University. Her art has been included in numerous catalogs and books, but she has never had a single catalog published about her art work. She has received numerous awards, fellowships, grants, and residencies. Stevens has given gallery talks, panel presentations, and artist presentations and served as visiting artist critic in universities and museums around the United States.

Stevens has been a recipient of many awards and honors such as 2005 Eiteljorg Fellowship Award from the Eiteljorg Museum in Indianapolis, Indiana, 2000 Artist Grant from the Andrea Frank Foundation in New York and in 1998 Sculptor Award from The Joan Mitchell Foundation, Inc. in New York. She has exhibited at numerous museums, including the C. N. Gorman Museum, University of California at Davis, Davis, California; Eiteljorg Museum of Indian Art, Indianapolis; Museum of Arts and Design, New York; Center for Contemporary Arts, Santa Fe, New Mexico; IAIA Museum of Contemporary Native Arts, Santa Fe, New Mexico; Gordon Snelgrove Gallery, University of Saskatchewan, Saskatoon, Saskatchewan, Canada; The Montana Museum of Art and Culture, Missoula, Montana; Boise Art Museum, Boise, Montana; Smithsonian National Museum of the American Indian, New York; and White Mountain Academy Gallery, Elliot Lake, Ontario, Canada.

NOTES

1. Museum of Modern Art, “Conceptual Art,” https://www.moma.org/learn/moma_learning/themes/conceptual-art.

2. C. Maxx Stevens, interview by Patsy Phillips, Institute of American Indian Arts, Museum of Contemporary Native Arts, April 14 and April 17, 2017.

3. National Archives, “American Indian Urban Relocation,” https://www.archives.gov/education/lessons/indian-relocation.html, published August 15, 2016.

4. Cherokee Nation, “Remember the Removal,” https://www.cherokee.org/about-the-nation/remember-the-removal/.

5. C. Maxx Stevens, interview.

6. Michelle McGeough. “C. Maxx Stevens,” in *Manifestations: New Native Art Criticism* (Santa Fe: Institute of American Indian Art, Museum of Contemporary Native Arts, 2011), 173.

7. C. Maxx Stevens, interview.

8. C. Maxx Stevens, interview.

9. Theresa Harlan, et al., *Watchful Eyes: Native American Women Artists* (Phoenix: Heard Museum, 1994), 32.

10. Centers for Disease Control and Prevention, “Global Health, What is Polio?,” https://www.cdc.gov/polio/about/.

11. C. Maxx Stevens, interview.

12. C. Maxx Stevens, email exchange, June 2017.

13. C. Maxx Stevens, interview.

14. C. Maxx Stevens, "Seeing One's Creative Process," *Expedition* 55, no. 3 (Winter 2013), https://www.penn.museum/sites/expedition/seeing-ones-creative-process/.

15. C. Maxx Stevens, interview.

16. Paul Trachtman, "A Brief History of Dada," *Smithsonian Magazine*, May 2006, https://www.smithsonianmag.com/arts-culture/dada-115169154/.

17. Justina M. Barnicke, "Rebecca Belmore, Review," *Art in America* 102, no. 9 (2014): 184–85.

18. Jessica Bradley and Jolene Rickard, *Rebecca Belmore: Fountain* (Vancouver, BC: Morris and Helen Belkin Art Gallery, 2005).

19. C. Maxx Stevens, interview.

20. C. Maxx Stevens, interview.

21. Gerald McMaster, "C. Maxx Stevens: If These Walls Could Talk: Environments That Tell Stories," in *Reservation X: The Power of Place in Aboriginal Contemporary Art*, ed. Gerald McMaster (Hull, QC: Canadian Museum of Civilization, 1998), 151.

22. Stevens, "Seeing One's Creative Process."

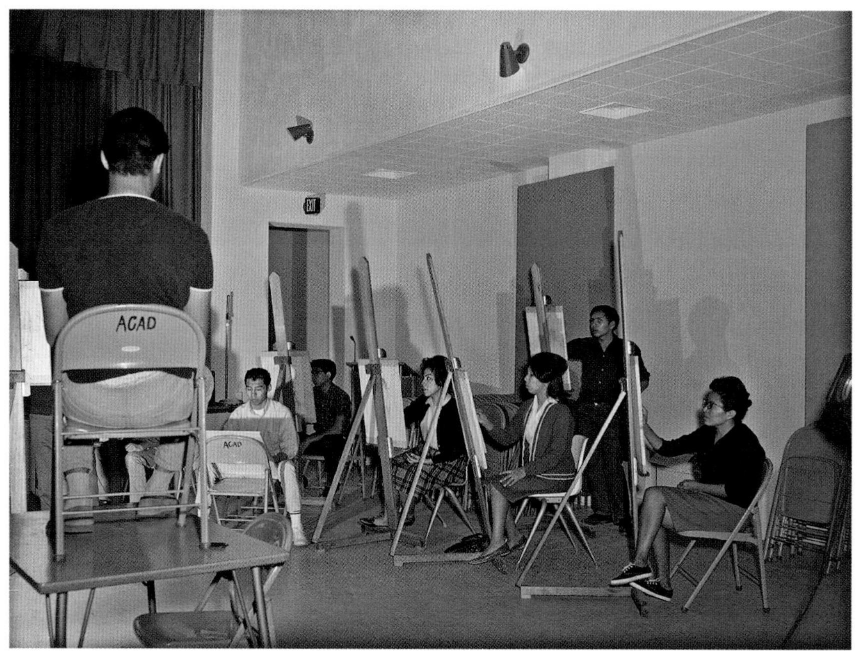

FIGURE 72 IAIA portrait class, 1963, photo by Kay V. Wiest, IAIA Archives (MS10.012.011).

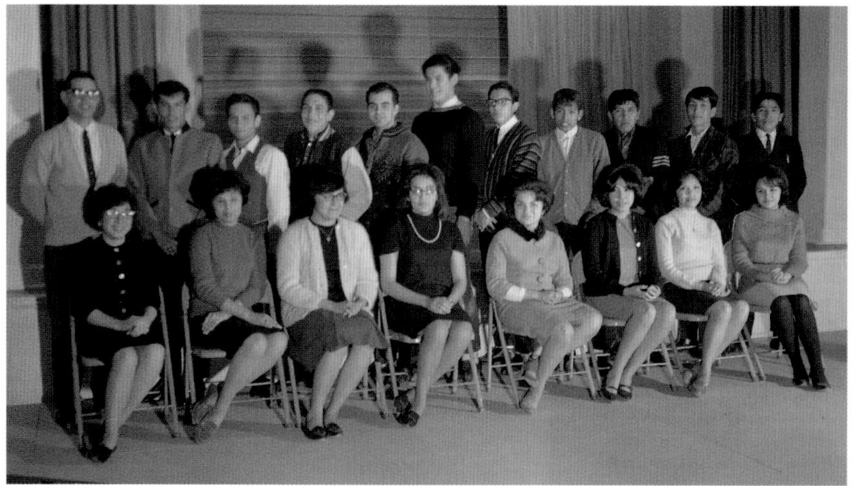

FIGURE 73 IAIA seniors, 1963, photo by Kay V. Wiest, IAIA Archives (MS10.028.001.01).

Historical Essays

About Professor Charles Dailey

JESSIE RYKER-CRAWFORD AND
STEPHEN C. FADDEN

There are scholars who, having made a vastly pronounced and positive impact in the field of Native American art and museology, are recognized through literature and laurels. A search of their names in bibliographical databases reveals a plethora of written materials testifying to their life's work.

And then there are others, extremely modest and discreet in their ways, who are only known through those who have had the immense honor to have crossed their paths. No less remarkable and inspiring, their glories and achievements have not been recognized adequately in written form. A huge debt of gratitude is owed to these seemingly invisible and nameless mentors.

Charles "Chuck" Dailey is one of the latter. This founder of the Institute of American Indian Arts (IAIA) Museum Studies Program (1971–2007), art historian, and prior director of the IAIA Museum, "Mr. D." (as he will always be lovingly called by his pupils) touched numerous lives throughout Indian Country as a passionate professor who guided hundreds of Native American students into becoming leaders in the professional fields of museums and the arts—fields that are so intertwined in our cultural heritage—and as a valued and insightful collaborator who has worked closely with tribal communities in their endeavors to form their own museums and cultural centers.

It is not surprising that the Institute of American Indian Arts was the birth of a museum studies and art history program "writ different." From the very beginning, its founders envisioned art, art history, and museum studies courses taught through a truly Indigenous lens. It was fortuitous that IAIA and Mr. D. found each other. For, beyond a vast knowledge of museology, this special man had an infectious passion for world art. Coupled with the ability to morph dry parchment text into epic drama through storytelling, he animated the artistic works and the people who created them. You knew that he loved the discipline, and he loved to share that with his students. He taught you to *think* about art rather than to simply *memorize* it.

Chuck recognized early on what other Native art writers would later describe: that Native American art has its own separate and distinct history from that of the West, and that it encompasses that history into its own telling, rather than acting as a mere appendage to the aesthetic study of the Western art world.

Buffy Dailey described how her father would instantly be recognized in tribal communities across the country. Once he was spotted in the powwow crowd, an honoring would be called for him and he would be showered with gratitude by those whose lives he had touched and changed. For he has touched many, too many to count. We are eternally grateful to this kind, humble, and passionate man. The outside world may not be fully cognizant of his teachings and his quiet way of empowering the people around him, but *we* know. And we move along our paths with the full knowledge that we owe it to Mr. D. to teach others what he taught us: that our voices count, and our words about our own cultures are of importance.

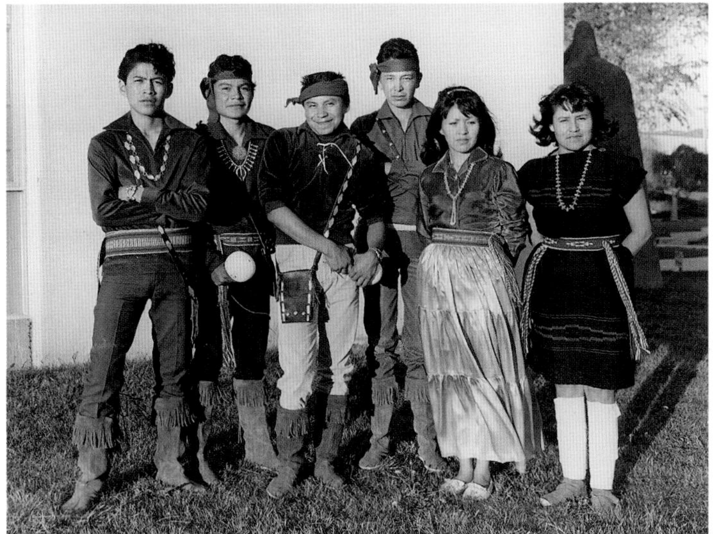

FIGURE 74 IAIA music students, ca. 1965, photo by Kay V. Wiest, IAIA Archives (RG03, Box 8, Folder 2).

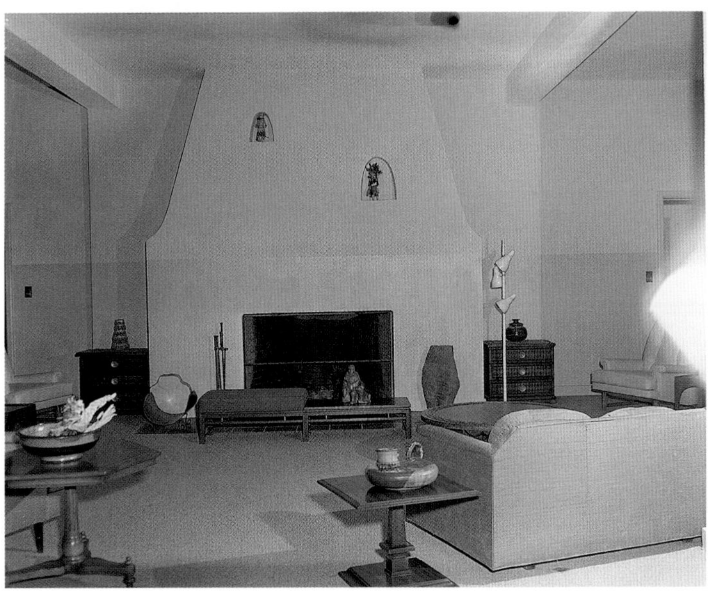

FIGURE 75 IAIA dormitory, ca. 1965, photo by Kay V. Wiest, IAIA Archives (MS10.015.001.03).

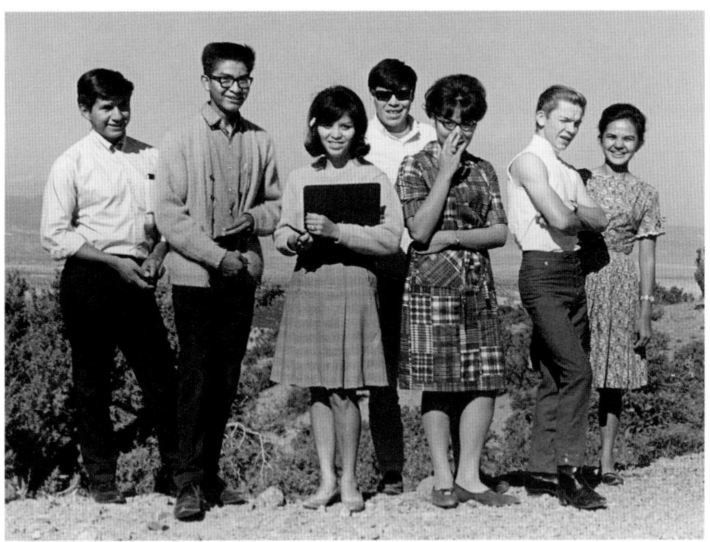

FIGURE 76 Students in the Commercial Arts class at IAIA standing on the Radio Tower Road overlooking Santa Fe and the Espanola Valley, 1965, IAIA Archives (RG03, Box 9, Folder 2).

FIGURE 77 IAIA student group, ca. 1965, photo by Milo, IAIA Archives (RG03, Box 8, Folder 1).

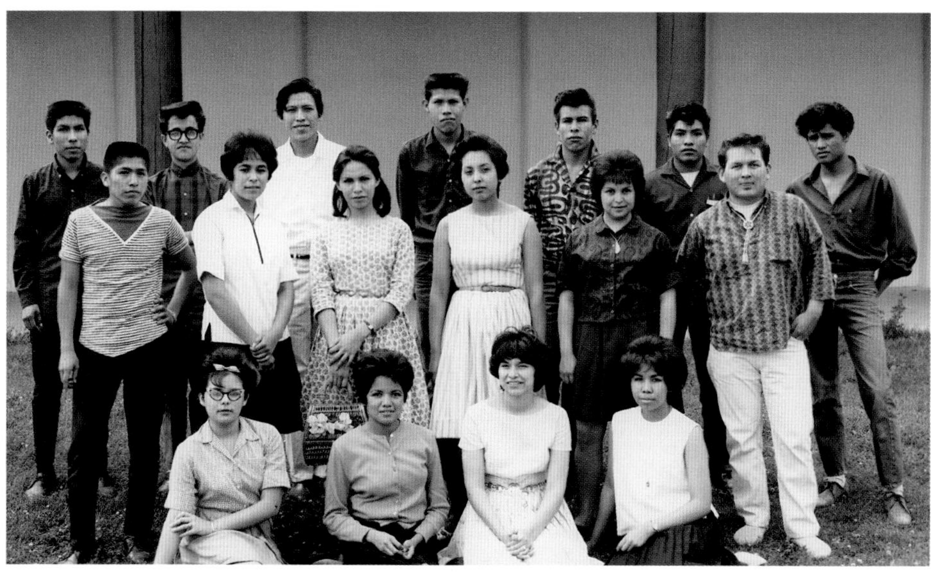

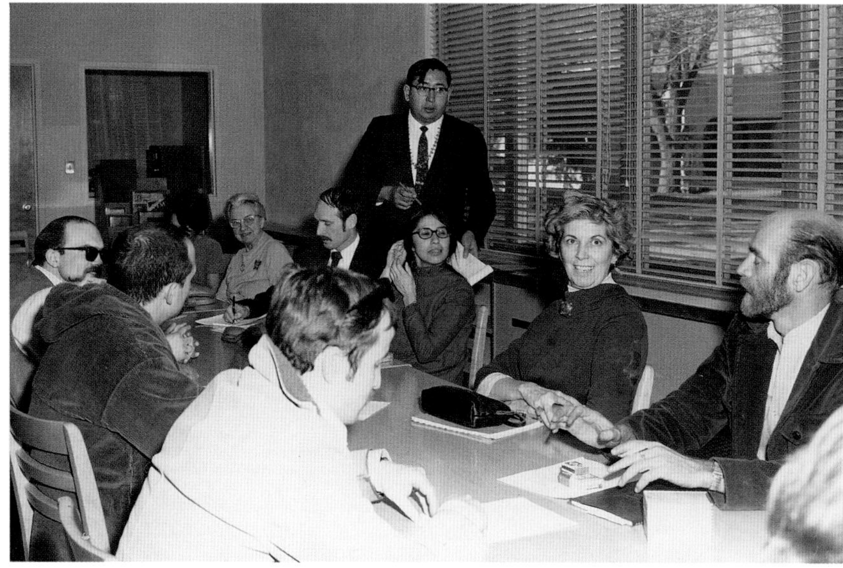

FIGURE 78 IAIA faculty meeting, 1967, IAIA Archives (RG03, Box 13, Folder 3).

Major Influences in the Development of Twentieth-Century Native American Art

CHARLES A. DAILEY

EDITOR'S NOTE *The following essay was written in 1982 by Charles Dailey, the founder of the Institute of American Indian Arts Museum Training Program, which began in 1971. I was enrolled in this program under Mr. Dailey in 1985 and am forever grateful for his mentorship.*

A beloved educator and guide to generations of American Indian museum professionals, "Chuck" was fond of saying that "we are too close in time to rationally examine and evaluate the lasting influence this Institute will have on world art."[1] This brief synopsis conveys something of Chuck's spirit and his absolute resolve to champion the IAIA's importance in the trajectory of Native art history.

As I read this piece, I was reminded how the IAIA educational approach fully embraced and even foregrounded the political and social currents that shaped and influenced the establishment of Native art programs, the curation of exhibits, and even the ability of artists to make the art they wished under government programs. Never one to shy from exposing colonial attitudes, Chuck's language in this brief historical overview is simultaneously romantic, somewhat nostalgic, and strident in his exposure of state-sanctioned violence. At the time this piece was published in 1991, his use of terms such as "trauma" and "extermination" was still unusual in typical writing about Native arts, which tended toward descriptive and celebratory analyses.

The following is an edited version of his essay "Major Influences in the Development of 20th Century Native American Art," which was included in the 1991 University of California Los Angeles American Indian Studies Center's publication Sharing a Heritage: American Indian Arts, *edited by Charlotte Heth, assisted by Michael Swarm.[2] We thank the UCLA American Indian Studies Center and Mr. Dailey for allowing us to reprint this piece.[3]*

The largest single misconception of the White society about the American Indian is that "all Indians are alike." There are over five hundred existing Native American Indian, Inuit, and Aleut tribes in America and no two tribes are alike in all aspects. Among the nineteen Pueblos of the Rio Grande Valley there are marked differences among even the neighboring Pueblos. Such diversity reflects on the nature of the influence which has affected Native American tribes since time began.

To set the stage of the influences on the Native American art forms one should keep some basic perimeters in mind. Basically, the Native American has always been nature-centered. Their lives were based upon ceremony and ritual revolving around the sun, wind, earth, rain, sky, lightning, water, moon, trees, plants, and animals. All of the tribes' music, dance, designs, ceremonies held spiritual and mystical powers and drew the performers into closer harmony with nature. The elaboration and decoration of ceremony masks, and even the seemingly utilitarian, gave magic religious meaning to the item. Art forms remained strong within tribes and correctness of detail many times determined how "these elements" responded to the appeal of the individual. When changes occurred in the art forms they generally were due to traumatic or dramatic shifts in religious or mystical forces of nature, or trading influences from other areas.

SEPARATION: NATIONAL POLICIES, 1492–1870

Influences in the development of Indian arts and crafts were felt by national policies from 1492–1870 when Indians were generally excluded from the social mainstream of the European/American society that grew up around them.

All Americans are aware of the drama of Indian contacts with the land seeking settlers into the late part of the nineteenth century. The total influence of these contacts on Native American arts and crafts was essentially that all of the general westward movement left the Native American population traumatized in the wake of excessive physical displacement, devastation of their social institutions, and severe policies of extermination. This exhorted the need, the desire, and the impetus to create and foster either traditional or new forms of art among the Native American population.

ASSIMILATION, CULTURAL SUPPRESSIONS: POLICIES OF 1870–1934

Congress appropriated $100,000 to operate federal industrial schools: Carlisle in Pennsylvania; Chemawa in Salem, Oregon; Chilocco in Oklahoma; and Haskell Institute in Kansas. By the early 1900s twenty-five such schools had been opened including Santa Fe, Carson City, Phoenix, and Flandreau. Still national policies influenced Indians which indirectly had a bearing upon Native American art forms during the early 1900s. For example, in 1917 Congress stopped appropriating federal funds to religious organizations for operation of Indian schools. In 1924 Congress finally gave citizenship to Indians via the Snyder Act . . . although some states did not support this legislation until the 1940s. Statistically, Native Americans were not yet approaching or completing post-high school programs. A survey in 1934 showed seventy-one Indians were in post-high school and only fifteen completed the year with none graduating. Again, in 1944 one hundred and thirty-three Indians were in a post-high school program with only twenty completing the year . . . none graduated. This was the trend in Indian education until the 1960s, which reflected that Indian students were still subject to a "military discipline" in schools, usually with their hair cut off, being made to wear industrial uniforms, and prohibited from speaking their own "Native" Indian language.

VOLUNTARY ASSIMILATION, 1934–1970

The Wheeler-Howard Act of 1934, which became known as the Indian Reorganization Act, was intended to end the land severalty policies, promised improved educational and medical facilities, restored religious freedom, supported Indian culture as a base for all programs, and encouraged self-government and economic betterment. A committee of one hundred, the Meriam Report reflected that "boarding schools were labeled as deculturization chambers, and the costs involved in their operation were questioned."[4] At this time there was new emphasis upon day schools being located near students' homes where feasible, resulting in the decline in boarding schools.

INFLUENCES OF SEPARATISM AND FORCED ASSIMILATION POLICIES

The harm which befell Indian social structures resulted in a dangerous collapse of cultural values and made many tribes doubt the dynamics of Indian life and their relation to the White society. Despite the pressures of the White society, reservation life, and sometimes, hopelessness, the underlying pride in a known way of life, a religious relationship to a nature-centered culture, and the remembrance of a life of the past handed down from generation to generation still lay rooted in the hearts of the People. The might of these traditions is revealed in the fact and degree to which they have survived despite hundreds of years of alien influences and hostile encounters that left no Indian tribe in the United States untouched. "Miraculously the threads of tribal cultural tradition have been carried forward and woven into the underpinnings of a significant segment of today's Indian tribal life. To the degree that such values have been preserved, so are Indian art expressions continued in traditional veins."[5]

DIRECT ART INFLUENCES: EARLY DAYS

J. Walter Fewkes, Anthropologist, working at Hopi Reservation in 1885 hired many local men to produce paintings to serve to record the Hopi Kachina. He gave them crayons, paints, pencils, brushes, and paper to work on. He was interested primarily in anthropological accuracy. Meanwhile in Santa Fe, a Dr. Edgar L. Hewett and Kenneth Chapman of the School of American Research encouraged early "secular" painting done by a number of San Ildefonso Pueblo artists including Crescencio Martinez, Julian Martinez, and others. Dr. Hewett was interested mostly with the emergence of latent artistic talent among Indian people. Dr. Hewett was also founder of the Fine Arts Museum in Santa Fe and an early sponsor of such newly immigrated East Coast artists as John Sloan, Robert Henri, and George Bellows. These early paintings were based on . . . elements in [the] preconquest past, but many new forms and motifs emerged. Early in the twentieth century a sales-economy centered upon the arts and crafts among the traders and ever-increasing tourists in the Southwest among the Navajos and Pueblos.

From 1918 to 1925 there was some activity in art at Santa Fe Boarding School, despite government policy prohibiting such cultural art. The superintendent, John D. DeHuff, and his wife Elizabeth had two Hopis, Fred Kabotie and Otis Polelonema, and a Pueblo Zia Indian, Velino Shije Herrera, begin to paint. Mr. Kabotie was allowed to be absent from his carpentry class to go to the home of Elizabeth DeHuff where he would sit in a little room of their house and paint for many hours. An "old lady" librarian complained to Washington about the DeHuffs, as well as the students painting things like the Kachinas.

In the Meriam Report, 1928, the federal government recommended that art be encouraged among Indian students. This influenced and climaxed in the Indian Reorganization Act in 1934 and the appointment of John Collier as Commissioner of Indian Affairs.

OKLAHOMA MOVEMENT

In the 1920s in Oklahoma there emerged a painting movement sponsored by White patrons who encouraged five young Kiowas to paint. The movement was centered in Anadarko, Oklahoma. The Oklahoma style which emerged was a colorful, bold figurative style, sometimes stencil-like and overly decorative.

SANTA FE INDIAN SCHOOL: DOROTHY DUNN STUDIO MOVEMENT

In 1932 Dorothy Dunn instilled in her students a firmly established preconceived idea of what Indian art should be: something instinctive as well as tribally specific and formulaic, a technique she felt could be taught. This developed into a clean, balanced, decorative style characterized by what J. J. Brody says is "good taste." It is the formulation of the so-called "Bambi" style of painting. Allan Houser was a student under Dorothy Dunn. He also became one of the finest sculptors in the soon-to-be-created Institute of American Indian Arts. "When I got to the studio, it was the old traditional style they wanted from you or none at all. Dorothy Dunn told me that if I was going to do things that are realistic, then you better go on out and take the first bus home. Everyone was encouraged to search their background for traditional things. That's all she permitted us to do. My only objection to Dorothy Dunn was this: She trained us all the same way. You either paint like this, Mr. Houser, or it is not Indian art."[6]

The Santa Fe Studio flourished under Dorothy Dunn for five years. She left in 1937. This period of art was the first classic revival of what is now called "traditional" Indian art. The Santa Fe Boarding School continued to build upon the formalism of their instructors and the commercial examples set by the older alumni, which included such great "old masters" as Pablita Velarde (Santa Clara), Gerald Nailer (Navajo), Allan Houser (Apache), Tsinijinnie (Navajo), Beaten Yazzie (Navajo), and many, many others. The period of 1945 to 1962 had many significant Indian artists, but most of them were continuing in the predictable continuation of earlier traditions.

Several major Indian artists have struggled to prominence across America in areas not in Santa Fe or Oklahoma. Many large National Indian art competitions like the Museum of New Mexico, Philbrook Art Institute, and Scottsdale National Indian Art Show were happening during this time with the intent of showing the dynamic and cultural art styles which were showing up all over Indian America.

FEDERAL POLICY IN 1960s

The Federal Policies in the 1960s emphasized treating Indians as co-planners and transferring programs to Indian communities. The federal government now began to work in partnership with Indians, ending paternalism and consulting with Indians before programs under which they must live are planned. The use of Indian arts as a ready vehicle for transmission of Indian culture and assisting Indian people in the amelioration of emotional tensions stemming from identity problems remains very neglected in the general education of the Indian. Other than the Institute of American Indian Arts in Santa Fe there are only twenty teachers in the visual arts throughout the entire BIA system up to the recent past. Only the first recognition of the methods of using values found in Indian cultural heritage as a springboard for positive human behavior are [*sic*] visible in the early philosophy of the Institute of American Indian Arts.

RENAISSANCE IN THE INDIAN ART OF THE TWENTIETH CENTURY

In recent years through education, political awareness, and the prestige of their art, Native Americans have acquired considerable strength as a People. From this has come a way of new traditional revivalism and cultural nationalism. Indians have entered almost every walk of life, doctors, lawyers, educators, physicians, college instructors, presidents of businesses, and well-known artists.

Art has become an increasingly important tool by means of which to reaffirm cultural identity and reinforce national pride. There has been a large change in creation of art from being essentially a tribally oriented expression serving tribal needs to an *individual-oriented expression system* serving individual needs. Art enters the realm of "art for art's sake." There are three major ways of approaching art forms of the new age: Many Native American artists who retain strong tribal affiliations and are deeply rooted in only traditional ways of seeing, thinking, or depicting arts spend their time reviving the past and old ways and trying to duplicate them in order to preserve the strong traditions of the past. Others are knowledgeable and are deeply rooted in the past, but abstract freely from traditional-based forms and innovatively adapt them to their own individual needs and art forms, and there are those who only occasionally use a tribal form or reference for their art forms.

It is the program of the Institute of American Indian Arts and the premise of this author that all forms of contemporary Indian arts are valid. It must be understood and appreciated for its own contribution. Many Indian arts and crafts are shown without the detail of tribal name or affiliation while others remain with strict adherence to a tribal group. All must be allowed to flourish and exist within its own realm and to be understood in this context. The Native American task is to examine and utilize all that is good in the traditional cultural heritage to strengthen their position in contemporary society. This is also seen as its roots of cultural greatness.

Native American arts are in the center of a renaissance of American Indian arts and crafts as firmly shown in important Indian exhibits, such as "Walk in Beauty" for the Festival of the Arts in Santa Fe, NM in 1981. It is notable to know that of the 150 artists invited from all over the United States over one-third were alumni or associated with the Institute of American Indian Arts in some way. With the opening of the Native American Center for the Living Arts (Turtle Museum) in Niagara Falls, New York in May 1981, the premiere exhibit and nationally selected Indian art exhibit had a selection of nearly two hundred Indian artists from across America including over one-third of the recognized artists who had roots or affiliation with the Institute of American Indian Arts.

American Indian art has its roots and its inspiration from the earth itself, extending as far as the great pyramids of the Aztecs and Mayan empires, emerging within the massive temple mounds of the Missouri and Mississippi valleys, being pushed, molded, and influenced by the White society for nearly four hundred years and now rebounding with the vigor and strength of a sleeping giant. Such is the contribution of this Indigenous art form in America.

INSTITUTE OF AMERICAN INDIAN ARTS, 1962–1982

In 1961 the Rockefeller Foundation funded an Indian art project at the University of Arizona where students from all over North America came to spend summers in new programs and to experiment and explore in different media and styles. Charles Loloma and Lloyd Kiva New were co-directors of that program.

The Indian Arts and Crafts Board of the U. S. Department of the Interior founded and sponsored the new Institute of American Indian Arts based on the University of Arizona project. The founding of the Institute occurred in

October 1962 with Dr. George Boyce as the first Superintendent and Lloyd Kiva New as the first Arts Director. There were one hundred and forty carefully recruited students in the first year.

The IAIA mandate stated, "To retain the valuable elements of Indian life and to strengthen the pride of Indian groups and the recognition by non-Indian as to the contribution of the Indian heritage to national life. To include information regarding the various Indian cultures in the school curriculum. To interpret Indian cultural values to non-Indian groups."[7]

This national Institute of Indian arts and crafts had the very best instructors from all fields of endeavor. Allan Houser, Charles Loloma, Otellie Loloma, Josephine Wapp, Lloyd Kiva New, and many others were some of the original instructors. The classes coupled a unique idea of relationship of traditional art classes with a holistic concept of relationships of one to another . . . of weaving a tapestry of one hundred and fifty tribes yet allowing each thread to be important and unique.

The young people at the Institute of American Indian Arts may discover strengths in themselves by virtue of differences as a base for sound personality development. The Institute of American Indian Arts constructs cultural bridges to serve students as members of two societies, enabling them to benefit from both as well as to contribute to both. The students were inspired from different cultural groups and so have unique and valuable contributions to make, using tradition as a springboard for personal creative action. Students are encouraged to become aware of themselves as members of a People tremendously rich in architecture, fine arts, music, pageantry, and the humanities, thereby giving the young person identification with cultural accomplishment of the highest order.

RENAISSANCE IN INDIAN ART IN THE TWENTIETH CENTURY

Art forms and programs are emerging from many different tribes. New programs are developing at Niagara Falls, New York; Seattle, Washington; Yakima, Washington; Davis, California and elsewhere. There is an emergence of stable Native American artists taking their place in the regional art scenes all across America. Contributions of Native American art are now being exhibited not only as an interesting cultural art form and anthropological exhibit, but as a recognition of an inherent art form which is accepted as a true art form able to stand on its own stature.

The future of Indian art lies in an ability to evolve, adjust, and adapt to the demands of the present, and not on the ability to re-manipulate, reinvent, and repeat the past. Art is a manifestation of the times and this is no less true of Indian art.

The soundness of such approaches must consider the rapidly changing Indian world and encompass the realization that Indians are human beings entitled to the same freedoms of self-determination as others. It must be realized that the validity of art expression of any group cannot be measured for its unique qualities alone, for one must consider the demands of aesthetics in terms of the universal principles about art. Above all, there must be an acute awareness of the Indian artist for his responsibility to society in general.

NOTES

1. Charles Dailey, "The Institute of American Indian Arts Museum: 1962 to 1992," IAIA Archives, n/d.

2. Charles Dailey, "Major Influences in the Development of Twentieth-Century Native American Art," in *Sharing a Heritage: American Indian Arts*, ed. Charlotte Heth (Los Angeles: University of California American Indian Studies Center, 1991).

3. http://www.books.aisc.ucla.edu/toc/sharinghert.html.

4. Margaret Connell Szasz, *Education and the American Indian: The Road to Self-Determination since 1928* (Albuquerque: University of New Mexico Press, 1974).

5. Lloyd H. New, *American Indian Art in the 1980s*, exhibition catalogue (Niagara Falls, NY: Native American Center for the Living Arts, 1984).

6. Charles Dailey, personal communication, n.d.

7. *Bureau of Indian Affairs Manual*, vol. 6, part 2, section 101.2, chapter 1, n/d. Quoted in *Indian Education Accountability: Hearings before the Subcommittee on Administrative Practice and Procedure of the Committee on the Judiciary, United States Senate, Ninety-Third Congress, First and Second Sessions, December 13, 1973 [and] August 22, 1974* (Washington, DC: US Government Printing Office, 1975), 66, https://books.google.com/books?id=iLk2eQCyMNAC.

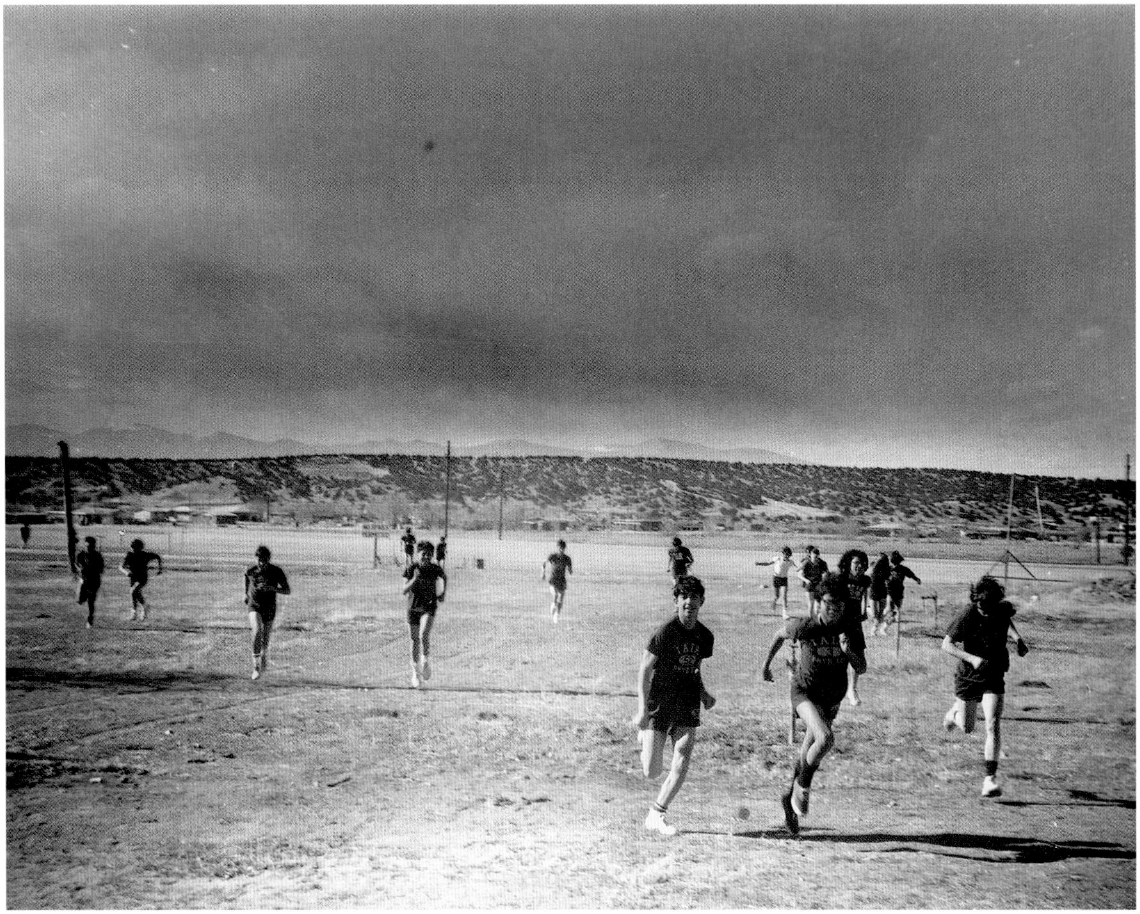

FIGURE 79 IAIA physical education class, ca. 1970, photo by A. R. Antone, IAIA Archives (RG03, Box 10, Folder 11).

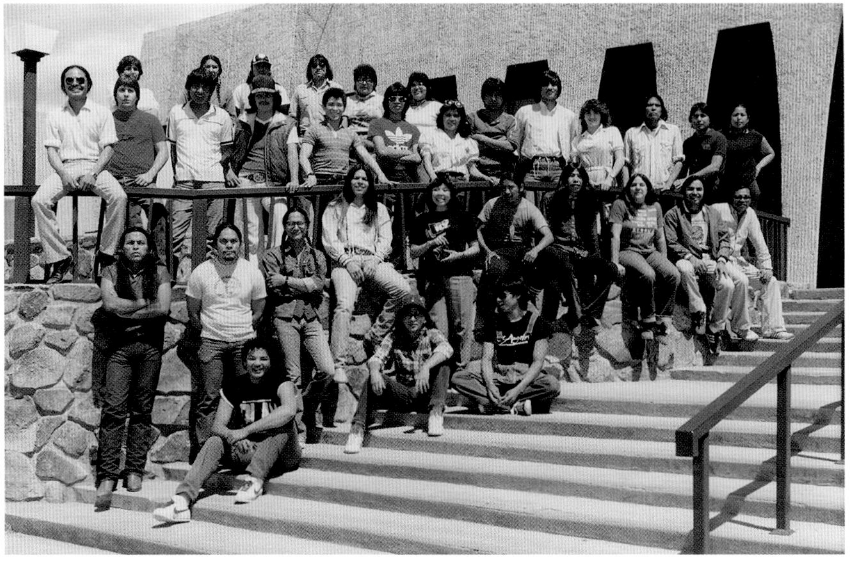

FIGURE 80 IAIA student group, 1972, IAIA Archives (RG03, Box 8, Folder 1).

Cultural Self-Determination

A Conversation with David Warren

NANCY MARIE MITHLO AND DAVID WARREN

EDITOR'S NOTE *Dave Warren (affectionately called "Dr. Dave" by his students and colleagues) is known as one of the primary architects of the American Indian arts movement. Throughout his long career, he has mentored countless students, professionals, and tribal leaders with his particular philosophical approach to Native ways of knowing. He devoted twenty years of leadership to the Institute of American Indian Arts (IAIA), holding positions including Cultural Research and Resource Development Center director and acting president. His positions with the Smithsonian Institution included special assistant for applied community research, Office of the Assistant Secretary for Public Service, and founding deputy director of the National Museum of the American Indian. A PhD recipient from the University of New Mexico in 1955, he also held teaching posts at Oklahoma State University, the University of Nebraska, and Colorado College.*[1]

In these excerpts from a conversation in 2008, one of many I was fortunate to have with him, Warren generously responded to my initial prompt, "We are talking about the history of American Indian art and, Dave, I am interested in what you want to say. You can start at whatever point of reference you want to, but I'm looking at problem-solving for where we want to go next in the scholarship dealing with American Indian art." He responded, "OK!" and promptly launched into this deeply engaged reflection on his life, his learnings, and his insights.

WARREN I think we have to remember, I hear this, I know this is a cliché almost, but these are unprecedented times in Native American history. And by that I mean we have seen a lot of change in the last generation, in the last twenty to thirty years, in the idea of self-determination. But most of it has been in political terms, and economic programs and development, casinos, is an example of tribes taking over the developing as self-directed and controlled kind of economic program. But I don't think we've looked carefully enough at cultural self-determination, and I think it's—you can do a lot of check-marking next to things like, well, the passage of the legislation for the National Museum of the American Indian, which did not only establish the museum but also had the provisions for the repatriation of cultural patrimony—ancestral remains as well as cultural materials. We saw, therefore, a whole new change of the relationship between the tribe, the studied, and those who studied them.

And that began an adjustment of institutions that were used to prerogatives that didn't take into consideration the viewpoint or the value system of the tribe with whom they worked. We also see a sweeping movement of Indian language programs all over. These are not only the programs, formal programs, in institutions, but they are community-based programs. They come out of the communities' own sense of how—why—they should try to maintain the language and how best to do that. And, in some cases, avoiding having to write it down. In many cases tribes had felt that if you write it down you literally freeze the language. Some have chosen to go ahead and write that language. Cherokee has been written, as we know, and Navajo has been transcribed and written and so . . . that's the choice of each tribe.

The language movement, however, is important because it is part of this cultural sovereignty issue, this cultural self-determination. The tribes want to maintain that which is critical and important to who they are . . . we worked with tribes in the program that I had at one time. . . . [T]he only funding we could find . . . was close to what they wanted to do was the ESEA [Elementary and Secondary Education Act] programs for bilingual education; I think it was Title VII. At any rate, those language programs were for transitional purposes, to move from Native language to English. The tribes didn't want to do that, they wanted to maintain that language. Today we are finding people and institutions aware that the priority is not transitional: it is maintenance and preservation for cultural integrity purposes.

We see a mapping program sweeping the Indigenous world. This is mapping of homeland—traditional homelands. And it raises all kinds of questions about, why a map? Maps have determined the fate of many tribes by placing all kinds of politically determined and other culturally determined borders, literal and figuratively, to who they are and where they are. Tribes are going back and looking at traditional homelands in terms of what they have always been: namely, the sacred content, the sacred significance of these lands in defining themselves within a much more cosmological setting. The repatriation of ancestral remains and cultural goods has had an effect that we really can't measure yet; and that is, internally there has been an implosion. I'm suggesting there has been an implosion of the effect of returning goods, and things, and remains that many felt would never be returned. So when you return something that had been lost, and you had in a sense reconciled yourself to that loss, the question becomes, well, they will be coming back, and "they" is spiritual as well as physical. How do we bring them back in the right way? Do we know how to bring them back? If we don't do it the right way, is there is consequence that we may not be aware of that could be a problem? Do we know the language, the prayers, so forth, necessary for that?

So this cultural sovereignty is very complicated and it is happening everywhere. It's made of all these kinds of changes, forces, policies, but it has its internal impacts that we will probably, in many cases, never fully understand or know about. When you, therefore, look at the expression of all this change, in the arts, or in the cultural discussions that take place, inside the Indian community, you're having to look at a transitional period that we have never seen anything like. In one way you could say that until the 1960s, the trend, whether it was policy, or psychologically through an educational system, everything was going away. You were taking, literally taking the children away to a boarding school. . . . You were taking the language *away* from the person. You were literally taking the person away from themselves. And to that extent you were trying to make them into that which they could never be. And Pratt, the superintendent at Carlisle, said it, but we haven't fully analyzed, "If you kill the Indian you save the man." Well, I'm not sure that you save anything except a hollow being that has lost its soul. Today we're seeing the effort to return that soul—literally, spiritually—and protect it once returned. And . . . we're asking people within the Native American community to explain that complicated process in whatever way they want to, care to, or can, to a world that is just trying to adjust to the fact that Native peoples, Indigenous peoples all over the world, are in a new process of taking a position that has been denied for centuries in every possible way. Whether it be by religion, by education, by economic determination, they have been marginal or nonexistent for the most part. So we're seeing the emergence in ways that we can't quite fully understand, and even the people, the participants themselves, may not fully comprehend that they are a part of. They're being swept along in something that nobody could have predicted.

So you see, the art, it seems to me, reflecting that experimentation on "How do I talk about something that I have not been allowed to talk about?

How do I project something that I am re-learning, that I know is critical to who I am? How do I define this new reality of my community finding itself and me as representative of that community presenting that discovery?" I don't know that any of us have had that experience until we've been denied what we were, or are, and then told it's okay, at some later stage to be what you've always been. And then you're trying to simultaneously shed a part of you and get adjusted to the new part. So I think these are all philosophical questions, but I think they are also very critical in understanding what we are looking at when we look at Native American or Indigenous art in general. We're seeing an expression that has been latent in many cases, but is coming through a series of filters that are obviously going to modify it, change it—but the content will remain the same, and, perhaps in some cases, be stronger for having to test itself against what it had to leave behind and not re-create so much as rediscover strength.

MITHLO As you talk, I think about how insightful you are about institutions and systems and those kind of larger paradigm shifts over time. And you have worked in both mainstream/academic and also community-based settings—and I don't want to necessarily position those in opposition, eternal opposition to each other—but speaking to that established academic genre, what do you see as challenges for Native people doing this renewal/revitalization within that setting? Is it like the language, for example, when you're talking about language retention and how most of the systems were set about making a transition—right?—into mainstream language . . . Is it the same for Native arts, you know, that Native arts are trying to make *into* the established discipline of art history, or other related disciplines? Is the system set up for that one-way direction?

WARREN I don't really know that it's. . . . I think we're seeing it, it is forming itself, whatever that may be, and I think that it is to be observed and to be nurtured to the extent that we can. To what extent is a Japanese art, or a Scandinavian art, trying to become some sort of a universal, international art? And we've looked at the exhibit in New York on primitivism and its role in twentieth-century art, as I recall that exhibit, they didn't label the so-called called primitive art so much as they just put it there as a juxtaposed image to what it had inspired . . . of a Max Ernst, so we called it, well, is it abstract, cubist, what are we watching at work here?[2] I think we are watching art forming.

Now, I think the academic world has to begin to look at the formation of art as a cultural expression in ways that they perhaps have not in the past because they have seen it happening in front of their eyes with the Native American and Indigenous world phenomenon. As I mentioned earlier, I went to Mexico to study Nawat (Nahuatl), and at that time (this would be in the late 1950s and '60s), at that time, there were outside of Mexico, there were probably five or six people who were interested in studying the language for whatever purpose; in this case historians were looking at it because there were a lot of documents written in Nawat. Nowadays you can go on the Internet and you can see title after title and resource after resource, including how to learn Nawat, and the world is full of people who are interested in Nawat. Now why? I have no idea, because they're looking at everything now, as I review the literature, from its linguistic and technical value all the way to its philosophical value. . . . We're finally beginning to learn about the philosophy and the aesthetics of the Nawat-speaking world. Well, I don't know that we'll come to that in the United States and yet, we may as people begin to appreciate the fact that there's no way in certain, in many cases, that you can explain the world in your language that others can understand. However, we may find the point where the dignity and the value of another person's language, as we're discovering with Nawat or Maya, is so important that we encourage the new generation of philosophy majors, and ethics majors, to look at their own language and tell us "what is the inherent lesson that is being taught through the language and worldview that only you can find?" We're assuming that that language will maintain itself through another generation.

So, I think we have to understand that we're involved in a very, very profound change, and we have to watch for the manifestations of that change, and accept them rather than impose anything that we feel from the outside as acceptable or understandable even. It will come forward; it will come out.

NOTES

1. For more background on his vast contributions to the disciplines of American Indian art and culture, see *Dr. Dave Warren and the Transformation of Cultural Studies: Speeches, Lectures, and Essays by Dr. Dave Warren*, compiled and edited by Ryan S. Flahive, Institute of American Indian Arts archivist (Santa Fe: IAIA, 2014).

2. See: Museum of Modern Art online archives for the exhibit "'Primitivism' in 20th Century Art: Affinity of the Tribal and the Modern," 1985, https://www.moma.org/calendar/exhibitions/1907.

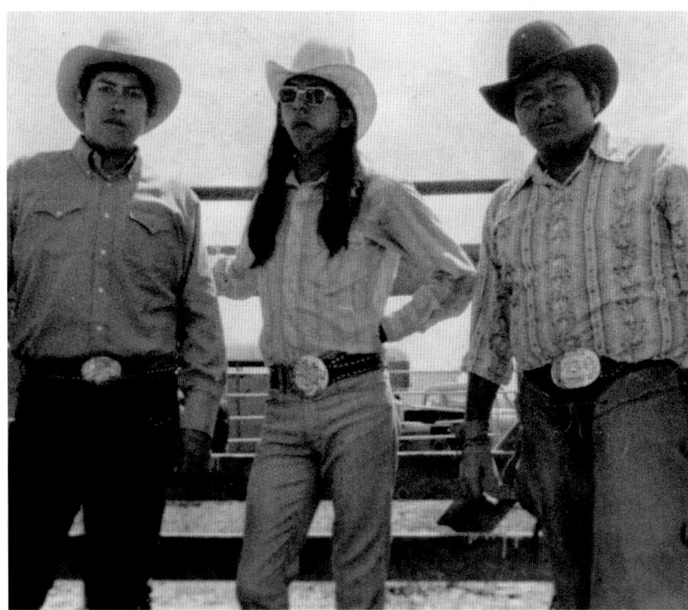

FIGURE 81 IAIA Rodeo Club members Robin Fohrenkam, DeVere Manning, and Leo Martinez prepare to ride in the All Indian Rodeo, 1973, IAIA Archives (RG02.1973.08).

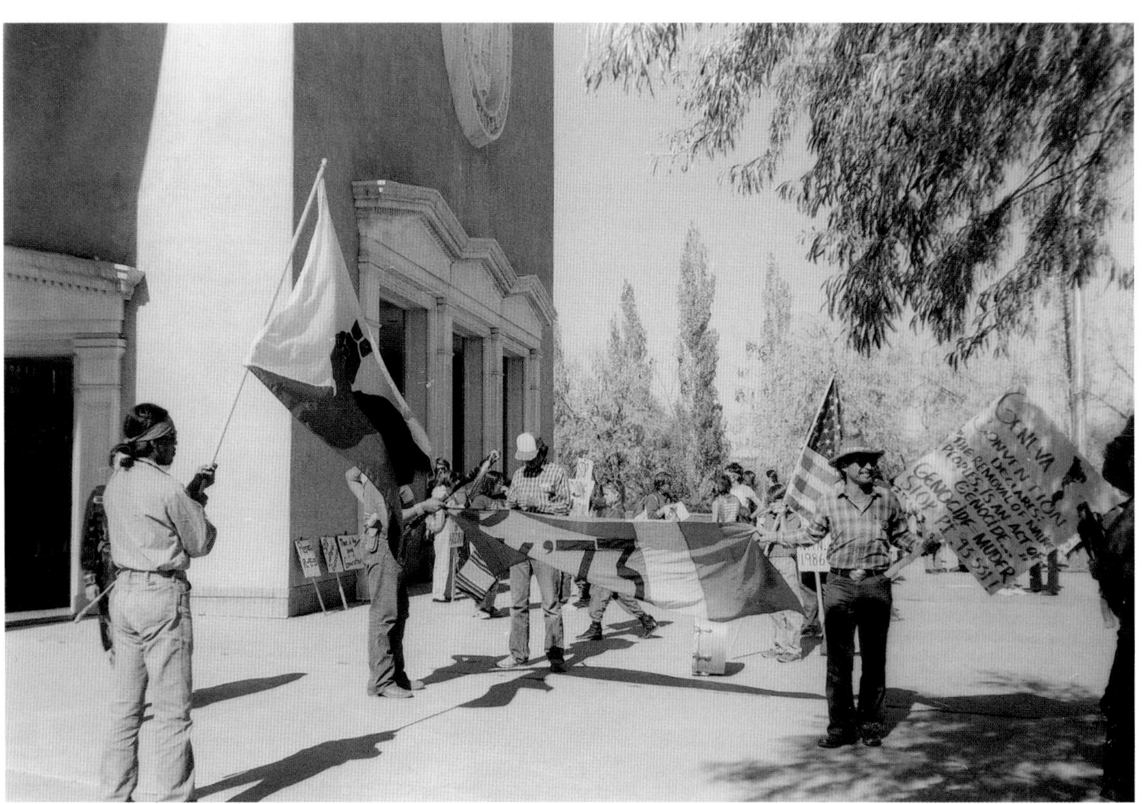

FIGURE 82 IAIA protest, 1973 (RG03, Box 8, Folder 3).

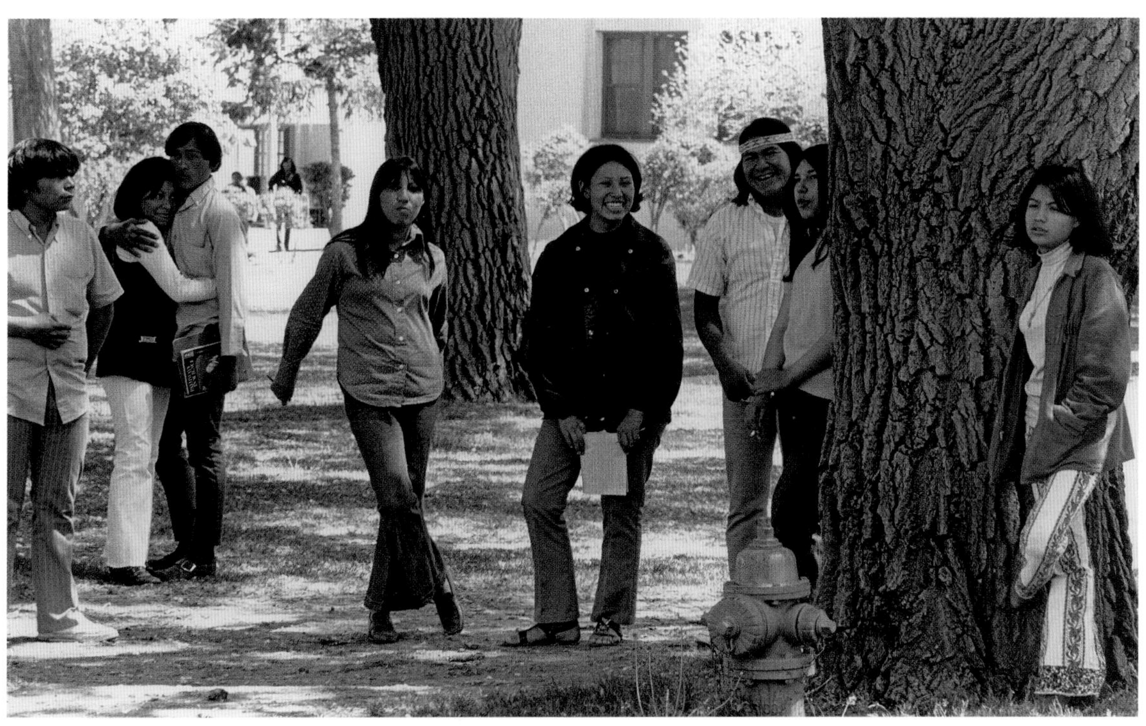

FIGURE 83 IAIA students on the Santa Fe Indian School campus, ca. 1975, photo by Karl Kernberger, IAIA Archives (RG03, Box 9, Folder 4).

FIGURE 84 Group of students at Soleri Theater, 1978, IAIA Archives (RG02.1979.08).

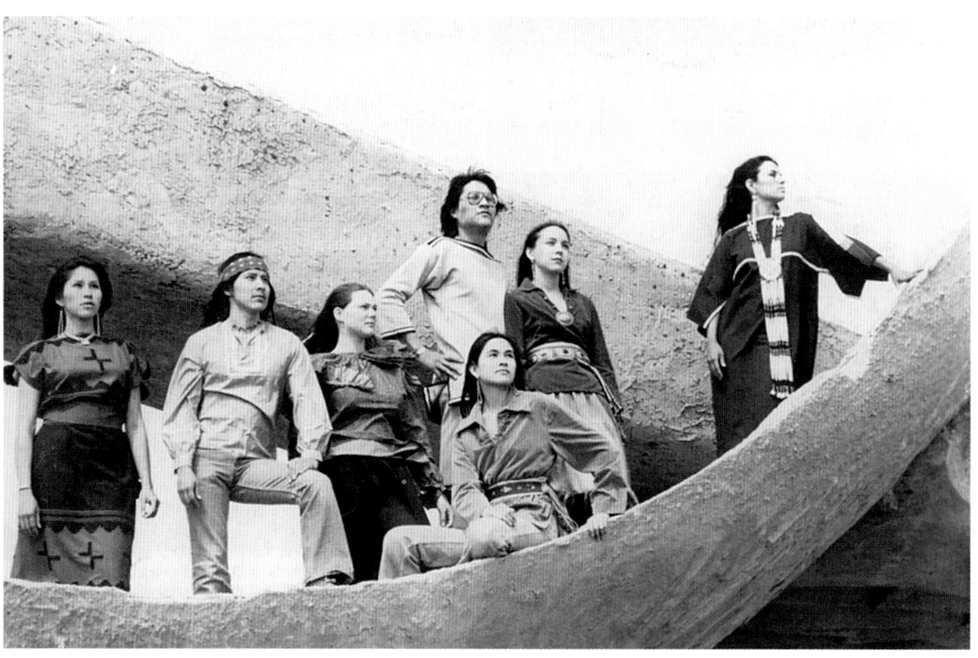

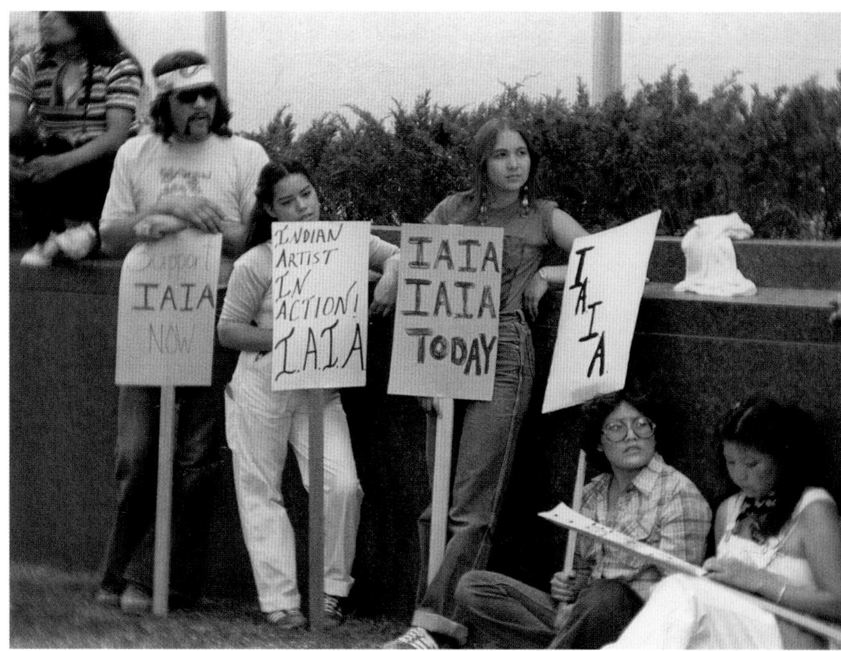

FIGURE 85 Protest by IAIA students, 1981, IAIA Archives (RG03, Box 8, Folder 3).

Teaching from Three Knowledge Spaces

The Native Eyes Project

DAVID WADE CHAMBERS

Editor's note: The Native Eyes Project (NEP), an online curriculum development program in Indigenous Studies, was set up in 1999 by a group of Indigenous scholars in North America and Australia.[1] *When it was implemented at the Institute of American Indian Arts in 2007, it was a revolutionary addition to the school's forty-year history of instruction for Native artists and scholars. Wade Chambers' strong commitment to ensuring the integration of visual, text, and audio narratives expanded the range of the IAIA curriculum model to consider visual and oral transmission through artistic images, architecture, song, dance, storytelling, agricultural and ecological practice, religious ritual, and the interpretation of historical artifacts, maps, and symbolic inscriptions. Under Wade's leadership, I developed courses in museums and visual studies for online delivery, a process that greatly enhanced my university teaching.*

The Native Eyes Project curriculum aimed to: 1) incorporate cultural and intellectual contributions of Native Peoples into mainstream teaching in the humanities and social sciences; 2) explore critical issues of knowledge and power, culture and society, from an interdisciplinary, multitribal, and liberal-arts point of view; 3) address social, cultural, ethical, and political issues important to First Nations and to Indigenous people around the globe; and 4) integrate a strong First Nations perspective, drawing input from tribal elders, tribal leaders, and prominent Indigenous writers and scholars.

Wade Chambers first presented the following essay as a paper at the World Indigenous Peoples Conference on Education held in 2005 in Aotearoa, New Zealand.

In the modern world, we find a remarkable array of highly varied approaches to teaching and learning, and perhaps we should not be surprised that many of the most exciting of these approaches are found in the Indigenous context. Most Indigenous educators wish to honor the knowledge traditions to which they are bound, while also respecting the constraints of the academic disciplines in which they have been trained. This means that we are indeed challenged, in ways that mainstream educators are not, to develop teaching content, protocols, and techniques that can provide for this complex pattern of cross-cultural allegiances.

Many writers reference the two main knowledge spaces within which Indigenous educators must work: on the one hand, the Western technoscientific paradigm, and on the other, Indigenous ways of knowing the world and of living in it. In addition to these two knowledge spaces, some have also suggested a third space in which multiple and diverse ontologies can interact without privileging one over another.

1. THE WESTERN SCIENCE KNOWLEDGE SPACE

In relation to this teaching space, we need say little. It is a place we all know well, one that has provided much of great value to the modern world of the twenty-first century. Yet it is also a space in which Indigenous knowledge has been, at best, neglected, and, at worst, denied, over long centuries of cultural oppression. It is the space in our societies in which a young person can become a "doctor, lawyer or merchant," but not an "Indian chief."

It is a space where knowledge is declared to be objective, rational, and universal, yet most Indigenous scholars know it as a highly political space in which the deadly forces of social, economic, and cultural colonialism are at work. Many scholars have vividly shown us how dangerous, and how compromising to cultural integrity, it can be for an Indigenous scholar to work in this space. Any Indigenous curriculum that operates here must contend with, and attempt to controvert, the ethos of exclusion, domination, exploitation, and assimilation that has long been a cornerstone of Western Scientific Knowledge.

For Indigenous educators to turn away from this knowledge space, with all its contending forces and entangling alliances, would be to deny Native young people leadership roles in government, in scholarship, in health, in technology, in science, and in the arts. Furthermore, Western knowledge in all its disciplinary configurations (sciences, social sciences, and humanities) can only profit from the input of the great Indigenous ways of knowing and being.

2. THE TRIBAL KNOWLEDGE SPACE

This teaching space is home to locally Indigenous ways of knowing and being in the world. Traditionally, this space was solely tribal, the responsibility of elders and those empowered with the transmission of knowledge across generations. With regard to secret, sacred, or ceremonial knowledge, such ethical restrictions remain in force; the authority mechanisms of control of such knowledge remain tribal. Notwithstanding these traditional restrictions, much Indigenous knowledge is about sharing and open participation. In Laurelyn Whitt's words, "Indigenous peoples across the planet are presently engaged in various and vigorous projects of recovery: of language and land, of law and sovereignty, and of ways of knowing and ways of living. At the deepest level, this project of recovery demands restoring and protecting knowledge systems. This story of resistance and recovery is essential to understanding not only the politics of Indigenous knowledge systems, but their substance, and their vital role in the world."[2]

In article after article, Indigenous scholars and activists speak of "an Indigenous renaissance," of how Native peoples are "taking control of their destiny," of the "revitalization of aboriginal societies." Evidence for this is plentiful and promising. It includes a range of initiatives to take control of education through the creation of tribally controlled programs as well as through curricular development commonly found in Native American and Indigenous Studies programs.

3. A THIRD KNOWLEDGE SPACE

This third teaching space, which has been called a "theater of diversity," constitutes a new sort of teaching venue in which (unlike in Mao's Cultural Revolution) a hundred flowers actually *do* bloom and a hundred schools of thought actually *do* contend.[3] This is a space of multiplicity and connection, in which persons, knowledges, practices, objects, and places are linked by narratives of relationship.

In this space, incommensurable knowledge systems, worldviews, languages, and theoretical constructs come together as useful stories without the need for common vocabularies, singular methodologies, or the resolution of apparent difference. This is a space in which knowledge accounts have distinct and heterogeneous components that can be compared, shared, joined, interwoven, or torn asunder.

This is a space in which the concept of knowledge itself is the subject of discussion and analysis. Here, ways of knowing the world are brought together in assemblages but not embedded together into coherent, procrustean configurations. To the extent that these systems of knowing are to be evaluated or appraised, it will not be in terms of how closely they measure up to the strictures of Western science: rather, the relevant criteria will be local, contingent, ethical, practical, and always culture-bound. Indeed, in this knowledge space, technoscience will be judged by these same criteria.

David Turnbull argues that working with multiple ontologies (including traditional knowledges) necessitates the production of a space in which these spatial and temporal narratives are held in tension with each other. Such a coproduced space would constitute what he terms an interstitial "third space," a type of trading zone in which differing traditions are narrated and performed together and in which actors can move, make connections, produce new spaces and trails in necessarily messy, contingent assemblages.[4]

Turnbull makes much of the "inherent irony of the narratological dimension" of this third space, the storytelling codes that he describes as "partial, incomplete and capable of being other."[5] The almost universal Indigenous trickster figure that so readily captures this narrative irony reminds us of the ways in which Indigenous knowledge systems are already fully practiced in dealing with diversity.

The performative possibilities of *emergent* mappings in a database are dependent on *emergent* protocols and strategies of connection. Importantly, these strategies and protocols could constitute the political architecture and practical ecology of a cultural commons. These issues bear directly and immediately on Native Eyes course structures, discussed below.

Working within the Indigenous web of *prescription* and *proscription*, the process of knowing requires attention to the meta level of understanding. Teaching in this fashion, and from this third knowledge space, is utterly essential if we are to provide a workable framework for Indigenous students who have professional aspirations but who do not wish to forsake their cultural heritage.

I think I can safely say that all Indigenous knowledge workers who work outside the traditional tribal setting, (i.e., in universities, museums, galleries, courts of law, hospitals, and even certain commercial enterprises such as tourism and hospitality) must constantly negotiate and renegotiate the boundaries between, the pathways through, and the connections among different ways of knowing and being. Teaching/learning experience in the third space is a vital dimension of properly training Native students to live and work in the larger world.

In summary, and from the point of view of the Native Eyes Project, we must acknowledge an obligation to teach from all three of the knowledge spaces: the first space, in which professional and disciplinary training can occur and that honors the best academic traditions; the second space, in which Indigenous ways of knowing are given prominence and respect, both for their past glories and also for their present and future significance; and the "third space," for bringing disparate knowledge systems and cultures together in dynamic tension to relate together in new and productive ways. In this regard, we have put together a more explicit, if also tentative, set of protocols for enabling this third space, ideally incorporating the following six characteristics. Native Eyes teaching spaces, then, would ideally:

> 1) enable the comparative study and analysis of images and texts representing multiple, often incommensurable knowledge systems, both "traditional" and "modern," in ways that do not privilege one system or set of understandings over another;
>
> 2) allow the direct juxtaposition and comparison of images, film and audio clips, texts (historical and/or interpretive), stories (oral or text-based), dance, landscapes, architecture, etc.;
>
> 3) allow for the inclusion of the above array of images and texts from multiple online databases, such as those found on many museum and Native websites;
>
> 4) encourage the making of new and unexpected cognitive and cultural connections, as has occurred with the remarkable development of the online Wikipedia;
>
> 5) strengthen the ability to make comparative judgments (ethical, aesthetic, practical, or intellectual) based on a variety of criteria specified and brought to bear by the user of the knowledge base; and
>
> 6) facilitate interactive learning exercises, utilizing all the above capabilities, in reference to specific student needs and interests: professional or scholarly, practical or theoretical, critical, or interpretive.

It goes without saying that ultimately achieving such a "third space" might well take a generation of collaborative work by scholars, technicians, elders, teachers, and students. Nevertheless, we believe that clearly stating these objectives will ensure a more viable conserving/teaching/learning enterprise in both the short and the long run. We believe the third space provides a means of globalizing, without westernizing, Indigenous knowledge.

THE NATIVE EYES PROJECT

The Native Eyes Project (NEP) at the Institute of American Indian Arts (IAIA) was founded in the year 1999 and offered courses until 2014. Versions of these courses were also taught internationally until the present at institutions including Deakin University in Melbourne, Victoria, Australia (Science and Technology Studies and Koorie Teacher Education Program); Brandon University, Brandon, Manitoba, Canada (Native Studies); and Charles Darwin University, Darwin, Australia. The aim was to construct an innovative major, principally in the humanities, which was taught both on and off campus utilizing interactive online teaching materials. While the interdisciplinary framework incorporates traditional humanities perspectives from disciplines such as history, philosophy, fine arts, cultural studies, literature, law, and anthropology, the program also integrates a strong Native American perspective, drawing upon significant input from tribal elders, tribal leaders, and prominent Indigenous writers and scholars from around the world.

Before any specific course subjects were considered, the following general aims were adopted: 1) the integration of Indigenous and mainstream perspectives and contributions; 2) encouragement of constant interplay of theory and practice; 3) significant interactive inculcation of visual and aural materials into the textual learning framework; and 4) the investigation of the relationship of abstract concepts, social life, and embodied knowledge texts with the objects of material culture through techniques of visual thinking.

The teaching program gains its focus from a common set of six core *dialectical* themes that provide continuity over the entire curriculum: 1) tradition and change; 2) nature and culture; 3) the local and the global; 4) self and community; 5) perception and representation; and 6) knowledge and power. Over the past generation, these themes have all been significant sites of conjecture and discussion in the humanities and social sciences. Furthermore, these themes are also on the cutting edge of debates within Indigenous educational communities.

The online format, which is seen as integral to the success of the project as a whole, is being designed to

- ensure that Native American students gain experience in the new technologies;
- capitalize on the unique capacity of electronic media in transmission of oral cultures;
- expedite access for off-campus students, particularly those in rural or remote sites;
- take advantage of electronic media's capacity to integrate modular materials to suit the needs of individual students;
- employ the resource of existing websites designed and managed by Indigenous peoples around the world; and
- facilitate information exchange and social interaction among people of diverse tribal affiliations.

The curriculum was intended primarily as a general education degree for Native Americans enrolled in tertiary courses at IAIA, but, through its placement online, was also made available to non-Natives and to Indigenous people in other parts of the world. Some of the materials are suitable for use at the graduate level.

Accepting the broad range of educational background and objectives of this proposed target audience, the Native Eyes Project hopes in some measure to individualize and personalize the instruction through specially designed tutorials, learning exercises, modular instructional materials, and writing assignments which could be chosen to relate to students' own particular ancestral backgrounds. Finally, the course was designed to enable students to better cope with, indeed to capitalize on, the multicultural environments that characterize the modern world.

Any educational program in the humanities needs to deal with how "culture" operates in the new technological environment and in the new global society. Native Eyes courses prepares American Indian and First Nations students to function effectively in modern society without loss of cultural identity. They further contribute to the humanities because they directly confront issues relating to education in a multicultural and pluralistic society. A significant number of students in US schools and universities share with Native Americans a profound sense of cultural disorientation. The modern American university is made up of students from many cultural backgrounds who also face continuous waves of social transformation and cultural disruption wrought by technological change and globalization. Teaching such students involves the difficult task of integrating disparate knowledge systems in ways that are intellectually productive and helpful to them.

In following these approaches, the purpose is not to set up a false dichotomy between academic and Indigenous points of view, but rather to make sure that the voice of the American Indian is heard, and integrated, within discussion of basic humanities concepts. It is also to relate these ideas to students' own lives and identities, communities and nations. The Indigenous knowledge systems approach is an emerging and powerful mode of inquiry.

"Objectivist" teaching methodologies, which assume that there is only one correct way of understanding the world, often fail at this task. In our experience, "relational" teaching methodologies, in which ways of knowing are related to social context and need, are more effective. Indigenous students who are taught to recognize the intellectual stature, cultural validity, and continuing social utility of traditional modes of thought actually become more, not less, able to integrate "Western" or "modern" ways of seeing and understanding into their worldviews. In other words, such students no longer feel required to choose between "expert knowledge" and the "wisdom of the elders."

In the beginning, an important objective of the Native Eyes Project was to build on the strengths and achievements of IAIA in the visual arts. In the intervening years, IAIA has had discussions with a number of museums to negotiate use of their databases of images and objects for teaching purposes that relate not so much to the ethnological dimension traditionally the focus of museum collections, but more to the third knowledge space considerations formulated above. In addition to their use in the study guides and for research purposes, a selection of these images has also been used in a series of online virtual exhibits accessible online to students. This approach enables images, video, and audio materials to be introduced into a multimedia learning framework. These exhibits utilize a range of learning techniques especially designed to promote visual thinking: problematic image juxtaposition; visual/verbal dialogue; visual narrative with verbal enhancement; verbal narrative with visual enhancement; nonlinear, multiple station-point narrative structure; and viewer interaction with exhibits.

While some might say that Native Eyes courses provide a "liberal studies" rather than "professional" orientation, the aim is to do both things: that is, to produce a new generation of Indigenous young people who are proud of their culture and at the same time able to wield traditional disciplinary skills and tools in the interests of both the individual and the community. Completing this degree, or parts of it, should well serve students intending careers in health, business and administration, law, policing, politics, teaching, art, creative writing, journalism, museums, social welfare, or indeed any career path in the modern world.

Appendix 1: An Applied Trajectory: Adapting the Third Knowledge System to the Visual Arts

The template below is provided to help schools and groups adapt the Third Knowledge System to the visual arts. Rather than present information about Indigenous arts from a regional or chronological frame, try incorporating the following conceptual tools found in the Native Eyes "Indigenous Voice Curriculum."

"Native Eyes; Indigenous Perspectives on Knowledge and Culture" proposes a course development initiative or "cluster" addressing the expressive forms of cultural production in Native North America. This area study is titled "Indigenous Voice." The aim of this component is to identify, examine, and seek to classify in new and culturally meaningful ways, key forms of representation in Native communities—both performative and material.

The goal of the "Indigenous Voice" curriculum is to uncover deeper understandings of cultural phenomena by adopting an interdisciplinary and inductive approach to learning in higher education. Four proposed key conceptual categories serve to link traditional disciplines such as anthropology, sociology, literary criticism, art history, film studies, religious studies, philosophy, music, and theater by focusing student discussion and research on certain cognitive themes. These themes include:

A) Relations—family, tribal, and adoptive means of relating oneself to a broader community using oral histories, genealogies, origin stories, archival research, digital technology, and photography;

B) Communications—conveying thought through language, storytelling, child development and training, leadership, visual signs and gestures, and myth by use of material culture studies, museum studies, ethnographic film, literature, and theater;

C) Life cycles—the characteristics of youth, maturity, and old age, gender, attitudes surrounding death and birth, naming, and change by examining life histories, enculturation, women's studies, and education;

D) Ceremony—ideas of contamination and cleansing, blessing, honoring, and resolution explored through religious studies, revitalization movements, dance and performance theory, ethnology, ethno-astronomy, environmental studies, and government.

Appendix 2: Native Eyes Courses

The seven courses described below were taught between 2000 and 2014 at IAIA in Santa Fe, New Mexico. Versions of these courses were also taught at Deakin University, Brandon University, and Charles Darwin University. The author would like to credit the following individuals who supported the development and implementation of the Native Eyes Project: Greg Cajete, LaDonna Harris, Barbara King, Toby Martinez, Nancy Marie Mithlo, Lloyd New, David Turnbull, David Warren, and Laurelyn Whitt. My gratitude goes out to the many other individuals who lent their time and expertise to this endeavor's aims and outcomes.

1) "Indigenous Perspectives on Knowledge"—In this course, students learn how ways of knowing relate to cultural values and social power, while they compare Indigenous knowledge systems to those of the dominant (European) culture. Students examine the value of Indigenous knowledge, particularly its potential contribution to sustainable development, to the alleviation of poverty, and to cultural survival and renewal.

2) "Indigenous Visual Studies"—This online course focuses on visual representation (photography, film, and hypermedia) both as a form of cultural documentation and as an exploration of unique visual worlds. Both the colonial project and Indigenous agency are presented as vantage points to understanding strategies of appropriation, commercialization, and political representation.

3) "Indigenous Perspectives of Place"—This course explores the nature of place and how different cultures conceive and orient themselves to it. As with all concepts, place does not exist in isolation. It is clearly directly connected to space and location, but also to time, narrative, identity, knowledge, and movement.

4) "How Indians Made America: History before Columbus"—Far from being a pristine wilderness, the environment of the pre-Columbian Americas was highly constructed and, by the global standard of the times, rather densely populated. The aim of this course is to bring that invisible historical reality back into focus with units on agriculture, cities, roadways and trails, knowledge systems, and remarkable social and intellectual achievements. This course will change the way students think about Indians as well as the way they think about America.

5) "Story Weaving: Ways of Knowing and Telling"—This highly innovative course approaches the honored Indigenous traditions of storytelling and weaving (rugs, baskets, etc.) as tools for the preservation and transmission of cultural, spiritual, ecological, astronomical, ethical, and historical knowledge. A special software tool called StoryWeaver has been developed especially

for this course and will enable even those students with minimal computer experience to create new stories that incorporate text, image, maps, oral history, tribal stories, and new media, including audio and video.

6) "Indigenous Perspectives on Nature"—This online course explores the way different peoples and cultures experience and understand nature, especially the relationship between humans and the natural world, looking at a range of ideas and theories from both mainstream and Indigenous traditions of thought. It is divided into two main sections: i) The Idea of Nature in Western and Indigenous Thought and ii) Nature and the American Indian.

7) "Indigenous Perspectives on Humor"—In this online course, students learn about the many roles humor plays in Native American life and culture. Students examine constructive and destructive uses of humor, racial and cultural stereotypes and how these work as colonizing forces, and laughter as an instrument of cultural liberation, as well as humor in art, literature, and oral tradition.

NOTES

1. The Native Eyes Project was funded by the W. M. Keck Foundation, the National Endowment for the Humanities, the National Aeronautics and Space Administration, the Victorian Education Foundation (Australia), and the American Indian Higher Education Consortium.

2. Laurelyn Whitt and David Chambers, "Knowledge Systems of Indigenous America," in *Encyclopaedia of the History of Science, Technology and Medicine in Non-Western Cultures*, ed. Helaine Selin, 1184–93 (Dordrecht, Netherlands: Springer, 2016).

3. David Turnbull, "(En)-Countering Knowledge Traditions: The Story of Cook and Tupaia," *Humanities Research* 1 (2000): 55–76, rpt. in *Science, Empire and the European Exploration of the Pacific*, ed. Tony Ballantyne, 225–46 (Aldershot, UK: Routledge, 2004).

4. Turnbull, "(En)-Countering Knowledge."

5. Turnbull, "(En)-Countering Knowledge."

BIBLIOGRAPHY

Barreiro, José. "The Search for Lessons." *Akwe:kon* 9, no. 2 (1992): 18–39.

Battiste, Marie. "Enabling the Autumn Seed: Toward a Decolonized Approach to Aboriginal Knowledge, Language and Education." *Canadian Journal of Native Education* 22, no.1 (1998): 16–27.

Battiste, Marie, and Sa'ke'j Youngblood Henderson. *Protecting Indigenous Knowledge and Heritage*. Saskatoon, SK: Purich, 2000.

Cajete, Gregory. *Native Science*. Santa Fe: Clear Light, 2000.

Castellano, Marlene Brant. "Updating Aboriginal Traditions of Knowledge." In *Indigenous Knowledges in Global Contexts*, ed. George J. Sefa Dei, Budd L. Hall, and Dorothy Goldin Rosenberg, 21–36. Toronto: University of Toronto Press, 2000.

Chambers, David Wade, "Seeing a World in a Grain of Sand: Science Teaching in Multicultural Context." *Science and Education* 8 (1999): 633–44.

——. "Story Weaver: el diseño de una aplicación web para reunir conocimientos dispares." In *Ensamblado en Colombia*, vol. 2: *Ensamblando heteroglosias*, ed. Olga Restrepo Forero. Bogotá: Universidad Nacional de Colombia, 239–51.

Chambers, David Wade, and Richard Gillespie. "Locality in the History of Science: Colonial Science, Technoscience and Indigenous Knowledge." *Osiris* 15 (2000): 221–40.

Chambers, David Wade, and Helen Watson (with the Yolngu Community at Yirrkala). *Singing the Land, Signing the Land*. Geelong, Victoria, Australia: Deakin University Press, 1989.

Chambers, David Wade, and Laurie Anne Whitt. *Concepts of Knowledge*. Online textbook for the Native Eyes Project at the Institute of American Indian Art. 2003.

Coffey, Wallace, and Rebecca Tsosie. "Rethinking the Tribal Sovereignty Doctrine: Cultural Sovereignty and the Collective Future of Indian Nations." *Stanford Law & Policy Review* 12 (Spring, 2001): 191–224.

Deloria, Vine, Jr. "Relativity, Relatedness and Reality." *Winds of Change* 7, no. 4 (1992): 34–40.

——. *Spirit and Reason*. Golden, CO: Fulcrum, 1999.

Ermine, Willie. "Aboriginal Epistemology." In *First Nations Education in Canada*, ed. Marie Battiste and Jean Barman, 101–12. Vancouver, BC: University of British Columbia Press. 1995.

Holmes, Leilani. "Heart Knowledge, Blood Memory, and the Voice of the Land: Implications of Research among Hawaiian Elders." In *Indigenous Knowledges in Global Contexts*, ed. George J. Sefa Dei, Budd L. Hall and Dorothy Goldin Rosenberg, 37–53. Toronto: University of Toronto Press, 2000.

James, Keith, ed. *Science and Native American Communities*. Lincoln: University of Nebraska Press, 2001.

LaDuke, Winona. *All Our Relations: Native Struggles for Land and Life*. Cambridge, MA: South End Press, 1999.

McGregor, Debbie. "Coming Full Circle: Indigenous Knowledge, Environment, and Our Future." *American Indian Quarterly* 28, no. 3 and 4 (2004): 385–410.

Momaday, N. Scott. "Native American Attitudes to the Environment." In *Seeing with a Native Eye*, ed. W. Copps, 79–85. New York: Harper & Row, 1976.

Scott, Craig. "Indigenous Self-Determination and Decolonization of the International Imagination." *Human Rights Quarterly* 18, no. 4 (1996): 814–20.

Shiva, Vandana. *Monocultures of the Mind: Perspectives on Biodiversity and Biotechnology*. London: Zed Books, 1993.

Silko, Leslie Marmon. *Yellow Woman and a Beauty of the Spirit*. New York: Simon and Schuster, 1996.

Simpson, Leanne R. "Anticolonial Strategies for the Recovery and Maintenance of Indigenous Knowledge." *American Indian Quarterly* 28, no. 3 and 4 (2004): 373–84.

Smith, Linda Tuhiwai. *Decolonizing Methodologies: Research and Indigenous Peoples*. New York: Zed Books, 1999.

Tafoya, Terry. "Coyote's Eyes: Native Cognition Styles." *Journal of American Indian Education* special issue (February 1982): 29–42.

Turnbull, David. "(En)-Countering Knowledge Traditions: The Story of Cook and Tupaia." *Humanities Research* 1 (2000): 55–76. Reprinted in Tony Ballantyne, ed., *Science, Empire and the European Exploration of the Pacific*, 225–46. Aldershot, UK: Routledge, 2004.

——. *Maps Are Territories: Science Is an Atlas*. Chicago: University of Chicago Press, 1993.

——. *Masons, Tricksters and Cartographers: Comparative Studies in the Sociology of Scientific and Indigenous Knowledge*. 2nd ed. London: Routledge, 2003.

——. "Multiplicity, Criticism and Knowing What to Do Next: Way-Finding in a Transmodern World." In *Social Epistemology* 19, no. 1 (2005): 19-32. Special Issue on Meera Nanda.

——. "Performance and Narrative, Bodies and Movement in the Construction of Places and Objects, Spaces and Knowledges: The Case of The Maltese Megaliths." *Theory, Culture and Society* 19, no. 5 and 6 (2002): 125–43. Special Issue on Sociality and Materiality.

Waters, Anne, ed. *American Indian Thought*. Boston: Basil Blackwell, 2004.

Whitt, Laurelyn. *Science, Colonialism, and Indigenous Peoples: The Cultural Politics of Law and Knowledge*. Cambridge, Cambridge University Press, 2009.

Whitt, Laurie Anne. "Biocolonialism and the Commodification of Knowledge." *Science as Culture* 7, no.1 (1998): 33–67.

——. "Indigenous Peoples and the Cultural Politics of Knowledge." In Michael Green, ed., *Issues in American Indian Cultural Identity*, 223–71. New York: Peter Lang, 1995.

Whitt, Laurie Anne, Mere Roberts, Waerete Norman, and Vicki Grieves. "Belonging to Land: Indigenous Knowledge Systems and the Natural World." *Oklahoma City University Law Review* 26, no. 2 (2001): 701–43.

Williams, Robert A. Jr. *Linking Arms Together: American Indian Treaty Visions of Law & Peace 1600-1800*. New York: Oxford University Press, 1997.

Wilson, Waziyatawin Angela. "Indigenous Knowledge Recovery Is Indigenous Empowerment." *American Indian Quarterly* 28, no. 3 and 4. (2004): 359–72.

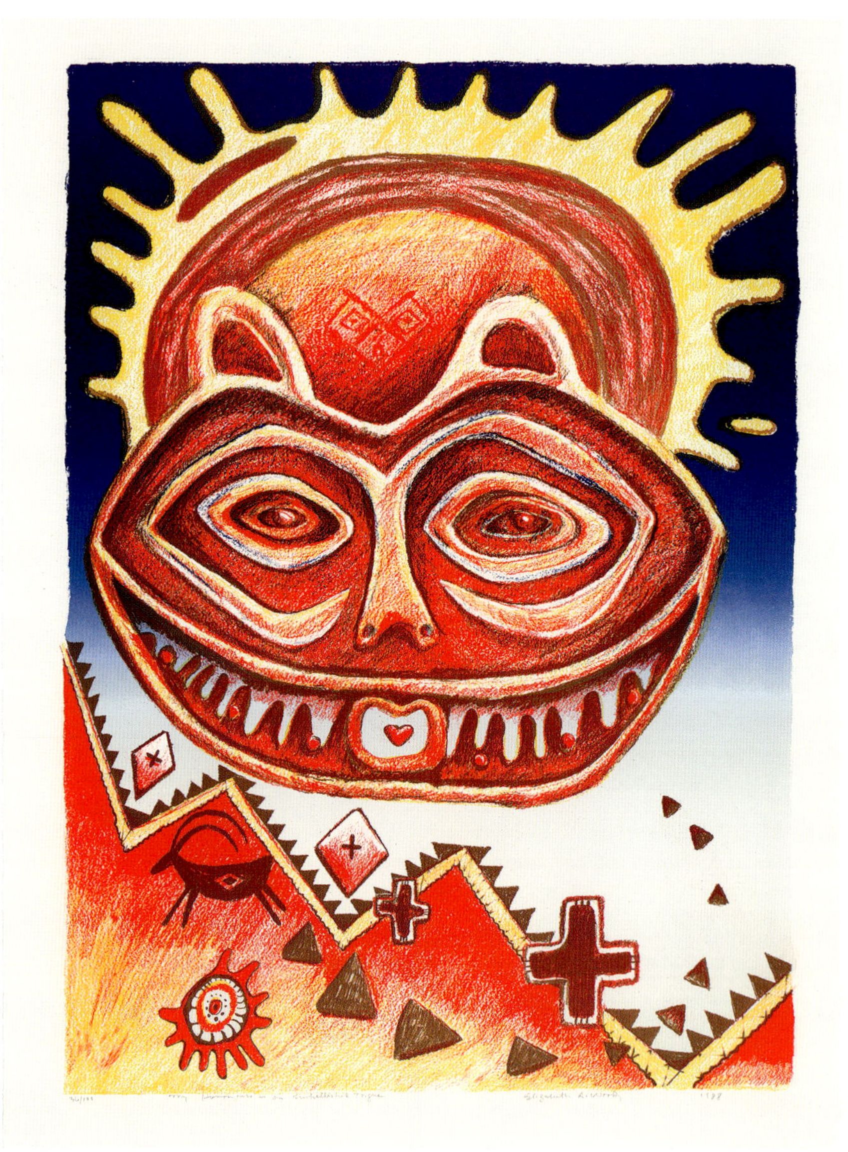

FIGURE 86 Elizabeth Woody (Wasco), *My Humanness Is an Embellished Tongue*, 1988, offset lithograph on paper, 30 in. × 22 in., MoCNA Collection, WAS-14 (photo by Jason S. Ordaz).

Illumination

POEM BY ELIZABETH WOODY

The irresistible and benevolent light
brushes through the angel-wing begonias,
the clippings of ruddy ears for the living room.
Intimate motes, debris of grounded, forlorn walks,
speckle through the vitreous quality of blush.
As fluid lulls turn like trout backs, azure-tipped fins
oscillate in the shallows, the clear floating
is dizziness.

Tender events are meeting halves and wholes of affinity,
the recurrence of whimsy and parallel streams
flush away the blockage of malaise.
Incessant gratitude, pliable kindness smolders
in the husk of these sweet accumulations:
abalone shells, the thoughtful carvings from friends,
the stone of another's pocket, the photo of mystified
moon over water, the smiles of worn chairs.

Austere hopes find pleasure in lately cherished flowers.
The blooms are articulate deluge, hues of delicacy.
Petals parted dim renderings, the viable imprint
of the blood-hot beam of light with reformed courage.
Beveling the finish to suppression, the blade of choice
brings the flourish of dividing while adequately doubling
worth by two. Multiplying. The luminescent burning of space.
The heat is a domicile as abandoned as red roses budding
their ascension from stem.

The sun has its own drum contenting itself with the rose
heart it takes into continual rumbling. The connection
of surface and hand. The great head of dark clouds finds
its own place of unraveled repercussions and disruption,
elsewhere, over the tall, staunch mountains of indemnity.

GALLERY FOUR

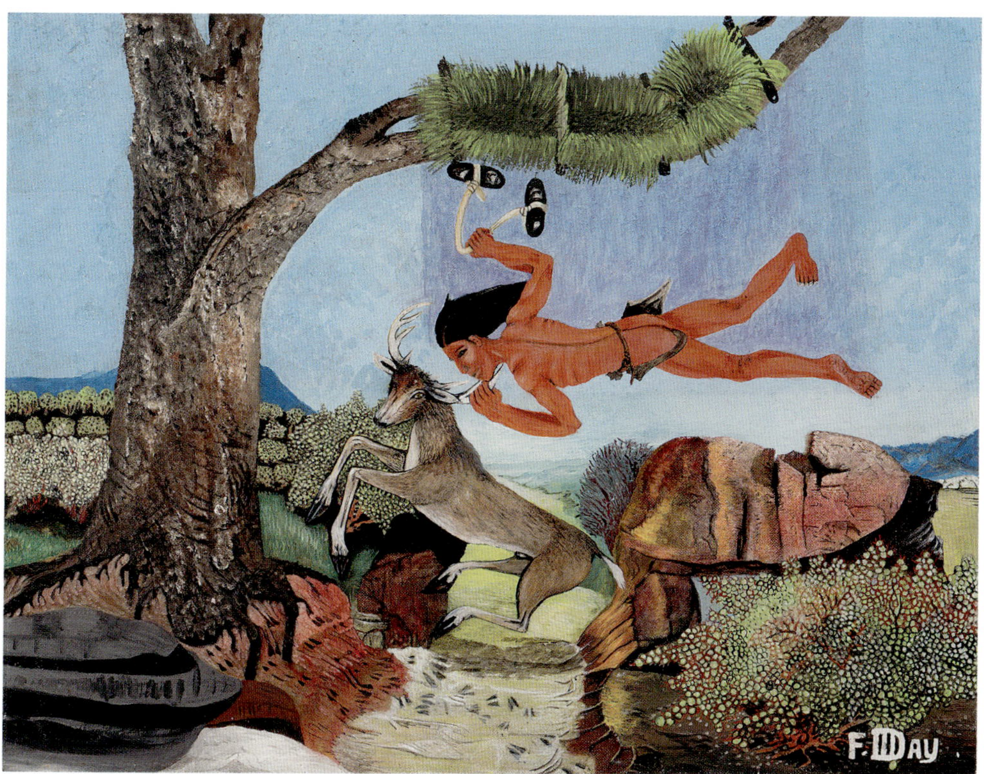

PLATE 71 Frank Day (Konkaw Maidu), *Stalking Deer*, 1967, oil on board, 18.75 in. × 22.75 in., MoCNA Collection, MA-6 (photo by Jason S. Ordaz).

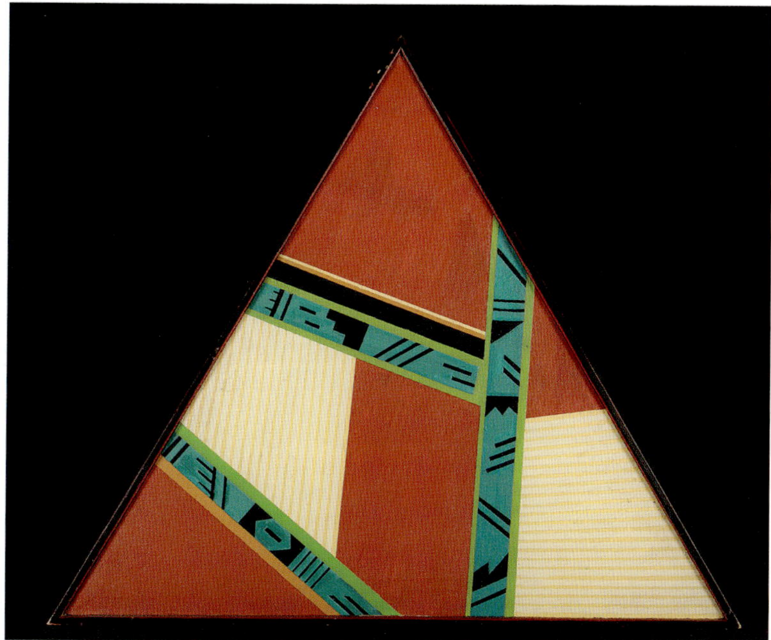

PLATE 72 Frances Makil (Hopi/Pima), *Triangle Painting*, 1968, acrylic on canvas, 28.38 in. × 28.38 in. × 28.38 in., MoCNA Collection, H-49 (photo by Addison Doty).

PLATE 73 Otellie Loloma, 1971, photo by Robert Nugent, IAIA Archives (RG01, S11, Box 2).

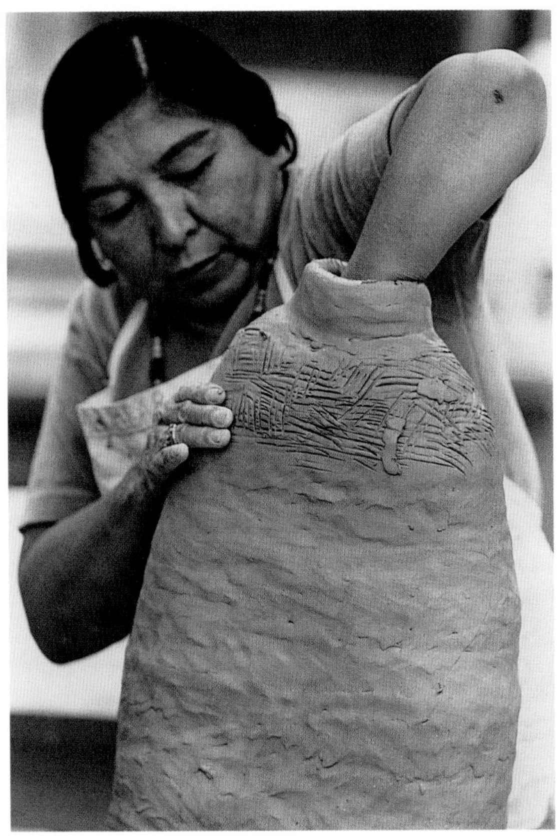

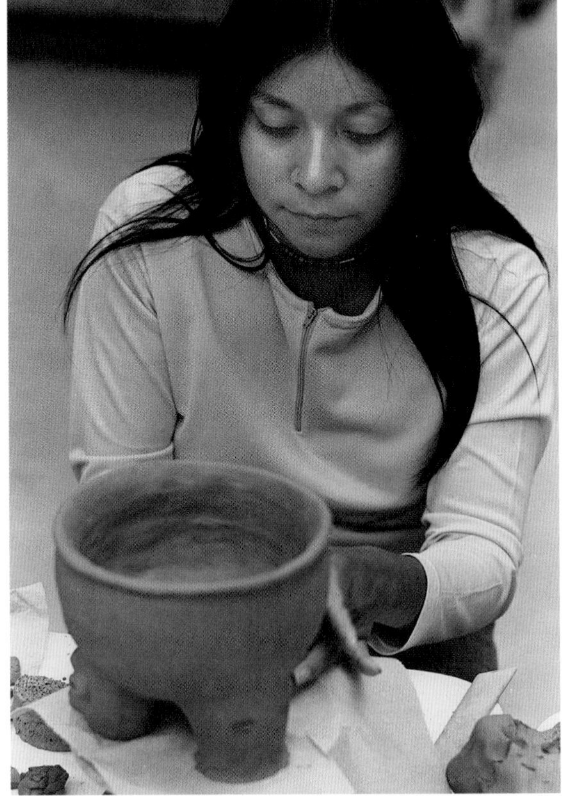

PLATE 74 IAIA student graduate Frances Makil with her clay piece teaching a two-day course on the Phoenix Art Van, 1971, photo by Robert Nugent, IAIA Archives (RG01, SG11, Box 2).

PLATE 75 Otellie Loloma (Hopi), *Tall Man with Bird*, ca. 1960–1971, clay, 36 in. × 11 in., MoCNA Collection, H-131 (photo by Walter BigBee).

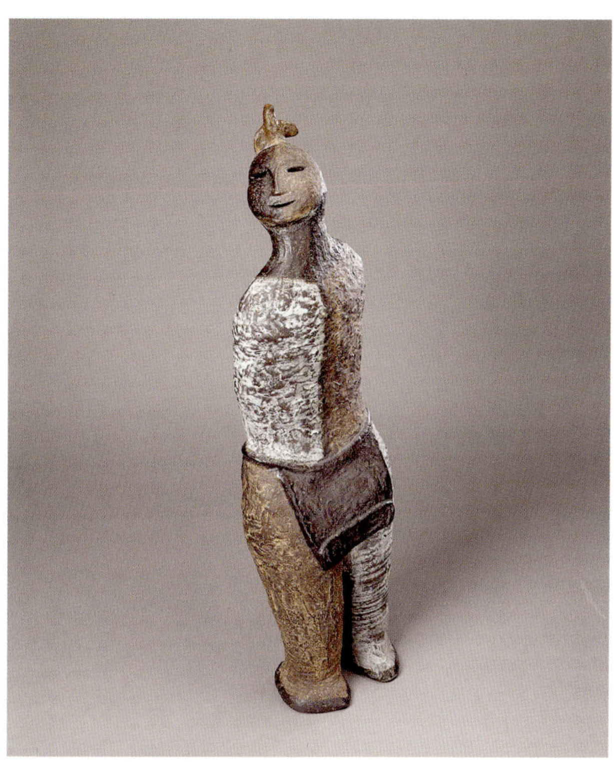

PLATE 76 Otellie Loloma (Hopi), *Bird Woman*, 1962, clay, turquoise, shell, 32 in. × 10 in. × 7, MoCNA Collection, H-371 (photo by Walter BigBee).

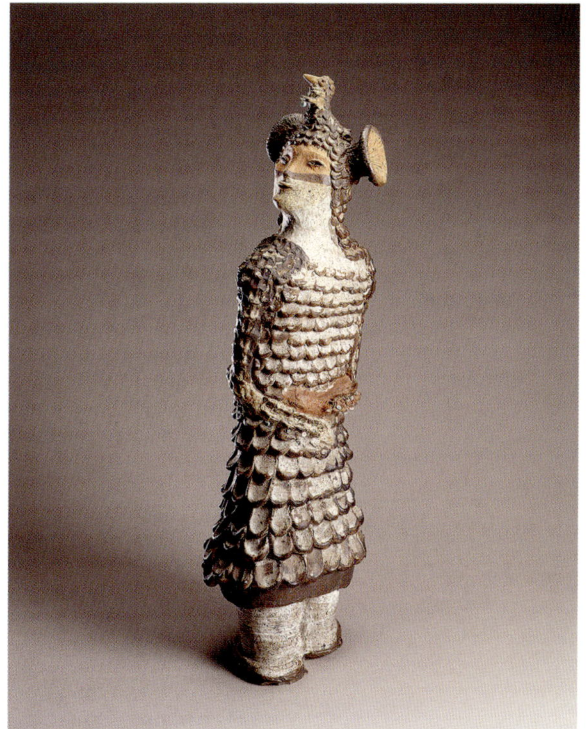

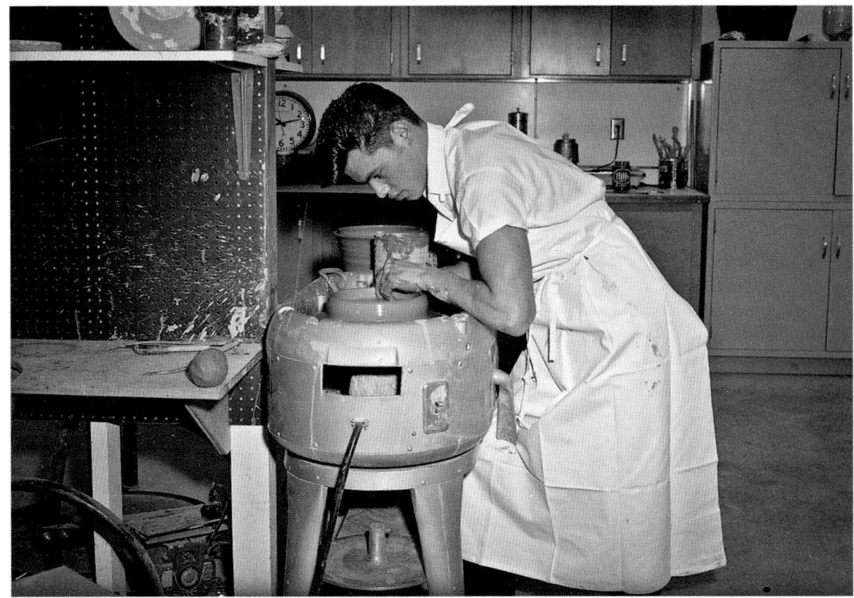

PLATE 77 IAIA student on pottery wheel, 1963, photo by Kay V. Wiest, IAIA Archives (MS10.010.090).

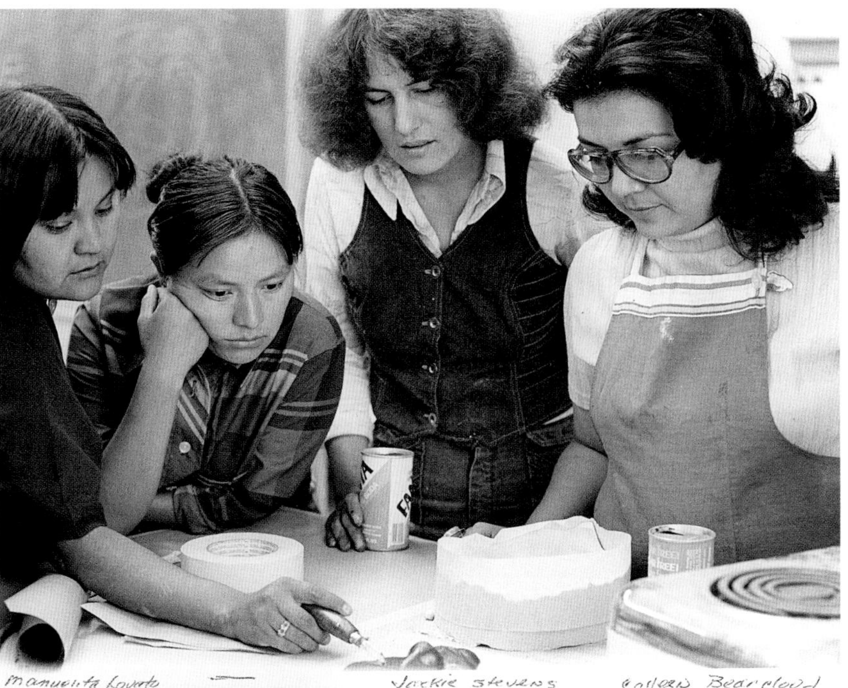

PLATE 78 IAIA students in class with instructor Manuelita Lovato (left to right: Manuelita Lovato, student unknown, Jackie Stevens, Colleen Bearcloud), ca. 1972, IAIA Archives (RG03, Box 9, Folder 4).

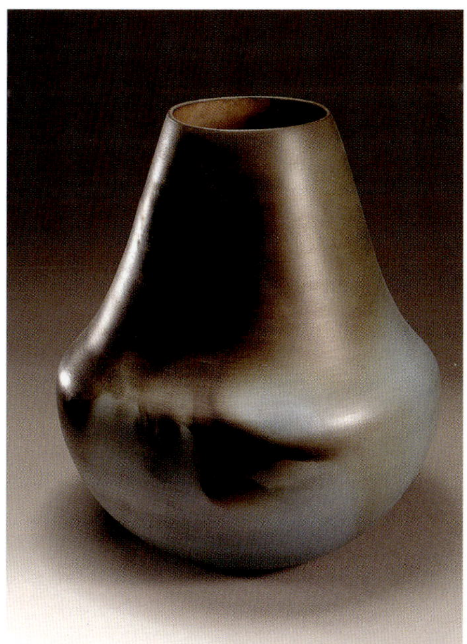

PLATE 79. Jacquie Stevens (Winnebago), Vase, 1985, micaceous clay, 14.75 in. × 39.50 in., MoCNA Collection, WIN-25 (photo by Walter BigBee).

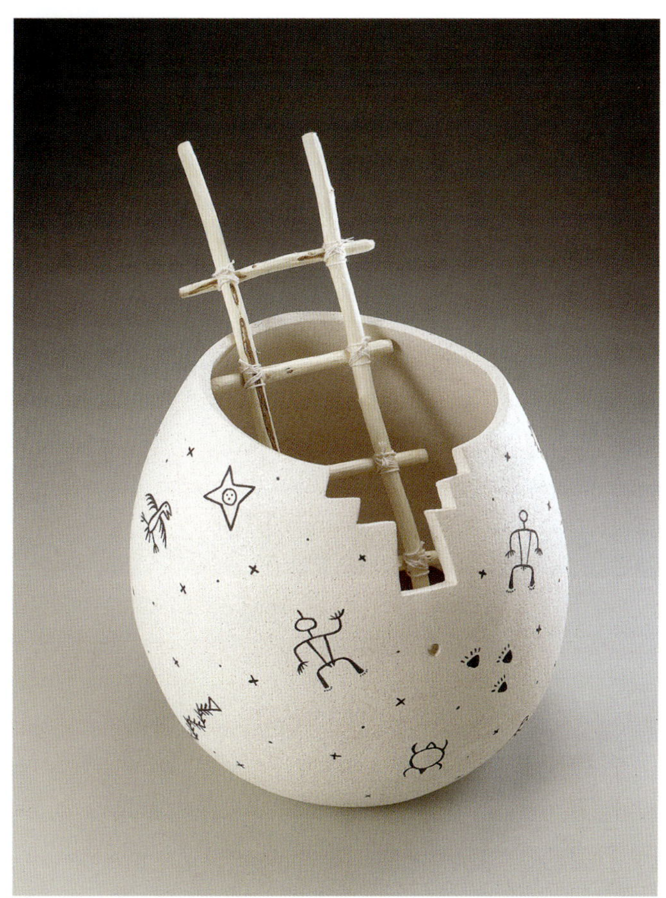

PLATE 80 Laura Fragua Cota (Jemez Pueblo), *Womb Bowl*, 1999, clay, sand, wood, 10.5 in. × 11 in., MoCNA Collection, J-86 (photo by Walter BigBee).

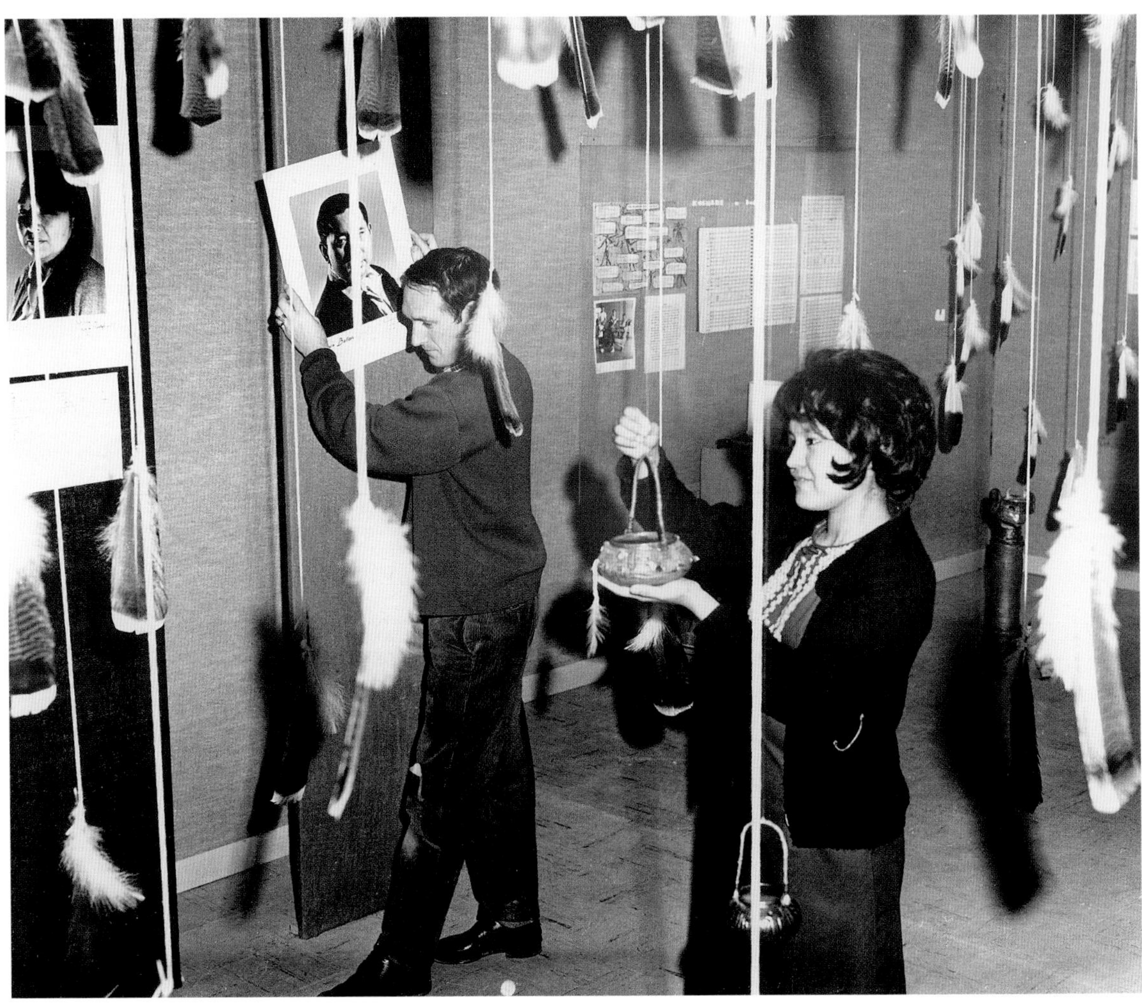

PLATE 81 James McGrath and Manuelita Lovato hanging 1966 IAIA Faculty exhibit, 1966, photo by Kay V. Wiest, IAIA Archives (RG03, Box 18).

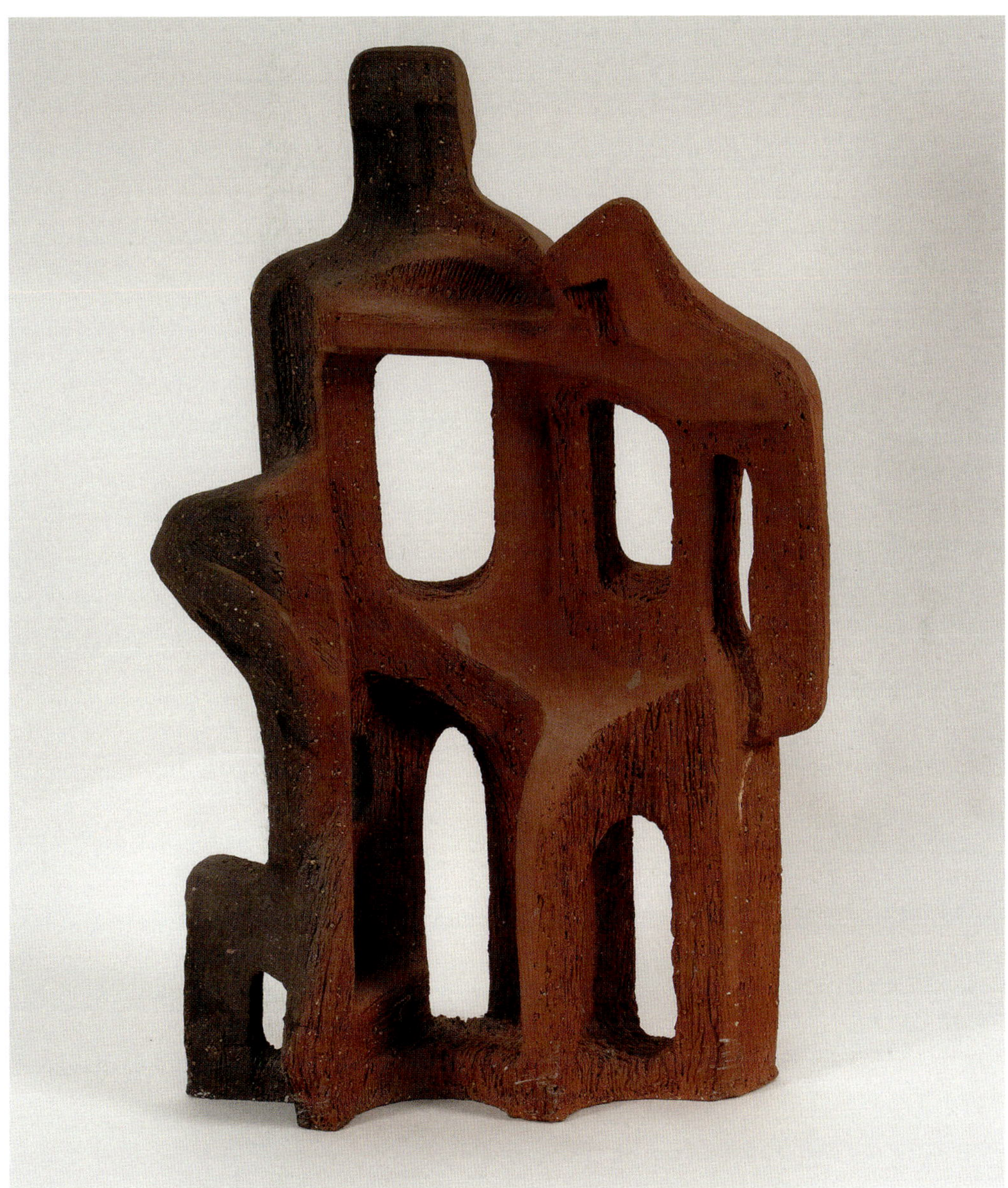

PLATE 82 Manuelita Lovato (Santo Domingo Pueblo), *Untitled*, ca. 1964, clay, 19.5 in. × 11.5 in. × 5.5 in., MoCNA Collection, PROP-221 (photo by Dianne Stromberg).

PLATE 83 Imogene Goodshot, a former student and an IAIA Traditional Techniques instructor, holds a photo of her grandmother who was the granddaughter of Crazy Horse, 1973, photo by Allen Thorne, IAIA Archives (RG02.1973.07).

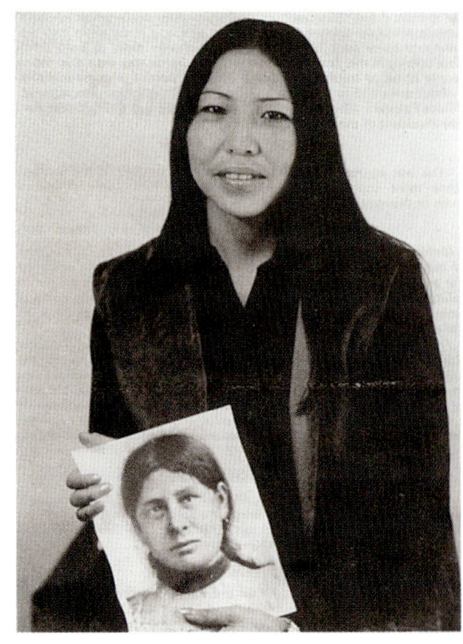

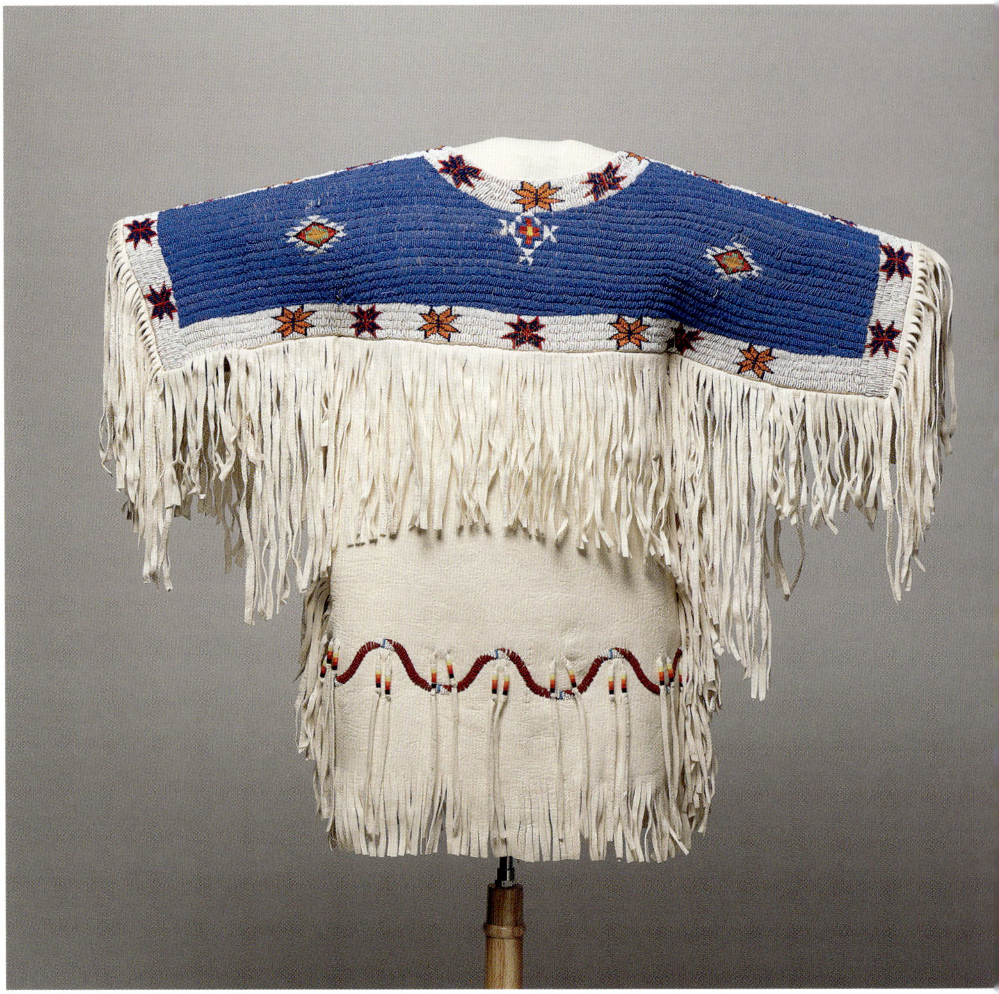

PLATE 84 Imogene Goodshot (Oglala Sioux), *Beaded Child Dress*, 1975, beads on buckskin, 14.25 in. × 33 in., MoCNA Collection, S-224 (photo by Walter BigBee).

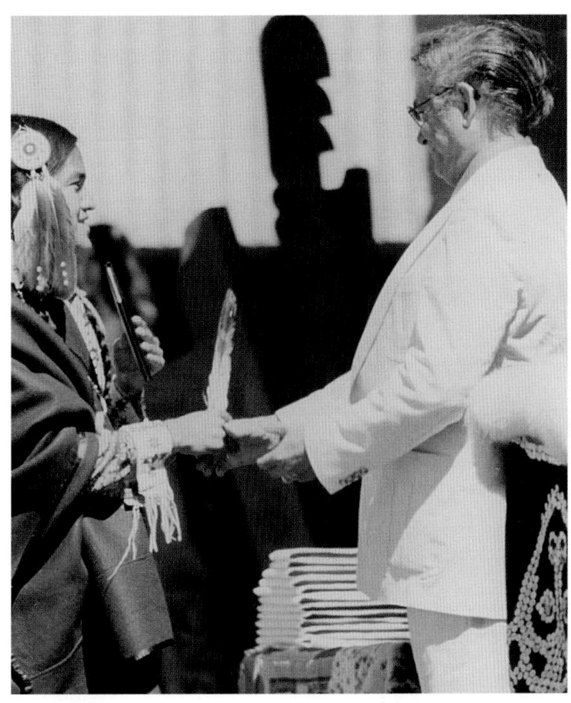

PLATE 85 *left* IAIA graduation with Lloyd New, ca. 1975, IAIA Archives (RG03, Box 8, Folder 1).

PLATE 86 *below* IAIA photography students screen printing, 1972, photo by Robert Nugent, IAIA Archives (RG03, Box 22, Folder 1).

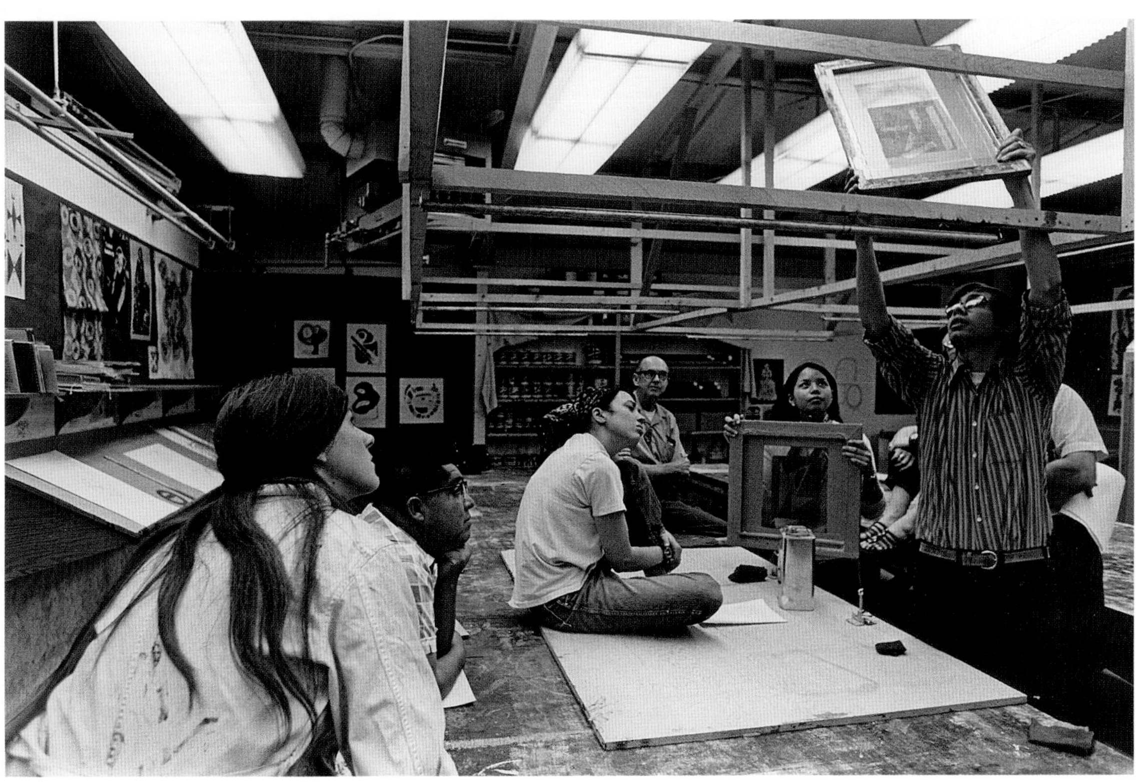

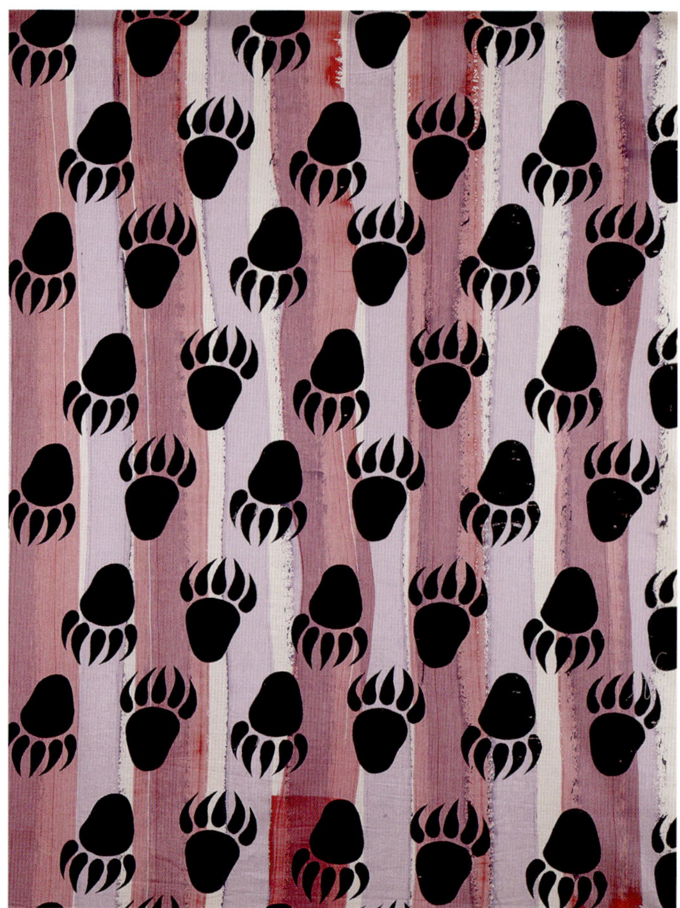

PLATE 87 *right* Mike One Star (Sioux), *Untitled (bear paws on stripes)*, 1976, fabric dyes on rayon, 175 in. × 46 in., MoCNA Collection, S-230 (photo by Walter BigBee).

PLATE 88 *below* Former students of IAIA return to join the instructional staff (L to R: Bill Prokopiof, Linda Lomahaftewa, Hank Gobin, Larry Ahvakana, Manuelita Lovato, Keith Conway, Grey Cohoe, Ted Palmanteer, and Larry DesJarlais), 1977, IAIA Archives (RG01.1977.10).

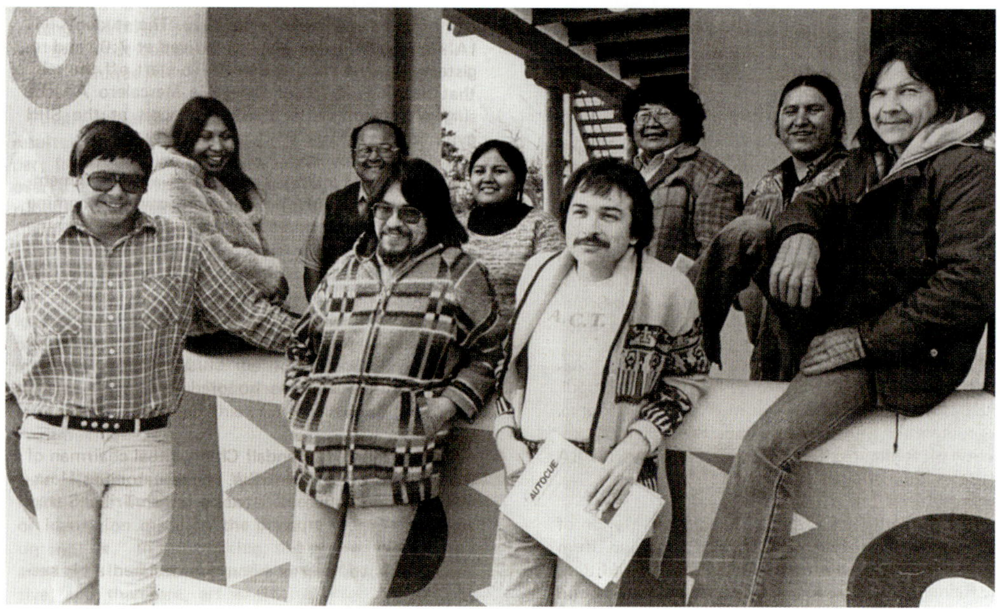

PLATE 89 Linda Lomahaftewa (Hopi/Choctaw), *Parrots Prayer Song*, Edition 36/40, 1989, offset lithograph on paper, 30 in. × 20 in., MoCNA Collection, H-412 (photo by Jason S. Ordaz).

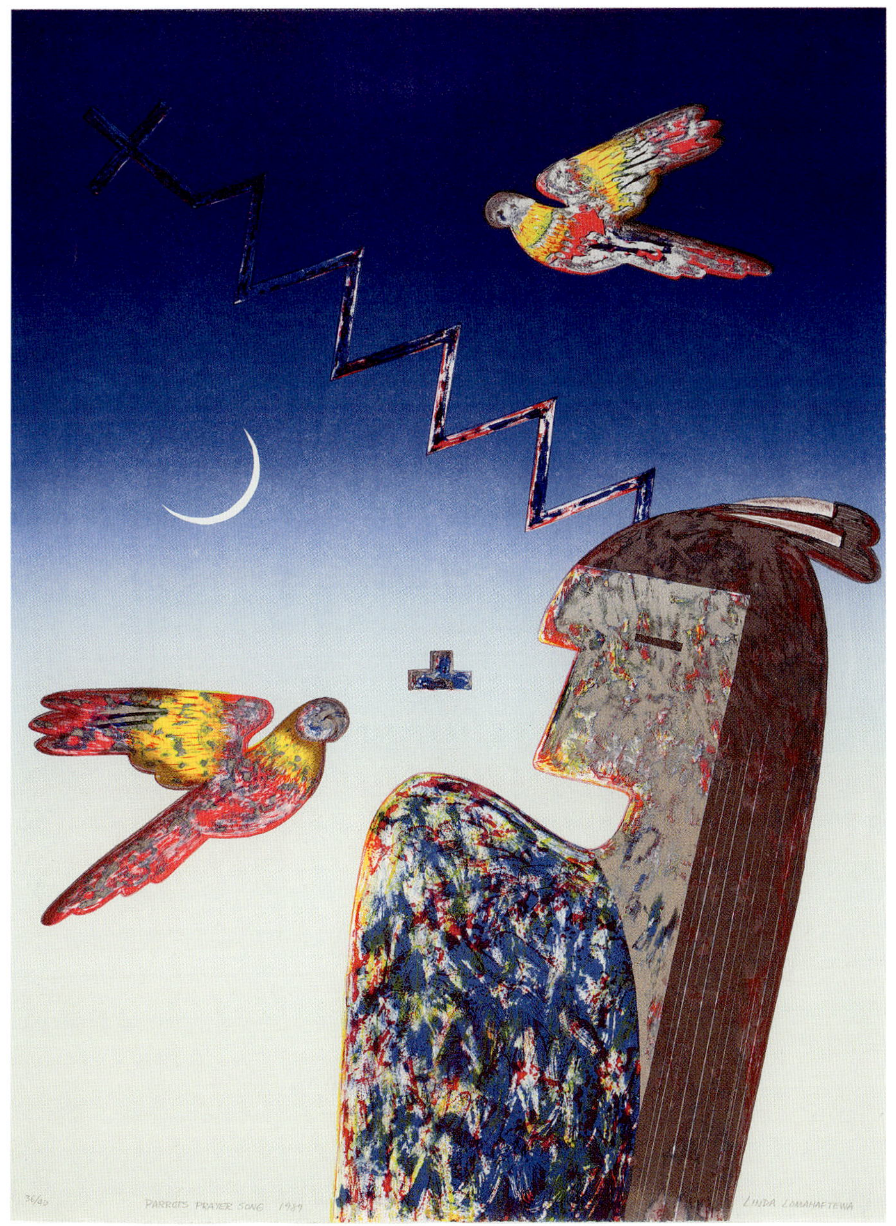

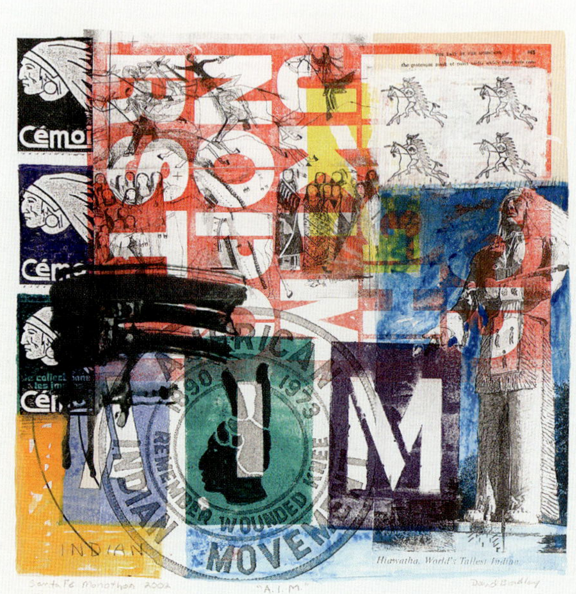

PLATE 90 David Bradley (Chippewa/Ojibway), *A. I. M.*, 2002, monotype on paper, 30 in. × 22 in., MoCNA Collection, CHP-174 (photo by Jason S. Ordaz).

PLATE 91 David Bradley (Chippewa/Ojibway), *The Married Woman*, Edition 9/48, 1980, lithograph on paper, 22.5 in. × 15.38 in., MoCNA Collection, CHP-149 (photo by Jason S. Ordaz).

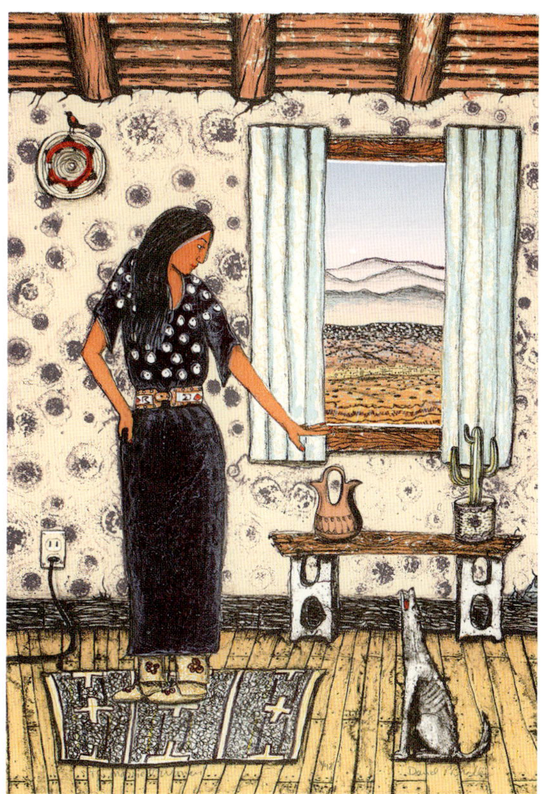

PLATE 92 Tammy Rahr (Cayuga), *Endangered Species*, ca. 1993, wood, cloth, beads, 34 in. × 14 in., MoCNA Collection, CA-1 (photo by Walter BigBee).

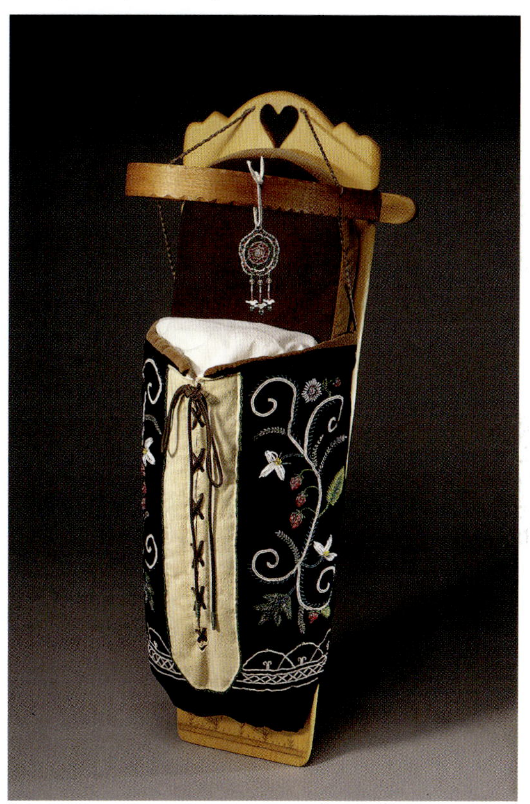

PLATE 93 Dolores Guerrero-Cruz (Xicana/Mexican), *El Veso*, Edition 36/100, 1990, offset lithograph on paper, 30 in. × 22 in., MoCNA Collection, MEX-37 (photo by Jason S. Ordaz).

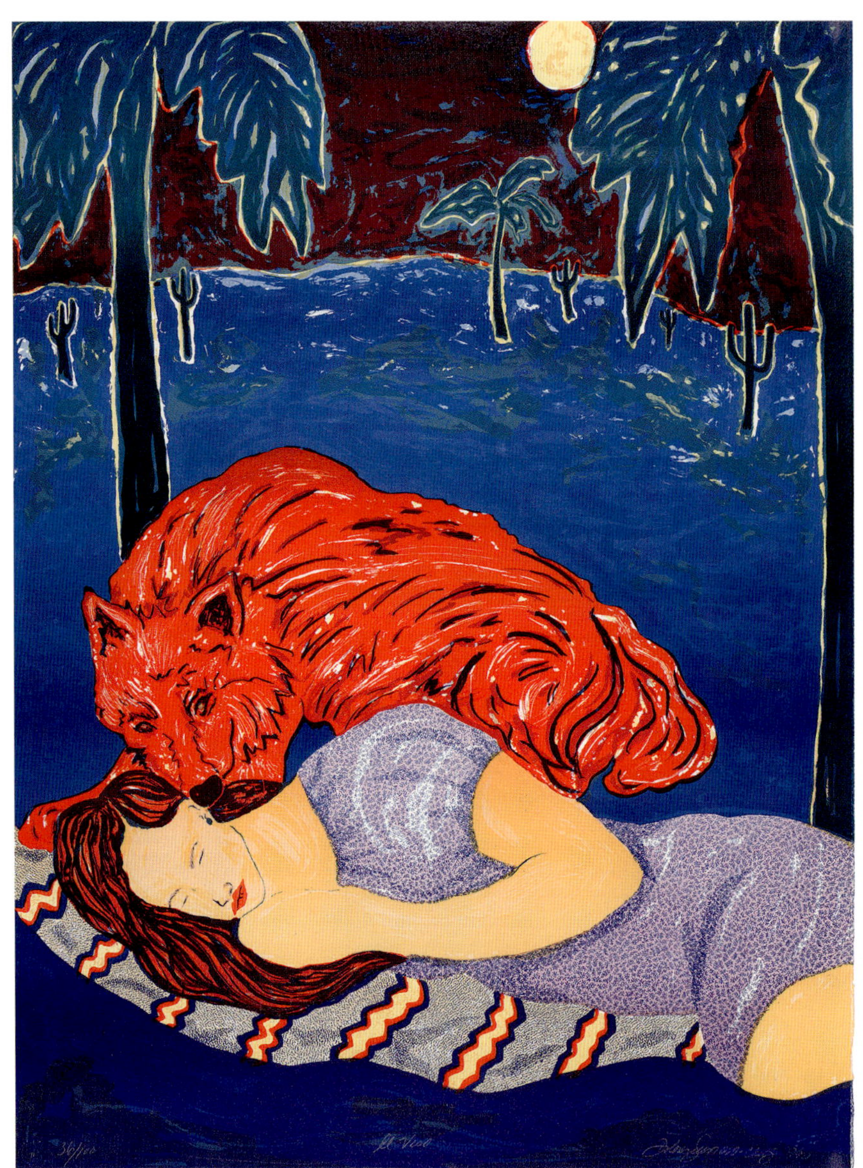

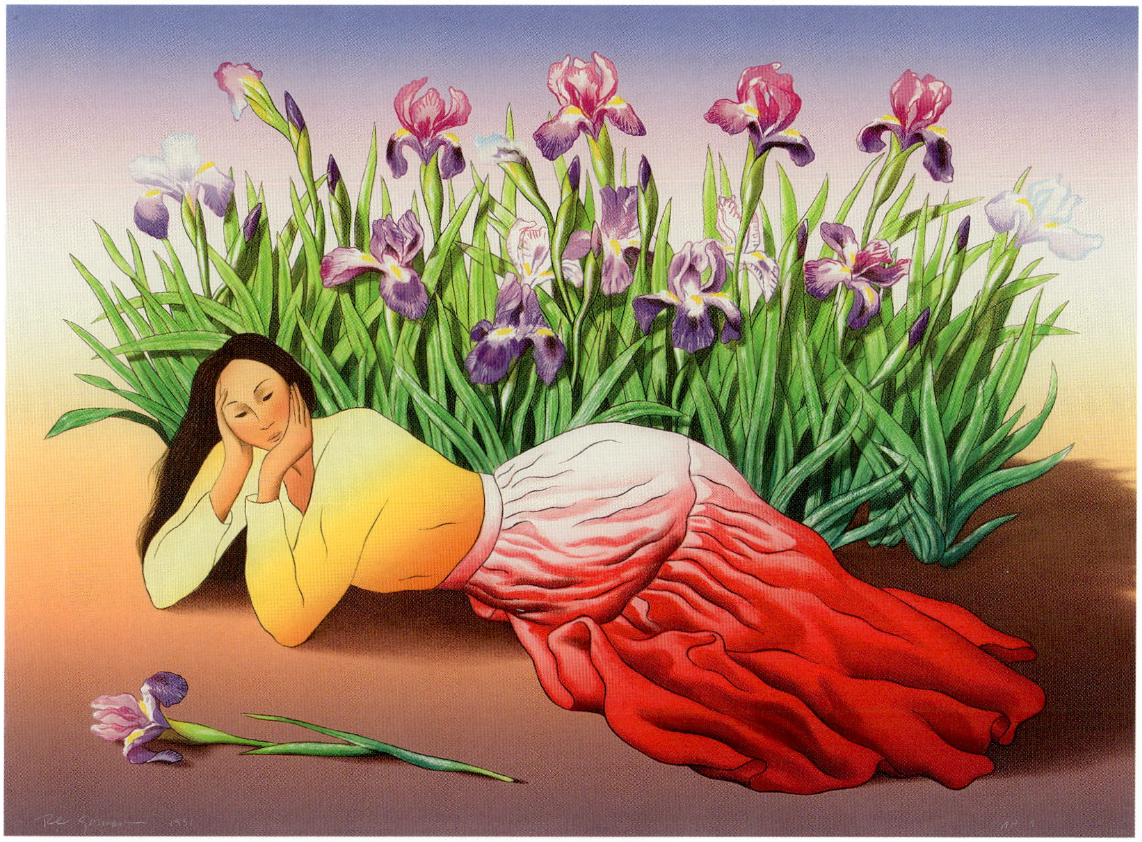

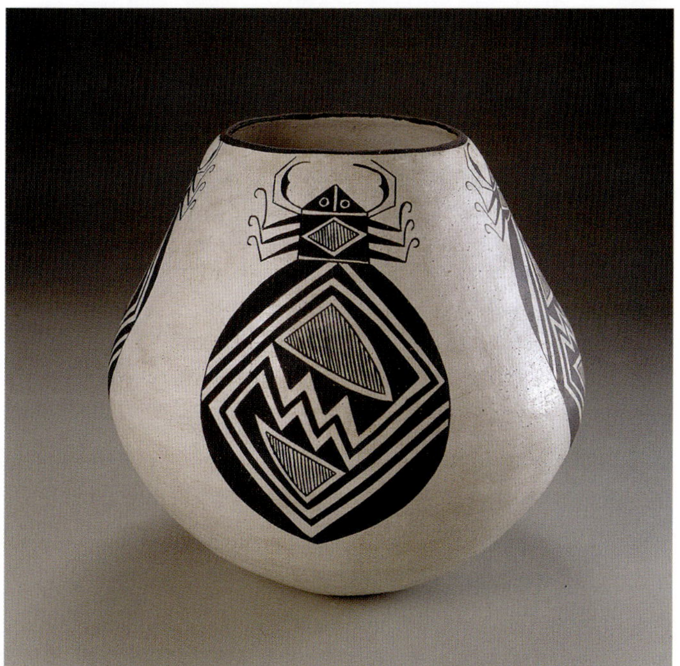

PLATE 94 *above* R. C. Gorman (Navajo), *Iris*, Edition A/P, Number 9, 1991, monotype, color pencil on paper, 27 in. × 36 in., MoCNA Collection, N-1133 (photo by Jason S. Ordaz).

PLATE 95 *left* Lucy Martin Lewis (Acoma Pueblo), *Beetle Design Bowl*, 1968, clay, 11 in. × 9 in., MoCNA Collection, AC-7 (photo by Walter BigBee).

PLATE 96 Susan A. Point (Coast Salish), *Black Bear Children*, Edition 24/45, 1992, color serigraph on paper, 21 in. × 20.875 in., MoCNA Collection, SAL-8 (photo by Jason S. Ordaz).

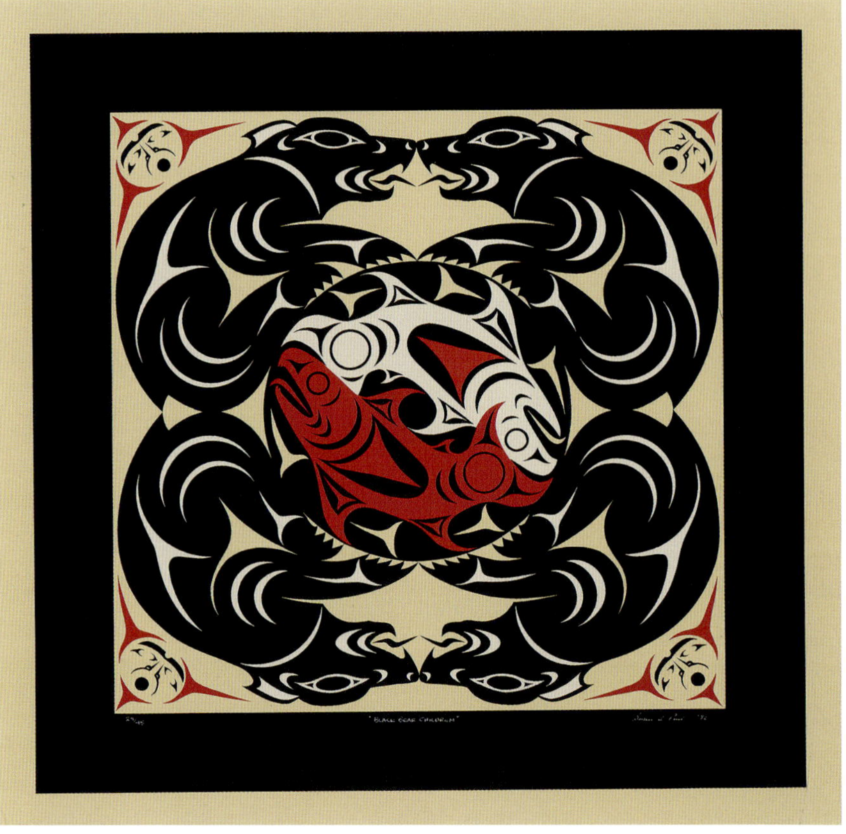

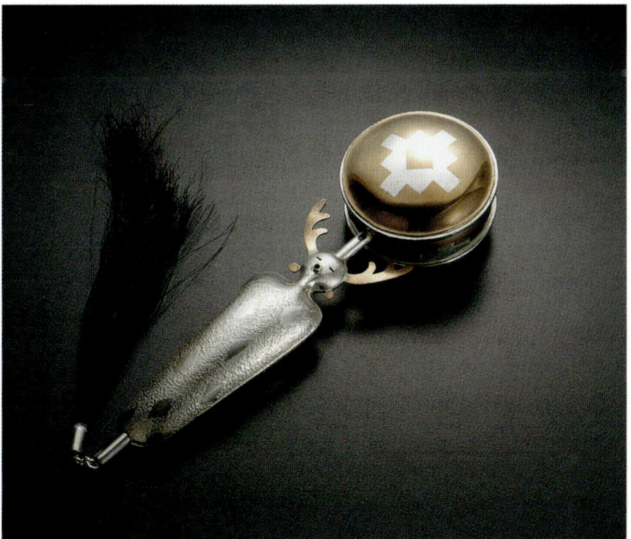

PLATE 97 Linda Lou Metoxen (Navajo), *Elk Spirit*, 1999, copper, horsehair on silver, 17.5 in. × 3 in. × 1.5 in., MoCNA Collection, N-1157 (photo by Walter BigBee).

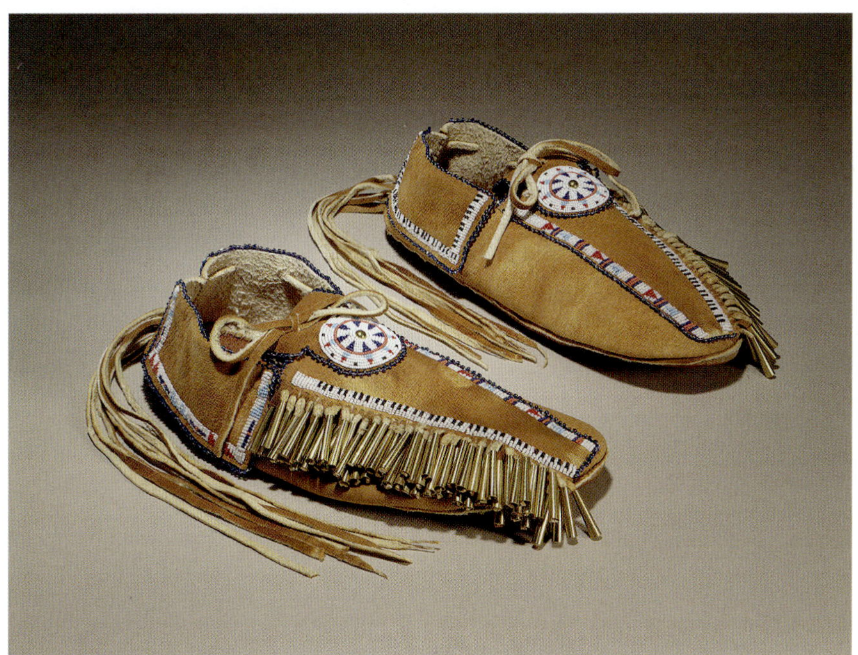

PLATE 98 Edward Wapp (Sac-Fox/Comanche), *Make Me Dance Ivories*, 2003, brass jingles and beads on buckskin, 3 in. × 10.25 in. × 25 in., MoCNA Collection, SF-34 (photo by Walter BigBee).

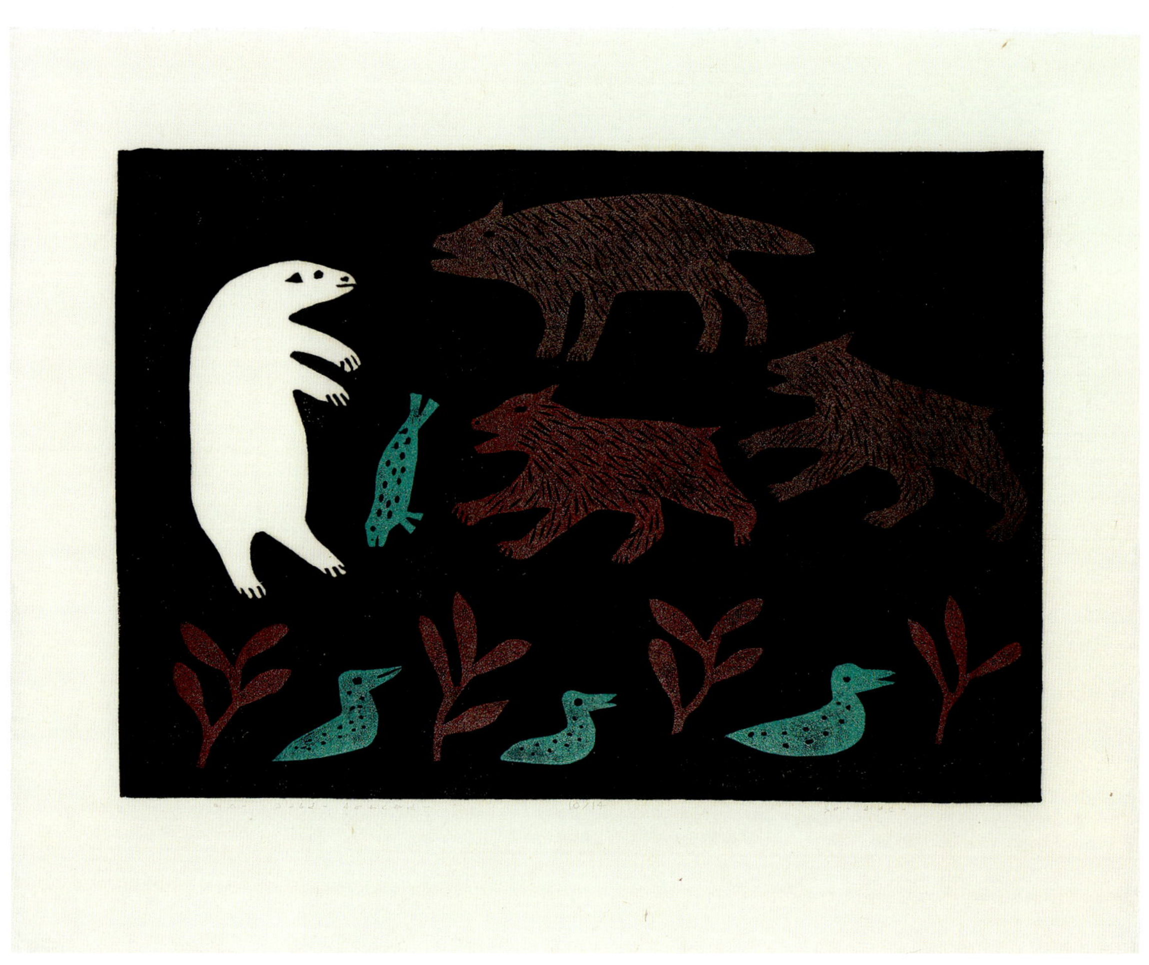

PLATE 99 Janet Nipi Ikuutaq (Nunavut, Baker Lake), *Fighting over the Dead Seal*, Edition 10/14, 1997, woodcut on paper, 21 in. × 25.5 in., MoCNA Collection, CAN-27 (photo by Jason S. Ordaz).

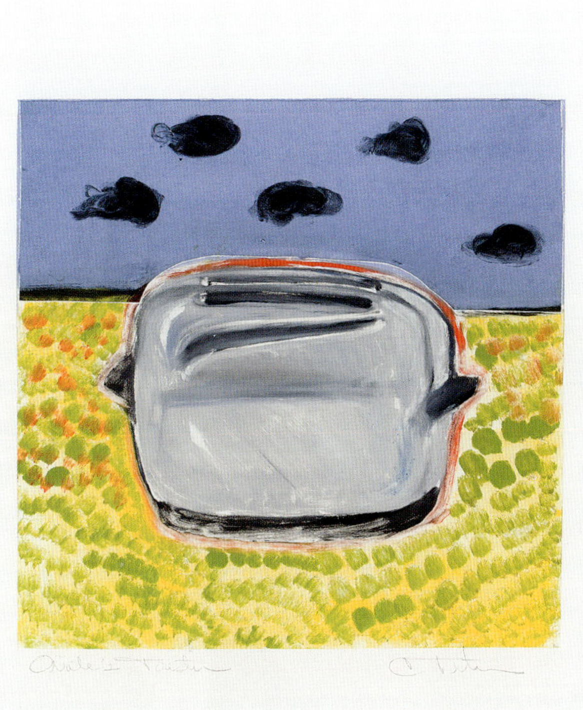

PLATE 100 *left* Charlene Teters (Spokane), *Oñate's Toaster*, 1999, monotype on paper, 29.75 in. × 22.25 in., MoCNA Collection, SPK-51 (photo by Jason S. Ordaz).

PLATE 101 *below* Roxanne Swentzell (Santa Clara Pueblo), *A Day at Cochiti Lake*, 2006, mixed media on paper, 14 in. × 35 in., MoCNA Collection, SC-162 (photo by Jason S. Ordaz).

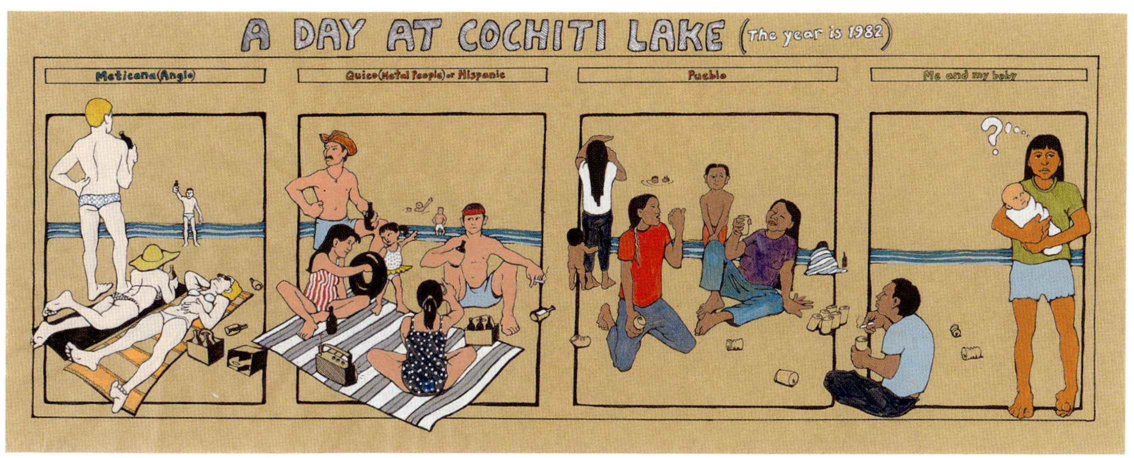

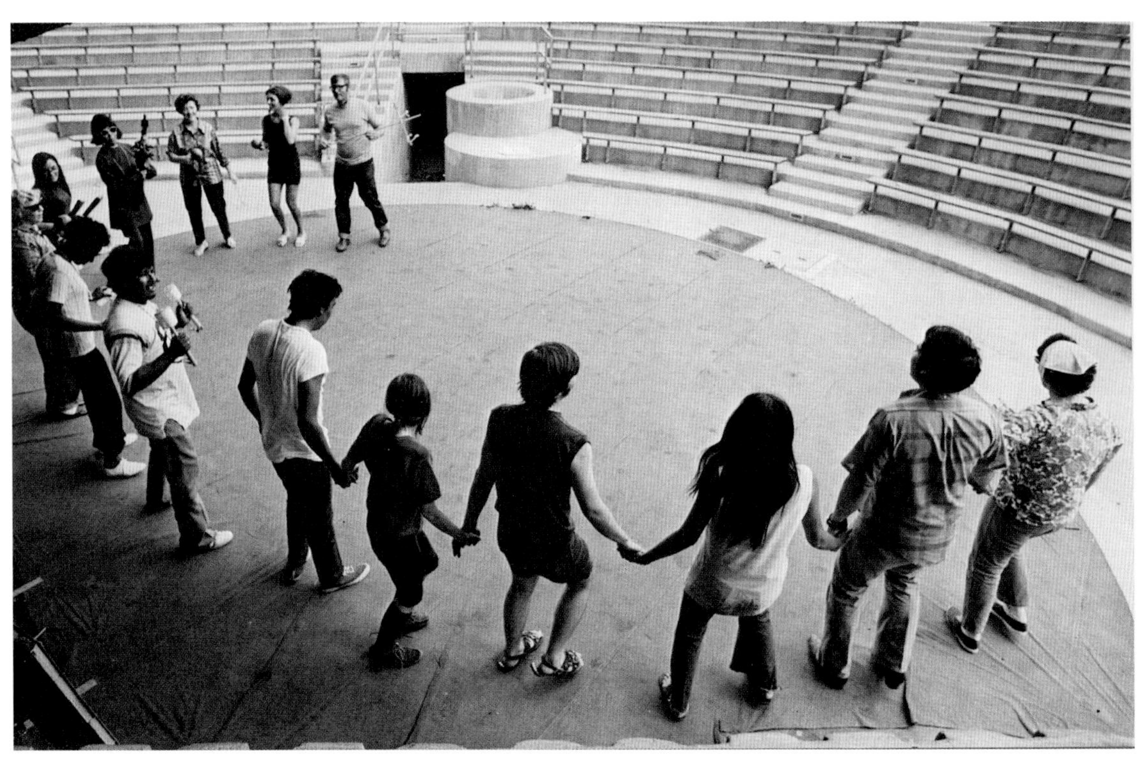

PLATE 102 IAIA students on stage at Soleri Theater, 1975, IAIA Archives (RG02.1975.01p39).

DAVID WADE CHAMBERS received his PhD (History of Science) from Harvard University in 1969 and completed a postdoctoral fellowship at the Smithsonian Institution. Between 1999 and 2011, he was Director of the Native Eyes Online Indigenous Studies Program at the Institute of American Indian Arts. Chambers is the author of eleven textbooks in the cultural studies of science and five in Indigenous Studies, including *Imagining Nature* (winner of the Australian National Book Award for Best Instructional book of 1984), *Imagining Landscapes*, and *Singing the Land/Signing the Land* (with Helen Watson and the Yolngu community at Yirrkala). He has published scholarly articles in such journals as *Isis, Osiris, Science and Education, Social Studies of Science*, and *Technology and Culture*, as well as the *Encyclopaedia of the History of Science, Technology, and Medicine in Non-Western Cultures.*

Chambers has also done significant work in the field of science education. Since his original development of the Draw a Scientist Test (DAST) in 1983, the test has been administered by educators in nearly one hundred countries around the world.

CHARLES A. DAILEY earned his BA in Fine Arts at the University of Colorado Boulder in 1962. He worked at the Museum of Northern Arizona and the Museum of New Mexico before serving in the post of Instructor of Museum Studies and Director of the Institute of American Indian Arts Museum starting in 1971. Dailey served as the inspiration for countless IAIA students and was a major force in forwarding the tribal cultural center movement. For over three decades, "Chuck," as he is affectionately known, consulted with dozens of tribal cultural centers, curated, designed exhibits, served as a juror, and trained many of the American Indian museum leaders of our time. In 2001 he received the New Mexico Governor's Award for Excellence in the Arts for art education. Dailey was named Professor Emeritus of Museum Studies at the 2007 IAIA commencement.

LARA M. EVANS is an artist, scholar, curator, and enrolled member of the Cherokee Nation. She earned her PhD in art history at the University of New Mexico in 2005; her specialization within Native American art history is contemporary art. Evans joined the Museum Studies department at the Institute of American Indian Art (IAIA) in Santa Fe, New Mexico in 2012 after eight years on the faculty at the Evergreen State College in Olympia, Washington. Since 2015, she has also been program director for the IAIA Artist-in-Residence Program, which brings twelve to fourteen Native American artists to campus for variable-length residency sessions each year. Evans' curatorial projects at the IAIA Museum of Contemporary Native Arts have included *Now is the Time: Investigating Native Histories and Visions of the Future* (2017) and *War Department: Selections from IAIA MoCNA's Permanent Collection* (2015–2016), and she has contributed essays to a number of exhibition catalogues.

STEPHEN C. FADDEN (Mohawk) is an educator, storyteller, motivational speaker, and performing artist. He holds an AFA in Museum Studies from the Institute of American Indian Arts, as well as BA and MA degrees in Communication from Cornell University. Before moving to Santa Fe, Fadden lectured in the Communication Department and American Indian Program at Cornell, where he won the Paramount Professor Award from the Greek Panhellenic Society for excellence in teaching and student motivation. He also worked throughout New York as a multicultural education consultant for public schools, examining the ways that stories can help students find connections and meaning in their educational experience. Fadden advised the Discovery Channel on the history of the Haudenosaunee (Iroquois) in its production of "Divided We Fall," an episode of the series *How the West Was Lost*. He has been a featured lecturer and performing artist for the National Gallery of Art, the Smithsonian Institution, the National Museum of the American Indian, and many storytelling festivals. He was awarded a National Endowment for the Humanities Fellowship to be the 2007 Visiting Scholar at the Institute of American Indian Arts, where he worked until 2017. He is currently the programming director at the Poeh Cultural Center at Pojoaque Pueblo, New Mexico.

RYAN S. FLAHIVE is the archivist for the Institute of American Indian Arts in Santa Fe, New Mexico. He has worked in several museum capacities in Missouri, Wyoming, and Arizona, including a four-year stint as director of research, archives, and publications at Sharlot Hall Museum in Prescott,

Arizona. Aside from his duties as archivist, he teaches courses in archives management and oral history methods at IAIA and is the managing editor of two publications, *Celebrating Difference: Fifty Years of Contemporary Native Arts at IAIA, 1962-2012* (2012) and *The Sound of Drums: A Memoir of Lloyd Kiva New* (2016).

SUZANNE NEWMAN FRICKE, PhD (Adjunct Professor in Art History, Institute of American Indian Arts, and Director, Gallery Hózhó, Albuquerque) earned her master's degree in Italian Renaissance art from the University of Chicago and a doctorate in Native American art history from the University of New Mexico. Currently, she teaches art history at the Institute of American Indian Arts and works as an independent curator. Fricke has taught a variety of art history courses for the past twenty years, including Native American, Renaissance, Southwestern, and Postmodern art. Her research into contemporary Native art includes an article on Bob Haozous in the anthology *No Deal! Indigenous Arts and the Politics of Possession* and the forthcoming publication *As We See It: Interviews with 10 Native American Photographers*. She curated five shows that traveled to different sites in the United States and internationally: *Octopus Dreams: Works on Paper by Contemporary Native American Artists*; *As We See It: Photography by Contemporary Native American Artists*; *Woven Together: Celebrating Grandmother Spiderwoman in Contemporary Native American Art*; *Borrowing the Earth: 5 Contemporary Native American Artists Celebrate Ecology*; and *Live Long and Prosper: Indigenous Futurisms in Contemporary Native American Art*. She edited and contributed to a special edition of *World Art Journal* about Indigenous futurisms. Dr. Fricke is a frequent contributor to *First Americans Art Magazine*.

ALEX JACOBS (Mohawk) earned an AFA from the IAIA a BFA in creative writing and sculpture from the Kansas City Art Institute. He writes, "I was doing Installation and Performance Art before it was a 'thing,' studying media (performance and video) at KCAI in '78–'79. Did three tours with *Akwesasne Notes*, Mohawk Nation, as poetry editor, associate editor and head editor, in the '70s, '80s, and '90s. Worked at CKON Mohawk Nation Radio as a DJ, news director, talk show host, and program director. Worked at IAIA Museum with Rick Hill on his American Indian Stereotypes Project. Won a 1996 NYS Foundation for the Arts Poetry Fellowship. Won the first Multicultural Spoken Word Fellowship at LOFT Minneapolis with fellow Mohawk poet Janet Marie Rogers in 2013. Won Best of Classification, Category, and Division at the Santa Fe Indian Market in 2006 for my fabric collage. I have developed a fabric collage technique based on my mother's and grandmother's quilt-making. Read at Talking Stick Festival in Vancouver, Nuyorican Poets Café in New York City, National Poetry Slams, and Taos Poetry Circus and at venues in Germany. My son, DJ Duran Flint, has produced several CDs of our spoken word and music. I sell my art at local markets in Santa Fe." Jacobs is a member of the Mohawk Nation at Akwesasne, historically the St. Regis Mohawk Indian Territory, which straddles the New York–Ontario–Quebec borders.

TATIANA LOMAHAFTEWA-SINGER (Hopi/Choctaw) is the Curator of Collections at the IAIA Museum of Contemporary Native Arts (MoCNA) in Santa Fe. She holds a BA in fine arts administration from the University of Arizona, Tucson. Some of Lomahaftewa-Singer's exhibitions include *Action/Abstraction Redefined*; *Linda Lomahaftewa: The Gift of Art*; *iCon: A Tribute to Allan Houser*; *Lloyd Kiva New: Art, Design & Influence*; *50/50: Fifty Artists, Fifty Years*; *Drawing from the Collection*; *Voices from the Mound: Contemporary Choctaw*; *Valjean McCarty Hessing Honored*; *Bon a Tirer*; and *Lifting the Veil: New Mexico Women and the Tri-Cultural Myth*. She sits on the New Mexico Capital Arts Foundation Board and the National Parks Arts Foundation Advisory Board and has juried numerous art programs, including the Southwestern Association for Indian Arts Fellowships and the Santa Fe Art Institute Visual Arts Review Committee.

ROBERT MARTIN (Cherokee) became president of the Institute of American Indian Arts (IAIA) on July 1, 2007. He has led the development of a comprehensive strategic plan and a campus facilities master plan, resulting in academic program expansion, growth in student enrollment, construction of five new buildings on campus, and the launch of a successful capital campaign. Prior to joining the IAIA community, Martin was the associate head of the American Indian Studies program at the University of Arizona. He also served as president of Southwestern Indian Polytechnic Institute in Albuquerque for eight years and of Haskell Indian Nations University for ten years. Under his guidance, Haskell made the transition from a junior college to a university offering baccalaureate programs. In addition, he served as the president of Tohono O'odham Community College (TOCC) in Sells, Arizona. During his tenure, TOCC achieved accreditation by the Higher Learning Commission and was designated as a 1994 Land Grant Institution by the US Congress.

Dr. Martin is an enrolled member of the Cherokee Nation of Oklahoma and received his Doctorate in Educational Leadership from the University of Kansas and bachelor's and master's degrees from Appalachian State University.

NANCY MARIE MITHLO, PhD (Chiricahua Apache) is a professor of Gender Studies at the University of California, Los Angeles and affiliated faculty with the American Indian Studies Center and Interdepartmental Program. She received her doctorate in cultural anthropology from Stanford University in 1993. Mithlo's curatorial work has resulted in nine exhibits at the Venice Biennale. A life-long educator, Mithlo has taught at the University of New Mexico, the Institute of American Indian Arts, Santa Fe Community College, Smith College, the California Institute of the Arts, Occidental College, and the University of Wisconsin–Madison. Her forthcoming book *Knowing Native Arts* will be published by the University of Nebraska Press. She is an enrolled member of the Fort Sill Chiricahua Warm Spring Apache Tribe of Oklahoma and New Mexico. http://www.nancymariemithlo.com/

PATSY PHILLIPS (Cherokee) is the director of the IAIA Museum of Contemporary Native Arts (MoCNA) in Santa Fe, New Mexico (2008 to present). Before joining MoCNA, she worked at the Smithsonian's National Museum of the American Indian (2000–2008) and Atlatl, Inc., a national service organization for Native Arts (1996–2000). Phillips holds an MA in Writing from Johns Hopkins University, a Graduate Certificate in Museum Studies from Harvard University, and a BA in Anthropology from Southern Methodist University. She is an enrolled member of the Cherokee Nation in Tahlequah, Oklahoma.

JOHN PAUL RANGEL, PhD (Mestizo: Apache/Navajo/Spanish descent) is a design, marketing, and communications professional as well as a scholar, writer, and artist/metalsmith. Rangel has a BFA from the University of Texas–Austin (1998), a master's degree in American Studies (2006), and a doctoral degree in education from the University of New Mexico (2012). He has worked with many Native institutions, including the Institute for American Indian Arts and the Santa Fe Indian Market. He is currently the creative director for his own design/marketing studio. Rangel has produced and exhibited jewelry since 2012, which he does simultaneously with his other professional pursuits, including writing about Native Art, marketing/advertising, and teaching.

JESSIE RYKER-CRAWFORD (White Earth Chippewa) is an associate professor of Museum Studies at the Institute of American Indian Arts. She received her PhD in sociocultural anthropology through the University of Washington in 2017, focusing on the Indigenization of the museum field. She has presented material on her studies at various conferences, including the National Congress of the American Indian and the International World Archaeological Congress. Ryker-Crawford currently sits on the board of the journal *Museums & Social Issues* and continues to act as a consultant for various museums and cultural centers across the United States.

DAVID WARREN is a member of the Santa Clara Pueblo. He earned his PhD in History at the University of New Mexico in 1955. For twenty years, he held various positions at the Institute of American Indian Arts (IAIA), including curriculum and instruction director, Cultural Research and Resource Development Center director, and acting president. During the Clinton administration, he was the first American Indian to be appointed to the President's Committee on the Arts and the Humanities, a national advisory body on cultural and educational policy. He was also a special assistant for applied community research at the Smithsonian Institution. In 1989, he was the founding deputy director of the National Museum of the American Indian. He held faculty positions at Oklahoma State University and the University of Nebraska, and was the first Native American appointed to the Hulbert Center Endowed Chair in Southwest Studies at Colorado College. He has served as a member of the National Council of the National Endowment for the Humanities, the National Council of the Smithsonian Institution, and the National Park System Advisory Committee. In 1994, he received an award from the New Mexico Commission on Indian Affairs for "lifetime commitment to the preservation and perpetuation of American Indian languages and cultures." In 2013 Dr. Warren was named a Santa Fe Living Treasure and awarded an honorary degree from IAIA and in September of 2014 was honored with an award for Excellence in the Arts from the office of the Governor of New Mexico.

ELIZABETH WOODY (Navajo/Warm Springs/Wasco/Yakama) has published poetry, short fiction, and essays and is a visual artist. Her first poetry book, *Hand Into Stone*, received a 1990 American Book Award. Her second and third collections, published in 1994, are *Luminaries of the Humble* (University of Arizona Press) and *Seven Hands, Seven Hearts, Prose and Poetry*

(Eighth Mountain Press). Woody is a Kellogg Foundation Fellowship alumna through the Americans for Indian Opportunity Ambassadors program. She was born into Tódích'íinii (the Bitter Water clan). She served as Oregon Poet Laureate from 2016 to 2018 and lives in Warm Springs, Oregon.

Page numbers in *italic* type indicate illustrations. Plates are indicated by "pl." preceding the plate number.

Absaloka Parfleche Belt (Gress), pl. 20
abstraction, 5, 19, 43, 69, 150
"Abstraction Serves Indigeneity," 28–39
accreditation, of educational program, 7, 182
Across Time (Kitsman-Jenike), pl. 22
advocacy, 54
aesthetics, 19, 77, 97, 112, 153, 159. *See also* Indigenous aesthetics
African Americans, representation of, 59, 61, 116
agency, in art, 18, 30, 36, 43; Native, 42; personal, 103, 107
ahtone, heather, 69, 74n35
Aikens, Carol Frazier, pl. 24
A. I. M. (Bradley), pl. 90
Akers, Norman, 65–69, *66*, pl. 55
Akulukjuk, Tronto Malaya, pl. 33
ambiguity. *See* Indigenous aesthetics; vocabulary, of Indigenous methodologies
American Alliance of Museums, 44n16
American Indian Curatorial Practice (Mithlo), 16, 42, 32–33; symposium, 2
America on Alert (Grandbois), *117*
Amerman, Marcus, pl. 68
anthropology, 96–97, 105, 148, 152, 168, 171
Antone, A. R., *154*
Apache Crown Dancers (Whitesinger), pl. 63
appropriation: of images, 85; of Native art, 71, 73n8, 88; of Native culture, 50; strategies of, 172
archaeology, 105, 96–97
art history: as established discipline,158; as narrative, 95–96; Native art in, 124, 141, 145; as study area, 96–116, 171. *See also* Indigenous aesthetics; pedagogy
Artist at 40 as a Buffalo (Scholder), pl. 69
artist: biography, 136–38; interviews, 136; permission, 136–37; statements, 115–16. *See also* Indigenous aesthetics; pedagogy
Ashevak, Kenojuak, pl. 38
assimilation, 58, 62, 77, 164; in boarding schools, 5; as Federal policy, 89, 122, 146–47
Aunt Nelly: My Story (Stevens), 124–25, *125*
authenticity, concepts of, 97–98

Bag Series #3 (Wood), pl. 56
Bambi Makes Some Extra Bucks at The Studio (Meredith), *6*
Barraza, Jesus, 54, *55*, 57, 67–68
Bartow, Rick, 7, *25*, 26–27
Baudrillard, Jean, 78
Beaded Child Dress (Goodshot), pl. 84
Beam, Anong, pl. 14, pl. 15
Beam, Carl, pl. 16, pl. 17, pl. 18
Bear Paws on Stripes (One Star), pl. 87
Beetle Design Bowl (Lewis), pl. 95
Begaye, Marwin, pl. 30
Beginning of Winter (Sevoga), pl. 60
Belmore, Rebecca, 131
Big Guy (McCabe), pl. 31
BigKnife, Heidi, 112–13, *113*, *119*
Bird Woman (Loloma), pl. 76
Birth (New Life) (Boyiddle), pl. 65

Black Bear Children (Point), pl. 96
Blomberg, Nancy, 98
Blue Feathers (Feathers), pl. 46
Bluejacket, Shawn, *117*, pl. 4
boarding schools, 5, 16, 37, 130, 147, 157. *See also* Federal policy and law
body and nudity: body reconsidered in, 40–43; "the gaze" in, 15–16; methodology on, 15–16; in "Patterns of Seeing," 16–44; prompts on, 42–43; "seen face" in, 16, 42; of women, 15; *See also* "Abstraction Serves Indigeneity"
Boone, Evans, pl. 52
Box Drum (Davidson), pl. 50
The Boxer (unknown) (Young Man) 116–17, *116*,
Boyiddle, Parker, pl. 65
Bradley, David, 6, pl. 90, pl. 91
Brandow, Heidi, *8*
Brody, J. J., 76, 90, 149
Brown, Melvin, 19, *20*
Bureau of Indian Affairs (BIA), 7, 84, 150, 153n7. *See also* Federal policy and law
Butterflies in December (Farmer), pl. 66
By the Water's Edge (Houser), 34, 35

Cachini, Ernest, pl. 47
Cannon, T. C., *117*, *123*, 123–24, pl. 9, pl. 40, pl. 62
canon: in art history, 21, 99; as classroom activity, 103–5
ceremony, 45–46, 88, 165, 171; celebration and, 112–13, *113*. *See also* Corn Dance
Chaco Canyon, 88
Chacon, Nani, *114*, 115–16
Chambers, David Wade, 179; Teaching from Three Knowledge Spaces: The Native Eyes Project, 163–75
The Change (Bartow), *25*, 26–27
Changing Woman (Hardin), pl. 25
Chaos Theory (The Whale of Our Being Series) (Beam, Carl), pl. 17
Childhood (Stevens), *127*
Children's Iron Lung, *126*
Christ, St. Vitalis, Bishop of Ravenna, and Archangels, *78*, 79
Circle of Life (Lomahaftewa), pl. 61
Civil.War. (Chacon and Fragua), *114*, 115–16
Clah, Alfred, pl. 21
Cohoe, Grey, pl. 35, pl. 43
colonialism, 33, 44, 57, 93, 95, 98, 112, 145, 164, 174
colonial project, 172
Columbus, 113; "History before," 172
Combattant de Liberté (Bluejacket), *117*, pl. 4
conceptual art, 121, 124–25, *125*, 133, 171
conflict: in art, 1; of interest, 33; in society, 24, 112–13, 115–16
connoisseurship, 95, 96, 98
continuity, 45, 62, 64, 68, 69, 70, 87, 168
Converse (Kahm), pl. 1
Corn Dance, 52, 87. *See also* dances of Southwest and West
Corn Dance Series (Romero), 50–52, *51*
Cota, Laura Fragua, pl. 80
Coyote, 75, *76*, 78, 89, 92, 93, 94, 175
Crown Dancer (Houser), *80*, 81, 82, 90
Cry I (Bartow), *25*, 26
culture, 5, 45, 47, 49, 50, 51, 52, 54, 57, 62, 63, 65, 69, 72, 74, 93, 112, 122, 123, 124, 130, 142, 163, 167, 169, 170; cultural sovereignty, 71, 157; European culture, 95, 172; Indigenous culture, 18, 45, 71, 147, 150, 152, 170; Native culture, 37, 46, 49, 50, 53, 61, 64, 66, 67, 68, 73, 75, 76, 77, 84, 86, 88, 90, 97, 98, 111, 121, 128, 173; Osage culture, 63, 64, 65, 67; Pueblo culture, 49, 51, 52; self-determination, 155–59; tribal culture, 97. *See also specific topics*
Curtis, Edward, 52

Dada, 131
Dailey, Buffy, 142
Dailey, Charles "Chuck," 141–42; 179; "Major Influences in the Development of Twentieth-Century Native American Art," 145–53
Dakota Access Pipeline (2016–2017), 40
Dance Land #2 (Fonseca), 75, *76*, 78–79, 89
dances, 42, 45, 46, 47, 49, 65, 67, 72, 112, 113, 146, 163, 167, 171; of Southwest and

West, 75–92; Fonseca on, 75–76, *76*, 78–79; ghost dance, 29; history related to, 77, 90n9; importance of, 77–78; law against, 77; materials in, 79; popularity of, 75–76, 90n7; questions on, 89–90; representations of, 76–79; vocabulary of, 88–89
Davidson, Reg, pl. 50
Dawn (Houser), 35, *36*
Dawn's Glow (Northwest Woman II) (Thomas), *21*, 21–23
Day, Frank, pl. 71
A Day at Cochiti Lake (Swentzell), pl. 101
Deam, Peggy, *27*, 27–28
Deceptus Magnus-October 12, 1492 (Solomon), *119*
decolonial practice, 95
decolonization, 33, 37, 43, 173, 174, 175
Deer Dancers (Fonseca), pl. 64
DeHuff, Elizabeth, 148
DeHuff, John D., 148
Deleuze, Gilles, 78
Deontic Koan (The Whale of Our Being Series) (Beam, Carl), pl. 16
diabetes, 131, 133–34, 135. *See also* Stevens, Maxx
Diplomacy (Moyah), *22*, 23–24
discourse, 1, 2, 46, 86, 88, 93, 115
Distortion (Moyah), *23*, 24
diversity, 71, 92, 99, 146, 165, 166, 169
Do Indian Artists Go to Santa Fe When They Die . . . ? (Whitman), *60*, 61–63
Dream Home (Stevens), pl. 49
dreams: and creativity, 128, 130
duality: in art, 18, 43; in nature, 18, 63
Dunn, Dorothy, 5, 50, 79, 149. *See also* Studio Style painting
Dutton, Denis, 97

eagle feathers, 115
Economic Sovereignty (Picotte), *119*
Eder, Earl, pl. 11
education. *See* pedagogy; Federal policy and law
Education (Yazzie, Melanie), *114*
Elk Spirit (Metoxen), pl. 97
Endangered Species (Rahr), pl. 92
Ernest, Marcella, *41*, 42
essentialism, 18, 43
ethnography, 7, 49–50, 52, 71, 97, 105; and gaze, 49, 72
Evans, Lara, 180; "Transforming Art History in the Classroom," 95–120; photograph of, *116*
Evolution (Houser), 82, *83*
exhibition, as classroom activity, 108–12, *109*
exhibition catalogs, 105, 120n8
exhibitions: 10n4, 37, pl. 81; *Emergence: John Feodorov*, 109; *The Human Figure in American Indian Art*, 43n2; *Ga.ni. tha*, 40; *Most Serene Republics*, 40; *Wah.shka*, 37; *War Department*, 112–19, *113–14*. *See also* Venice Biennale
Extra-Terrestrial Life Series (Gray), pl. 70

Fadden, Stephen C, 180; "About Professor Charles Dailey," 141–42
Family portrait, late 1940s, (Stevens), *122*
Farmer, Selina, pl. 66
Feast Day Selfie (Garcia), 47, *48*, 49–50
Feathers, Kirby, pl. 46
Feddersen, Carly, pl. 8
Federal policy and law: of 1960s, 150; of assimilation, 146–47; Elementary and Secondary Education Act, 156; Indian Arts and Crafts Law (1990), 85–86; Indian Relocation Act (1956), 62, 122; Indian Removal Act (1830), 122; Indian Reorganization Act (1934, aka Wheeler-Howard Act), 147–48; Meriam Report (1928), 147–48; Native American Graves Protection and Repatriation Act (NAGPRA), 3; and religious freedom, 61; of separation, 146–47; Snyder Act (1924), 147; Violence Against Women Act (2003), 39; White House Initiative on American Indian and Alaska Native Education, 2–3
Feminine Sacred (Goshorn), 37, *38*
Feodorov, John, *109*
Fields, Anita (née Luttrell), 63–65, *64*, pl. 28

Fife, Phyllis, 6
Fighting over the Dead Seal (Ikuutaq), pl. 99
Fire Dancer (Houser), 82, *83*
Flahive, Ryan S., 180–81; “Introduction to the IAIA Museum of Contemporary Native Arts Collection and the IAIA Archives,” 5–10
Fonseca, Harry, 75, *76*, 78–79, 89, pl. 19, pl. 64
Ford Foundation, 2. *See also* symposia
Forms in Beadwork (Eder), pl. 11
Fragua, Jaque, *114*, 115–16
Freedom (Gauthier), 58–59, *59*, 61
Fricke, Suzanne Newman, 181; “Presentations and Representation: Images of Dances from the Southwest and West,” 28, 30, 43n2, 46–47, 54, 62–67, 75–94, 115, 124, 127, 130, 131, 158, 167, 168
Frightened Baby Becomes a Ptarmigan (Ukpatiku), pl. 42
Fringed Cuffs (Amerman), pl. 68
Fry, Aaron, 76

Gachupin, Maxine, pl. 67
Garcia, Jason, 47, *48*, 49–50
Gaseoma, Clara LaRose, *26*, 27
Gauthier, Anthony, 58–59, *59*, 61
the gaze: as concept, 34, 42; ethnographic, 49, 72; male, female, 15, 19
gender, 15–16
Ghost Dance. *See* dances
Ghost Dance II (Soza), 28
Giant Symbols (Winters), pl. 10
Gilpin, Laura, pl. 36, pl. 37
Gina Gray (Fields), pl. 28
Gobin, Hank, pl. 48
Goodshot, Imogene, pl. 84; portrait of, pl. 83
Gorman, R. C., pl. 94
Goshorn, Shan, 37, *38*, 39, *119*
Grandbois, Dorothy, *117*
Gray, Darren Vigil, pl. 41, pl. 70
Greenberg, Clement, 33
Gress, Robert, pl. 20
Group of students at Soleri Theater (1978), *162*
Guerrero-Cruz, Dolores, pl. 93

Haozous, Bob, 33, pl. 44
Hardin, Helen, pl. 25
Harjo, Joy, 124
Hawk Woman (Hoover), pl. 23
health: diabetes, 131, 133–34; polio, 125–26; radioactivity, 113, 115
Heap of Birds, Edgar, 52–54, *53*, 73nn14–15, 73n17
heteronormative looking, 15, 42
Hewett, Edgar L., 148
Hill, Richard, 18–19
historical essays, 141–73
Hogarth, William, 91n18
Holden, Brenda, pl. 32
homelands, 45, 47, 61, 63, 64, 65, 66, 67, 71, 86, 122, 124, 156–57
honoring, 39, 46, 63, 67, 69, 72, 141–42, 171; of dreams, 130; the past, 135; of tradition, 164, 167, 172. *See also* ceremony
Honors Collection, 5–6, 7
Honor the Treaties Collective, 115–16
Hoover, John, pl. 23
Hopi Clowns (Fonseca), pl. 19
Horton, Jessica, 90n9
House of Constant Rotation (Stevens), 128, *129*
Houser, Allan, 33, 34, 35, 36, 37, 39, 77, *80*, 81–82, *83*, 84, 90, 149, 152
The Human Figure in American Indian Art, 43n2
humor, 93, 94, 173; of artists, 77, 135; Indigenous, 106
hyperreality, 78, 89

IAIA. *See* Institute of American Indian Arts
IAIA, photographs of: dormitory, ca. 1965 (Wiest)*143*; author Lara Evans photographing *The Boxer*, n.d., *116*; faculty meeting, ca. 1967, *144*; Former students of IAIA return to join the instructional staff (1977), pl. 88; graduation with Lloyd New, ca. 1975, pl.

85; James McGrath and Manuelita Lovato hanging 1966 IAIA Faculty exhibit (Wiest), pl. 82; music students, ca. 1965 (Wiest), *143*; photography students screen printing, ca. 1972 (Nugent), pl. 86; physical education class, ca. 1970 (Antone), *154*; Pima, Zuni and Santo Domingo potters (Frances Maki), 1971 (Nugent), pl. 74; portrait class, ca. 1963 (Wiest), *140*; portrait of Imogene Goodshot, former student and instructor, 1973 (Thorne), pl. 83; Rodeo Club members, 1973, *160*; seniors, 1963 (Wiest), *140*; student group, ca. 1965 (Milo), *144*; student group, 1972, *154*; student on pottery wheel, 1963 (Wiest), pl. 77; students in class with instructor Manuelita Lovato, ca. 1972, pl. 78; students in Commercial Arts class, 1965, *143*; students on the Santa Fe Indian School campus, ca. 1975 (Kernberger), *161*; student protest, 1973, *160*; student protest, 1981, 162
iconography, 70–71; abstracted, 29; Christian, 19, 78, *20*, *79*; human/animal, 27
Ikuutaq, Janet Nipi, pl. 99
"Illumination" (Woody), 177
Indian Affected by Anti-Indian Backlash (Bradley), pl. 6
Indian Arts and Crafts Law (1990), 85–86. *See also* Federal policy and law
Indian Land (Barraza), 54, 55, 57
Indian Relocation Act (1956), 62, 162. *See also* Federal policy and law
Indian Removal Act (1830), 122. *See also* Federal policy and law
Indian Reorganization Act (1934), 147, 148. *See also* Federal policy and law
"Indian with a Watch" (Jacobs), 11, 13–14
Indigeneity: "Abstraction Serves Indigeneity," 28–39; in aesthetics, 68–71; epistemologies, 72; "Indigenous Voice," 171; *intellectual apparatus*, 2; knowledge production, 28, 34, 37, 39, 40, 46, 47; knowledge systems, 1, 18, 50; mapping, 72; materials, 46, 72; 171; place, 45, 172; scholarship, 164; space, 45–46, 72. *See also* mapping Indigenous space and place
Indigenous aesthetics, 45, 68–71, 171
Indigenous Methodologies (Kovach), 68
Inside Joke (Bartow), *7*
Institute of American Indian Arts (IAIA), 1; accreditation for, 7; distinction of, 5, 7–8, 10n2, 151–52; Honors Collection in, 5–6, 7; Museum of Contemporary Native Arts (MoCNA), xvi–xvii, 5–10, 15, *109*, 121, 131; Native Eyes Project and, 163, 170; Stevens and, 123; student exhibitions in, 10n4; teaching philosophy of, 5. *See also specific topics*
Instructor In Green (Cannon), 123, *123*
International Council of Museums, 44n16
interviews: as classroom assignment, 106–7, 136
Iris (Gorman), pl. 94
iron lung machine, 126, *126*

Jacobs, Alex, *12*, 19, *20*, 21, 30, 36, 181–182; "Indian with a Watch," 11, 13–14
John Wesley Hardin, Killer of Men . . . (Soza), 30, *31*, 32
Joseph, Chief, as subject, 58–59, *59*

Kahm, Jeff, pl. 1
Katchina No. 1 (Tsabetsaye), pl. 26
katsinim (*katchina*, *katsinas*), 79, 91n15, 148
Keene, Adrienne, 73n8
Kelliher-Combs, Sonya, pl. 6
Kernberger, Karl, *161*
Kill the Indian Save the Man (Begaye), pl. 30
King, Martin Luther, Jr., 59, *59*, 61
King, Patti Jo, 77
Kitsman-Jenike, Bobbie (neé Meeks), pl. 22
knowledge, 33, 36, 46, 52, 62, 64, 65, 67, 68, 69–70, 93, 127, 128, 130, 163–75; systems of, 72. *See also* Native Eyes Project
Kovach, Margaret, 68
LaMarr, Jean, *118*, pl. 51

land, 39, 40, 42, 51, 53, 54, 57, 62, 64, 67, 68, 88, 115, 130, 146, 147, 165
land as container of culture, 45–46, 65, 71–72. *See also* space
landscape, 40, 42, 45, 53, 63, 64, 65, 66, 167
language, 2, 3, 40, 45, 46, 52, 53, 58, 65, 67, 68, 70, 72, 89, 98, 122, 124, 130, 145, 147, 156, 157, 158, 159, 165, 171, 184
Last Supper (Stevens), 131, *132*, 133–34, 135; detail of, *132*
Lee, Tony, pl. 13
letters, to artist. *See* pedagogy, classroom activity
Lewis, Lawrence, pl. 27
Lewis, Lucy Martin, pl. 95
Life on the 18th Hole (Neel), *114*
Little Dog (Yazzie, Melanie), pl. 58
Loloma, Otellie, pl. 39, pl. 73, pl. 75, pl. 76
Lomahaftewa, Linda, pl. 61, pl. 89
Lomahaftewa-Singer, Tatiana, 182; "Introduction to the IAIA Museum of Contemporary Native Arts Collection and the IAIA Archives," 5–10
Loneman, Charlene, pl. 45
Louis, Joe, as subject, *116*, 116–17
Lovato, Manuelita, pl. 74, pl. 78, pl. 81, pl. 82

Maiden Voyager (Tohee), pl. 29
Make Me Dance Ivories (Wapp), pl. 98
Makil, Frances, pl. 72, pl. 74; portrait of, pl. 88
Making Frybread at Crownpoint School 1960 (Gilpin), pl. 37
Malotte, Jack, *118*
Manifestations: New Native Art Criticism, 3
mapping, 106, 156, 166
mapping Indigenous space and place, 52, 88; accessibility of, 67–68; continuity in, 45, 64; in *Corn Dance Series*, 52; discourse in, 46–47; in *Do Indian Artists Go to Santa Fe When They Die . . . ?*, 61–63; dynamism in, 46; in *Feast Day Selfie*, 47, 49–50; in *Freedom*, 58–59, 61; geography in, 45; in *Indian Land*, 54, 55, 57; Indigenous aesthetics in, 68–71; questions on, 71–72; in *Sorting Out Blind Sensations*, 65–67; in *Telling Many Magpies, Telling Black Wolf, Telling Hachivi*, 52–54; vocabulary of, 72; in *When More Than Knees Have Been Wounded*, 57–58
The Married Woman (Bradley), pl. 91
Martin, Robert, 3; Foreword, xv–xvii
Martineau, Jarrett, 37
Mashburn, Keli, 40, *41*, 42
material culture, 70, 96, 97, 100, 156, 168, 171
materiality, 69–70
materials, 28, 57, 68, 71, 81, 89, 100, 103, 121, 126, 156; availability of, 79, 91n14; Indigenization of, 46, 72; use of natural, 69, 130–31. *See also* Indigenous aesthetics; individual artwork captions
Maytwayashing, Mary, 42
McCabe, Michael, pl. 31
McGrath, James, pl. 82
meaning layers, 32
Medal of Dishonor (BigKnife), *119*
memory, 15
Memory Prom Dress (2005), pl. 2
Meredith, America, 6
meridian, 87, 89
Mesa Mirage from Tocito Rain (Cohoe), pl. 35
metaphor, 24, 43n2, 51, 58, 59, 61, 63, 65, 66, 67, 68, 69, 96, 120n1
Metoxen, Linda Lou, pl. 97
misrepresentation, 50; *See also* appropriation
Mist in the Morning (Fife), 6
Mithlo, Nancy Marie, xvii, 183; "Cultural Self-Determination: A Conversation with David Warren," 155–59; "The Gaze in Indigenous Art: Depictions of the Body and Nudity," 15–44; 155–59; "American Indian Curatorial Practice: State of the Field," 1–4
MoCNA. *See* Institute of American Indian Arts (IAIA), Museum of Contemporary Native Arts
modernism, 36, 90n7, 93, 120n7

Montoya, Geronima Cruz, 113, *113*
Morgensen, Scott Lauria, 33
Mother and Child (Brown), 19, *20*
Moyah, Courtney, *22*, *23*, 23–24, *24*, 26
My Backyard Larry (Deam), *27*, 27–28
My Father was a World War II Warrior (Tsinhnahjinnie), *119*
My Humanness Is an Embellished Tongue (Woody), *176*
My Mother, Myself (Ashevak), pl. 38

names, 50, 53–54, 62, 68, 141. *See also* Heap of Birds
National Museum of the American Indian, 50, 52, 57, 61, 63, 94, 122, 155, 156, 180, 183, 184
national policies. *See* Federal policy and law
Native American Center for the Living Arts (Niagara Falls, New York), 151
Native American Graves Protection and Repatriation Act (NAGPRA), 3
Native American art, 46, 77, 92, 94, 97, 99, 100, 106, 111, 120n8, 123, 141, 142; categorization of, 71; culture in, 146; early days of, 148; expression system in, 150; federal policies in, 147–48, 150; IAIA 1962–1982, 151–52; major influences on, 145–53; nature in, 146; Oklahoma movement in, 149; Santa Fe Indian School, 149; traditions in, 147–48, 150–51. *See also* Dunn, Dorothy
Native Appropriations website, 73n8
Native Eyes Project, 163–75; courses in, 172–73; dialectical themes in, 168; diversity related to, 165–67, 169–70; goal of, 168, 170; IAIA and, 163, 170; individualization of, 169; "objectivism" and, 164, 170; online format of, 168–69; third knowledge space, 165–67, 171; tribal knowledge space, 165; Western science knowledge space, 164
Native peoples, 15, 36, 40, 46, 50, 64, 72, 75, 87, 88, 97, 98, 115, 130, 131, 133, 157, 163, 165; in *Freedom*, 59, 61; in *Picture Tour of Arizona*, 85; stories of, 121; in *Telling Many Magpies*, 52–53. *See also* health; tribal nation(s)
nature, 18, 39, 42, 66, 67, 147; in ceremony, 76; in dance, 88; as dialectical theme, 168; duality in, 63; harmony with, 146; Indigenous perspectives on, 173; metaphors for, 65; symbolism of, 64. See also "Illumination"
Neel, David, *114*
Neuf Paintings, 53, 73n15
New, Lloyd Kiva, 5, 10n1, pl. 85
New Mexico Red (Cannon), pl. 62
Nibiin Water Song (Ernest), *41*, 42
The Night after Columbus (BigKnife), 112–13, *113*
nostalgia, 79, 87, 89, 145
nude, as Earth Mother, 43n2
Nugent, Robert, pl. 73, pl. 74, pl. 86

Obama, Barack, 2–3
Object: Hand + Mechanism (Brandow), *8*
objectivity: in knowledge, 164; objectivism, 170; in scholarship, 33–34
The Offering (Scholder), pl. 5
Oklahoma movement. *See* Native American art
Oñate's Toaster (Teters), pl. 100
On Drinking Beer in Vietnam in 1967 (Cannon), *117*
One Navajo (Scholder), pl. 34
One Star, Mike, pl. 87
Onyx Mosaic (Wood), pl. 57
Otellie Loloma, 1971 (Nugent), pl. 73

Pablito, Roy, pl. 54
Painting the Underworld Sky (Romero), 50–51
Parrots Prayer Song (Lomahaftewa), pl. 89
Parsons, Elsie Clews, 91n10
Pedagogy, art history, 96–116
Pedagogy, classroom activities: art experiences, 107–16; artist statement, 115; bibliography,105–6; canon formation, 103–5; field trips, 107; library scavenger hunt, 105–6, 120n8; reading, 102–3; research, 105–7; terminology, 42–43

Peña, Alex J., pl. 7
performance, 46, 88, 175; in art, 71–72, 75, 106, 111, 131, 171, 181; and Indigenous space, 46, 88
Phillips, Patsy, 183; and Harry Fonseca, 75; "'No Rules Make Art': The Work of C. Maxx Stevens," 121–35
philosophy, 5, 37, 40, 99, 150, 158–59, 171
Picotte, Seth, *119*
Picture Tour Map of Arizona (Yazzie, Melanie), *85*, 85–86
poems: by Alex Jacobs, 11, 13–14; by Elizabeth Woody, 177
Point, Susan A., pl. 96
popular culture, 15, 47, 50, 58, 71, 100
primitivism, 158; exhibition, 159n2
protests and civil unrest, 115–16, *160*, *162*
Pultz, John, 40
pyramidal composition, 81, 82, *83*, 89

Quintana, Teresa, *118*

racism, 52, 61, 69; in cultural authenticity, 97; among Native people, 58; toward Native people, 58
Rahr, Tammy, pl. 92
Rangel, John Paul, 88, 183; "Mapping Indigenous Space and Place," 45–74
reciprocity, 2, 16, 32, 40, 65, 68, 69–70, 72
Red Meridian (Romero), 86–88, *87*
Red Print II (Gobin), pl. 48
repatriation, 156–157. *See also* Federal policy and law
representation, 15, 21, 37, 39, 171–72; as hyperreality, 89; as Indigenous framework, 70, 73; study of, 84; symbolic, 64. *See also* Fricke, Suzanne Newman
research, 105–7, 111–12
Research Is Ceremony (Wilson), 68
Residential School (Nightmare Koan I) (Beam, Carl), pl. 18
Revolution (The Evolver Series) (Beam, Anong), pl. 14
Ritskes, Eric, 37
Romero, Mateo, 50–52, *51*, 86–88, *87*
Roosevelt, Franklin D., 81
Rose (fictitious character), 75, 78
Ryker-Crawford, Jessie, 184; "About Professor Charles Dailey," 141–42

sacred, 65, 86, 89, 91; dances, 86; eagle feathers, 115; homelands, 64, 156–57; images, 77; kiva, 91n10; knowledge, 165; number, 73n15
Sani, Atsidi, 46
Santa Fe Dude #4 (Jacobs), *12*
Santa Fe Indian School, 79, 81, 149. *See also* Dunn, Dorothy
Scholder, Fritz, 30, *84*, 84–85, 90, 123, pl. 5, pl. 34, pl. 69
Scott, Sasha, 76
Screaming Eagle Blues (Malotte), *118*
seeing, 15–16; traditional ways of, 150. *See also* the gaze
self-determination, 153, 155–56, 165, 174
"selfie," 47, *48*, 49–50, 52, 73n4
Self-Portrait (Lewis), pl. 27
Self-Portrait (Soza), 30, *31*
Self Portrait in the Studio (Cannon), pl. 40
serpentine lines/S-curve, 81, 82, 91n18
Settler, 33, 44, 146
17 Navajos Gathered (Gilpin), pl. 36
Sevoga, Nancy, pl. 60
sexuality, 19, 34, 43
sexual violence, 23, 24, 39
simulacra, 78
Simultaneous Advance (The Evolver Series) (Beam, Anong), pl. 15
Sioux Blue (White Hawk), pl. 3
Smith, Shawn, 37
Smithsonian National Museum of the American Indian, 126
Snake Dancer (Scholder), 83–85, *84*, 90
Snapchat, 47, 73n4
Soldier Boy Ring (Quintana), *118*
Solomon, Floyd, *119*
Sometimes It Happens That Way (LaMarr), pl. 51
Somewhere in South Dakota (Winters), pl. 53
Sorting Out Blind Sensations (Akers), 65–67, *66*
Sotomayor, Sonia, 134
sovereignty, 13, 70, 156, 157, 165, 174

Soza, Bill (War Soldier), 28–30, *29*, *31*, 32–33
space, 19, 24, 45-74, 89, 104, 131, 163–75; activation of, 72; arrangement of, 109; in dance, 88; discursive, 46; Indigenization of, 88; perceptions of, 78–79, 81-82. *See also* mapping Indigenous space and place; Native Eyes Project
Spirit Dance of the Moon and Sun (Cohoe), pl. 43
spirit realm, 134, 91n15
spirituality, 28, 45, 54, 57, 61, 64, 66, 67, 70, 71, 76, 77, 79, 88, 89, 124, 134, 157; in ceremony, 146; in knowledge, 172; technology related to, 49
Stalking Deer (Day), pl. 71
Standing Bear, Luther, 39
Standing Rock, 40. *See also* Dakota Access Pipeline
Stevens, C. Maxx, 126, *127*, 128, *129*, *132*, *134*, 133–35, 137–38, pl. 2, pl. 49; conceptual art of, 121, 124–25, *125*; Dadaism and, 131; family of, 122, *122*, 124–25, 134, 135; health of, 125–26, *126*, 133; IAIA and, 123; philosophy of, 126
storytelling, 22, 49, 65, 70, 141–42, 166, 171; tradition of, 172
StoryWeaver, 172–73
Studio Style painting, 5, 79, 81, 84
Swentzell, Roxanne, pl. 101
symbolism: 13, 59, 65, 66, 67, 68, 71, 87, 95, 99, 125, 128, 163, 69–70, pl. 10; of fertility, 18–19; of spiritual realm, 134; of warfare, 113–15
symposia, American Indian Curatorial Practice, 2
Szabo, Joyce, 99

Tale of a Bigfoot Incident in American Vernacular (Cannon), pl. 9
Tall Man with Bird (Loloma), pl. 75
Tamahnous Pro-Being (Thoms), pl. 12
Tangerine Walrus Family (Kelliher-Combs), pl. 6
"Teaching from Three Knowledge Spaces." *See* Chambers; Native Eyes Project
technology, 67, 164, 171; spirituality related to, *48*, 49–50
Telling Many Magpies, Telling Black, Telling Hachivi (Heap of Birds), 52–54, *53*, 73nn14–15, 73n17
terminology. *See* vocabulary
Teters, Charlene, *118*, pl. 100
Thomas, Yvonne, *21*, 21–23
Thoms, William, pl. 12
Thorne, Allen, pl. 83
Thursday Blues (Jacobs), 19, *20*, 21, 36
time, 11, 12–14, 16, 19, 22, 24, 27, 32, 39, 46, 49, 59, 61, 64, 67, 72, 76, 77, 79, 82, 86, 87, 96, 100, 101, 117, 124, 125, 126, 128, 130, 133, 135, 145, 146, 147, 149, 150, 153, 155, 156, 158, 159, 170, 172; pre-Contact, 89; Indian Time, 11; as timeline, 103–4
To Cry in the Dark (Moyah), 24, *24*, 26
Tohee, Ken, pl. 29
Tooth and Twine Necklace (Fedderson), pl. 8
traditions, 23, 36, 37, 40, 42, 45–46, 47, 52, 63, 65, 68, 69, 72, 98, 112, 128, 131, 135, 146, 147–48, 149, 150–51, 152, 164, 165, 166, 167, 168, 170, 171, 172, 173, 174, 175; in carving, 27; celebratory, 112; homelands, 156–57; related to knowledge, 164; Western, of art, 22, 70–71. See also Indigenous aesthetics
Triangle Painting (Makil), pl. 72
Tribal Colleges and Universities, 2–3
tribal knowledge space, 165
tribal nation(s), 49, 70–71, 123, 146; of artists, *See* captions in text
Trickster, 75, 89, 90n3, 166
Tsabetsaye, Robert, pl. 26
Tsinhnahjinnie, Hulleah, *119*
Turnbull, David, 166

Ukpatiku, Magdelene, pl. 42
University of California Los Angeles, American Indian Studies Center, 145
University of Wisconsin-Madison, 2
Unrelenting-Number 1 (Gray), pl. 41
Untitled (Abstract Humanoids) (Boone), pl. 52
Untitled (Aikens), pl. 24

Untitled (*The Boxer*) (unknown), *116*, 116–17. *See also* Institute of American Indian Arts (IAIA)
Untitled (Cachini), pl. 47
Untitled (Clah), pl. 21
Untitled (Cover Girl Series) (Lamarr), *118*
Untitled (Fields), 63–65, *64*
Untitled (Holden), pl. 32
Untitled (Lovato), pl. 81. *See also* IAIA
Untitled (Wolf), 16, *17*, 18–19
Untitled Lines #19 (Peña), pl. 7

Venice Biennale, 37, 40, 52, 131, 183
El Veso (Guerrero-Cruz), pl. 93
Vessel (Goshorn), 37, *38*, 39
Violence Against Women Act (2003). *See* Federal policy and law
visual representation. *See* Native Eyes Project
vocabulary, 72, 88–89, 99, 102, 113
vocabulary, of Indigenous methodologies, 88–89

Wah.shka: exhibit, 37; film, 40–41
Wanting Fish (Akulukjuk), pl. 33
Wapp, Edward, pl. 98
War Dance (Montoya), 113, *113*
War Department, 112–15
War Makers Back in Town (Teters), *118*
Warning Call (Akers), pl. 55
Warren, David, 184; "Cultural Self-Determination/A Conversation with David Warren," 155–59
War Soldier. *See* Soza, Bill
Watcher (Gaseoma), *26*, 27
Water Study #1 (Mashburn), *41*
Watt, Marie K., *56*, 57–58
We Come as Clouds (Loloma), pl. 39
West, Richard "Dick," 122–23
Western science knowledge space, 164
When More Than Knees Have Been Wounded (Watt), *56*, 57–58
White Hawk, Dyani, pl. 3
White House Initiative on American Indian and Alaska Native Education, 2–3. See also Federal policy and law
Whitesinger, Don, pl. 63
Whitman, Richard Ray, *60*, 61–63
Whitt, Laurelyn, 165
Wíčazo Ša Review, 3
Wichita House (Stevens), *134*
Wiest, Kay V., *72*, *73*, *74*, *76*, *77*, pl. 77, pl. 82
Wilson, Shawn, 68
Winters, Raymond, pl. 10, pl. 53
Wisdom (Lee), pl. 13
Wolf, Wesley, 16, *17*, 18–19
Womb Bowl (Cota), pl. 80
Women, 47, 49, 62, 63, 64, 93, 121, 123, 135, 138, 171; and duality, 18; and nudity, 15; as subject, 15–44
Women in Mourning (Loneman), pl. 45
Wood, Margaret, pl. 56, pl. 57
Woody, Elizabeth, *176*, 184–85; "Illumination," 177
Words Are Our Weapons (Goshorn), *119*
Working with Pima, Zuni and Santo Domingo potters (Frances Makil) (Nugent), pl. 74. *See also* Institute of American Indian Arts (IAIA)
World Indigenous Peoples Conference on Education. *See* Native Eyes Project
Wounded Knee Massacre (1890), 29, 58
Wovoka, 28, 89

Yazzie, Larry, pl. 59
Yazzie, Melanie, *85*, 85–86, 90, *114*, pl. 58
Ye'ii Impersonator (1984), pl. 59
Yellow Cat (Haozous), pl. 44
Young Man, Alfred, *116*, 116–17

Zuni Shalako Dancer and Mudhead (Pablito), pl. 54